KHOMEINI

Life of the Ayatollah

KHOMEINI

Life of the Ayatollah

Baqer Moin

THOMAS DUNNE BOOKS
St. Martin's Press ☙ New York

THOMAS DUNNE BOOKS.
An imprint of St. Martin's Press.

KHOMEINI. Copyright © 1999 by Baqer Moin. All rights reserved.
Printed in the United States of America. No part of this book may be used or
reproduced in any manner whatsoever without written permission except in the
case of brief quotations embodied in critical articles or reviews. For information,
address St. Martin's Press, 175 Fifth Avenue, New York, N.Y. 10010.

www.stmartins.com

ISBN 0-312-26490-9

First published in Great Britain by I.B. Tauris & Co Ltd

First U.S. Edition: June 2000

10 9 8 7 6 5 4 3 2 1

Contents

Preface		vii
1	The Orphan: Childhood in Khomein	1
2	In the Seminary: Student Years in Qom	21
3	In Search of Perfection: Taking Refuge in Mysticism	39
4	The Formation of a Politician: Reza Shah and After	53
5	Challenging His Majesty: Khomeini and the Shah in Conflict	74
6	The Leader: Khomeini and the 1963 Uprising	92
7	Arrest and Imprisonment: The Emergence of a Political Ayatollah	107
8	In the Den of Snakes: Exile in Turkey and Iraq	129
9	Waiting in the Wings: Iran Prepares for Revolution	160
10	Khomeini in Paris: The End of an Empire	182
11	Revolution: The Return of the Imam	199
12	The Ruler: Creating an Islamic Republic	223
13	The Warrior and his Theocracy: Khomeini Defies the World	245
14	The Rise of the Phoenix: Khomeini's Last Months	270
15	Khomeini's End: Death of a Patriarch	299
Notes		315
Select Bibliography		335
Index		341

Preface

I began this biography over a decade ago as a journalistic endeavour designed to make Khomeini explicable to the general reading public. An Iranian working abroad, I had for many years been bombarded with questions about the background and motives of a very tenacious and complex character, and had spent much time trying to correct misconceptions about him and the cultural context in which he flourished. It would, I felt, be helpful to write about him within a serious, but non-academic framework.

I have been, from the outset, well aware of the difficulties of trying to offer a reasonably accurate and objective account of a life that spanned most of the twentieth century and lived in a rapidly changing society. Very little reliable material is available on Khomeini's personal life and early career and many memoirs of him are deeply tinged by the emotions aroused by his political career. Where facts are a scarce commodity, accuracy is not easily attainable. Objectivity – though a relative term in itself – is even more difficult to achieve when passions run high over a man the consequences of whose actions, sayings and thoughts have touched all our lives.

Ten years after Khomeini's death, history has gradually taken over from emotional and political considerations. The release of more documents, and the information that is now trickling out, will provide opportunities for a deeper and more comprehensive portrait in the future.

This book, for what it is worth, could not have been conceived without my early education as a seminarian in Khorasan – my spiritual home. My first teacher was my father, a tolerant and enlightened *mojtahed* who spent his life as a farmer near Neishabur. He taught me the love of Persian and Arabic poetry and spoke to me of revelation, mysticism, and philosophy; but above all he showed me how to think and to have an open mind. Through him, I met men of remarkable knowledge and spiritual attainment. I am indebted to them and to my teachers in the Mashhad seminaries. Being the black sheep of the family, I ended my time in Iran in quite different circles: among students in Tehran University and my colleagues in the Franklin Book Program. I am much indebted to people I encountered in this period for helping me to see another side of life, especially the late Dr Hamid Enayat, Abdolmohammad Ayati, Mohammad Reza Hakimi, Dr M. R. Shafi'i Kadkani and Karim Emami.

In writing this book I benefited from my journalistic work in Iran and with the BBC Persian Service, which gave me unique access both to ordinary men and women and to leading players on the political and cultural scene. I would also like to thank the BBC World Service, and in particular John Dunn, Mark Dodd, James Norris, William Crawley and David Page of the former Eastern Service for their help and encouragement.

It was in Oxford, where I lived for some time, that I initially began my research. I spent many fruitful hours at the Middle East Centre, St Antony's College and at Wadham College's Persian Library. For these privileges I owe thanks to Dr John Gurney and Dr Derek Hopwood. I should thank Professor Algar of the University of California at Berkeley for generously offering me access to his source material. I am also grateful to many people in Iran, whose names I have not mentioned, for help with sources. Thanks are due to Elahe Mohtasham, Mehrdad Nabili, and especially to Setareh Alavi who kindly read my early drafts. In addition I am grateful to the late Albert Hourani, Dr Homa Katouzian and Dr Mansur Farhang for their advice on earlier versions of the book.

Finally, in finishing this book I was greatly helped by Trevor Mostyn, the late Dr Reza Navabpour, and the late Dr John Cooper.

Above all I am most grateful to my editor Anna Enayat, who completed and edited the text, not only making it more comprehensive but also making me intelligible.

KHOMEINI

Life of the Ayatollah

1

The Orphan
Childhood in Khomein

Khomein lies deep in the vast semi-arid areas of central Iran some 200 kilometres to the north-west of Isfahan, the magnificent capital of the Safavid Shahs, and 40 kilometres south of the city of Sultanabad-Arak. At the beginning of the twentieth century it was the administrative centre of Kamareh, a district of Golpayegan province. Yet in today's terms it was no more than a large village with a population of around 2,000 divided into 800 households. Built on the west bank of a tributary of the Qom river, it consisted of a main street fed by numerous alleys, a small shrine covered with blue and white tiles, three caravanserais, three bath houses and a great cluster of mud-brick houses plastered with a mixture of clay and straw to protect them from the eroding effects of the occasional downpour of rain and the ever-blowing wind. The little town was constantly threatened by marauding tribesmen. For this was the country of the Lurs, notorious for their unruly ways until the 1920s when they were pacified under Reza Shah. Khomein was all the same a rather prosperous place. A constant traffic of carts, donkeys and camels made its way through the market place carrying goods along one of the main trade routes between the Persian Gulf ports in the south and the capital, Tehran, to the north. It was surrounded by rich fields of grain, abundant orchards and good pasturelands all watered by the carefully channelled melting snows of the

nearby Zagros mountains. A little further afield were some of the finest
vineyards in the region from which a dozen or so Jewish families in the
nearby village of Lilian produced a very fine *araq* (spirits).

Ruhollah Khomeini was born on 24 September 1902 in a house that
stood in a large garden on the eastern edge of the village. A spacious two-
storied structure built around three courtyards in a style common to the
homes of the prosperous throughout provincial Iran, it had cool balconies
and two tall watchtowers – one overlooking the river to the fields beyond
and the other the surrounding streets and gardens. Throughout Khomeini's childhood this large fortified compound was alive with activity. His
widowed mother Hajieh Khanum rented the *andaruni*, the old family and
women's quarters, to the provincial governor's deputy in Kamareh who
used the first floor as his offices and the second as a billet for his guards.
Hajieh Khanum herself lived with her five children, her sister-in-law, her
co-wife and their guards and servants in what was known as the *biruni*, the
outer courtyard of the house normally used for guests and as the men's
quarter.[1]

Outside the house, on almost any warm evening, noisy groups of boys
would play in the street. A favourite game among them was 'the thief and
the vizier' (*dozd-o-vazir*) in which a thief is captured by guards and brought
to the court of a king who commands his vizier to have the wretched man
punished. Ruhollah Khomeini loved *dozd-o-vazir*. He was a particularly
striking boy of above average build, and he had a decorum that betrayed
his membership in one of the more prominent families of the area. Even
his friends seem to have noticed the difference between themselves and
this charismatic child, for whenever he joined the game he was at least the
vizier, if not the Shah himself. 'Even as a youngster, my father always wanted
to be the Shah in the games he played,' says Khomeini's son Ahmad.[2]

Khomeini's family are Musavi seyyeds; that is they claim descent from
the Prophet through his daughter's line and the line of the seventh Imam
of the Shi'a, Musa al-Kazem. They are believed to have come originally
from Neishabur, a town near to Mashhad in north-eastern Iran. In the
early eighteenth century the family migrated to India where they settled
in the small town of Kintur near Lucknow in the Kingdom of Oudh whose
rulers were Twelver Shi'a – the branch of Islam which became the official
state religion in Iran under the Safavids and to which the majority of Iranians adhere today. Ruhollah's grandfather, Seyyed Ahmad Musavi Hindi,
was born in Kintur and was a contemporary and relative of the famous

scholar Mir Hamed Hossein Hindi Neishaburi whose voluminous history of the religion, the *Abaqat al-Anwar*, is sometimes described as the pride of Indian Shi'ism.

Seyyed Ahmad left India in about 1830 to make a pilgrimage to the shrine city of Najaf in present-day Iraq, and possibly to study at one of its famous seminaries. He never returned. In Najaf he struck up a friendship with Yusef Khan Kamareh'i, a landowner who lived in the village of Farahan not far from Khomein who persuaded Ahmad to return to Iran with him. It is thought that the two men made the journey around 1834. Five years or so later, in 1839, Ahmad purchased the large house and garden in Khomein which was to remain in his family for well over a century and a half. Whether he had brought money with him from India or made it in Iran, he was clearly at this time a man of substance as the 4,000-square-metre property cost him the very large sum of 100 tomans. He had already married two wives from the district, Shirin Khanum and Bibi Khanum, and in 1841 he took a third, his friend Yusef Khan's sister Sakineh. Ahmad had only one child from his first two marriages, but Sakineh gave him three daughters and a son Mostafa, who was born in 1856. The family continued to prosper as, over the next decade, Ahmad bought land in the small villages of the region, and in Khomein itself an orchard and a caravanserai. He died in 1869 and, as he had instructed in his will, the family took his body by mule to the holy city of Karbala for burial.

Still a young boy at the time of his father's death, Khomeini's father Mostafa, as was customary in those days, trained for the family's religious profession. He studied first in a seminary in nearby Isfahan and then in Najaf and Samarra. He seems to have arrived in Najaf in 1891 with his first wife, Hajieh Agha Khanum, the daughter of Mirza Ahmad Mojtahed-e Khonsari, a high-ranking cleric well-known in central Iran. For a young member of a clerical family this was an exhilarating time to be in the holy city. Just a few months earlier, the Qajar king of Iran, Nasser al-Din Shah, had granted a monopoly over the country's large tobacco business to the British Imperial Tobacco Company in return for an annual payment of £15,000. The measure had enraged all kinds of people – the landlords and peasants who grew tobacco crops, the large merchants who exported them, the more humble tradesmen who sold tobacco in the country's bazaars and the many Iranian men and women who habitually enjoyed the water pipe with their friends and family. Responding to the anger, in December 1891 Mirza Hassan Shirazi, the leading divine of the

Shi'a who lived in Najaf, issued a *fatwa* banning the use of tobacco by the faithful. Throughout Iran, even in the royal harem, people obeyed his call, forcing the Shah to climb down and cancel the concession. Whether Mirza Hassan himself had issued the *fatwa*, or whether, as one historian persuasively argues, it was dreamt up by the country's threatened tobacco merchants, the effect was to vastly increase the prestige of the clergy in Iran's great trading cities and to mark the beginning of their active involvement in contemporary politics.[3]

Mostafa studied in the Atabat or 'sacred threshholds', the collective name given to the Shi'i shrine cities of Iraq, until 1894 when, at about the age of thirty-nine, he received what is known as 'permission to exercise *ejtehad*' (*ejazeh-ye ejtehad*), a qualification that allowed him to issue his own interpretations of religious law and principle and put him in the senior rank of the Shi'i clerical hierarchy. His first child, a girl, was born in Najaf soon after he and his wife arrived there. Five more children followed his return to Khomein, three sons and two daughters. The eldest son, Morteza, was born in 1896 and lived to be 101; the second, Nureddin, became a lawyer in Tehran; Ruhollah was the third. The family was still wealthy and when Mostafa died he left them an annual income of 100–200 tomans from his properties, a very considerable sum in days when it was calculated that an individual required just one toman a month for his or her upkeep.

In a memoir written in his old age Morteza, Mostafa's eldest son, remarks that his father took no part in the 'religious affairs' (*omur-e shari'*) of Khomein.[4] Although he does not elaborate, it is probable that by this he means that Mostafa did not carry out, or live by, any of the many specific functions that the clergy carried out in traditional Iranian society. Mollahs supervised not only people's personal religious affairs but also social, educational and judicial matters. Often, especially in larger towns, these functions were separated. Private tutors who worked with children educated beyond the level of the traditional primary schools were nearly always mollahs who would teach a range of subjects – language, calligraphy, mathematics, literature as well as the religious sciences. Or a mollah might have specialised in legal matters acting as a notary public or, if he was properly qualified (had gained his 'permission' in other words), as a judge at one of the country's many religious courts which in those days enjoyed wide, often vaguely defined jurisdiction over both criminal and civil matters. Or he may have concentrated on one or another of the purely spiritual functions of the clergy and worked as a prayer leader, a preacher or a chanter of religious stories (*rowzehkhan*).

A good mollah in a smaller place often combined many of these functions. A sort of country vicar extraordinary, he was at the same time spiritual guide, judge, notary, teacher, preacher and entertainer. He would be asked to speak the word of God in a child's ear after it was born, Islam's form of baptism. He often taught children and young people the principles of Islam. He officiated at their marriages and legalised their divorces, acted as notary to sign and seal their land, household and water transactions. He preached to them, eulogising the martyrdom of the saints and the Imams. Above all he guided them in their daily religious practices from the cradle to the grave. For the ordinary believer, whatever his or her social class, the mollah was an essential companion in the most intimate moments of life: birth, prayer, marriage and death. And he was especially needed to ensure their entry to paradise.

This wide-ranging remit meant that the Iranian clergy as a body enjoyed a special prestige among a highly religious and deeply superstitious people; and individual clerics were particularly valued if, like Khomeini's family, they could claim descent from the prophet. Yet a rather low social status was attached to some of the specific functions they carried out, and the whiff of corruption that sometimes surrounded even the more prestigious occupations, such as that of the *shari'a* judge, meant that members of landed clerical families would usually stand aloof from such work. They nevertheless maintained the tradition of religious learning which gave them the social influence and the country-wide social connections that were so vital to maintaining a family's position in nineteenth and early twentieth-century Iran.

Mostafa seems to have belonged firmly to this category and to have lived the life of a landed provincial notable whose clerical background, wide-ranging connections in the region, and strong personality enabled him to become something of a community leader. Inevitably, hagiographical accounts of Mostafa's character have, given the almost god-like status achieved by his youngest son and the lack of contemporary records, proliferated since the 1979 Iranian Revolution. These tend to portray him as a man who came to be a popular and influential figure because he was 'close to the ordinary people' and, unlike many clerics and chiefs 'stood by the small farmers and peasants in their problems with the landlords and government officials.' There may well be an element of truth in such claims. But the noble qualities they attribute to a man of this period were of a different kind than those implied by the vocabulary of modern populist politics. The role a man like Mostafa played in his community should be seen against the background of the lawlessness and insecurity that prevailed in many areas of provincial Iran in his day and the idealised function, in such circumstances, of the good 'notable'.

Rural society in nineteenth-century Luristan was made up of a complicated, chaotic web of settled and migrating tribes and sub-tribes, large and small landowners and the peasantry who worked the land. Disputes over rights to land and water and, where landowners behaved unfairly with their peasants, over the division of crops, were rife and the settled population lived in constant fear of raids by armed and highly mobile tribesmen. Although it had its officials in the area, central government was not strong enough to have much of a presence. Tax collection and the business of maintaining order were usually farmed out to powerful local landowners who kept private armies, and all too often exploited their position to enrich themselves at the expense both of ordinary people and the government. 'The khans and the princes were very powerful at the time,' Mostafa's eldest son Morteza recalls: 'They had guns. They were oppressive ... princes and khans oppressed the governor and the governor oppressed the people.'[5] In this context, people needed the protection that a well-connected wealthy man like Mostafa could provide.'Our father,' says Morteza, 'was well-supplied with rifles and riflemen which he used not only to protect his land but to help others.'

But such a position carried its own dangers. On a cold day in March 1903, less than six months after the birth of his third son Ruhollah, Mostafa was shot and mortally wounded on the road from Khomein to Arak. He was only forty-seven-years-old.[6] A number of imaginative stories have circulated since the 1979 revolution about this incident. One of these suggests that Mostafa had ordered the execution of a man for publicly violating the Ramadan fast and that he was murdered by the man's relatives in revenge. Khomeini's son Ahmad tells another, very different tale tinged with both illicit romance and a strong hint of populist political motive. The Shah was at the time on a visit to Arak and had summoned Mostafa to his presence. On hearing of the invitation Mostafa's sister Sahebeh became anxious about her brother's safety and insisted that he take armed men with him. Mostafa refused, left Khomein on his own and was murdered on the way to Arak. The distraught Sahebeh immediately organised a party to track down the murderer. However, it soon became apparent that her daughter was in love with one of the assassins, and tried on several occasions to warn him of his imminent arrest. The men were eventually discovered by reluctant local officials who took them to prison in Tehran. Sahebeh and her daughter were also taken to the capital as witnesses at the interrogation. On the journey the desperate girl pleaded with her mother to show mercy and to stop the execution, but Sahebeh adamantly refused. When they returned to Khomein her daughter dressed for months in mourning black, ostensibly for her Uncle Mostafa; but it was an open secret that the man for whom she was mourning was in fact her lover and her uncle's assassin.[7]

An account that is undoubtedly closer to the truth and just as intriguing is that given by Morteza, who was only eight-years-old at the time of his father's death, but, as his eldest male heir, was deeply involved in the events that followed it. It is worth paraphrasing in some detail for the vivid picture it provides of the society into which Khomeini was born.[8]

In the second and third years of the twentieth century, life for the people of Khomein was, Morteza relates, made particularly miserable by three local khans – Bahram, Mirza Qoli Soltan and Ja'far Qoli – whose predatory ways oppressed the population. The worst of them, Bahram Khan, was arrested and jailed by Heshmat al-Dowleh, a powerful Qajar prince who owned huge tracts of land in the region. Bahram Khan was later killed or died in prison, but his two companions continued to harass the people. As the situation got worse, Mostafa decided that something must be done and that he would go to Arak to ask the provincial governor, the Shah's son Azod al-Soltan, for help.

When they heard about Mostafa's plans, Mirza Qoli Soltan and Ja'far Qoli Khan approached him pretending they wanted to seek a position from the governor, presumably on the grounds that if they had a stable source of income they could afford to stop living by pillage and extortion. They asked Mostafa to allow them to travel with him. 'My father replied,' says Morteza: 'There is no need for you to come. I'll get a job for you from the governor.' Meanwhile, the wife of one of the khans, who was a daughter of Sadr al-Ulema, a local religious dignitary and a relative of the family, warned Mostafa that 'they bear you ill will'. But Mostafa ignored her. 'They won't dare to do a damn thing,' he said. He left for Arak, which was about two-day's journey from Khomein, with ten to fifteen horsemen and armed guards. The next day, as he was riding ahead of the party flanked by only two of his guards, Ja'far Khan and Mirza Qoli Soltan appeared on the roadside. They were unarmed. 'You were supposed to stay in Khomein,' said Mostafa. 'Well we didn't obey you,' they replied. 'They offered our father sweets and then suddenly seized a rifle [from one of the guards] and … aimed at his heart. The bullet went clean through the Qor'an my father had put in his shirt pocket and pierced his heart. He fell from his horse and died instantly.' The assassins escaped before the rest of the party could catch up.

News of the murder was taken without delay to Arak and a large group of clerics set out to collect Mostafa's body and accompany it back to the city. 'Life in Arak came to a complete standstill that day' and elsewhere. In Tehran, Isfahan and Golpayegan, the news of Mostafa's murder was heard with dismay and services were held to mourn him. 'In Khomein itself,' Morteza recalls, 'there were displays of public grief and groups of mourners came to our home to offer their condolences … the killer's house was burned down though I do not know whether this was the work of the government or the people. I was only eight and no one told me. But I saw the flames from the top of our watch tower. Their houses were burnt and their property confiscated.' They were, however, he adds in a footnote, 'later returned to their heirs at the request of our family.'

The murderers had meanwhile escaped to the nearby villages of the Aligudarz area. Finding that no one was prepared to give them shelter they moved on to Khonsar, a small town many miles away, thinking that they could find sanctuary with Haj Mirza Mohammad Mehdi Khonsari 'an important cleric who also had numerous difficulties with the government and so was always armed and had a great many riflemen.' But he, too, refused them. Finally, they returned to the environs of Khomein to hide with their families in an abandoned fortress in the village of Yujan. The prime minister, Amin al-Soltan, who had been informed of the incident by Seyyed Mohammad Kamareh'i, Mostafa's son-in-law who resided in Tehran,[9] had by this time ordered their arrest. Meanwhile, Mostafa's family had gone to the governor's court in Arak to demand *qesas* or retribution – the customary procedure under Islamic law in such cases. But the wheels of justice proved to be painfully slow.

Despite Amin al-Soltan's orders, Ja'far Qoli and Mirza Qoli remained undisturbed in their hideout for the next six months, perhaps longer, until a new prime minister, the notorious Qajar strong man Ayn al-Dowleh, came to power. By this time Mostafa's heirs had obtained the support of Tehran's most powerful clerics - Seyyed Abolqassem the young Imam

Jom'eh of Tehran, Seyyed Mohammad and Zahir al-Islam. The three men were brothers and the senior members of a family from whose ranks the Friday Imam (*imam jom'eh*), the leader of Friday prayers in the capital – the most important religious position in the country and the only position in the Shi'i hierarchy that was a government appointment – had been selected ever since the Safavid era. Zahir al-Islam was also, through his mother, the grandson of Nasser al-Din Shah.

On the brothers' request, Ayn al-Dowleh ordered Nasrollah Khan Sardar Heshmat, the son of Heshmat al-Dowleh, to arrest Mostafa's assassins. 'Sardar Heshmat, who kept an armed troop in his village Heshmatieh, set out with his men for Yujan ....' The soldiers surrounded the fort but Ja'far Khan and Mirza Qoli refused to surrender. Eventually, when all [other] efforts failed, the governor [*sic*] ordered his men to dig a tunnel under the fortress. The murderers resisted until their last bullet was spent ... and were finally arrested with members of their family and were taken to Tehran.' According to a report in the newspaper *Adab* the battle had lasted for three days.[10]

Mirza Qoli Khan died in prison. But nothing was immediately done about Ja'far Qoli who, for reasons Morteza does not explain, had found a patron in Mozaffar al-Din Shah's court minister, Amir Bahador-e Jang. Amir Bahador had insisted that '... the past is the past ... we should not execute Ja'far Khan,' and had even instructed groups of ritual mourners commemorating the heroic death of Imam Hossein in the holy month of Moharram (1322) – March 1904 – to attack the prison and free him. But the plot was foiled when the prime minister ordered Ja'far Khan to be moved to a different prison just before the attack was scheduled to take place.

At this point Seyyed Abolqassem, Seyyed Mohammad and Zahir al-Islam, together with leading ulema in Sultanabad, intervened once more by issuing a decree condemning Ja'far Qoli to death. But their judgment was not immediately pursued, presumably because Amir Bahador was still protecting the man.

So back in Khomein Mostafa's family decided that if justice was to be done they would have to travel to Tehran to seek the intervention of the Shah. Before they left, the young Morteza and his seven-year-old brother Nureddin were invited to the home of Heshmat al-Dowleh with their male relatives. As a mark of the nobleman's respect and sympathy they were presented with the customary gift of new clothes, a turban and *abba*, the long woollen cloak worn by mollahs. Little Morteza was deeply impressed. The gift of a clerical outfit made of the finest material – as was usual with such ceremonial gifts, known as *khalat* – marked a coming of age. 'We became turbaned,' he recalls, using a slang expression for the clergy.

We set out for Tehran in April 1905 in the company of Nureddin, my elder sister, my aunt Sahebeh Khanum, our mother Hajieh Agha Khanum, our father's [second] wife Shahzdeh Agha, our mother's uncle Sheikh Fazlollah Raja'i and our servant Abbasqoli Abarqu'i. Imam [young Ruhollah], who was 4 months and 22 days old when our father was killed, and our two sisters, stayed behind with our servants. The journey took us ten days ... When we arrived in Tehran we rented a house in Abbasabad in the south of the city.

Once they had settled in, the whole family headed for the palace of Ayn al-Dowleh. They were taken to the prime minister's audience chamber where, as usual, a large crowd was gathered. The now ten-year-old Morteza, as Mostafa's eldest male heir, had been thoroughly schooled in the way to make a formal plea for retribution.

When we moved forward to meet the prime minister he ordered some ten people to move back. He wore a long robe and had a huge moustache. I moved forward and took hold of [the hem] of his robe. I had been taught my lines with care and said to him in a sarcastic tone: 'if you are just, we are not. Give us the killer and we will execute him ourselves.' Ayn al-Dowleh replied 'No. I will execute the murderer. But Mozaffar al-Din Shah himself decreed that his own father's assassin should not be executed in the [holy] months of Moharram or Safar. We won't kill anyone in Moharram or Safar. If we don't kill him after that you can complain.' I replied 'We will take sanctuary and remain in this building until you kill him.' He said 'Fine. You stay here. My feet are aching and you have kept me standing too long. I'm tired.' Then they brought Zahir al-Islam to speak to us ... [and] he persuaded us to go home and wait.

Shortly after this audience Ayn al-Dowleh left Tehran to accompany Mozaffar al-Din Shah on a trip to Europe. The acting prime minister was Moshir al-Saltaneh who Morteza describes as 'a Sufi learned in theology.' The family pursued their case with him. 'We saw him in his garden and he took me in his arms and sat me on his knee. He treated us with great respect and said "the death warrant has been issued for the murderer. I will kill him".'

Later, probably as a means of demonstrating the court's sympathy for their case, the two young orphans were taken to the Golestan palace to visit the crown prince Mohammad Ali Mirza. 'He had ordered that Nureddin and I should go alone ... I was ten and Nureddin was eight. We both wore our turbans. [The Crown Prince] stood next to a big pond in a court yard surrounded by trees. When he saw us he said "go back now".' The boys were conducted to an adjacent building and on the way they spotted Ja'far Qoli Khan with his neck in a chain held by a guard. 'He was brought in and he sat down. He was an old man and he had become very fat. He swore that "I am not the murderer. They are lying. Please let me go."'

But the children showed no mercy and soon afterwards, on 9 May 1905, Ja'far Qoli was taken to the Baharestan, and area of Tehran where public executions were held, to meet his fate. 'My brother and myself were not allowed to watch and were told to go home ... but others went to watch. The condemned man, the executioner and the Shah [sic] all wore red, as was the custom in those days. Ja'far Qoli was beheaded. The executioner took his head to the bazaar where he showed it to the merchants and shopkeepers who offered him tips.'

Justice done, the family left Tehran immediately – just a few months before the Constitutional Revolution of 1905–6, the most momentous event in the history of early twentieth-century Iran, began to gather steam. In fact one of the first incidents of the build-up to the revolution had occurred just as they arrived in Tehran, although Morteza does not mention it. The capital's merchants, who were deeply upset by new customs tariffs drawn up by Monsieur Naus, the Belgian head of the customs administration, in an effort to find extra sources of income for the government, had closed their shops and taken sanctuary (bast, a traditional form of protest in Iran) at the shrine of Shah Abdolazim. At the same time, a photograph of Naus dressed in mollah's robes for a fancy-dress ball had been circulated among the clergy arousing huge indignation and guaranteeing their firm support for the merchants' cause. The merchant–clergy alliance which, a decade earlier, had succeeded in forcing the Shah to withdraw the Imperial Tobacco Company's concession, was once more on the move against an increasingly impecunious government.

This time, however, there was more at stake than just forcing a climb down over the customs tariffs. For one thing a sharp economic recession was producing generalised discontent in the urban areas of the country. But even more important, from the mid-1890s demands for political reform and for an end to British and Russian intervention in the affairs of the country, advanced at first by a small elite of intellectuals, bureaucrats and merchants who were deeply aware of the backwardness of Iranian society, had, with the advent of newspapers, begun to find a wider audience.

The demand for reform surfaced for the first time on the streets in December 1905 when the undercurrent of unrest which had simmered all summer burst out into the open when the prime minister ordered a group of prominent Tehran merchants to be bastinadoed in public for putting up the price of sugar. Their colleagues took sanctuary (*bast*) at the Shah mosque and crowds of people led by a coalition of religious figures and secular intellectuals, many of them reforming bureaucrats, began to fill the streets. The crowd demanded not just the dismissal of the prime minister Ayn al-Dowleh, but also an end to despotic rule and the establishment of a 'house of justice', a sort of judicial council whose functions would be to abolish favouritism and to make all subjects equal before the law and which would be made up of representatives of the clergy, merchants, craft guilds and landowners and to be presided over by the Shah.

A month later Mozaffar al-Din Shah promised action, but he did nothing until he was forced by a more serious crisis which blew up in the summer of 1906. This time the trouble began with the death of a *talabeh* (a seminary student) who had been demonstrating in a crowd that was fired upon by the Shah's Cossack guard. Subsequently 14,000 people, many of them clergymen, took *bast* in the grounds of the British Embassy in Tehran and stayed there for around a month – a demonstration perhaps comparable in scale, given the very much smaller population of the capital in those days, to the huge demonstrations that ushered in the Iranian Revolution seven decades later. By that time the demand of the crowd had developed into one for a full-blown Western-style constitution and a representative assembly. In October the first National Consultative Assembly – the Majles-e Showra-ye Melli, known for short as the Majles, was opened, and in December 1906 the Shah signed the Constitutional Law on his deathbed.

Although it heralded a major political change and caused much excitement and gossip throughout the country, the Constitutional Revolution did not immediately affect the daily life of people in places like Khomein, and certainly did not help to increase security. In fact the revolution severely weakened the central government's already fragile authority in the provinces and Morteza recalls that this was a time of widespread thievery and, for Khomein, frequent raids by the Lurs. He describes one such raid that took place on a cold March day just after the Iranian New Year, which falls on the Spring solstice. He and the rest of the family were paying the customary new year visit to friends in a different part of the town when the warning cry went up. 'We got up and returned to our homes. When we got home we found that the gendarmerie had taken over our house and were shooting from the watch tower. I went up the tower and saw the tribesmen on their horses 100 to 200 *zar'* from Khomein, but the attack was repulsed.' All the same, *korsis*, charcoal burners covered by low tables and cotton-stuffed eiderdowns, were set up around the family's home so that the people of Khomein could take refuge there and sleep peacefully guarded by constables and by Morteza and Nureddin who gave them an enthusiastic helping hand.

The young Ruhollah was brought up in this bleak, somewhat hair-raising environment by his mother, his wet nurse Naneh Khavar and his Aunt Sahebeh, who had no children of her own and had moved back into the family home to help with her brother's orphaned brood. (There is no record of how this affected Sahebeh's relationship with her second husband, a wealthy landowner and merchant; her first, a certain Shokrollah Khan whose brother had become an outlaw, was killed in a skirmish.) Sahebeh seems to have been a major influence on the family and legends of her strength and courage abound. Ahmad, Khomeini's son, says that in the absence of a *shari'a* judge in Khomein, Sahebeh had once carried out his duties for a few days until a replacement could be appointed. If this story is true it is most unusual since in Islam women are not allowed to become judges. Ahmad also relates that: 'Two rival groups of the people of Khomein were involved in a shooting incident. Sahebeh interfered and placed herself between the feuding factions, ordering them to stop shooting. Her power and charisma were such that they immediately obeyed her.'

Whether as a result of his genes, or of influences such as Sahebeh, Ruhollah was clearly a spirited child. The family recalls that he was very energetic, playing all day in the streets and coming home in the evening with his clothes dirty and torn, often bearing the wounds of scraps with his friends." He was also physically strong and his abilities meant that as he grew older he became something of a champion at sports. He could beat other boys in wrestling, but his favourite game was leapfrog and in this he was considered the local champion.

Like most other boys in Khomein – and throughout Iran at the time – when he was seven Ruhollah was sent to a local *maktab* run by a certain Akhund Mollah Abolqassem. In Arabic *maktab* means 'place of writing', but in effect it was a 'place of reading'. The teacher was usually, like Abolqassem, an old mollah or woman who taught the alphabet, the Qor'an and popular religious stories. Each child would take his food and a piece of cloth or an animal skin rug to sit on. Learning was by rote and the children would repeat in chorus the lines spoken by their teacher. In lessons of this kind their chanting gained its own musical momentum and on a quiet day could be heard from several hundred metres away.

Regulations in the *maktabs* were very harsh and punishment for mispronouncing a Qor'anic word was by today's standards torture. The suffering of the children who attended them was legendary. One of the nursery rhymes of those days was: 'Wednesday I think. Thursday I enjoy. Friday I play. Oh unhappy Saturday: my legs are bleeding from the strokes of cherry-tree branches.'[12] Schoolchildren dreaded Saturday, the first day of the Islamic week, and when the days lessons were over they felt as if they had been freed from prison.

At the *maktab* and at home Ruhollah would have first been taught to memorise by heart the last few chapters of the Qor'an, as well as a few phrases and words in Arabic about the Prophet and the Imams. In the absence of his father, the elders of the family – his brother, his aunt or his mother – would have taught him to recite the principles and precepts of Islam. Children are made to repeat these principles without any idea of the meaning of the words. For them the regular cadences of Persian made the task seem just like reciting a nursery rhyme: first, the oneness of God; second, the prophethood [of Mohammad]; third, justice; fourth, the imamate (the leadership of Mohammad's twelve successors) and fifth, the resurrection on the day of judgement.

Another channel through which Ruhollah would have been socialised into the culture of Shi'ism, this time in its popular form, would have been through the many religious festivals in the Shi'i calendar which, in the days before cinema and television, provided the main form of entertainment in a place like Khomein and were eagerly looked forward to. Most such festivals mark the birthdays of the Imams and the anniversaries of their martyrdom. For young and old alike their high point comes in the month of Moharram when children join in colourful processions, passion plays and the recitation of elegies and eulogies of the Imams and other martyrs.

Moharram is the first month of the Islamic lunar calendar, but for the Shi'a it is the month of mourning for the third Imam, Hossein, and his companions who were killed in the battle of Karbala on 10 October 680, the tenth day of the lunar month, known as Ashura. The events of that day are commemorated throughout the Shi'i world with great intensity. For the Shi'a, the martyrdom of Hossein is a historic moment rich in religious symbolism. It is represented in scholarly works, poetry and architecture, passion plays and other popular rites and evoked everywhere by orators, clerics, monarchs, politicians, revolutionaries, reactionaries and men of literature. This one moment acts as a focus for the sentiments of all Shi'i believers and was used later in his life by Khomeini as a point of departure for the mass movement he staged against the Shah.

The tragedy of Hossein was the culmination of a long dispute over the succession to the Prophet and the nature of religious and political leadership in early Islam. It is also the great issue which divides the Shi'a from the Sunnis. The Shi'a believe that, before his death, Mohammad designated his cousin and son-in-law Ali as his successor – as a divine act, not a personal choice. But Ali did not become the temporal leader or caliph of the community. Abu Bakr, the closest of the Prophet's 'Companions' was elected by a congregation of the elders of Medina, Mohammad's capital, while Ali and his wife Fatemeh, the Prophet's only surviving child, were occupied with the funeral arrangements.

Abu Bakr survived for only two years and on his deathbed he appointed another leading Companion, Omar, as the new caliph. Omar, in his turn, appointed a council of six men, including Ali, to designate his successor and Osman ibn Affan was declared the third caliph. Osman was the longest serving of the early successors to Mohammad; but he became very unpopular and was accused of nepotism and corruption. He was eventually assassinated in 656, and Ali, who had by this time acquired a considerable following, was finally acclaimed the fourth caliph. Ali had not involved himself in the wars of conquest that had begun within two years of the Prophet's death and which had, by this time, brought large swathes of territory in the Middle East under Muslim control. He also, unlike many other members of the Meccan aristocracy, lived a simple ascetic life devoting himself to preaching and writing.

Nevertheless, Ali faced enormous difficulties, because the provincial governors of the Islamic Empire had been appointed by Osman, mostly from his own family, the Umayyads. The most powerful of these, Mo'awiya, the governor of Syria, refused to acknowledge Ali as caliph. In this he was supported by one of the Prophet's wives, Ayesha, who led an army against her son-in-law near Basra. Ali won the battle, but his efforts to guide the community and set it back on the correct Islamic path brought him more and more enemies. Two years later Mo'awiya marched an army against him at Siffin in Iraq. Ali's forces were on the point of victory when Mo'awiya's general ordered his soldiers to fasten Qor'ans to their spears, a signal that only God could decide the issue. Arbitration followed, largely to Ali's disadvantage. Not long afterwards Ali was mortally wounded in Kufa by an assassin, probably by one of a group of rebels known as Kharijites who believed that he should never have submitted to arbitration at Siffin. The caliphate passed to Mo'awiya; but for Ali's followers he was succeeded by his son Hassan, the second Shi'i Imam.

For the Shi'a, Mo'awiya's takeover signalled even greater decline in the purity of the Muslim community. When he was succeeded by his son Yazid it must have seemed that Islam as a religious movement was in grave danger. Yazid was well-known for his love of wine and the pleasures of court life and he showed little respect for the moral and legal changes that Islam had inaugurated. The growing discontent was led by Hossein, Ali's second son who had become the Imam upon the death of his brother Hassan. He first moved from Medina to Mecca to escape swearing allegiance to Yazid and, while there, he received messages from Kufa urging him to set up a rival government with the support of the townspeople. Hossein set out with a small armed detachment and several women and children, including his family. But Yazid had, meanwhile, frightened or bought off the Kufans. As a result, when Hossein reached the plain of Karbala he was met by some 4,000 of Yazid's troops.

Hossein seems to have been aware that a battle was impending, for he had several times urged his followers to leave him. His armed men are said to have numbered a mere seventy-two. A massacre ensued; all the fighting men were killed, and Hossein was the last to fall. His infant son Ali Asghar was struck by an arrow and the women and children were taken prisoner, first to Kufa and then to Yazid in Damascus. Hossein's surviving son Ali – better known as Zein al-Abedin – now became the fourth Shi'i Imam and he and the family were eventually allowed to return to Medina.

The passion plays staged in Iran during Moharram, known as *ta'zieh*, are a ritual re-enactment of this story. There are many different versions, each emphasising a different aspect in order to convey a particular religious truth. For example, on the day of Ashura the focus is usually on the battle of Karbala itself depicting the bravery of Hossein and the cruelty and corruption of his enemies. On other occasions the focus may be on Hossein's sister Zeinab, her journey in captivity with the rest of his family, and her brave and dignified conduct in the court of Yazid.

These same stories are also related throughout the year in another ritual of popular Shi'ism, the *rowzehkhani*. *Rowzehkhanis* are held in people's houses or in neighbourhood mosques. Most of the preachers who conduct these ceremonies have a repetoire of a dozen or so stories about the different personalities of the Battle of Karbala which they will be asked to relate as the occasion demands. For example, if a family loses a child they may ask for the story of little Ali Asghar through which they can mourn their own loss. These are always highly charged, emotional occasions and, even if the *rowzeh* is organised to mark a happy occasion, a skilled preacher will construct the plot of his story in a way that will, without losing the flow, relate it to the martyrdom of Hossein and bring his audience to tears.

Through these popular ritual observations children are indoctrinated with the Shi'i version of history. The constant themes of sadness and morbidity in them reflect the ever-present sense among the Shi'a that they are an oppressed community who have been wronged historically. The Prophet and all Imams and saints were wronged by their enemies, and it is the duty of the faithful to seek revenge. This struggle between truth and falsehood, *haq* and *batel*, and the resulting tendency to see things in black and white is imprinted on children's minds and can remain with them for the rest of their lives. There are no grey areas and it is only through revenge that things can be put right.

But Shi'ism was not the only element of the cultural environment in which the children of literate families, even very strict religious families, grew up. The great classics of Persian literature were also read to them from a very early age and they would be encouraged to learn poetry by heart. On long winter nights families would sit together around the *korsi* to read and recite passages from the *Shahnameh* (Ferdowsi's *Book of Kings*), tales from *A Thousand and One Nights* or the poetry of Hafez and Sa'di. These and other great works of literature inject a more complex picture of life which has an altogether more questioning feel about it. The culture of literature and the culture of religion often blatantly contradict one another; and yet they have coexisted for centuries in the Iranian psyche.

There is much to suggest that Khomeini's family was no exception to this pattern. His brother relates that, by the time he reached his teens, Ruhollah had memorised hundreds of verses by different poets, both religious and classical. There is indeed hardly a major poet whom he has not quoted in his later writings.[13] He also, from his teens, knew how to versify and would often, later in life, write his own poetry as a pastime. This was a skill learnt by boys in clerical and other literate households through the *mosha'ereh*, or verse contest, a game in which two or more would exchange lines of poetry. The rules of *mosha'ereh* are varied, but the most common form is to begin a line of verse with the same letter used at the end of the competing side's line.

Ruhollah remained in the *maktab* until he was about seven and then attended a school built in Khomein by the constitutional government as part of its effort to modernise Iran's educational system. In addition to Persian language and literature, at this school he would have had an elementary training in subjects such as arithmetic, history, geography and some very basic science. He also had private tutors: Sheikh Ja'far his mother's cousin, Mirza Mahmud Eftekhar al-Ulama who had been his brother's tutor and whom Morteza describes as 'not very literate' (and certainly a much inferior teacher to Mirza Mahmud's mother who would stand in for him when he took his annual trip to Isfahan) and Sheikh Hamza Mahallati who taught him calligraphy.[14] When he was fifteen he started learning Arabic grammar in a serious fashion with Morteza, who had studied Arabic and theology in Isfahan. Morteza, who had a good hand, also worked with his younger brother on his calligraphy and relates how their handwriting became so alike that he would write half a letter, give it to Ruhollah to complete, and then wait to see whether anyone could tell the difference. The brothers' conspiracy was never discovered![15]

Khomeini's childhood drew to a close towards the end of the First World War when his mother and aunt both died in the terrible cholera epidemic that raged through Iran in 1918. He was sixteen and about to enter the seminary. But political events in far off Tehran during his childhood and adolescence meant that the country he was to live in as a young man was very different from the society in which he had been born and brought up.

The Constitutional Revolution had gone through many ups and downs since the victorious months of late 1906. Aided by the Russians, Mozaffar al-Din Shah's successor, the reactionary Mohammad Ali Shah, had in 1907 moved against the constitutional government and had eventually succeeded in abolishing the Majles and arresting the constitutionalist leaders. Riots had flared up all over the country and armed revolutionaries took the northern city of Tabriz declaring the Shah deposed. By this time, however, the constitutional cause was a truly nationwide affair and in the summer of 1909 tribesmen from the great Bakhtiari confederation marched on the capital from the south while, simultaneously, a hastily assembled army of constitutionalists approached from Rasht in the north. Mohammad Ali Shah was deposed and succeeded by his eleven-year-old son, Sultan Ahmad.

The Shah's counter-revolution had been supported by a group of clergymen led by Sheikh Fazlollah Nuri, Tehran's most learned cleric and one of Khomeini's heroes in his later life. Like many of the clergy, Sheikh Fazlollah had at first sympathised with the constitutional movement's opposition to tyranny and the demand to apply the law. However, after he had attended a few sessions of the first Majles, he realised that its function was to make laws.[16] For Sheikh Fazlollah, Man could not make law and the role of a parliament should only be to ratify and enforce shari'a-based laws. Some of the clergy still argued in favour of the Majles – generally on the grounds that the Qor'an enjoined consultation and in the modern world the Muslim community was in need of legislation not provided for in the shari'a, as long as the new laws were not incompatible with Islam. Many other pro-constitutional clerics shared Sheikh Fazlollah's doubts but, rather than actually oppose the Majles, opted out of active involvement in politics. Only Sheikh Fazlollah and his followers took their argument to its logical extreme, concluding that in the absence of the Hidden Imam, an absolutist government which applies Islamic law is the best government. The despotism of the Shah was, in other words, for Sheikh Fazlollah the lesser of two evils and he had campaigned vigorously, from the pulpit and through pamphlets, for this point of view.[17]

Sheikh Fazlollah was a man of conviction and considerable courage. When the constitutionalist forces entered Tehran, instead of fleeing to a place of sanctuary, he encouraged the local roughs, armed by the Shah, to defend the Sangelaj district of Tehran where he lived. Their resistance was, however, quickly broken and Sheikh Fazlollah was arrested. He was put on trial on 31 July 1909 before a special tribunal consisting of 'ten members drawn from the occupying forces, the former assembly, the press and others, mostly of a radical persuasion chaired by a reformist *mojtahed*, Sheikh Ebrahim Zanjani',[18] and condemned to death. The execution took place in public immediately after the trial.

Soon afterwards the second Majles was convened. By then the secular reformists, for whom the image of law was derived primarily from the tradition of the French Enlightenment, had won the day and the Iranian state began to develop decisively in the direction of a modern state – though not in the end the democracy the constitutionalists had envisaged. In the course of this evolution, many clerics cast aside their turbans and were absorbed into the new order, often as teachers, intellectuals or lawyers. But for the clergy as a body the end result was marginalisation, the loss of many of their functions and of their authority in society. As we shall see, many of them became increasingly bitter about the events of this period.

2

In the Seminary
Student Years in Qom

Khomeini had left his birthplace and a turbulent childhood behind him. He was, by all accounts, a determined, assertive and serious young man. But beyond this little is known about him. Had the murder of his father created in him a spirit of revenge, not against the murderers or their families, but against the supposed instigators of the murder, the authorities? We do not know. But if his brother's account is correct this seems highly unlikely. Nor was his family in any way marginal to Iranian society. True, Khomeini spent his youth in a small provincial town, but he was brought up in a well-connected household whose prosperity was based on land and whose economic position is unlikely to have been dramatically affected by the death of its master. The picture painted for him of his father as a man who campaigned for 'truth' and opposed 'falsehood', unbelievers and oppressors, may well have deeply affected his impressionable mind and provided a model of conduct for him to look up to. But in the end all that can be safely concluded about him is that he was destined by family tradition for the seminary, though not necessarily the active priesthood.

He may well have aspired to go to Najaf for the next stage of his education; but with the collapse of the Ottoman Empire at the end of the First World War the great shrine city was in turmoil. Furthermore, young men usually went to Najaf when they had already completed several years in a seminary – known in the Islamic world as a *madraseh*. So, after much consultation with his brother Morteza, it was decided that he would go to Isfahan, the nearest important town to Khomein and a centre of Shi'i learning for several centuries. Before long, however, Ruhollah heard that a certain Sheikh Abdolkarim Ha'eri, a learned and pious man, had created a theological college of outstanding quality in nearby Sultanabad-Arak,[1] where he was supported by the wealthy mollah, Haj Mohsen Araqi.[2] For a student whose dream was Najaf this was an exciting opportunity.

Sheikh Abdolkarim, who had spent many years in the shrine cities of Iraq, first settled in Arak in 1900, two years before the birth of Khomeini. However, six years later, on the eve of the Constitutional Revolution, he had left Iran to live once more in Najaf. Unlike many of the senior clergy of his generation, Ha'eri believed that a mollah should not be involved in politics, and went to great lengths to keep aloof from the fray. Unfortunately for him, Najaf in 1906 was rapidly turning into a political hotbed which mirrored the conflict raging in Tehran. Supporters of the Constitutional Revolution had written to the three leading clerics of the holy city – Akhund Mohammad Kazem Khorasani, Haj Mirza Hossein Khalil Tehrani and Sheikh Abdollah Mazandarani – asking for an opinion on the following question: 'What would be your view of an assembly set up from among the elders and wise men of the country to eradicate or reduce tyranny?' Their reply was unambiguous: 'It is a divine duty'.[3] Despite the authority of these men, clerical factions supporting and opposing the Constitutional Revolution were soon locked in passionate dispute which came to a head when crowds under the influence of the anti-constitutionalists attacked their rivals in the streets of Najaf killing many religious students. Ha'eri moved to Karbala. But in 1913, as the Shi'i clergy of the shrine cities began to agitate against British rule in Iraq, he was forced to move again – this time back to Sultanabad.[4]

Khomeini's attitude to politics in his mature years was the polar opposite of Ha'eri's. Nevertheless Ha'eri's pious and ascetic ways exerted a lifelong influence on him. In the medieval atmosphere of a seminary the clergy competed with each other for status. They would vie for the best seats at a meeting. Those who could afford it would go everywhere surrounded by their riflemen and, to prove their popularity, with their supporters. Ha'eri was quite different. He would walk on his own with his *aba* or cloak under his arm, an example Khomeini was to follow in later years. Unlike many mollahs, he had no interest in the material world and he cared scrupulously for his blind wife, personally attending to her every need.[5]

Although only recently established, the seminary Ruhollah entered as a slim, rather tall seventeen-year-old was not very different from seminaries throughout the Islamic world. In most a large door with a smaller inset door for ordinary daily use leads into a symmetrically laid-out courtyard, similar to the quadrangle of a medieval European college but without cloisters. A path runs around the edge of the courtyard, giving access to the ground-floor rooms and the courtyard is often laid out with flower-beds and paths leading to a central space with a pond or a flower-bed. In the climate of Iran shade is essential, so the flower-beds have large trees under which the students can sit out of direct sunlight.

The emphasis which Islam places on learning has given the *madraseh* a position of prominence in society on a par with the mosque. 'Search for knowledge from the cradle to the grave,' the Prophet Mohammad is quoted as saying. The first *madrasehs* were, in fact, the mosques themselves, combining the place of worship with that of learning, although there was no formal organisation or curriculum.[6] In the early days of Islam, the learned were those who could recite and teach the Qor'an, interpret obscure meanings or grammatical constructions and relate the *hadith* or sayings of the Prophet, and the *sunna*, the path or way of life of the Prophet. As the Islamic Empire spread and Islamic learning flowered the scholars became itinerant, travelling vast distances in search of knowledge. Acquiring knowledge meant hearing as many as possible of the *hadith*, traditions of the Prophet (and in the case of the Shi'a, the Imams) from leading authorities and then passing them on to other scholars. It also came to mean arguing and applying criteria for distinguishing a true *hadith* from a false one. Other religious sciences such as theology (*kalam*) and grammar developed along similar lines. Circles for the study of these subjects evolved around the major scholars who met in mosques or sometimes their homes. Students would be likely to attend several of these circles in widely different locations before settling down (if they reached the required status) to teach themselves.

It was only in the eleventh century that *madrasehs* were established as distinct institutions, set up with large endowments by sultans and their viziers. They had a standardised curriculum based on the teaching of Islamic law, the *shari'a* and the study of Arabic grammar and rhetoric, logic, theology and jurisprudence. Both the curriculum and the teaching methods in today's religious colleges have changed little since then. The verbatim memorising of texts plays an important part although, as he advances, the student is increasingly encouraged to seek the meaning of the texts he is studying and to evaluate the arguments used.

In many cases the students' textbooks have also been in use for centuries. Thus, as a beginner in Ha'eri's *madraseh* Ruhollah studied an Arabic grammar known as the *Suyuti*, written by the sixteenth-century Egyptian scholar Jalaleddin Suyuti (or al-Usyuti). The *Suyuti* is, in its turn, a commentary on another book, the *Alfiyya*, or 'One Thousand (Verses)', composed by the thirteenth-century Andalusian grammarian Ibn Malik, who, in turn, was summarising an earlier work on syntax. As an intelligent and serious student Khomeini would have dedicated all his time to learning grammatical rules and memorising the words and verses used in this book as examples of those rules. He may even, like many other *talabehs*, have learnt them so thoroughly that he could, quite literally, recite them backwards.

An anecdote from this period related by Ahmad, Khomeini's son, illustrates his uncompromising determination to progress. 'One day when he was studying *Suyuti* with other students in the courtyard of the school, Ha'eri was teaching advanced studies to other *talabehs* and the noise disturbed my father. Having never bothered to mince his words, he turned to Ha'eri and told him, politely but firmly, to speak more softly.'[7] Ha'eri was astonished to be chided in this way by a student.

By this time, Ruhollah wore the customary turban, a sign that he was a fully-fledged *talabeh* or 'seeker'. If, having spent some time at the *madraseh*, a young man decides that he will commit himself to religious learning, he goes through an initiation ceremony at which he exchanges his skull cap and short jacket for religious garb. He is given his turban, or *amameh*, by a respected religious figure, someone of the status and position of Ha'eri, and this publicly commits him to his new way of life. Not only does the turban bring with it the respect which religious learning attracts in a Muslim society, but it also the responsibility to uphold the moral and religious values which a religious figure is expected to embody. When he assumes the turban, the student also dons the long coat or *qaba*, which he wears most of the time, indoors and out – and the *aba*, the floor-length cloak, usually black, which is worn mostly outdoors over the *qaba*. There are religious rules which prescribe the desirable length and other qualities of these garments. If he can afford it, the *talabeh* may have both winter and summer versions of them.

Because he was a seyyed, Ruhollah's turban was black; non-seyyeds, known as sheikhs if they are members of the clergy, wear white turbans. As a sign of respect for his black turban, he was from then on called Seyyed Ruhollah Musavi Khomeini, although in his identity card and his passport he was Ruhollah Mostafavi – the name chosen for him by his brother when Western-style surnames were introduced to Iran in 1925.[8]

It was probably quite soon after his initiation, in the summer of 1922, that Khomeini followed Ha'eri to a new theological centre at Qom, 90 miles to the south of Tehran. Two years earlier Ha'eri had made a pilgrimage to Qom, which houses the shrine of Fatemeh, the sister of the eighth Shi'i Imam Reza. As he approached the outskirts of the city he was met by the whole of its clerical community with a petition requesting him to move his teaching circles from Arak. Qom had once been a major seat of religious learning, but had fallen into decline after the death of its most famous theologian, Mirza-ye Qomi in 1815. The city had, nevertheless, remained an important Shi'i centre because of its shrine. In 1916 Ayatollah Feiz-Qomi had begun to reclaim the old buildings which were used as barns and shops. However, it was only when the British authorities expelled the Shi'i leadership from Najaf early in 1920 that a concerted effort was made to turn Qom into a centre that could provide an alternative home for the religious communities of the Atabat.[9]

At first, Ha'eri was unwilling to move his teaching circle; but after an *estekhareh* or 'search for guidance' from the Qor'an and much persistence on the part of Qom's clergy, he agreed.[10] This was such a momentous decision that, after his arrival in Qom towards the end of 1921, Ahmad Shah made a special trip to the city to welcome him. Qom soon began to buzz with activity as Ha'eri set about laying the foundations of a major religious institution with teachers in all branches of Islamic learning. Before long, most of the clergy who had been with him in Sultanabad-Arak and a number of leading divines from other cities joined him.

The euphoria that surrounded the city's revival in the early 1920s did not, however, last long. For in 1921 the political process that would make Iran into a secular state and deprive the clergy of many of its functions received a new boost. In February a little educated, but exceedingly capable Cossack colonel, Reza Khan, had ridden into Tehran at the head of his troops to arrest a weak prime minister, his cabinet and, for good measure, some fifty political notables of all colourings. In the wake of the coup the young Ahmad Shah had appointed Reza Khan as commander-in-chief of the army and his co-conspirator, a pro-British politician named Seyyed Ziaeddin Tabataba'i, as prime minister. Within a few months Reza Khan had managed to rid himself of Seyyed Zia and, as minister of war in a succession of cabinets, he embarked on a vigorous and successful effort to create a centralised modern army.[11]

This enterprise was widely supported by Tehran's politicians, including many democrats and nationalists who had fought for the constitution. Ever since the Constitutional Revolution Iran had suffered from a succession of weak governments and over the difficult period of the First World War the authority of the state in many provinces had broken down entirely. Tribal rebellion, separatist political movements and bands of highway robbers had thrown the country into turmoil. In such a situation, the consensus went, there was a pressing need for a strong military force to revive the power of the state, bring peace to the countryside, and enable the government to collect taxes. Most progressive politicians went a step further, believing that the country could only rid itself of the poverty, disorder and the foreign interference that had gone on for so many decades by adopting Western institutions and creating a modern economy.

Reza Khan played to this constituency with great skill, and very soon gained the support of a large section of it, not only for his military ventures but also for his appointment as prime minister in October 1923. Once he had secured a dominant position in government, he began to make plans to rid himself of the last obstacle to supreme power, the Qajar dynasty. In the summer of 1924 a bill to abolish the country's ancient monarchy and declare a republic was put before parliament. The Qajars were not particularly popular. Ahmad Shah, who had succeeded to the throne in 1909 at the age of eleven, was regarded as a weak and vacillating figure and in any case had already left the country. But the idea of a republic did not command much support either, and among the ulema it was vehemently opposed. In neighbouring Turkey, the abolition of the sultanate after the First World War had been rapidly followed by the abolition of the caliphate. Not surprisingly, Iran's religious establishment feared that the destruction of the monarchy would undermine its own position – and pose a danger to Islam itself. In Tehran influential clergymen quickly set about mobilising their traditional allies, the bazaar merchants, who obliged by staging a violent demonstration outside the parliament on the day the bill was to be debated.

The wily politician in Reza Khan sensed trouble, and an opportunity. He knew that the clergy were still a political force to be reckoned with, and from the beginning had taken care to hide his anti-clericalism – by ordering his troops to organise mourning ceremonies during the month of Moharram – events in which Khomeini recalls participating as a young *talabeh* [12] – or by paying his respects to the divines who had fled from Iraq to Qom. [13] Faced with the possibility that the opposition to republicanism would strengthen the Qajar's position and clerical agitation would force his hand, he executed a swift u-turn and extracted a promise from the anti–republican members of parliament that if he dropped the bill they would not support Ahmad Shah. Immediately afterwards he set out for Qom, where he met with Ha'eri, the much venerated Ayatollah Na'ini and Seyyed Abolhassan Isfahani, the most eminent and respected of all the Shi'i leaders. [14] After the meeting he issued a proclamation promising that he would respect 'public opinion' and abandon plans for a republic. 'From my very first day in office, my personal aim was, and still is, to protect the grandeur and welfare of Islam and the Muslims, to safeguard the independence of Iran and the sovereignty of the country and nation … All the country's armed forces and myself are ready to protect and preserve the glory of Islam.' [15] Meanwhile, the three divines dispatched a telegram to Tehran announcing that 'representation for a republic which was not suitable for the country had been made and when the prime minister came to Qom we demanded that he stop his agitation and send a proclamation to all towns. He complied with our request.' [16]

In the weeks that followed Reza Khan worked hard to exploit this new-found rapprochement with religious leaders, helping Na'ini and Isfahani to negotiate with the British for their return to Najaf, providing an armed escort for their journey and, finally, himself paying a visit to Najaf in January 1925. Ten months later he was in a strong enough position to introduce a new bill deposing the Qajars and to convene a Constituent Assembly which proclaimed him the new monarch. Only six members of parliament, all committed democrats, opposed this development. Among them was Seyyed Hassan Modarres, a prominent and in many ways 'progressive' *mojtahed* who had sat in the Majles for years and had an unblemished record as a constitutionalist and nationalist. But Modarres was the only clergyman to raise his voice. Qom remained silent, thus implicitly favouring the new dynasty.

At his coronation, Reza Shah swore to work for the propagation of the faith and for a while afterwards he paid frequent visits to the holy city. He even bowed to clerical protests against a conscription law introduced in 1927, eventually agreeing to exempt students of theology from military service. But within months the cordial relationship between Qom and Tehran broke down.

The crunch came on New Years Day of 1928, 21 March, which in that year fell in Ramadan, the month when Moslems fast. The Queen had gone to the shrine of Fatemeh at Qom to attend the traditional service and during the proceedings she unveiled her face. The gesture enraged the assembly. It would be five more years before Reza Shah introduced his notorious law forbidding women to wear veils. But already men were required to wear European hats and suits and mollahs had to suffer the humiliation of applying for a permit from the Ministry of Education in order to keep their religious garb. Hearing that the Queen was 'immodestly dressed' Ayatollah Bafqi, who was present at the shrine, sent a message to her: 'if you are not Muslims why are you coming to the Shrine? If you are, then why have you not covered your hair and face?' When his reprimand was ignored, Bafqi rose to deliver an impromptu sermon in which he criticised the Shah and incited the crowd to demonstrate. Retribution was swift. Reza Shah marched to Qom with an detachment of troops, entered the shrine without taking off his boots, horse-whipped Bafqi and had him arrested. Ha'eri, in order to calm the situation down and to save the clergy from further humiliation, issued a *fatwa* forbidding any discussion on the incident. He later intervened with Reza Shah who agreed to let Bafqi go into internal exile in the shrine town of Rey, near Tehran where he was visited by mollahs including Khomeini.[17]

Khomeini's *madraseh* in Qom was known as the Dar al-Shafa, or 'hospital'. It was built in the early nineteenth century by Fath Ali Shah, but had fallen into disrepair after Mirza-ye Qomi's death and was turned by a Qajar prince into a hospital. When Khomeini took up residence there, conditions were spartan for there had been neither the time nor the money to reconvert it. Nevertheless, he quickly settled down to work. One of his first teachers was Mohammad Reza Masjed Shahi, with whom he studied rhetoric and poetry but who was also to interest him in a new topic, Darwin's theory of evolution. Masjed Shahi was one of the many mollahs who attempted to refute Darwin, and Khomeini was soon to learn and discuss his book, *A Critique of Darwin's Philosophy*. He also studied the principles of jurisprudence (*osul-e feqh*) with Mohammad Taqi Khonsari and semantics with Mirza Mohammad Adib Tehrani.

Ruhollah's day would begin before dawn, although it was not unusual for the oil lamps to be alight at three and four in the morning while some keen *talabeh* pursued his studies. He would rise with the other *talabehs* and perform the ritual ablutions, followed by the morning prayer. Immediately afterwards he would attend the first lecture of the day which could last for one or two hours. Only when it was over did the *talabehs* have their breakfast of tea, bread, and some white cheese or dried fruit. After breakfast there were more lectures, followed by discussions. In each lesson students were paired with a debating partner with whom they would discuss questions arising from the lecture or their readings. Lectures were held in the hall of the *madraseh*, in a mosque or in a quiet and shaded corner of the courtyard. The lecturer would sit either on the floor or on a low stool, depending on the number of students – anything from one to several hundred – who would sit cross-legged around him in a semicircle. When they were taught by well-known scholars or learned and skilled orators, these 'circles' gained widespread renown.

The number of lectures a *talabeh* attended was up to him. Some would go to very few and instead pay a particularly learned man to be their private tutor. The fee was small, intended to establish the sincerity and dedication of the student rather than to reward the lecturer whose satisfaction lay in the pursuit of and passing on of knowledge. Outside the formal lectures some students might spend time memorising the Qor'an, while others read history, poetry, mysticism or philosophy.

The afternoon was for further study, attending to routine affairs, shopping for food or washing one's clothes. Towards evening the *talabehs* would gather again in the *madraseh* to prepare for evening prayers. As in every institution of learning, some students enjoyed diversions and at night ventured into the streets hoping to find a woman to 'marry' for the night or the week. In Shi'ism there are two types of marriage, the permanent and the temporary or *mut'a* marriage, which is for a specified period. Although Islam encourages permanent marriage as soon as possible, it makes exceptions for those treading the path of knowledge. It is an oft-repeated piece of wisdom in *talabeh* circles that 'knowledge is obliterated in the embrace of a woman'. Theological centres are as a consequence renowned for the number of women they attract who are available for temporary marriages. Such women are often retired prostitutes who come to spend the rest of

their lives serving the 'men of God' so that their 'sins' may be forgiven, or
widows, mostly too old to bear children.

Aqa Najafi Quchani has left a vivid description of the kind of evening
some of the *talabeh* might have enjoyed. Recalling his days as a student in
Najaf at the turn of the century, he writes:

One day I was on my way to a house often frequented by women who were
past their menopause. I had been there before, accepted on credit. I arranged
that day to borrow one *qeran* [a unit of old Iranian money made up of 40
puls] to repay my debt, enter upon yet another blessed deed and buy myself
some meat with the change as the foundation of a stew to share with a friend.
On my way I saw something shining in the dust in the street. It felt as if the
whole world had been given to me. I almost died of happiness. Even Pharaoh
could not have been as thrilled by his sovereignty as I was with this *qeran*.

Fortunately, the woman was at home and I married her for a while. When
I had quietened my desire and enjoyed the pleasure of the flesh from my
lawful income, I gave the woman the *qeran* so that she could take her 12 *puls*
for the last time and 12 *puls* for this time and give me back the remaining 16
puls. She asked me to leave the rest with her on account for the next week or
the next month. I replied: 'Woman, I have many plans for the remaining 16
puls.' There was a pond of cold water in that house where I performed my
obligatory ablutions after the [sexual] act by dipping myself in the freezing
water. From there I went straight to the Shrine of Imam Ali (peace be upon
him) to say my prayers.

Ali saw me and he was pleased with me. I left the Shrine and I spent the 16
puls on meat as well as 3 *puls*-worth of peas and 3 *puls*-worth of charcoal. I
came back to my room in the *madraseh* and prepared a stew. Now hear what
that *qeran* had done! It is reported that the Imams have said that whoever
makes love legitimately has in effect killed an infidel. That means killing the
lascivious spirit. It is obvious that when a *talabeh* has no problem with the
lower half of his body he is happier than a king.[18]

No one knows whether the young Ruhollah was interested in temporary marriage, but it seems unlikely. His wife has said that he was a virgin
when he married her and that she remained the only woman in his life.[19]
Furthermore, even in the prime of his youth he was deeply involved in his
studies and it would have been out of character for him to pursue worldly
pleasures. He is more likely to have dealt with the frustrations of his semi-
monastic way of life in the same way as most young Iranians deal with

their enforced separation from the opposite sex, through sublimation. It is common for young *talabehs* to use the expression *wasf al-a'ish nesf al-a'ish* (half the pleasure lies in talking about the pleasure) and read and repeat lyrical and highly erotic pre-and post-Islamic Arabic poetry as a substitute for the lack of sensuality in their lives.

Khomeini's lifelong interest in poetry, and in particular love poetry, flowered during this period. In the atmosphere of the *madraseh*, where art forms such as music and painting are forbidden, poetry and calligraphy are often taken up by students as a recreation and as a way of developing the imagination. In addition to the Persian poetry he had memorised in his childhood, Ruhollah had by now learnt Arabic poetry from his grammar books and he began to try his hand at writing verse. His poems from this period indicate a certain sense of humour – and that he was aware of the temptations of beautiful girls with their habit of winking from beneath their veils in the shrines of Qom. But he had a ponderous style, and the discipline he imposed on his mind would not allow his subconscious to assert itself and kept his emotions from surfacing. He was to try his hand at lighter verses in later years .

Yet Khomeini's life in the seminary was not entirely without warmth, for he became close friends with a boy from the small village of Lavasan, to the north of Tehran. Mohammad Sadeq Lavasani, who was not dissimilar in looks to Ruhollah, was mesmerised by his energetic, dare-devil and intelligent companion. The two spent a great deal of time together discussing the finer points of theology and poetry. Often in the morning Ruhollah would encourage Lavasani to walk with him near the river and would take a kettle and cups with him to prepare tea for them both. A confirmed, robust walker, as a student he developed a habit which he never forsook. 'In the street, he always walks on the right-hand side, like a car, with a heavy and military style and pace – head up and body erect.'[20]

Ruhollah and his friend also went on trips together. Ruhollah was fascinated by all he had heard of Tehran, so at the first opportunity the two boys went off to the capital where they had their first photograph taken in full clerical attire. Every summer the nostalgic Ruhollah would take Lavasani to Khomein to visit his brother and sisters and to bask in the reverence of the local boys.

Despite these excursions, the cloistered routine life of the *talabeh* obviously restricted Ruhollah's knowledge and experience of life outside the *madraseh*. Although an idealistic *talabeh* may genuinely suffer in the pursuit of his vocation, he may at the same time know very little about the daily hardships of ordinary people. He usually leads a modest, even ascetic life; but the endowments which support the *madrasehs* mean he can be reasonably certain – even if his family does not have the means to support him, as Ruhollah's certainly had – that he will never starve. Those who remain all their life within the innermost circle of the theological schools, the grand ayatollahs, often have little or no contact with or conception of the world in which their followers live and suffer. As a result, their *fatwas* (religious edicts or legal opinions) are sometimes totally irrelevant.

Through the ages, this detached existence, and the sterile formalism it all too often creates, has been attacked by Persian poets and philosophers. Omar Khayyam's world-famous verses expressed his disillusionment with the hypocrisy and sterility of the scholastic way of life, while Hafez, the most accomplished of Persian poets, rejected the obscurantism of his fellow thinkers, choosing instead to serve 'the beloved and wine'. Poetry such as this also expresses, metaphorically, a thread which runs through Shi'i learning: that it is not enough merely to acquire the outward accomplishments of learning, it is also necessary to train the heart. Even Ruhollah later used the language of the lover of wine and the tavern, writing:

> Keep the door of tavern open for me night and day,
> Farewell seminary, farewell mosque,
> Let me go my way.[21]

Financially, the *talabehs* are dependent either on their families, on stipends from leading teachers, or on the *madraseh's* own endowment fund. Ruhollah received some money from his brother in Khomein, and this was supplemented by donations from Ha'eri, who in the 1920s gave single students 10 and married men 15 rials a month. This money came mainly from religious taxes donated by the ordinary people and bazaar merchants. One measure of the power and popularity of a religious figure (such as Ha'eri in his day) is the amount of money he is able to bring to theological establishments. This, in turn, reflects his dual role as a teacher and a religious figure in the outside world to whom devout Muslims send their religious taxes. The more followers a religious figure has in the world beyond the *madraseh*, the more religious taxes he receives and the more he can afford to reward the *talabeh* within it. But, by the same token, it is often through the unswerving loyalty of his *talabehs* that a good teacher acquires a popular following – for it is they who will propagate his name beyond the seminary.

The extraordinary position of teachers among the leading Shi'i clergy and the populist, almost charismatic, link between a leading clergyman and the community as a whole can be traced back to the way in which Shi'ism defines the function of the clergy. For, according to Shi'i doctrine, there must always be a group of people who devote themselves to the study of religion, particularly religious law, who will act as guides so that ordinary people can be sure of fulfilling their religious obligations. One of the proofs used to support this position is the Qor'anic verse: '... why should not a party from each section of [the believers] go forth, in order that they may gain understanding in religion, and that they may warn their people when they return to them, so that perhaps they will beware?'[22] There is thus a clear division in the Shi'i community between those who have studied and are learned, who are known as the ulema (from the Arabic singular noun *alem* or learned man), and the rest; the first group guides and the second is guided. The name given to this principle of guidance is *taqlid* which literally means imitation.

Shi'ism invests the principle of guidance in an individual or several individuals known as the *marja'-e taqlid*, or 'source of emulation', who stand at the peak of the religious hierarchy and whose authority is accepted by lesser clergy as well as ordinary believers. A *marja'* must be someone who has devoted himself to the study of Islamic law until he is qualified as a *mojtahed* or *faqih* (jurist), which means that he can derive his own legal rulings and issue edicts on religious law. But, unlike the Catholic pope or Christian bishops, he is not chosen by an electoral college, or by any other formal procedure. It is incumbent on every believer or 'imitator' to make his or her own choice of *marja'-e taqlid* on the grounds that he is the most learned *mojtahed* of his time and a man of great moral probity.

Of course, most ordinary people are not in a position to judge who is the most learned, so believers are instructed either to inquire of two upright and knowledgeable persons who are not contradicted by two other, similar persons, or to satisfy themselves on the evidence of a group of learned and upright persons. In practice this means that most people rely on the assurances of their local mollahs, who in their turn will be influenced by people they respect or are further up the religious hierarchy. Hence the importance to any leading divine of a following among students and the lesser clergy, who will promote his position in this informal process of consultation.

The ideal to which the Shi'i community has aspired over the past 150 years is that there should be one *marja'* who is universally recognised to be above everyone else in knowledge. This has obvious social and political advantages, for such a *marja'* can effectively mobilise the whole community should the need arise, as for example, over the controversy surrounding the tobacco concession in the late nineteenth century. However, the element of personal choice and the process of consultation that goes into the recognition of a learned divine as *marja'* has meant that such consensus has been hard to achieve and for much of the period people have been able to choose between several *marja'* at any given time.

We do not know whether the young Ruhollah dreamt of becoming a *marja'*, for to openly express such an ambition would have been presumptuous in the extreme and would have marked him down as lacking in some of the moral qualities that are an essential precondition of such pre-eminence. In any case, to become a *mojtahed* or *faqih* (jurist), an interpreter of religious law, is the highest point to which a religious education can in itself lead and ambition enough for a young man. Not every *talabeh* has such aspirations and among those who do only a minority succeed, for the course of study required to reach this rank is arduous and takes many years. Traditionally, studies in the Shi'i theological centres are divided into three main levels. To complete each level can take more than four years and a total of fifteen to twenty years will be needed to complete the whole cycle.

Ruhollah began the preliminary stage of the cycle with a tutor in Khomein, continued in Sultanabad and completed it in Qom. At this stage the student learns to understand the basic texts in Arabic grammar, logic and rudimentary theology. Once they have completed the course, about 30 per cent of *talabehs* leave the seminary to join the ranks of junior mollahs. Men who have studied to this level can become a *mas'aleh-gu*, an 'explainer of problems'. The *mas'aleh-gu*, who stands at the bottom of the religious hierarchy, holds informal meetings on a daily, weekly or monthly basis for an audience of either sex (but generally female) to answer their questions on the precepts of religion, usually those affecting day to day complexities of observing Islamic rules of cleanliness, or personal, domestic and social problems. A few men who have completed the first cycle manage to move a step further up the hierarchy to become *va'ez*, preachers whose task it is to educate people in the principles of religion and entertain them with tales of heaven and hell and the tragedies of martyrs, particularly Imam

Hossein. A good *va'ez* can attract immense local popularity and enjoy the influence and perhaps wealth which accompanies popular adulation.

In the second cycle the *talabeh* begins to teach students at the first level and, at the same time, to study more advanced texts. The main subject is now the *shari'a* or Islamic law, and the student is schooled not only in the substance of the law and the sources from which it is derived, but also in the general principles on which legal rulings are based. So along with the *shari'a* he has to study linguistics, logic and legal philosophy. At the second level texts are studied in classes at which the teacher will read a section and then expound on the meaning of the passage, with students raising points and questions and engaging in argument to further clarify the matter under discussion. These exchanges between students and teacher can often become quite heated, and serve in part as occasions for the students to display their understanding and mastery of the subjects. They also reflect the general style of the texts themselves, which take the form of a basic text, and commentaries in which later authors argue with that text, refining and, sometimes, disagreeing with the author's conclusions.

Students who complete this level generally have a good all round grasp of the bases of *feqh* and the principles of religion, but they are not qualified to make their own rulings on legal matters or offer their own interpretation of theological issues. The majority leave the *madraseh* at this stage to become the mollah in charge of a local mosque in one of the quarters of a major town or in remote townships or villages. They live on alms donated by the local population or by their *marja'*, who they represent in the locality for the purpose of collecting religious donations or providing guidance on religious problems.

Khomeini studied *feqh* (religious law) and its principles with a teacher from Kashan eleven years his senior, Ayatollah Ali Yasrebi-Kashani, and completed the second cycle in the mid 1920s. As a student of the third level, known as the *dars-e kharej* or 'studies beyond the text', Khomeini attended Ha'eri's own classes. At this final level of the cycle there are no set books and students work towards forming their own opinions on given legal issues. The teacher starts his lecture on a topic by first referring to a Qor'anic verse and then quoting what the Prophet and the Imams are reported to have said about it, basing his information on the work and accepted opinions of previous jurists. Finally, he will outline his own judgement and the students will then argue with him over the issue, expressing themselves in a free and friendly atmosphere. In theory the student will, by the end of his training, learn to derive a ruling for every eventuality, a ruling which carries with it the degree of certainty which can assure those who must comply with it that they are pleasing God by their actions. In practice only a handful will ever acquire such authority.[23]

Those students who feel they have reached such a level of learning and do not need to emulate other clerics on the topic under discussion will set forth their own thoughts on it and submit them to their teacher. If he finds their reasoning and knowledge of the sources is of a sufficient standard, the teacher will issue them with permission to derive their own rulings. Such students will then have the right to practice *ejtehad* (interpretation) in that area of law. If the student shows himself capable of deriving rulings across the whole spectrum of the law, his teacher (or teachers) will issue him with permission to practise unlimited *ejtehad* and derive rulings in every area of the law and indeed, because of the all-encompassing aims of Islamic law, for every human activity. He will then have become a fully-qualified *mojtahed*.

Khomeini seems to have achieved his 'permission' around the time of Ha'eri's death in 1936, at the age of thirty-two or thirty-three and some fifteen or sixteen years after he had begun the cycle.[24] Even by the standards of leading ulema, this was an impressive record. The handful of students who reach this level automatically enter the higher ranks of the clergy. Some become the sole prayer-leader of a medium-sized town or the Friday prayer-leader of a major town, a very important position in society, in religious, social, and – since the 1979 Revolution – political terms. Others, like Khomeini, remain as teachers in the religious centres of Qom, Mashhad, Isfahan and Tehran, or in centres outside Iran, such as Najaf.

Mojtaheds are given the honorific title 'hojjat al-Islam' (proof of Islam), and in recent times those who go on to achieve a reputation for outstanding learning and piety become known as an 'ayatollah' (meaning 'sign of God'). The title 'ayatollah' was introduced at the time of the Constitutional Revolution of 1906 to honour those clerical leaders who signed the constitution. After that it became acceptable to call the *marja'-e taqlid* ayatollah. But in the 1920s the use of the title as a sign of respect for great religious leaders proliferated and eventually the term 'ayatollah al-ozma' (literally, grand sign of God) was coined to distinguish the *marja's*.

By the time he became a 'hojjat al-Islam' Khomeini was himself a well-established teacher in Qom. He began to take classes in jurisprudence (*feqh*) just after he entered the third stage, and at the age of twenty-seven had already assembled his own circle of admiring students who visited his home regularly or met him at the shrine or *madraseh*. He also developed his own method of teaching. One of his students from this period, Ayatollah Ja'far Sobhani, who now lectures in Qom, recalls that instead of conducting his lectures as a dialectical argument between teacher and students, as was the custom, 'He put forward a topic in a decisive manner, first explaining other opinions and then his own before looking for arguments. He never introduced issues that were unclear in his own mind, preferring to do his homework and reflect upon topics before discussing them.'[25] Khomeini was never particularly interested in discussion for its own sake, and he maintained this approach throughout his teaching career. The qualities of autocracy, decisiveness and self righteousness that were to stand him in such good stead in his later political career were already well ingrained in Khomeini the young teacher.

Outwardly, too, he differed from other mollahs. Those who considered themselves to be unworldly paid little attention to their dress, rough and worn-out material being a sign of piety – and for the more unscrupulous, a way of attracting donations. Khomeini was always neat and clean, and would explain that wearing old and torn clothing might in the past have been a sign of holiness, but now it was a mark of a beggar. Clergymen should not look like beggars.

He was by this time a very presentable bachelor, and his early show of promise meant he was in a position to make a good marriage. Being a hard working and serious student, Khomeini was regarded by many, including Ayatollah Mirza Mohammad Saqafi, a wealthy Tehran cleric, as 'learned, intelligent, chaste and pious'. Saqafi became acquainted with Khomeini through Lavasani, who was a family friend. It was Lavasani who put the idea of marriage into Khomeini's mind:

'Why don't you want to get married?' he asked Khomeini.

'I have no one in mind and don't want to marry a girl from Khomein,' answered Khomeini.

Lavasani said 'Mr Saqafi has two daughters, who are, I am told by my sister-in-law, good for marriage.'

Thus in 1929, at the age of twenty-seven, he requested the hand of Qods-e Iran, known to family members as Qodsi, Saqafi's fifteen-year-old daughter, who was a schoolgirl at the time. It was not easy, and to begin with she refused Ruhollah.[26]

In an interview with the press after the 1979 Revolution Qodsi has said that Lavasani's mother, who was responsible for negotiating the liaison, was persistent and when she again visited the family she found that a dream had persuaded the girl to change her mind: 'The night after I refused Ruhollah's hand,' recalls Qodsi, 'I saw the Prophet Mohammad's daughter, Fatemeh, in my dream. She told me to marry him and so the next day I told my parents that I had changed my mind.'[27] She adds in the same interview: 'When we married he told me that he was not an obscurantist who expected me to undertake extra duties, his only request was that I should observe the rules of Islam.' She was to be the first and the only wife of Ruhollah and their lifelong companionship was to last for sixty years.[28]

3

In Search of Perfection
Taking Refuge in Mysticism

While still a young student, Khomeini yearned for a higher knowledge that could not be acquired within the formal framework of the *madraseh*. Besides law and jurisprudence, the subjects taught there were limited in scope and the attitude of obedience demanded of students left little scope for an exploration of the rational or mystical spheres towards which his searching mind impelled him. Soon after he arrived in Qom he began to search for masters with whom he could study two of Islam's great mystical and philosophical traditions – *erfan* and *hekmat*.

Erfan is an Arabic word meaning gnosis, the mystical knowledge of the inner world of Man seeking intimacy with God. It is a spiritual tradition found mainly in the Shi'i world which parallels and shares many doctrines with Sufism, the form of Islamic mysticism most familiar to people in the West. There are, however, some important differences between *erfan* and Sufism. Sufism is closely associated with religious brotherhoods, groups linked by a definite spiritual chain of masters to a person whose proximity to the Prophet would guarantee the authenticity of the master's spiritual knowledge. *Erfan* is not practised through organisations such as these although, as in all esoteric traditions, there is always a strong link between master and pupil. *Erfan* is also highly theoretical, whereas within Sufism there are both intellectual and anti-intellectual currents. Because of its strong intellectual bias, within Shi'ism *erfan* has always been closely connected with the study of philosophy, particularly of the philosophical tradition known as *hekmat* (literally 'wisdom').

In Shi'ism *erfan* is, however, a river into which many streams have flowed. Strangely, despite its distinctly Shi'i character, many of the leading contributors to its development – intellectuals, poets and mystics – have not been Shi'a. This has been a source of criticism from the more legalistic Shi'i ulema.[1]

Hekmat (literally 'wisdom') provides the main intellectual stream of *erfan*. This philosophical tradition traces its lineage back to the eleventh-century scholar Ibn Sina, known in the West as Avicenna (980–1037), and can be followed in a more or less uninterrupted line down to the present day. It is characterised both by a thoroughly logical and scholastic system of thought and by an experiential exploration of the nature of ultimate reality. Its leading thirteenth-century exponent was the great Shi'i scholar Nassir al-Din Tusi, who systematically defended the metaphysical writings of Avicenna against the attacks of unorthodoxy levelled at them by theologians, in particular the criticisms of Ghazali, who accused Avicenna and his followers of heresy. Both Avicenna and Tusi were masters not only of metaphysics, but also of peripatetic logic, natural philosophy (Tusi was an important mathematician and astronomer) and, in the case of Avicenna, of medicine.

Two other figures, both slightly earlier than Tusi, stand out as representatives of the more gnostic and mystical aspects of *hekmat*. The first, the great mystic Ibn Arabi (1165–1240), was born in Arab-ruled Andalucia in today's Spain and died in Damascus. The central idea of Ibn Arabi's mysticism is a transcendent state which he called 'opening', through which direct knowledge of God and the unseen is achieved. To reach this elevated state it is necessary to discipline oneself through religious law and the practices of the spiritual path, but 'opening' is ultimately a gift of God. Because he wrote of the knowledge he had received through his 'opening', Ibn Arabi suffered a great deal and was, for a while, imprisoned. He claimed that he had met the beatified Mohammad, that he knew God's greatest name (*esm-e a'zam*), and that he had acquired his knowledge not through his own labour but through direct inspiration. His enormous body of writings integrated the teachings of Sufism into the mainstream of the Islamic intellectual tradition. His encyclopaedic *al-Futuhat al-Makkiyya* (The

Meccan Openings) expounds practically the whole range of Islamic sciences – theology, law, philosophy, psychology, physics – within the framework of the Oneness of God and in terms of the unfolding of human perfection.

Ibn Arabi's major contribution to the subsequent development of *hekmat* was the concept of *vahdat al-vojud*, the unity of existence. He saw the constituents of existence as many and at the same time one, one but at the same time many. This concept was another occasion for accusations of heresy against the practitioners of *hekmat* by the orthodox ulema, who took exception to its implications of pantheism.

The other, slightly earlier, figure was Sohravardi (1154–91), who was executed at the age of thirty-seven for his supposedly heretical views. His philosophy of illumination (*hekmat al-eshraq*) was again a masterly systematic fusion of mystical experience and analytic thinking. In one of his works he, too, expounds the principle of the indispensability of these two paths: 'In the same way as the follower of the Path [i.e. the mystic] falls short of perfection if he lacks the power of intellectual enquiry, so also does the intellectual who has no direct experience of the signs from the divine realm.'

These various strands in the tradition of *hekmat* were gradually brought together in the Persian world by figures such as Qotb al-Din Shirazi (d. 1311) and Seyyed Heidar Amoli (d. after 1354). However, the most important time for the development of *hekmat* in Persia was that of the Safavids, most notably in the person of Sadr al-Din Shirazi, better known as Mollah Sadra (d. 1641). His works, of which *al-Asfar al-Arba'a* (The Four Journeys) is the most masterful representation, are based on what he called the 'transcendent wisdom' (*al-hekmat al-muta'aliyya*), the source or moment of direct awareness of the true reality of being, which comes with the realisation of the oneness of the intellectual subject and object, as well as an awareness of the intellect itself.

Another stream which flowed into the river of *erfan*, and one which is also important with respect to Khomeini, is the contribution of Persian mystical poetry. Again, it was not only the poetry of the Shi'a which made this contribution; two of the most renowned Persian poets, who remain among the most important mystical poets in Persian, were Sunnis. The first, Jalal al-Din Rumi (d. 1273), is perhaps the most highly regarded of all Sufi poets. He was born in Balkh in what is today northern Afghanistan, but his father fled from the devastating Mongol invasions and the family ended up in Asia Minor, present-day Turkey. He attracted a large following in Konya and left behind two masterpieces of Persian mystical poetry: the *Mathnavi*, a long didactic work, and a collection of lyrical poetry usually referred to as the *Divan of Shams-e Tabrizi*, after the wild and ascetic dervish who became the most elevated object of Rumi's mystical love. Rumi is also revered as the founder of the Whirling Dervishes or Mevleviyya, a brotherhood which was probably brought into existence by his son. The second poet, Hafez of Shiraz (d. 1389 or 90) is considered by many to be the finest of all the Persian poets. Hafez was not, in fact, a Sufi in the strict sense of the term. Indeed, he frequently criticised the Sufis along with the mainstream clergy for being hypocrites. Hafez is a link between *hekmat* and *erfan*, combining the rational issues of his time raised by such philosophers as Omar Khayyam, with the mystical approaches of Sufi poets like Rumi.

Khomeini's own interest in poetry must have helped him to move towards *erfan*, and soon after arriving in Qom he found three teachers who undertook to teach him both *erfan* and *hekmat*, mainly in private. He began with Mirza Ali Akbar Yazdi, a pious old teacher of philosophy and mysticism with whom he studied the *Sharh-e Manzumeh*. Written in the mid-nineteenth century by the philosophical teacher, Haj Mollah Hadi Sabzevari (d. 1872), this work is a basic philosophical text for the *talabeh* in the *madraseh* system and is rooted in the tradition of *hekmat*.

Although logic is an obligatory part of a *talabeh's* studies, this is not the case with *hekmat* and metaphysics. Nevertheless, many students study the *Manzumeh*, even if few do so out of a desire to advance along the spiritual path. It is often taught in a purely formal way, aimed simply at acquainting the student with metaphysical terminology and at exercising the mind. This was not the way it was taught by Yazdi, who had himself been a student of Sabzevari. Because of his deep commitment to the subjects he was teaching, Yazdi left a powerful impression on Khomeini who quotes him often in his books.

When Yazdi died in 1924, Khomeini continued his studies with Mirza Javad Aqa Maleki Tabrizi, another ascetic who taught ethics and mysticism privately. Khomeini lost this teacher in the same year. He then began to study and discuss Mollah Sadra's *Four Journeys* together with a fellow student before going on to another teacher, Seyyed Abolhassan Rafi'i Qazvini (d. 1976), to continue studying this text. From these three men Khomeini learnt the fundamentals of philosophy and some mysticism. However, the man to whom he felt most indebted was Mirza Mohammad Ali

Shahabadi (d. 1950), an ascetic who, perhaps more than any of his other mentors, captured Khomeini's imagination as a model of a good teacher, disciplined, thoughtful, unpretentious and introverted.

Khomeini's first encounter with Shahabadi is best described in his own characteristically deadpan words.

I met him in the Feiziyeh, where I asked him a question on mysticism. When he began speaking, I soon realised that he was the man [I sought]. I told him that I wanted to study under him but he was unwilling [at first] to teach me. I [continued to] insist until he agreed to teach me philosophy. He thought that I was a seeker of philosophy. [However], when he agreed I told him I had already studied philosophy and that I had not come to him to study philosophy but to study mysticism. In particular I wanted to study the *Sharh-e Fusus*.

The *Sharh-e Fusus* is a commentary by Sharaf al-Din Davud Qeisari (d. 1350) on the *Fusus al-Hikam*, one of Ibn Arabi's works, which gives a mystical exposition of the divine attributes reflected in the prophets from Adam to Mohammad. In 1937 Khomeini wrote a commentary on the *Fusus* in 1937.

He refused, but I insisted so strongly that he eventually relented. [So,] I studied mysticism with him, most of the time on my own but sometimes with a third person. During the weekends and on holidays I read the *Mafatih al-Gheib* with him. At the same time I wrote a commentary on the *Mafatih al-Gheib*. I also read the *Manazel al-Sa'erin* [The Stages of the Wayfarer by the eleventh-century Sufi, Ansari of Herat, which describes the progress of a spiritual seeker in a hundred stages] with him on my own and occasionally with one or two other people who left after a while. Once I said to Shahabadi: 'What you are saying is not in the book. Where is it from?' Shahabadi replied: 'It is said', by which he implied: 'It is my own opinion.'[2]

Shahabadi also influenced Khomeini's political views, and for seven years Khomeini studiously followed his lectures. Unlike the majority of mystics, he did not believe in quietism and was one of a small group of mollahs who actively opposed Reza Shah's policies. For a period he had to take refuge in the golden shrine of Shah Abdolazim in Rey, to the south of Tehran, to avoid arrest.

Shahabadi emphasised the importance of planning in order to educate and organise Muslims. He would advise his students to simplify difficult subjects for a wider popular appreciation, something which the Prophet had encouraged when he said: 'Talk to people according to the level of their intelligence.' This was a lesson that was to be practised, most effectively, by Khomeini in future years.

Constantly urging his students to work towards the salvation of the Muslim community, Shahabadi, who had clearly been influenced by early-twentieth century nationalist discourse, even set out the following guidelines: (i) to publish a religious magazine in order to propagate religious thought and activities among the people; (ii) to practise frugality in everyday life and overcome harmful habits; (iii) to form an Islamic company to promote trade, agriculture and industry and to produce Islamic and Iranian goods and clothing; (iv) to establish a fund for granting interest-free loans to prevent usury, which harms people in this world and the next.[3] Khomeini acknowledged the influence Shahabadi had on him, stating that he was not only a perfect theologian and mystic but also a combatant (mobarez), these being the three key facets of Khomeini's own personality.[4] When, after the 1979 Revolution, one of Shahabadi's sons was killed at the front in the Iran–Iraq War, Khomeini wrote a lavish letter of condolence in which he praised Shahabadi as 'my spiritual father and teacher'.

By the age of twenty-seven Khomeini was well versed in mysticism and its terminology. A book he wrote in 1929, which is a commentary on a prayer known as 'The Dawn Supplication' (Do'a al-Sahar), shows his mastery of the subject. He quotes his teachers and offers his own opinion on the text. Most Iranians have heard the Supplication over and over again on the radio during the holy month of Ramadan. Khomeini, however, highlights issues that an untrained mind would fail to notice. He writes about this text as someone who has read the major sources of Islamic mysticism in Arabic and Persian, in poetry and prose.

Seyyed Ahmad Fehri, a student of Khomeini who edited the book, points out in his Sharh Do'a al-Sahar that 'Khomeini is considered [in his commentary] to have demonstrated the conformity of the shari'a with the logic of mysticism and the conformity of mysticism with the logic of the shari'a.' He argued that there is no intrinsic contradiction between erfan and Sufism on the one hand and a strict adherence to the shari'a on the other. Of course, there are some mystics who shun the restrictions of the shari'a, considering themselves to be already on the path (tariqa) of God and, therefore, above divine law, but they are likely to fall prey to the hedonism and decadence which is so widespread among the followers of some marginal Sufi orders. To take an opposite example, Ibn Arabi was himself scrupulous about legal matters, and he was certainly not generous or kind in his attitude towards non-Muslims, or even towards the Shi'a.

It is perhaps difficult for a modern Westerner to reconcile what might appear as two conflicting attitudes; the gentle and contemplative facing the rule-bound and legalistic. But Khomeini's developing personality conformed with Islamic tradition, just as his mentor Shahabadi's had done. As an intelligent, introverted and frustrated young man embittered by the decline and decay of the clerical establishment, discovering the inner illumination of mysticism was a turning-point for Khomeini. He was neither satisfied nor fulfilled by the orthodox version of religion so common among the majority of the clergy. However, to reveal the secrets of mystical knowledge carries its own dangers. Unpopularity, threats, excommunication, exile, isolation and even death have rewarded many of those who have proclaimed their belief in this secret knowledge. The mystical theologian Mansur Hallaj was actually crucified in 922 for 'telling the world at large', and boasting, that 'I am the truth and the people.' Ibn Arabi was condemned as a heretic for having claimed to have seen the Prophet. As we have seen, Sohravardi was also executed. Another mystic, A'in al-Qozat (d. 1131) of Hamadan, not far from Khomein, was hanged and his body burnt with oil and marshreed. Mollah Sadra, the last great philosopher of Islam and the founder of transcendental theosophy, a tradition which was followed by Khomeini, was driven out of his home town, Shiraz.

What all of these mystics said can be viewed as echoing, in different ways, what Hallaj had propounded. As Ibn Arabi wrote: 'Everything in the world is nothing but fantasy or imagination, or images in the mirror, or shadows.'[5] Fear of persecution forced many mystics and philosophers in the Islamic world to hide behind a language which the common man would not understand. One such was Mir-Damad (d. 1631), whose work Khomeini came to know in later life. Mir-Damad, who lived in Isfahan, the Safavid capital, brought together mysticism and the esoteric aspect of Shi'ism but was, at the same time, a scholar in the traditional mould of the ulema. His language was so complicated as to be almost incomprehensible. Legend has it that when, at the moment of his death, the angels Nakir and Monkar, descended to interrogate him, and, in the Muslim tradition asked: 'Who is your creator?', the philosopher replied in a mixture of Arabic and Greek: *ostoqoson fawq al-ostoqossat* ('an element above all elements'). The angels of death reported their conversation back to God, adding 'We cannot understand this creature of yours, this Mir-Damad fellow.' The Almighty responded: 'Don't worry. Nobody in the world understands him.'[6] This was how Mir-Damad remained safe from the zealots' wrath.

Another story relates exactly why Mir-Damad's famous student, Mollah Sadra, was less fortunate. Mollah Sadra saw his master in a dream after his death and asked him: 'Why have people accused me of heresy, while they did not accuse you? My school of thought is not very different from yours.' Mir-Damad replied: 'I have written in such a way that even learned people cannot understand my intentions, while you have vulgarised philosophy so much that even a simple mollah can understand your language. That is why I was not accused of heresy and you are.'[7]

Righteousness and piety are encouraged by the more orthodox Shi'i ulema, as is asceticism, within certain bounds; but they ascribe practices or ideas which they regard as excessive, or of which they disapprove, to the influence of Greek, Manichaean, Indian, or other non-Islamic currents, and label those who practise them as deviants. Of the three paths to God, the only one they accept is that of total obedience and devotion. The other two, the rationalism of philosophy and the illumination of mysticism, have always been viewed as incompatible with what was revealed to the Prophet. Books by 'heretical' philosophers and mystics were always frowned upon. The mollahs even openly advised their followers to avoid books such as Rumi's *Mathnavi*, which had to be removed with pincers from the homes of pious Muslims, like a piece of dirt. Anyone who brought the *Mathnavi* to a seminary would be excommunicated as an infidel.

Khomeini's public posture from his early days as *mojtahed* was always to conform to the general trend of the clergy and shun what they regarded as suspicious subjects like philosophy and mysticism in favour of the mainstream disciplines of law, jurisprudence, the sciences of the Qor'an and the *sunna* (traditions) of the Prophet and the Imams. He wrote in a simple and clear language both on these subjects and mysticism. But he kept his mystical writings under wraps. This was clearly sensitive territory in which it was all too easy to be accused of heresy or isolationism.

Islamic history is punctuated with incidents in which jurisprudents, mystics and philosophers have fought one another, sometimes physically and sometimes to the death. Jurisprudents value and use revelation, the simplest of the three messages after mysticism and philosophy. However, mysticism in its devotional form is seen to be the most direct path to God, which is why it has been so attractive to converts. The militants, however, have found less to value in it. Khomeini was, in a sense, one of the few to have reached the stature of a leading jurisprudent, the highest level of theoretical mysticism and also to have become a highly-regarded teacher of Islamic philosophy. He was unique in being at the same time a leading practitioner of militant Islam.

The philosopher whose writings captured Khomeini's imagination as he pursued his studies of mysticism was Ibn Arabi. Ibn Arabi was influenced by the Neo-Platonic idea of *logos* (the Perfect Man), and the Shi'i doctrine of the pre-existence of the Prophet, a doctrine which made his views more acceptable to the Shi'i mystics. The concept of the Perfect Man fascinated Khomeini, since it provided him with a new and more effective mode of expressing the decay in Islam. Logos is central to the mystical understanding of the universe and Man's place in it. For the Islamic mystic, all the universe which is not God in His full essence is divided into the macrocosm, the universe as we see it looking out, and the microcosm, the inner world of Man. These two worlds are reflections of each other, and Man has the unique opportunity to perfect his being and 'polish his soul' until he reaches the stage at which his microcosm and macrocosm become, as it were, congruent. Man is able to perfect himself through disciplining himself according to the guidance of the divine law until he reaches the stage where he assumes the outward form of the divine essence. It is then that he has realised the stage of the Perfect Man.

For Khomeini and other Islamic mystics the Perfect Man is a copy of God. He is 'the centre and animating principle of the whole created universe, the spirit and the life of things', and, more importantly, 'a channel through which God imparts knowledge of himself to his worshippers and endows them with every spiritual gift.'[8]

It is important not to confuse the non-Shi'i Sufi treatment of Light and the Perfect Man, the sheikh and the saint, with the Shi'i view, the Imam. The term *vali* (deputy, regent) is common to both. For the Sufi a *vali* or 'saint' is designated either by virtue of his inheritance of a position in a chain of esoteric initiation, or, as was supremely the case with Ibn Arabi, by virtue of his inward visions. But for the Shi'i the *vali* is always the Imam. The Shi'i mystic can ultimately only rise to identification with the 'Imam of the Age', whereas the non-Shi'i Sufi takes the Prophet as the model of the Perfect Man. There is arguably a grey area where the 'extremist' view that the Imam is spiritually superior to the Prophet overlaps with the possibility of his rising to a point of imitation of the Prophet. What is most interesting is the theory that after the physical death of the Prophet there are viceregents, Imams, saints and *valis* who carry on the prophetic torch. At this stage the love of the Prophet gives the mystic a place far superior to that of those who venerate him. When a mystic claims oneness with God he is naturally very close to the Prophet, the embodiment of the Perfect Man, and it is through the mystic that the special relationship between the Prophet and God can be passed on to others. Both the *valis* and saints feel that they inherit this mystical inward aspect of Mohammad's nature described as 'cosmic guardianship' (*velayat-e takvini*) or 'creational guardianship', which as far as they are concerned is far more important than the legalistic and outward appearance of Mohammad as an apostle and a Prophet (*velayat tashri'i* or 'legislating guardianship'). Mystical saints are Mohammad's personal representatives, to whom he has delegated his functions as *viceregent* of God. Without their invisible governance (*velayat*) the world will fall into disorder and ruin.

In his commentary on 'The Dawn Supplication' Khomeini quotes major Islamic mystics such as Ibn Arabi, Mollah Sadra, Hafez and Rumi to support this view: '... the Perfect Man', he writes, 'is the holder of the chain of existence, with which the cycle is completed. It is the beginning and the end, it is the external and the internal, the totality of the Divine Book. He is God's great sign, created in God's image. Whoever knows the Perfect Man has known God.'[9]

Having accepted Ibn Arabi's view on the Perfect Man, Khomeini then turned to his hero, Mollah Sadra, whose transcendental theosophy (*hekmat-e mota'aliyeh*) drew on the *erfan* of Ibn Arabi, the illuminationist philosophy (*falsafeh-ye eshraq*) of Sohravardi, the rational philosophy (*falsafeh-ye mashsha'i*) of Avicenna's followers, and on Shi'i *kalam*. In bringing together these schools of thought in his transcendental theosophy, Mollah Sadra produced a unique mystical philosophy.[10]

Mollah Sadra aimed to create a new philosophical system in the hope of ending some of the controversies among the four schools of Muslim thought. Although orthodox opposition prevented him from doing this, his views came to be the most influential among the intelligentsia of the last three centuries. Khomeini studied his *Four Journeys* thoroughly, later becoming the most respected teacher of the book in Qom.[11] For Khomeini, Mollah Sadra was the man who had enabled him to understand the path of perfection. Ibn Arabi believed that this path follows a journey of purification which has been formulated into four journeys. However, Mollah

Sadra examined the issues involved as an intellectual as well as a spiritual journey, rationalising his argument with mystical and philosophical explanations.

Khomeini took this a step further. For him the first journey was 'from Mankind to God' (*min al-khalq ila al-haqq*), in which the traveller (*salek*) in search of 'truth' strives to leave the domain of human limitations. Before starting the journey, the traveller must have purged his soul of all earthly, carnal desire by practising all the religious duties, immersing himself in piety and asceticism, and robing himself with total submission in certitude and love of the Almighty. It is only after this that he can leave the physical world and cross some of the metaphysical, spiritual barriers in order to reach God's essence. The second journey is with God in God, and that is when the traveller is acquainted with His essence, and having achieved certitude in Him begins his journey with God's help. He will submerge into oceans of secrets and mysteries to acquaint himself with the beauty of God's names and attributes, witnessing their real manifestations, influence and governance. The traveller will also learn from God the qualities of love, anger or disaffection and see them among the people. The third journey is one in which the traveller returns to the people, but is no longer separate from God, as he can now see His omnipotent essence. The fourth and final journey is one in which the traveller has acquired godly attributes with which he can begin to guide and help others to reach God. This is the crucial stage. It is here that *velayat* (viceregency) and prophethood are realised, giving the traveller the mission to preach God's word. He must strive towards God, appreciating His beauty and glory, whilst inviting others in the name of revelation to do likewise, and he must recognise the manifestation of God in the community. That is, he must guide people from multiplicity to unity, from blasphemy to faith, from polytheism to the oneness of God, from imperfection to perfection. More importantly, by establishing rightful policies, the government of absolute justice and a reign of divinity, the Perfect Man will guide society towards absolute perfection.

Having studied these texts and learnt about all four journeys in his twenties, Khomeini's interest was so great he began writing about them with mastery and confidence. He was to write many books over the coming years on a variety of topics. One is *The Ascension of the Traveller and the Prayer of the Mystics* (*Me'raj al-Salekin wa Salat al-'Arefin*). On the surface it is about the daily prayers of Muslims, but in reality it is a book about the travels of a seeker who embarks upon the four journeys.[12] Deploying a cautious language so as not to alienate the uninitiated, Khomeini uses the mystical terminology of Ibn Arabi, Mollah Sadra and others demonstrating clearly that he knows his subject minutely.

In his books on jurisprudence Khomeini discusses prayer for ordinary believers. He mentions the type of prayers, the intent, the time, the physical cleanliness of the supplicant and the correct pronunciation of the Arabic words. It is here that one either takes refuge in one's inner self or establishes separate systems for 'commoners' and 'the elite' (awamm wa khawass). Several verses of the Qor'an clearly state that 'the majority do not think ... the majority do not understand ... the majority do not appreciate.' This was undoubtedly a problem for a man with a mystical life. Khomeini's language in this book is very much the language of a mystic imbued with the love of God. The theosophical belief in the relationship between God and Man is always kept in mind when he discusses this relationship. Prayer (salat) is the most important element in the life of an Islamic mystic. Such prayer is quite different from the habitual daily prayer which a Muslim must practise. Outwardly the same, but inwardly different, Sufi prayer is a supplication, a dialogue between God and Man. Khomeini perceived prayer as a ladder to climb to the state of perfect manhood, the viceregency of God. Heart plays an important role in prayer for the traveller. To Khomeini, the process of teaching one's heart the remembrance of God through prayer is important if the traveller is to climb the ladder and thereby reach a state of perfection. Although to begin with the task is a difficult one, not unlike teaching a child to talk, once mastered it gives the body joy, such as is felt by parents when their child has learnt to speak.

For the traveller there are many stages and preparations, but prayer, supplication and litany are the ways used to begin the journey. After some sixty pages of his book The Prayer of the Mystics, discussed above, Khomeini closes with a consideration of the four journeys: '... the secret of praying is in essence the journey to God, the journey in God and the journey from God.' He then goes on to say: ' ... when one has left the people and is in the presence of the Almighty ... the fourth journey which is from people to people will end ... And this truth needs more explanation than I'm able to give and people are able to hear.' In fact the last sentence is borrowed from a poem attributed to Sa'di: 'I am a dreamer who is dumb, and the people are deaf. I am unable to say, and they are unable to hear.'[13]

Khomeini never openly claimed to have reached this final stage, but mystics are traditionally hesitant to 'reveal the secret' of being at one with God and Mankind. It is while a mystic is in the fourth journey that, whenever he or she speaks, it is as if God has spoken. Mehdi Ha'eri Yazdi, the son of Ayatollah Ha'eri, a former student of Khomeini and a leading Iranian scholar who is well versed in both Western and Islamic philosophy, believes that Khomeini, not unlike Hallaj, considered himself as having completed the fourth journey, which implies a belief in the words: 'I am the truth and the people' (*ana al-haqq wa'l-khalq*). The only difference is, says Ha'eri, that Hallaj 'having secrets in his charge' told 'the world at large' and was crucified, but Khomeini succeeded. 'Khomeini is not a philosopher,' says Ha'eri Yazdi. 'He has no mathematical mind. Nor has he the disinterested attitude to qualify him as having one.' However, in Ha'eri Yazdi's view, Khomeini was in his time 'the greatest living theoretical mystic'.

Khomeini did not publish much from his mystical books before the 1979 Revolution. Had it not been for the social and political upheaval, and had the traditional clergy been as powerful as in other periods, he himself might have become the victim of the orthodox faction. Khomeini was aware of this antagonism towards the mystics, and was careful to justify all his utterances, first through Qor'anic verses and then through the sayings of the Prophet and the Imams. In fact, during his televised commentaries on the Qor'an, broadcast after the 1979 Revolution, he referred to one of his own teachers, Mirza Ali Akbar Hakim, who had been the subject of much insult for teaching mysticism and philosophy. 'When I went to Qom,' he told the viewers, '... a certain pious man said:" ... see the level to which Islam has fallen; the doors of Mirza Ali Akbar are open to receive students."' When he died there was so much suspicion surrounding him that certain preachers found it necessary to testify from the pulpit that they had seen him reading the Qor'an.' The antagonism towards him implied that the clergy would have considered someone who taught mysticism as being 'beyond the pale.'[14]

Khomeini studied and later taught mysticism privately. Because he had taught philosophy he was branded as unfit to be a senior theologian and was isolated. During his period in Qom, the battle against the philosophers and mystics took on a more formulated structure. In Mashhad a new school of thought called *tafkik*, or 'separation', was led by a cleric called Sheikh Mojtaba Qazvini, who, like Khomeini, trained many students but was a recluse. Qazvini taught philosophy only to those whom he considered to be qualified (*ahl*), that is to those who would avoid falling into the trap of the mystics and other philosophers. He believed that there should be a separation between philosophy, mysticism and revelation, and that Islam should be solely concerned with the latter, as it is God's revelation that should be obeyed. Ironically, he was as much of a mystic as anybody could be. Qazvini was not interested in titles, followers or publicity, and he was unwilling to appear during the day at the holy shrine of Imam Reza to avoid drawing attention to himself. Nevertheless, when Khomeini was arrested he went to see him, recognising Khomeini's aura of leadership.

Khomeini's relationship with God was something of a puzzle for many people. His son Ahmad says that he understood from his mother and friends that his father believed he had a special relationship with God with whom he was at one, often speaking with frightening enthusiasm about his beloved Lord.[15] Occasionally, after the 1979 Revolution, when officials came to see him with great problems or a major crisis, he would talk about God as if nothing else existed, oblivious to the great political, social and economic forces he had unleashed.

A student of Khomeini who published his reflections on 'The Dawn Supplication' says of him:

If the Western philosophers consider the world as a mixture of conflicts and strife, it is possible to call this man the centre of contradictions and the pivot of divergent tastes and feelings. The man who talks about issues of theosophy and mysticism (the mystical path and liberation from all material inclination) can simultaneously think about the establishment of Islamic government, justice for the oppressed and the implementation of Islamic law.[16]

The question was how Khomeini would go about achieving these objectives.

4

The Formation of a Politician
Reza Shah and After

Graduates of Shi'i theology colleges require prudence, expediency and a developed ability to manoeuvre in order to become fully recognised teachers and aspiring ayatollahs. Obviously Khomeini the mystic who indulged in the concept of the Perfect Man had also to face reality. In clerical politics, factionalism, lobbying and populism are the norm. Teachers and advanced students are the main actors and extras who turn a man into a grand ayatollah or destroy him. By the age of twenty-seven Khomeini had begun to assemble his own circle of admiring students who visited his home regularly or met him at the shrine or *madraseh*. He had also developed his own method of teaching. In the best seminaries, dialectical argument between teacher and students was the norm; but Khomeini had no patience with discussion for its own sake. He would set out the issues, explain the various opinions on them and end with his own views, leaving little room for argumentation.[1] He never introduced issues that were unclear in his own mind and was scrupulous about preparing and reflecting on his topics before discussing them. This single-mindedness was to remain a lifelong habit which was to stand him in good stead beyond his classroom.

Khomeini's devotion to mysticism and his preoccupation with teaching did not curb his interest in what was going on in Qom and the country at large. Driven by what he perceived to be the moral degeneration of Iran, in the 1930s he began to teach ethics. He later recalled how during this period the people '... were selfish, feeble and sluggish', so that 'they were unable to resist the dictatorship of Reza Shah'. To Khomeini his fellow countrymen lacked the necessary moral fibre to combat this decay, 'and Iran, as a nation, thus lay dormant'.[2] Khomeini's lectures were given at the Feiziyeh School at Qom. His choice of a prominent public venue next to the Shrine of Fatemeh, and his choice of Thursdays and Fridays, ensured that his reputation spread far beyond religious circles. Indeed, many people travelled from neighbouring towns and villages and even from Tehran just to hear him speak. The authorities very quickly perceived the threat he posed to public order, and tried to dissuade him from lecturing, even in the seminaries. Khomeini's response was uncompromising: 'I am duty-bound to continue with these lectures. If the police want to stop them, they will have to come themselves and physically prevent them from taking place.'[3] The police ignored this challenge; but the pressure they exerted forced Khomeini to move his lectures from the prominent Feiziyeh to the more obscure Haj Mollah Sadeq School of Theology.

The ulema had long since discovered that their support for Reza Khan's accession to the throne would not protect them from secularisation. In the late 1920s Reza Shah's new administration, which had an intensely nationalistic outlook, had introduced a series of major reforms designed to turn Iran into a modern state. In two vital areas, the legal and educational system, these measures continued the process begun after the Constitutional Revolution which eroded the most important prerogatives of the clergy outside the strictly private and spiritual domains. The new criminal and commercial codes were based on French law, and although the civil code enacted in 1928 was largely derived from Shi'a legal theory, its administration was secularised and brought under the control of the Ministry of Justice. No longer could the ulema exercise their right to interpret and enforce the *shari'a* through their own private courts or register commercial transactions. Nor did their long, difficult training in jurisprudence in itself qualify them to practise under the aegis of the new Ministry of Justice, which set up its own law school and examination system for aspiring members of the legal profession. Mollahs were admitted to the school to be re-trained, but unless they attended they could not practise under the new system. Meanwhile, as the state invested more and more money in modern schools and introduced qualifications for civil service jobs that could only be acquired in the new educational system, the *maktab* and *madraseh* lost their attraction for ambitious parents and students at all levels of society.

In the 1930s Reza Shah embarked on far more provocative policies. He was fascinated by what he had heard of Turkey's progress under Atatürk, and in 1934 he visited the country to see for himself what had been achieved. Deeply impressed, as soon as he returned to Iran he announced at the border town of Maku: 'We have been to meet a very great man. We must bring our people to the same level of development and progress as his.' From then on he plunged into an accelerated programme of social and economic modernisation. But many of the decisions he took in this period were hastily conceived and arbitrary. Among them were decrees forcing men to wear European hats, forcing mollahs – with the exception of those who had qualified as *mojtaheds* – to discard clerical attire and, most unsettling of all for the traditionalists, forcing women to discard the veil or any other modest form of head covering. In the streets the new dress laws were strictly enforced by policemen who had orders to fine anyone who did not observe them, and to tear the veils from the heads of women who dared to venture out in them. Not surprisingly, many older women simply stayed at home.

The mollahs, who had shown little open opposition to the legal and educational reforms, were outraged by the new dress laws, but helpless.[4] Ayatollah Hossein Qomi left his home in Mashhad for Tehran hoping to persuade the Shah to change his mind. He was even reported to have said that he was 'willing to kiss Reza Shah's feet if he drops his plan'. However, the Shah refused to receive him and he took sanctuary in the shrine of Shah Abdolazim in Rey before being exiled to Iraq.[5] By early July 1935, the story of Qomi's humiliation and his anti-government sentiments had sparked off protests in the Gowharshad mosque in Mashhad in which many people were shot dead. Even the politically quiescent Ha'eri, still the leading figure in Qom, now came under such pressure from his flock to do something about 'the infidel Shah', that he openly attacked Reza Shah; but to no avail.[6] If they were to survive, the clergy felt they had no choice other than to keep their heads down. 'Had Ha'eri uttered a word, they [Reza Shah's regime] would have destroyed the theological centre of Qom,'[7] explained Ayatollah Saduqi, many years later.

During this time Khomeini did little to provoke the wrath of the determined Shah and the secularist politicians who drove his programme of

reform. He was for one thing still too junior, and for another he was content to go along with the passive attitude of the majority of the ulema and
adopt the Shi'i practice of *taqiyya* or dissimulation which permits people
to deny their faith in order to continue its practice. This highly pragmatic
doctrine has allowed the Shi'a in times of danger to trim their sails, reverse their positions or simply to lie in the interests of self-preservation
and, when prudence demands, it is called upon by even the most single-
minded devotees. Given the brutality with which Reza Shah was implementing his policies – with imprisonment and death often the reward for
those who crossed him – most of the ulema preferred to bide their time.

One of his students recounts Khomeini's visit to Bafqi, an ayatollah
who had incurred the Shah's displeasure and returned to Qom after a
period of internal exile. Bafqi was very upset because the religious community had allowed the authorities to demolish part of the Imam mosque
in Qom in order to build a road. He castigated Khomeini, saying: 'You
were here and let them demolish the Imam's Mosque?' Upon which Khomeini replied with a *hadith*: 'Dissimulation is my path and the path of my
forefathers.'[8]

There were, of course, many Iranians who did not share the view that
Reza Shah was an absolute evil. They admired his attempt to use force to
modernise the country, and the fact that he had united the country, reduc-
ing the power of local notables, tribal lords and reactionary clerics. Certain nostalgic nationalists praised him for glorifying pre-Islamic Iran and
for preferring Iranian nationalism to 'backward Arab culture', meaning Islam. Even the intelligentsia, the Left and other progressive politicians, who
despised Reza Shah for his corruption, brutality and despotism admitted
the positive side of his reforms. So too did some of the clergy. Part of this
group left the clerical establishment to take positions in government or
become secular lawyers or teachers. Others attempted to rally support for
modernising reforms.

One scholar who jolted his fellow clergymen was Shari'at-Sangelaji, who
dared to criticise the religious establishment as an anachronistic body which
should rid itself of the superstitions it had imposed on Islam. Benefiting
from the anti-clerical ethos of Reza Shah's period, Sangelaji was able to
write with remarkable frankness on several religious topics. For example,
he published a refutation of the concept of *raj'at* or the physical return of
the Imams. And, on even more sensitive ground, he attacked the concept
of *taqlid* or imitation, the very cornerstone of clerical influence, as a major

cause of backwardness which prevented people from thinking for themselves.

In 1935 other religious reformers began the journal *Homayun*, of which eleven issues were published before it was finally suppressed as a threat to public order. The editor of *Homayun* was Ali Akbar Hakamizadeh, whose father, Sheikh Mehdi Pa'inshahri, a friend of Ha'eri's, has been described by one religious historian as a 'man of great zeal who implemented Islamic laws by flogging drunks and fornicators'.[9] Hakamizadeh and his colleagues were frustrated by the 'backwardness, ill health and addictions of society in general and the religious community in particular'. Famous anti-clerics as well as prominent religious figures contributed to his journal. Among them was Ahmad Kasravi, who had been educated as a mollah but became a secular lawyer and widely respected historian of the constitutional period. Kasravi was an idealist who formulated his own rationalist religious ethic. In one of his articles he suggested that Iran had only three choices: 'to remain in ignorance, to become Westernised, or to follow a path which is guided by reason and supported by knowing God and belonging to the People.'[10] Another contributor was Seyyed Ali Akbar Borqa'i, a clergyman who admired Reza Shah's reforms, referring to him in phrases such as: 'His Majesty the Shah of Iran, may his reign continue.' Borqa'i later became a sympathiser of the left. Mohammad Taqi Eshraqi, a leading preacher whose son later married Khomeini's daughter, was also a contributor.

In the autumn of 1941, in the middle of the Second World War, Reza Shah fell victim to his pro-German sentiments, which had become increasingly evident in the late 1930s. The Allies needed to secure the supply route from the Persian Gulf to Russia and, using the presence of the German technicians and businessmen the Shah's policies had brought to Iran as a pretext, they invaded the country in the autumn of 1941. A few days later, on 17 September, the Shah was forced to abandon his throne and the twenty-one-year-old Crown Prince Mohammad Reza was presented as the new monarch. Mohammad Reza had attended Tehran's military high school and a boarding school in Switzerland. A mild-mannered youth, his style was very different from that of his charismatic, overbearing father and at first he was eager to play the constitutional game. People were astonished to see him behaving like an ordinary man, offering cigarettes to his visitors and chatting with them in a relaxed way, despite his shyness. But Mohammad Reza very quickly mastered the intrigues and

machinations of Iranian politics. Nevertheless, more than a decade of relative political freedom followed his succession, in part guaranteed by the
Allied presence. In the more relaxed atmosphere, the social and political
agenda of those who had tasted Reza Shah's repressions could be revived.
This included the clergy, whose expedient passivity under the old king
could now be reversed.

Throughout Iran the ideals of the Constitutional Revolution sprang to
life once more. The coalition of clergymen, intellectuals, merchants and
the local and tribal chiefs who had staged the revolution again became
active in the Majles. Newspapers blossomed, revelling in the opportunity
to criticise the old Shah and the Pahlavi family. Turbaned men and veiled
women reappeared on the streets without fear of arrest. Political detainees were released from prison, and very soon the Marxists among them
were busy forming a communist party – known as the Tudeh Party – with
the grace of the Soviet Union.

The evident popularity of the Tudeh among educated youth and its
potential for becoming a potent weapon of Russian influence within Iran
was, from the beginning of Mohammad Reza's reign, a matter of concern
to the ruling politicians, and to the Western powers. So to help counter
the spread of revolutionary ideology, religious activity was encouraged.
Once again Qom became a place of some importance in the life of the
nation. Ministers and officials began to visit leading mollahs in their homes,
apologising for the misdeeds of the past. Indeed, in 1943 when Ayatollah
Hossein Qomi, who after the death of Isfahani became, for a brief period,
senior *marja'*, and who Reza Shah had exiled to Iraq, paid a triumphal
visit to Iran, the five demands he made of the government were politely
received. These included the reimposition of the veil and entrusting the
management of theological schools and endowments to the clergy.

However, it was no longer possible to turn the clock back. Thousands
of women brought up under Reza Shah had no desire to go back to the
veil, the secular schools and universities were flourishing and the restoration of the clergy's judicial privileges was unthinkable. Furthermore, the
clergy no longer enjoyed a monopoly of ideology and teaching, or unique
access to the means of spreading ideas. The pulpit, although still important, had to compete with the radio, newspapers and periodicals, as well as
the political gatherings now in vogue. New forms of art such as theatre
and cinema, banned by the clergy, had found their own enthusiastic following. Among the educated there was a genuine sense of liberation from

religious superstition. This active and increasingly large minority could no longer be treated simply as a flock seeking a shepherd. It was clear that Reza Shah's secular policies would have a lasting impact. Not only had they helped, irreversibly, to create a secular section in society, but they had also intensified the divisions that already existed among Muslim intellectuals over how they should deal with the military, political, economic and, more importantly for Muslims, the ideological and cultural Western offensive.

Most of the clerical elite accepted that the situation could probably not be changed, even though, as diehard religious conservatives, many of them found it distasteful. Under the leadership of Ayatollah Borujerdi who in late 1946, after Qomi's death, emerged as the sole *marja'-e taqlid* of the Shi'a, they opted to strengthen the religious institution and to establish an amicable relationship with the state. Borujerdi was popularly known as 'the renewer of the faith' – an apt title, for he combined immense piety and knowledge with unusual administrative ability. He brought much-needed reform to the theological colleges of Qom, and by rationalising the collection of religious alms he revived the city's economic fortunes. He also vigorously guarded the non-political status of the 'source of emulation', and in 1949 successfully persuaded a large gathering of clergy to agree that they too should keep out of the political fray.

Outside the clerical elite there were two other religiously-oriented groups. The first was made up of Muslim intellectuals with liberal and reformist tendencies including Mehdi Bazargan, Mahmud Taleqani and Mohammad Taqi Shar'iati. These men were critical of the inability of the religious conservatives to respond to the requirements of the modern age and attempted to present a modern interpretation of Islam, especially to the young who were attracted by secularism. The second consisted of mollahs and laymen who, rather like the Muslim Brotherhood in Sunni countries, were fundamentalists and wanted to revive the golden age of early Islam and establish Islamic government. They believed that Islam was capable of answering all problems and organising every aspect of life and that liberation from the power and influence of the West could only be achieved through the proper implementation of the *shari'a*.[11] Led by a junior cleric called Navvab Safavi, in 1945 this group formed the Feda'iyan-e Islam which advocated – and on several occasions used – violence, in particular assassination, to pursue their goal.

Khomeini's own political position during this period was somewhere between that of the clerical establishment and the Feda'iyan. On the one hand, as a believer in religious authority and the need for solidarity among the clergy, Khomeini was a firm supporter of Borujerdi. Indeed, although he was still a junior, he had been among the mollahs who helped to raise Borujerdi to the rank of *marja'*. For a time during the 1940s he also appears to have been an adviser to him. On the other hand, as the only two political statements that come from this period show, he was radically opposed to secularism, believed adamantly in the rule of the *shari'a*, and had activist tendencies. He had absorbed, in other words, some of the ideas of the Feda'iyan perhaps in the course of conversations with Navvab Safavi who, according to the latter's widow was a frequent visitor to Khomeini's home.[12]

The shorter of his two statements was recorded in 1944 in the visitors' book at a mosque in Yazd. At the top of the page Khomeini wrote: 'To be read and put into practice.' He began with the Qor'anic verse: 'Say: I do admonish you on one point, that you do stand up for God, in pairs or singly.' In the lines that followed he spoke of the importance of staging an uprising in the name of God: 'It is our selfishness and abandonment of an uprising for God that have led to our present dark days and subjected us to world domination. It is selfishness that has undermined the Muslim world.' Disappointed with the performance of his fellow Muslims, Khomeini urged them to take a lesson in dedication and determination from the Baha'is, whom he otherwise regarded as hated heretics.[13]

The second statement was more elaborate and more important. It took the form of a short book called *Kashf al-Asrar* (The Discovery of Secrets),[14] which Khomeini appears to have completed in 1942 and published anonymously. The book is an attack on secularism. Skilfully deploying the polemical style he had learnt at theological school, in it Khomeini describes Reza Shah as 'that illiterate soldier who knew that if he did not suffocate them [the clergy] and silence them with the force of bayonets, they would oppose what he was doing to the country and religion.' He continues:

Reza Shah spent some time unsuccessfully trying to win over Modarres ... Realising that Modarres could not be bought, frightened or influenced by the power of his logic, he became convinced that there were other clerics like him who were not going to co-operate with him. It was then that he decided to go ahead with his plans to destroy the clergy in order to 'serve his masters' [the British]. They resisted him, of course, but the laxity and sluggishness of the people, who form the power-base for the implementation of any plan, aborted their resistance.[15]

Khomeini then paints a vivid picture of the results of Reza Shah's anti-clerical propaganda. During his reign the mollahs, wrote Khomeini, had lost their influence over the people to such an extent that no one was prepared to give them a lift in their car. If a mollah was by any chance given a lift, any fault that developed in their car was promptly attributed to his 'evil presence'. 'I myself saw a car run out of petrol in the middle of the road,' writes Khomeini. 'The driver said that it was because of the presence of this ill-omened mollah but because I was a seyyed I was not bothered.'[16] The poor mollahs had indeed fallen from grace, and the stage was left open for 'the players of the golden age'[17] – an expression used to describe the secular intellectuals and politicians who were active during 'the golden age' of Reza Shah's reign, modenisers eager to leave their stamp on society, many of whom ended up in prison and some dead.

Khomeini then goes on to bitterly reprimand those who, in his estimation, had not learnt from the grim days of Reza Shah:

When his dark dictatorship was over, one would have expected people to become aware of the causes of the malady which had beset them, learnt from the violations committed against their lives, honour and property during those twenty years, and taken it upon themselves to punish those who had been left in that bankrupt golden age. One would have expected them to trample over those who wanted them to abandon their religion. But the people who have taken over are still asleep and have forgotten their darkest days of exploitation, using the opportunities afforded by the nation's refusal to stand up for its own legitimate rights. It is they who are now subduing the clergy, challenging religion and belief itself and trampling the rules of the Qor'an so that they can get on with the implementation of their corrupt and poisonous intentions.[18]

However, the real target of *Kashf al-Asrar* was not Reza Shah but the 'renegade' clergymen who in Khomeini's eyes had 'actively collaborated with him'. Indeed it was a direct response to an attack on the clerical establishment in a pamphlet called *Asrar-e Hezar Saleh* (Secrets of a Thousand Years) written by Hakamizadeh, the editor of *Homayun*. Khomeini later recalled that when he saw the work of this 'twisted person' he was inflamed with rage. Despite problems he was having at the time with his eyes, he saw no alternative but to take forty-eight days off from his teaching obligations to reply to the accusations.

On the subject of Hakamizadeh and men like him, Khomeini maintained that while the world had been enveloped in the hellfire of war, and nations were trying to salvage themselves, such 'mindless' people were trying their utmost to spread disunity and mischief instead of helping their brethren who had been pushed into war. These people had taken the 'criminal step' of spreading their 'poisonous' ideas against the clergy. He considered it his duty to bring these facts to people's attention so that the sources of Iran's corruption and misery could be traced.

One reformist trend that had been gaining ground, and which Khomeini particularly reviled, argued that Shi'i rituals and the rituals of some Sufi sects had little to do with the original religion founded by Mohammad. This view, which was advocated by Ahmad Kasravi and a number of former mollahs, was in a sense not unlike that espoused by the puritanical Wahhabi sect in Saudi Arabia. So Khomeini accused its propagators of being 'the followers of the camel grazers of Riyadh and the barbarians of Najd, the most infamous and the wildest members of the human family.'[19] 'If you think these camel-grazers are a model for development,' he wrote 'why don't you invite advisors from the Saudi royal court to teach you civilisation and eradicate superstition from among you?'[20]

Parts of Khomeini's book were more sober. In these he proceeded systematically, selecting and refuting doubts about God's unity, the imamate and religious leadership, the clergy, government, law and the *hadith*. Exploiting to the full his knowledge of philosophy, logic and polemics he would challenge his opponents, explain the background to his subject-matter and then put forward his case. Another technique he employed was to appeal to his readers' sense of patriotism and religious sentiments. Conscious of how widely secular nationalism had spread among educated people, and how alienated those who had studied in the new schools and colleges had become from the clergy, he addressed the young with words such as: 'O you dear Persian-speaking readers, you educated youth who love religion, and you enlightened university and high school students.'[21] Or again he appealed to 'the conscience of Persian-speaking Iranians for the sake of whose religion, faith and homeland these pages are being written',[22] to 'judge for themselves and see who the source of these nonsensical absurdities is.'[23] Unusually for a mollah of his generation he even made constant use of a philosophical term fashionable at the time among the anti-clerical element, namely *kherad*, or the power of reason:

This irrational person has taken it for granted that religious people have tram-pled upon the rule of 'reason' and have no regard for it, thus revealing his own ignorance. Is it not religious people who have written all our books on phi-losophy and the principles of jurisprudence? Have they not looked upon thou-sands of philosophical and theological issues in the light of reason and intel-lect? Is it not these leaders of theology who consider reason as one of the binding issues?[24]

Yet such displays of political sensitivity were interspersed with pure invective. When he launched a counter-attack on the clergy's opponents Khomeini would often lose control, accusing them of stupidity, treachery, ignorance and heresy. But as he embarked upon the final statement of his polemic, he wrote in an offensive tone that those who see themselves as protectors of religion must 'smash in the teeth this brainless mob with their iron fist' and 'trample upon their heads with courageous strides'.[25]

There is yet another layer to *Kashf al-Asrar*. Significantly – for here we see the first statement of Khomeini's ideas on the constitution of an Is-lamic state – he advised his readers to look at the chapters on government and the clergy with particular attention. Government, he argued, can only be legitimate when it accepts the rule of God, and the rule of God means the implementation of the *shari'a*. All laws that are contrary to the *shari'a* must be dropped, because 'only the law of God will always stay valid and immutable in the face of changing times.'[26] Western civilisation and for-eigners have, in this respect, 'stolen the reason and intelligence from mis-guided Muslims'.[27] The form of government, he said, did not in itself mat-ter as long as the law of Islam was enforced. But if the government were to be a monarchy the king should be appointed by the *mojtaheds* who would choose 'a just monarch who does not violate God's laws, will turn from oppression and wrongdoing and will not violate men's property, lives and honour.'[28] On a rather chilling note, he expected the government of Islam to 'follow religious rules and regulations and ban publications which are against the law and religion and hang those who write such nonsense in the presence of religious believers.' The 'mischief-makers who are corrupt-ers of the earth, (*mofsed fi'l-arz*) should, he said, 'be uprooted so that others would avoid betraying religious sanctity'.[29]

Another indication of Khomeini's political ideas at the time was his admiration for Ayatollah Seyyed Abolqassem Kashani (1882–1962) who from 1945 was closely linked to the Feda'iyan-e Islam. Kashani came from a long line of ulema. As a very young man he went to study in Najaf, and later he joined his father and other leading clerics in opposing British rule over Iraq following the collapse of the Ottoman Empire after the First World War. He fled to Iran in 1921, just as the Qajar dynasty was on the verge of collapse.[30]

Prominent enough to merit a warm welcome from the young Qajar king, Ahmad Shah, Kashani soon joined parliament as a member for Tehran. He later became a member of the Constituent Assembly, with whom he voted to depose the Qajars and to establish the Pahlavi dynasty in 1925. In 1941, after the fall of Reza Shah, Kashani's anti-British sentiments landed him in trouble once again, and in 1942 he was arrested and interned by the occupying British forces for pro-German sentiments. He became a popular figure with junior and middle-ranking mollahs as a result, and his release in 1945 was enthusiastically celebrated by them.

Khomeini was a frequent visitor to Kashani's home and admired his courage and stamina. He shared his views on many issues such as anti-colonialism, Islamic universalism, political activism and populism. But the two men also differed in many ways. Kashani was the urbane politician willing to be flexible, while Khomeini was more austere and less accommodating. While Kashani severed his links as a teacher at theological centres, Khomeini continued to advocate a united clerical leadership, and he was not prepared to break ranks with the clerical elite in Qom and Najaf who controlled the theological centres.

The late 1940s and early 1950s were a period of militant anti-colonialism in Iran, directed against Britain and British oil interests. In this ferment the Shah and his court were viewed by many as instruments of foreign domination, the issue around which Iranian political life revolved at this time. Borujerdi's non-interference in politics in a period of major political upsurge did not go down well with the constitutionalists and nationalists, who expected support from the clergy. In 1949 Dr Mohammad Mosaddeq founded and assumed leadership of the National Front, a loose coalition of political groups and parties, journalists and other private individuals. An aristocrat and doctor of law, Mosaddeq had an impeccable reputation for honesty and public service. With his charismatic personality and unique political style he was able to mobilise mass popular support both for the nationalisation of Iran's British-owned oil industry and for his attempts to limit the Shah's powers.

When Mosaddeq became prime minister in 1951, many leading clerics declared their support for the nationalisation of the Anglo-Iranian Oil Company, although they did little else to help Mosaddeq's cause. In addition, a handful of clerical deputies allied themselves with the National Front in parliament. However, the only mollah of importance to play a leading part in the movement was Kashani. In 1949 the government had exiled Kashani to Lebanon because it suspected, although it could not prove, that he had been involved in an attempt on the Shah's life. But he was allowed to return to Iran a year later after Ayatollahs Borujerdi and Khonsari had interceded with the Shah on his behalf. Ignoring Borujerdi's quietist policy, Kashani immediately plunged into political activity, issuing one statement after another in support of Mosaddeq and organising demonstrations and strikes. He even at one point, when it was rumoured that the British were considering the use of military force against Iran, threatened to declare a *jihad* against them.[31]

However, as the political crisis deepened the alliance between Mosaddeq and Kashani began to crumble. It finally broke down in the early months of 1953, after Mosaddeq requested an extension of emergency powers the Majles had granted to him the previous autumn. By this time the clerical establishment also viewed Mosaddeq with alarm. The anticlericalism of some of his supporters worried them, but above all the conservative ulema, who feared the spectre of communism, were suspicious of the National Front's secular and reformist orientation, which began towards the end of 1952 with Mosaddeq's assumption of emergency powers.

In this confused situation there was a battle of wills between several interested parties: the Feda'iyan-e Islam wanted to loosen the links between the conservative clergy and the Shah, while the Shah himself aimed to prevent any nascent secular–clerical axis. Dr Mosaddeq wanted the support of the clergy, but he was unwilling to submit to the Feda'iyan and their clerical allies' demand for the literal implementation of the *shari'a* and would not befriend the clergy at the expense of his own convictions and his reformist wing. During this period Khomeini was involved with the Feda'iyan, a fact that could not have escaped Borujerdi's attention; but his belief in central authority amid the confusion of the clerical centres meant that he always stopped short of airing any public criticism of Borujerdi's policies.

Khomeini's attitude towards the political events of this period is indeed not at all clear. But he was close enough to Kashani to accept his

version of events when he withdrew his support from Mosaddeq's government. 'Mosaddeq,' he commented after the 1979 Revolution, 'meant well
and wanted to serve the nation, but his main mistake was not to have got
rid of the Shah when he was strong and the Shah was weak.'[32]

In August 1953 Mosaddeq was overthrown in a *coup d'état* led by General Fazlollah Zahedi but organised by the CIA and the British. Kashani
played an important role in the whole enterprise, helping to mobilise the
anti-Mosaddeq crowd. After the *coup* clerical support for the Shah intensified and a period of harmony between Qom and the court ensued which
lasted until the late 1960s. During this period, under the leadership of
Borujerdi, the clergy attempted to remain above the political fray; but in
effect their tacit support went to the Shah. In return, in the early post-*coup*
years the Shah made some concessions to them. These included a free
hand to counter the growth of Baha'ism, which the clergy reviled as heretical. Baha'ism was seen as a nineteenth-century schism lead by Mirza
Hossein Ali Nuri (1817–92), known as Baha'ollah, who proclaimed himself a new prophet, despite Islam's fundamental credo that Mohammad is
the 'seal' of the prophets. Even more sensitive for the Shi'a, Baha'ollah, by
claiming that the Bab was a personification of the Hidden Imam, undermined the theory of the return of the Imam who will bring peace and
justice. In later years Baha'i proselytising activities increased Muslim animosity towards them as did, perhaps, the secularism and modernism of
the Baha'is which, given that they accepted many of the tenets of Islam,
may have lead the clerical establishment to perceive them as a threat. Animosity towards the Baha'is had thus existed from the beginning. But the
fact that Baha'ollah was buried in Acre in Palestine and the Baha'i Universal House of Justice, its main administrative centre, was in the port city of
Haifa made matters worse after the creation of Israel in 1948 when anti-
Baha'i feeling found a stronger pretext.

In 1953 a well-organised society, officially known as the Hojjatieh
Mahdavieh Charity, was set up in Tehran to fight Baha'i influence. Its
founder was Sheikh Mahmud Halabi, a well-known preacher from Mashhad who had been a prominent supporter of Dr Mosaddeq. The Shah not
only tolerated the activities of Halabi and his fellow anti-Baha'i clergymen, but allowed the clergy's fight against the Baha'is to be aired from the
government-controlled media. In an unprecedented move in 1955, Tehran
Radio broadcast a series of anti-Baha'i sermons by Mohammad Taqi Falsafi,
Iran's leading preacher. Soon, however, the Shah came under international

pressure, decided to drop the plan after allowing his officials to destroy a Baha'i temple and unleashing mob rule against the Baha'is.

Borujerdi did not pursue the matter, but Halabi and others finally obtained a *fatwa* from the leading clerics, including Borujerdi, which banned transactions with the Baha'is. The *cause célèbre* was the *fatwa* which forbade Muslims to buy or drink Pepsi-Cola since the Iranian franchise belonged to Habib Sabet, a Baha'i. Interestingly enough, the anti-Baha'i clergy, including Sheikh Mahmud Halabi, were apolitical and highly conservative. Khomeini, however, who did not favour Borujerdi's co-operation with the Shah to begin with, now wanted Borujerdi to continue with his anti-Baha'i campaign. But as Khomeini complained later: 'I went every day to encourage His Holiness's anti-Baha'i activity in order to rid the administration of Baha'is, but by the following day he had gone cold on the issue.'

Khomeini remained silent during these years since 'he did not feel duty-bound to talk while Borujerdi was in charge of the theological centres.' Privately, however, he did not hesitate to use his influence for whatever it was worth. When Navvab Safavi was under the threat of execution following attempts to assassinate the prime minister and the minister of court, Khomeini tried to persuade Borujerdi to petition the Shah for his release, but failed. It was then that he himself wrote letters to a former prime minister, the Shah's religious adviser and Ayatollah Behbehani, a pro-court cleric who had been instrumental in the overthrow of Mosaddeq. The plea failed and Navvab was executed. Later Khomeini disdainfully commented to a friend: 'I do not recognise Mr Behbehani's handwriting and I do not know his political lines. But I think he dictated the answer to my letter to a twelve-year-old boy to write.'

A religious historian considered Khomeini in the early 1950s as 'one of the great teachers and prominent figures of Qom's theological centres.' In the ornate literary style used in such chronicles he described him as 'the learned philosopher, the discerning jurisconsult by whom the eyes of the theological centre are enlightened.' He went on to say that Khomeini was '... the centre of attention for many students and people from Qom, Tehran and other cities, whose lectures on ethics were, until interrupted after eight years, attended by hundreds of virtuous people from the centre itself and from other places.' Of his lectures on theology, he wrote that they were 'better than any others', and speculating on Khomeini's future he added that 'much hope is now attached to him.'[33] Years of teaching ethics, theology, transcendental theosophy and philosophy were bearing fruit, as his 200 or more students were spread all over Iran and amongst the Shi'i community abroad. Some had become leading local clerics representing one of the grand ayatollahs, others were prayer leaders, teachers of theology or preachers. Khomeini was perhaps aware that it had been said of the Prophet Mohammad that he 'made little headway as a prophet until he became a successful politician; but at the same time, political opportunity depended upon his credentials as a prophet.'[34]

Khomeini's involvement in politics has been compared by his followers with that of the Prophet Mohammad. This was not only because of the distinction that is drawn between the Prophet's early, idealistic period in Medina and the Meccan period when he set up his administration and became a shrewd political operator. Mohammad's whole methodology changed as he gradually introduced a ban on alcohol and restrictions on slavery and there is little doubt that Khomeini modelled himself on the Prophet. The twenty-three years of personal leadership are an example that modern Islamicists, including Khomeini, have attempted to revive. Khomeini often referred to Ali's attempts to establish justice and to Hossein's courage in the face of tyranny and corruption. A gradualist, Khomeini established his credentials as a prominent religious leader before moving on to the political arena in order to both strengthen his standing within the religious establishment and widen his power base in general.

Khomeini regarded his two main patrons, Kashani and Borujerdi, as two facets of Mohammad: Kashani the political and Borujerdi the religious leader. Neither of them was ideal for Khomeini, although both are said to have pointed to him as a future religious leader. Khomeini's political instinct taught him to express his often unconventional and radical views, and persuade others to adopt similar positions, while at the same time adhering to the consensus of the Qom establishment under the patronage of Borujerdi as grand ayatollah. Theologically speaking, Khomeini was not in a position to become another Borujerdi, as he was young and there were too many ageing senior ayatollahs living. Many clerics have faced the same predicament, including Ha'eri and Na'ini both of whom had reached the highest level of learning but neither of whom had the chance to achieve ultimate leadership, to become senior *marja'-e taqlid*, because of the longevity of their seniors.

On the other hand, Khomeini did not want to become another Kashani, whom he saw as misunderstood by the clergy of Qom and Tehran, and from whom religious nationalists such as Mehdi Bazargan, Ayatollahs Reza and Abolfazl Zanjani and Mahmud Taleqani distanced themselves, blaming him for Mosaddeq's downfall. Alluding to the post-Mosaddeq period in which the clergy and, in particular, Kashani were heavily criticised for the Shah's return, Khomeini recalls, as an example of Kashani's isolation after Mosaddeq's downfall, that he was in a religious gathering when 'the late Mr Kashani entered. No one got up to offer him a place. I got up and offered him my place.'

Having the Feda'iyan-e Islam and Kashani as examples of forces who did not have the support of the majority of the clerical establishment and who were eventually isolated and suffered defeat, Khomeini did not want to break with the theological circles. In fact, his criticism of Kashani was that instead of trying to Islamise politics, he politicised Islam. Khomeini's aim was to ensure that this did not happen to him.

Following the benign role that the clergy played in the restoration of the Pahlavis in 1953, the rest of the 1950s were a period of relative tranquillity in clergy–state–court relations. These held fast until 1960/61 when, under pressure from the incoming Kennedy administration, the Shah decided on a land reform programme. Alarmed, the country's landowners turned to Borujerdi, begging him to declare that the relatively innocuous law submitted to the Majles by Manuchehr Eqbal's government violated the principles of Islam. Borujerdi and many other leading clerics were themselves worried about the prospect of a land reform. They believed that private property was sanctified by the *shari'a*, and were also concerned about what would happen to the endowments of land on which many religious activities depended if the reform eventually snowballed. So, breaking his principle of non-interference in politics for the first time, Borujerdi lodged a strong protest against the bill.

The land reform bill was in fact modified by the landlord-dominated parliament to the point that it 'became useless as an instrument of reform'.[35] The Shah kept silent on the issue, but he was by this time increasingly confident of his political position and no longer willing to pay the ageing Borujerdi the traditional visits to his home. His final meeting with the old man before his death was nothing less than a deliberate humiliation. Frail and sick, Borujerdi was taken in a horse-drawn carriage to the shrine at the centre of Qom, where he was made to wait almost an hour for the Shah's arrival. As the Shah approached, two army officers helped him to his feet. But the Shah, not even bothering to shake the

hand he had kissed so many times in the past, merely spoke the customary greeting 'ahval-e Aqa cheh tor ast?' (How are you, sir?), and moved on
without even waiting for a reply. The Shah's affront was not lost on the
younger clergy like Khomeini who venerated the old man.

Borujerdi died on 30 March 1961. On the seventh day after his death,
Ayatollah Behbehani invited the leading divines of Qom to form a group
to look after the theological colleges and possibly find a replacement for
Borujerdi. There were at the time seven or eight senior Shi'i ayatollahs
and none of them was a clear candidate. The royal court appeared to favour Ayatollah Mohsen al-Hakim, who lived in Najaf and to whom it
sent a long telegram of condolence on Borujerdi's death. However Hakim
was an Iraqi citizen popular among the Shi'a of Iraq and Lebanon. He did
not have much of a following in Iran and the court's interference in an
affair the mollahs considered to be their own caused considerable resentment. Behbehani's meeting was therefore indecisive and the whole issue
was put aside for a time. Khomeini, still only fifty-nine at the time, was a
very junior candidate, if a candidate at all. In Qom alone he was outranked
by the older and better-known Ayatollahs Shari'atmadari, Golpayegani
and Mara'shi Najafi. He was by now considered to be a *marja'-e taqlid*, but
with so many others in the running his youthfulness counted against him.
He himself gave the impression that he 'wanted to be known only as a
teacher' and not as a 'source of emulation'. To a student who asked him to
put himself forward he is reported to have replied: 'Leave me alone to continue with my teaching. If one day the Muslims need me I will be available
but now there are others. Leave me alone.'

Throughout 1960 and the early months of 1961 political discontent had
been simmering below the surface – and breaking into the open with increasing frequency. The underlying cause was economic crisis. For more
than five years increased oil revenues and large quantities of American aid
had brought unprecedented prosperity to the country and enabled the
government to launch ambitious development plans. But poor economic
management had created a huge budget deficit, growing inflation and a
runaway import bill. By the autumn of 1960, excessive imports had
completely eaten up the foreign exchange reserves. Forced to introduce a
draconian stabilisation programme prescribed by the International
Monetary Fund, the government created a severe recession which lasted
for almost three years bringing misery to many people. Workers, especially
those who had laboured on the mushrooming building sites of the boom

period, suddenly found themselves unemployed; bankruptcy threatened bazaar merchants who had grown prosperous on the lucrative import trade. The country's numerous state employees, notoriously underpaid, were forced to live on frozen salaries.

As the economic crisis deepened a political dispute was raging over the elections to the twentieth Majles held in July and August 1960. Bowing to American pressure, the Shah had announced that the elections would be free and 'independent' candidates (except for people associated with Mosad-deq) would be allowed to participate. But the elections were so obviously rigged that, faced with growing public resentment, he had to cancel them and schedule a new round for January 1961. The January elections were also rigged and, for the first time since the 1953 *coup*, the Second National Front openly organised protest demonstrations at Tehran University, even-tually forcing the authorities to close the campus. The unrest continued with a teachers' strike in late April and a massive street demonstration which ended in tragedy when a teacher was killed by armed police.

The newly elected Kennedy administration in the United States was by now seriously worried, and in May 1961 the Shah, under strong Ameri-can pressure, dissolved the twenty-first Majles and appointed Ali Amini as prime minister with special powers for six months. Dr Amini was an aristocrat whose mother, Fakhr al-Dowleh (facetiously called by Reza Shah 'the only man in the Qajar dynasty'), was the daughter of Mozaffar al-Din Shah, the king who signed the Constitutional Edict in 1906. He had served in one of Mosaddeq's cabinets and in Zahedi's cabinet of the *coup d'état* and was regarded as an 'independent'. He acquired considerable fame as a result of his election campaign, and was one of the very few politicians who did not play sycophant to the Shah. According to Amini himself, the Shah was suspicious of him because of his family links to the Qajars and never trusted him. 'He thought I was a republican at heart or was trying to revive the Qajar dynasty.' But with political tension and the economic cri-sis mounting, the Shah tolerated Amini because he needed American sup-port – although his silent intrigues against Amini never ceased.

Amini survived as prime minister for fourteen months. During this period he introduced economic austerity measures, conducted a campaign against corruption in government and on 7 January 1962 announced a sec-ond land reform law. The law was drafted by Hassan Arsanjani, Amini's visionary and very knowledgeable minister of agriculture. It was radical compared with the bill introduced by Eqbal's cabinet, and there was an obvious danger of clerical opposition. So on 2 January, the birthday of Imam Ali, Amini set out for Qom to congratulate the leading ayatollahs on the occasion and discuss his plans with them. Despite discontent among the conservative clergy, neither Shari'atmadari, Golpayegani nor Mara'shi Najafi voiced any objection. Nor did Khomeini, whom Amini visited as Qom's fourth-ranking theologian. Amini had, as a young man, himself studied as a *talabeh* in Najaf and for this reason he enjoyed good personal relations with many mollahs. Over tea and Persian biscuits he indulged in a lively debate with Khomeini on the role of the clergy and the clergy's expectations of the government. According to Amini, the only immediate problem that appeared to be on Khomeini's mind was the divorce proce-dures, which Amini assured him would be revised.

Despite his independent stand, and the inclusion in his cabinet of in-novators such as Arsanjani and Derakhshesh (the minister of education), Amini did not attract the support of the National Front because he re-fused to hold free elections. By this time the Front again wielded consid-erable influence on the streets of Tehran and it continued to organise dem-onstrations attended by thousands demanding an end to rule by decree and a properly constituted parliament. On Amini's orders the Front's lead-ership was eventually arrested, but after a short lull the demonstrations began again. Matters came to a head when, on 21 January 1962, in a move designed to weaken Amini, the Shah ordered commando units of the army to attack striking students at Tehran University, where they inflicted such great injury and damage to property that the chancellor resigned in pro-test. Meanwhile, conservative agitation against the land reform gathered pace. With both the Right and the Left ranged against him and the economy still in recession, Amini was forced to resign. He was replaced on 19 July 1962 by Asadollah Alam, a well-known landlord and close personal friend of the Shah, unashamedly servile to him. Where Amini had signed his reports to the Shah as 'Ali Amini, Prime Minister', Alam would sign his as 'Your home-born servant'.

By now the Shah had gained political confidence and believed that he no longer needed clerical support for plans that had possible religious implications. Initially he had been nervous about the reforms demanded by the Kennedy administration but now, with Amini out of the way, he was determined to adopt the programme as his own and carry it through at all costs. In Alam, he had a tough and faithful deputy. And precisely because of his servility, which attracted the Shah's trust, Alam immediately became a more powerful figure than Amini, and far more adept at implementing policies than his master.

Meanwhile Borujerdi's death had liberated Khomeini from the implicit restraints that the presence of this venerable old ayatollah had imposed on his radical view of the relationship between religion and politics. With the Shi'i hierarchy, whose traditions he respected so deeply, now without a leader of undisputed stature, Khomeini finally had a free hand to act according to his beliefs and instincts. Where previously he had worked in private, after Borujerdi's death he campaigned in public to eradicate the stigma attached to an *akhund-e siyasi* or 'political mollah'. Politics and religion are one, he often declared. He no longer had to worry about the stigma attached to being a political mollah.

5

Challenging His Majesty
Khomeini and the Shah in Conflict

For Ayatollah Borujerdi the survival of the faith had been dependent on co-operation with the Shah; but Khomeini believed that Islam could only prevail by confronting the secular order. The Shah had already indicated that he no longer needed the mollahs. By the late 1950s he had, with the clergy's help, regained his confidence in his struggle with the democratic nationalists and the Left. His priority was now to proceed with his father's secular revolution. Khomeini sensed this and, in every meeting he attended with fellow clerics, and every statement he made, he reminded his listeners of bleak days ahead unless they united to resist the Shah's 'sinister plans'. Khomeini continued to support Borujerdi's leadership, despite his private misgivings; but this was a tactical move born of his desire to see a strong and united leadership. Drawing on Shi'i references and traditions, he hinted that Ali, in order to preserve unity among Muslims, had sacrificed his right to become caliph. For the same reason he, Khomeini, had himself been reluctant to claim personal leadership.[1] He was well aware of the autonomous tendencies within the clergy in general, and among the top-ranking ayatollahs in particular. At the same time he knew that without a centralised authority the clergy would be unable to protect its own interests and act as a point of reference in turbulent times.

After some twenty years of relative harmony between the turban and the crown, the first clash of wills was to be won by the clergy, with Khomeini the main benefactor. The Shah, emerging from his short period of weakness following a challenge to his authority by former premier Ali Amini, and still under pressure from the Democratic administration of President Kennedy and the International Monetary Fund, began to carry out reforms begun by Amini aimed at undermining the resurgence of a new generation of opposition, mainly of leftist activists. Within weeks of Amini's resignation, the cabinet announced a new and provocative local council election bill which allowed women to vote for the first time and did not require the candidates to be Muslims (they could take their oaths of office on any 'Holy Book', such as the Torah or Bible, as well as the Qor'an).

Khomeini had been looking for an excuse to start his political campaign against the Shah without being seen to be too political – the marginalisation of the highly politicised Ayatollah Kashani was a lesson not to be ignored.[2] Unlike many other senior divines he had not opposed the land reform law. But the opening of the local councils to non-Muslims and the proposed enfranchisement of women gave him a clear-cut opportunity to draw attention to the 'threat to Islam' posed by the government. 'The son of Reza Khan,' he confided to one of his colleagues, 'has embarked on the destruction of Islam in Iran. I will oppose this as long as the blood circulates in my veins.'[3]

For Khomeini and, as he well understood, the clergy as a whole, votes for women were the last straw – the final stage in the Pahlavi dynasty's attack on traditional Islam. No other issue could possibly have had such resonance among the mass of the people.

Khomeini moved quickly. The new bill was announced in the Tehran press on the afternoon of 8 October 1962 and that same evening he invited Ayatollahs Shari'atmadari and Golpayegani to meet him at the house of their late master, Ayatollah Ha'eri. The venue was diplomatically chosen, for Borujerdi had no undisputed successor and divines who aspired to the position of *marja'* would have refused to visit any colleague's home, since this would have implied recognition of his seniority. Khomeini's qualities as a political leader were already emerging. At the meeting he proposed that the ulema present a united front against the government's plan and urged that they should constantly keep their followers informed of what was happening. This, he argued, would keep the people's interest alive, leaving little room for the regime's rumour-mongering and propaganda. But although they talked long into the night, the three ayatollahs could not agree on the wording of the protest they intended to make to the Shah and eventually had to settle for separate telegrams. Shari'atmadari and Golpayegani were in addition reluctant to make the contents of their telegrams public; but after some arm twisting from Khomeini, they agreed to do this and to meet at least once a week for consultation. 'Even at this very early stage, it was evident that Khomeini was after power while my father wanted only to be a spiritual guide,' recalled Shari'atmadari's son in November 1989.[4]

Six days later, the Shah's reply was sent to Qom. He was unrepentant. Addressing the three divines as 'hojjat al-Islam', which implied that he did not recognise them as grand ayatollahs, he wished them well in their task of 'guiding the populace' and in their 'non-interference' in politics. He bade them to look at the situation in other Islamic countries and to take into account the times they lived in and promised that he would pass their telegrams to 'the government'.[5]

Incensed by the Shah's attitude, Khomeini convened a second clerical summit in which it was decided to write to Prime Minister Alam. Meanwhile, both sides rallied support for their positions. The government's newspapers projected a mood of impatience with 'meddlesome' mollahs and attempted to appeal to women and the educated middle class by portraying the clergy as a reactionary force which lived in the Dark Ages. For their own part, the clergy used their large circulation religious monthly, *Maktab-e Islam*, to mobilise the faithful over the question of women's franchise. The magazine quoted Western scholars and intellectuals who pleaded that the East maintain its spirituality and not sell out blindly to the West. 'We Muslims,' it wrote, 'are unfortunately in need of Western science and technology but we don't need the West's morality, social behaviour and customs ... .' *Maktab-e Islam* attacked the participation of women in social and political affairs as 'blindly aping the West', arguing that even in Europe there were countries such as Switzerland in which women did not have the right to vote. Leading clerics from Najaf, including Ayatollahs Hakim and Kho'i, also joined the attack by warning the Shah not to pass 'such blasphemous laws against Islam and Shi'ism, but to learn a lesson from what has happened in other Muslim countries.'[6] They were referring, of course, to countries like Iraq, which had overthrown their monarchies and become republics.

Protest against the local government bill spread among other opponents of the regime. A statement issued by eighteen leading merchants called on the government to abandon its 'un-Islamic' bill and Mehdi Bazargan's Freedom Movement declared: 'The government does not respect the votes of men, what is the good of giving women the right to vote … ?'[7] The Freedom Movement was a group of pro-Mosaddeq liberal modernist Muslims founded in 1960 which mistrusted the mollahs for their role in the 1953 coup, but which now began to warm to the new political awareness among them. Bazargan and his colleagues, Ayatollah Taleqani and Dr Sahabi, were impressed by Khomeini's shrewd exploitation of this issue. In a second statement the Freedom Movement acknowledged the clerical leadership, adding that: 'Some fifty-six years after their role in the Constitutional Revolution … freedom-seeking Muslims are once more looking forward with admiration and hope to a collective return to law and religion, which [the revolution] saw as complementary.'[8] The ayatollahs, it continued, should not restrict themselves to campaigning against the local election bill, but refer as well to autocracy and authoritarianism, the real sources of the nation's malaise.

For the clergy who, as a body, had either been tainted by their collaboration with the Shah during the coup against Mosaddeq, or had shown indifference to the political situation, these words of approval from a progressive force signified a positive change. Khomeini had displayed an impressively accurate sense of timing. Thus encouraged, he now adopted an Islamic–constitutional recipe in his speeches to appeal to secular nationalist forces, just as in the early 1940s he had laced his language with Persian expressions to combat accusations that the clergy were influenced by Arab culture. Indeed, the constitution of 1905–6 came to play a crucial part in the polemics of both sides, with the clergy emphasising its Islamic nature and the Shah claiming that it had 'guaranteed the rights of every citizen, men and women alike'.

Several weeks passed and still Alam did not reply to the ayatollahs' telegrams. The ayatollahs met once more and decided to step up their pressure on him with yet more requests to abandon the new law. Khomeini penned another telegram to the Shah himself. Referring to the Shah's remark, 'I wish you success in the guidance of the populace,' he wrote: 'Your Majesty's statement is in line with the *hadith* of the Prophet: "When heresy appears among my people the *alem* [theologian] must enlighten them, otherwise God's damnation will be upon him."' But, he added, the 'heretic Alam does not listen to God's word, the constitution, the law of the Majles, the orders of Your Majesty, the advice of the clergy or the demands of the people.' As in his other telegrams, Khomeini still made no direct reference to the issue of women's suffrage, but instead advised the Shah not to listen to servile flatterers 'who, with their anti-Islamic and anti-constitutional actions, are weakening the foundations of the nation and monarchy ... if Mr Alam does not repent of the insult he has committed against the holy Qor'an, I will have to remind Your Majesty of other issues in an open letter ... .'⁹ Khomeini followed this telegram with another harshly worded missive to the prime minister accusing him of wanting to abandon the Qor'an and return to the 'anachronism' of the Zoroastrian and other Holy Books.

Throughout the country mollahs were given the go-ahead to criticise Alam's government. A new era had dawned, for until then sermons were usually devoted to purely religious themes such as the praise of the Prophet and the Imams, descriptions of the martyrdoms of the various saints, or moral and spiritual advice. In Tehran the leading preacher, Hojjat al-Islam Mohammad Taqi Falsafi, who had been firmly on the regime's side in the 1950s when his shrill anti-Baha'i and anti-Communist speeches were regularly broadcast on the radio, now spoke out. He referred to Alam's background as a major landowner and feudal chief: 'There was a time when titled men were able to write laws as they wished,' declared Falsafi sarcastically, 'but people campaigned and paid with their blood to establish constitutionalism in order to limit their power. Now, once again, we see that Mr Alam has shut out the Majles in order to forge laws undermining the constitution and to impose feudalism and tyranny upon us. But Mr Alam must know that one cannot turn the clock back. Constitutionalism cannot be turned to tyranny.' Falsafi's speech met with cries of 'Allahu akbar!' (God is great!) from ecstatic crowds who took up his closing line as their slogan and poured into the street to demonstrate outside the radio station.

As opposition to the local government bill escalated, some six weeks after its introduction Alam made three concessions – that candidates and voters be restricted to Muslims, that all oaths be sworn on the Qor'an, and that the question of female franchise would be left to the new parliament. He also convened a press conference to announce the contents of his tardy reply to the telegrams sent to him in October by Ayatollahs Shari'atmadari and Golpayegani, but ignored Khomeini. If Alam's gestures had been intended to soothe the situation and isolate Khomeini, they failed.

Shari'atmadari and Golpayegani were dissatisfied because the issue of votes for women had only been deferred, and they were certainly not going to let themselves be manipulated by the government into disunity with a fellow ayatollah.

Alam's snub to the author of all these fiery political statements thus inadvertently accorded him the status of the regime's principal political foe. Khomeini's camp was quick to exploit the opportunity. It arranged for a group of bazaar merchants to issue an *istifta* (a request for the edict of a cleric on a legal and religious question) on the matter of the cabinet's concessions. Carefully choosing his words, Khomeini argued in his reply that Alam's telegram and press conference had no legal validity. As it had been passed by the cabinet, the franchise bill would have to be cancelled by the cabinet because it posed a great threat to the independence and existence of the country.

To keep up the pressure the Tehran clergy planned a major religious meeting in the bazaar mosque of Seyyed Azizollah. But on the eve of the meeting the cabinet realised that the fuss was not going to die down and decided to abandon the local council election bill completely. The expectations of the great majority of the clergy had now been fulfilled, and they told their supporters to celebrate. However, Khomeini, ever eager to prise the maximum concessions from the Shah, suggested that his fellow ayatollahs demand Alam's resignation for insulting Islam and turn their attention to the prolonged unconstitutional closure of the Majles. He got no response from them and, feeling frustrated by what he perceived to be their cowardly and over-cautious approach, he issued a short statement thanking the faithful for having participated in 'this vital affair' but adding that Muslims should 'remain alert and more than ever united'.[10]

Khomeini's ability to mobilise a vast number of people was not only due to his powerful speeches or religious credentials. He also sustained popular zeal through his organisational ability and through the quality of those he chose as his lieutenants. From 1962 he began to encourage his supporters in Tehran to consult him more often and to make contact with other groups who were active in propagating his views. These were largely members of the bazaar guilds, the same social stratum which, during the late 1940s, had been the most important source of support for Ayatollah Kashani's Mojahedin of Islam and Navvab Safavi's Feda'iyan of Islam. Khomeini excited the loyalty of such men not only because he represented the views of the religious middle class, the bastion of religious orthodoxy, but also because they felt their livelihood threatened by the Shah's at-tempt to shift power away from the traditional bazaar towards the new commercial and industrial bourgeoisie.

After the repeal of the local election law, a group of bazaar merchants visited Khomeini in Qom where he told them that the repeal was merely a test by the regime '… to see how prepared we are in responding to their plan, which is to destroy Islam'. 'Don't think,' he said, 'that they will give up. They are readying themselves for a new assault on Islam. Be prepared, strengthen your ties and expect a new move.'[11]

One of the merchants, Sadeq Eslami, declared that they were willing to do whatever Khomeini asked: 'If you give the order we are prepared to attach bombs to ourselves and throw ourselves at the Shah's car to blow him up.' Khomeini replied: 'It won't come to that. [When] you come here, if there is something to be done, you will be asked to do it.'[12]

From this time, acting as a link and a guide for different groups of bazaaris, Khomeini helped them to establish an organisation known as 'The Coalition of Islamic Societies'. The Coalition's founding members were twenty-one bazaaris who had been involved in three different study circles and societies – the groups of the Sheikh Ali mosque, the Aminodowleh mosque, and the Esfahaniha mosque.[13] The religious and social activities of the first group dated back to 1948, and some of its founder members, who were self-taught even in jurisprudence, came to occupy important positions after the 1979 Revolution. The second group was led by Habibollah Asgar Owladi, who became minister of trade after the revo-lution. Scores of ministers and officials of the Islamic Republic were the offspring of these groups, whose members were to form the core of the Islamic Republican Party.

Asgar Owladi has recently given an account of the origins of the Is-lamic coalition. Khomeini, he recalls, sent a messenger to the representa-tives of the bazaar missions with the following invitation: 'I am coming to you from the clergy of Qom, in particular from Haj Aqa Ruhollah Kho-meini, who says the distance between Tehran and Qom is short and does not cost much to travel. Why don't you keep in regular contact with Qom under these exceptional circumstances? We may have something to tell you, [and] you may have something that you want us to know.'[14]

In the audience which followed, Khomeini said to the merchants: 'I have some questions for you which you should study carefully. The first question concerns the precepts of "ordering the good and forbidding the evil, and calling for *jihad*". My question is: "Are not these precepts part of religion? Why, then, is there no mention of them in the practical religious manuals?" Find out when they were removed, why and who has removed them."[15] In Khomeini's opinion 'ordering the good and forbidding evil' (*amr be ma'ruf va nahy az monkar*) and the defence of the boundaries of Islam (*jihad*) were the duty of the Prophet and must be carried out in his absence by the clergy. If these precepts were to be followed they would bring the clergy and the authorities into open conflict over social as well as political issues, which, of course, is exactly what Khomeini wanted. Under Ayatollah Borujerdi and his predecessors, these topics had been dropped from the practical manuals for the faithful. Khomeini explained the concept of *amr* (an order) to his fascinated audience: 'It is an order and not "please". Order means that the nation of Islam has established a power to be able to order good and forbid evil. Now go and find out who they thought would be the loser when they dropped it from the manuals.'[16]

Khomeini's goal was to undermine the position of other clerics who were not interested in challenging the authorities, and his instruction to the merchants gained him even more support among bazaari activists. From this point onwards he became their undisputed spiritual leader and, by channelling considerable sums of money to him, the bazaaris helped him to increase his influence among the clergy by spending it in the theological centres.

Khomeini's most trusted students such as Morteza Motahhari, Mohyeddin Anvari, Mohammad Hosseini Beheshti, Mohammad Javad Bahonar and Abdollah Mowla'i took charge of the Coalition and acted as its supervisory body. Each of the three groups chose three members to join a central organisation, overseeing an executive committee, a financial committee and a propaganda committee. The Coalition also established branches and contacts with other bazaaris in major cities such as Mashhad, Isfahan and Tabriz, actively supporting militancy, distributing Khomeini's statements and publishing its own papers and leaflets clandestinely like a fully organised party with its underground cells, each consisting of ten members linked to central councils via contacts.[17]

After the repeal of the Local Council Election Bill a fragile peace seemed to reign between government and clergy, although the media continued their propaganda against 'the retrogressive and reactionary elements of society'. The secular opposition was divided over what to do, some expressing admiration for Khomeini for 'rubbing the government's nose in the dirt', others believing that the danger of rising fanaticism would prevent any kind of reform. But through the activities of the Coalition Khomeini was building up wide support among the people. In addition, by using his network to keep the faithful in constant touch with events, he was able to exert more pressure on leading mollahs who would otherwise have publicly opposed him – a tactic he used successfully throughout his political and religious career. He began to speak with the confidence of a man who could influence events and shape the future. No longer in the defensive mood of the post-Reza Shah period, when his words were like a sick man's curse against the diseases around him, he began to broaden his demands. He became a swaggering warrior defying an enemy who must ultimately be destroyed.

Khomeini's speech in his first post-crisis lecture on 2 December 1962, less than two months from the day he had first embarked on his public career, was a review of his past and future political plans. He offered many justifications for his twenty years of political quiescence. 'Ali co-operated with the caliphs,' he told his congregation of students, 'because they appeared to be acting according to the rules of religion. When Mo'awiyah turned the caliphate into a monarchy, which was contrary to [the principles of] Islam, there was no other choice for him but to incite resistance and uprising.'[18] By this he meant that he had had previously been silent because there was no danger to Islam.

With reference to people like Ayatollah Shari'atmadari and other well-wishers who advised him to strengthen his position before taking on the Shah, Khomeini said that 'those who advised Ali not to tackle Mo'awiyah before he had strengthened the caliphate were ignorant of the fact that, had he waited, he would have been criticised by the Muslim community, and, once Mo'awiyah had strengthened his position, it would have been impossible to remove him.' Khomeini also felt that it was now time to clarify his position vis-à-vis the constitution: 'If we talk about the constitution, it is because the government uses it to justify its existence, and we want to beat them at their own game. We neither care about the constitution nor want anything to do with it. Our constitution is the law of Islam.' At the end of his speech he challenged the regime to 'leave the people free to decide, and then see who they support.'[19]

The Shah, however, was determined to surge ahead with reform, and in January 1963 he decided to out-manoeuvre both the clerical establishment and the secular opposition by appealing directly to the people. He was confident that he could tackle the social, political and economic problems of the country alone without having to ally himself with the political Left or the clerical Right. He announced a six-point reform bill that came to be known as the 'White Revolution' or the 'Revolution of the Shah and People'. It included distribution of land among the peasants (the reform begun under Amini), the sale of government factories to the private sector, the right of women to vote and to stand as candidates in elections to parliament and local government bodies, the nationalisation of natural resources, a literacy corps for remote towns and villages, and an industrial profit-sharing scheme. The whole programme was to be put to a referendum on 26 January 1963.

Once again Khomeini was swift to warn other clerics that the long-term consequences of the Shah's plans would be to further 'weaken their role and that of Islam in society'. But a long evening of discussion with Shari'atmadari, Mara'shi Najafi and Golpayegani, who were in no mood for a new confrontation, left him frustrated and unhappy. He later confided to a student that:

These gentlemen are not ready for a struggle, I'm afraid. Shari'atmadari says: "If we go too far they will put a policeman on our doorstep." What can I do with this gentleman who says if they put policemen at our doors we will be dishonoured, we will be insulted? I tell them that the path of prison, torture and martyrdom is the right path. But he says we will be insulted.

He added bitterly: 'If I protest against their political stance, they say: "I am a *mojtahed* and I know my religious duties." I cannot tell someone who says: "This is my religious duty" that they are wrong. I know that they are not the men for the battlefield.' [20]

Eventually an inter-clerical meeting in Qom decided that the Shah should be asked to send a representative to clarify his intentions. But after talks with a high-ranking court official it became apparent that no solution was possible and that the court was merely trying to buy time. Khomeini sent one of his students to Khorramabad in the western province of Lorestan to ask an old friend, Ayatollah Ruhollah Kamalvand, to try to persuade the Shah not to go ahead with his reforms. Kamalvand agreed. A lean, affable man with large eyes, he had in the past acted as Borujerdi's emissary to the Shah and was at ease with him. But this time when the two men met in Tehran the atmosphere was tense. Kamalvand's warnings went unheeded by a monarch who saw the reforms as his only means of survival. 'I will have to carry through these reforms, come what may,' he said. 'If I do not I will be swept away and others will take my place who believe neither in you nor in your ideology, who will destroy these mosques over your head and get rid of you.'[21]

The Shah then tried to appease Kamalvand by promising to listen to him and do whatever he asked for the clergy as long as they agreed to the reforms and did not create any obstacles. But his mood changed suddenly: 'The Iranian clergy,' he spat out, 'should learn from the Sunnis who publicly remember the king at the end of each prayer and pray for him. Of our clergy, the less said the better.'

Kamalvand reminded the Shah that the Sunni clergy, like Iranian government officials, were paid by the government for their prayers, but that the Shi'i clergy never had been in their entire thousand-year history, and never would be, government servants. He also pointed out that Mosaddeq had been charged and tried after the 1953 coup for the crime of staging a referendum and yet this was precisely what the Shah now planned. The Shah, however, claimed that what he intended was not a referendum but a request for 'national ratification' of his reforms. Khomeini's emissary returned to Qom empty-handed. There was disagreement among the top clergy over the approach they should now take. Again, some called for compromise, well remembering the manner in which Reza Shah had silenced them in the 1930s. But, as usual, Khomeini was far bolder:

Gentlemen, you must note that what has happened makes our future bleak and our responsibility heavy and difficult to bear. What is happening is a calculated plot against Iranian independence and the Islamic nation, and it is threatening the foundation of Islam ... One should not treat this incident like the quarrel over the [local government] bill. In that instance we were, at least superficially, against the government. That defeat was also a defeat for the government ... now we face the Shah himself, who is poised between life and death. He himself has said that his retreat over this issue would cause the destruction of his regime. So not only will he refuse to retreat, he will confront any opposition with force and savagery ... Nevertheless, we are duty-bound to resist him because what now threatens the people is of such enormity that it cannot be ignored or faced with indifference.[22]

After some discussion a consensus emerged that the clergy must, as a body, boycott the referendum, and that each ayatollah should issue a statement to this effect. Other leading clerics such as Ayatollah Kho'i and the conservative and quietist Tehran Ayatollah Khonsari, even the pro-court Ayatollah Behbehani, issued statements condemning the referendum. Tension began to rise between the religious establishment and the government while the media intensified their attacks on 'the retrogressive, reactionary, and parasitic' clergy.

Khomeini's network went to work to mobilise his supporters, to create distance between the Shah and those of the clergy who had supported him in the past and to pressurise the apolitical conservative clergy out of their traditional isolationism. On the morning of 23 January 1963 many people walked out of their work. Shops and trading offices in Tehran's vast covered bazaar were closed as everyone marched towards the apolitical Ayatollah Khonsari's home at the southern end of the bazaar to persuade him to lead them. The whole affair was organised with such secrecy and spontaneity that the police were unable to obtain an order to confront the demonstrators.

By late morning a large crowd had gathered and, with Khonsari at its head, it began to march along the main thoroughfare in the bazaar area, Buzarjomehri Avenue. Shouting the Qor'anic slogan *'nasrun min Allah va-fathun qarib'* (with God's support victory is near), the demonstrators moved towards the home of Ayatollah Behbehani in the small alley of Sarpulak near the north-east corner of the bazaar. He greeted them at the door but then retired into the house with Khonsari. While the people waited, the two aged mollahs conferred about what was to be done. Much to the activists' annoyance it took two hours for them to emerge again to lead the crowd towards the Seyyed Azizollah mosque.

At the mosque the fiery orator Mohammad Taqi Falsafi went to the microphone and asked the people to listen carefully. To create a charged atmosphere he unrolled a round of his turban and passed it under his chin, a common clerical practice at prayer-time and funerals known as *taht al-hanak* (the under-chin). Falsafi denounced the referendum as anti-Islamic. 'Iran is the land of oppression,' he said. 'Death to oppression ... If you knew what crimes they intend to commit under the guise of this referendum, you would go mad. They want to martyr Hossein once again and take his sister Zeinab into captivity. They want to bring about another Karbala.' Falsafi then read out a joint statement by Ayatollahs Khonsari and Behbehani announcing that the Tehran bazaar would remain closed for three days as a sign of protest.

The stage was now set for a major confrontation between the clergy and the regime. The crowd was asked to go to the Seyyed Azizollah mosque at three o'clock the next afternoon, where the two ayatollahs would join them. Then they dispersed, chanting Falsafi's slogan 'Iran is the land of oppression. Death to oppression.'

The first of many confrontations took place that day. By one o'clock the government was beginning to appreciate the level of unrest, but the Shah and Alam decided that no concessions would be made and that they had to act swiftly to avoid being overtaken by events. The police were ordered to confront the demonstration. It was still early afternoon when clashes between demonstrators and baton-charging paramilitary police broke out near the bazaar in Buzarjomehri Avenue. Broken bricks, empty bottles and sticks and stones flew everywhere. Spirits were high as their newly gained solidarity began to take hold of the crowd. More police and security men were drafted in to seal off the Seyyed Azizollah mosque, and the Shah, who was personally in command of the operation, ordered the police not to allow the two aged ayatollahs to join the demonstration there – a difficult decision for him, since this was Khonsari's own mosque.

Khonsari, a fragile seventy-five at the time, left his home accompanied by hundreds of people chanting the slogan: 'The clergy is victorious, death to the enemies of Islam.' When they reached the crossroads leading to the mosque, the order came to cordon off the crowd, now estimated to number several thousands. Police moved in with force, surrounding those gathered around Khonsari. The cordon became tighter to rule out any possibility of the crowd being able to throw missiles of stones and bricks in retaliation. Nevertheless, clashes broke out and many people were beaten, arrested, then taken away in military trucks. By the time they managed to reach Khonsari at the centre of the fray, some of the policemen were angry. They hurled abuse and threats at him, pushing him over until he lost his balance and hurt his foot. Injured, pushed and shoved, the old man who had been a symbol of piety and quietism to his supporters, returned to his home.

The militants' attempt to turn the demonstration into a counter-referendum failed. But the Shah's silencing of the two prominent conservative clerics who had helped him in the past forced the opposition to take a more radical stance and find their natural leader in Khomeini. Skirmishes in and around the bazaar continued on the next day. The general atmosphere of unrest was reinforced by a quite separate National Front campaign around the slogan 'Reforms, Yes! Dictatorship, No!' which lead to the arrest of its leadership and a great number of student supporters shortly before the referendum.

Tension was also running high in Qom. The first anti-referendum statement had been issued the previous day, and news of the Tehran riots was causing a mixture of excitement and alarm. The city's bazaar merchants and religious students streamed towards the homes of religious leaders in a display of solidarity. To add to the tension and excitement the Shah had announced a visit to Qom for the next day, a gesture of piety to mask a show of strength. Not to be outdone, Khomeini instructed his supporters to close all offices and shops and to remain indoors in protest against both the referendum and the Shah's visit to the city.

While local officials set up victory arches and coloured lights to welcome the Shah, a group of demonstrators headed by clergymen suddenly appeared from the south, chanting 'We are the followers of the Qor'an, we do not want a referendum.' Pro-Shah demonstrators, including plainclothes policemen specially drafted in, began to shout their own slogan – 'Long Live the Shah' – provoking skirmishes and riots which were only calmed after several truckloads of soldiers arrived from the nearby Manzarieh barracks.

At about lunchtime that day Khomeini issued a statement warning the government that it was losing popular support. 'Despite our advice and expression of our duties,' he wrote:

... today a group of thugs and government officials ran through the city of Qom attacking innocent people, injuring, arresting and imprisoning them. They broke into shops and looted them. There was nobody to come to the aid of the faithful and the clergy. Is this the meaning of government support for religion and is this the meaning of freedom of voting and voters? We leave this for public opinion to judge.[23]

Khomeini's words were calculated to encourage the leading clergy in Qom to break completely with the regime, and to a degree he was successful.

On the morning of 24 January the bazaar and schools of theology remained closed. Not even the pro-Shah mollahs dared to venture out, although many people were brought in from Tehran and the surrounding areas to welcome the Shah. Within the shrine a number of peasants were waiting to be presented with land deeds in a ceremony designed to show publicly how simple villagers would benefit from the land reform

programme. When the presentation was over the Shah, ignoring all pro-
tocol, delivered a memorable impromptu attack on the clergy. A shy man
whose command of literary Persian was at best defective, he usually read
prepared speeches. But on this occasion he put his text aside and his voice
shook with anger as he mouthed one muddled phrase after another:

They were always a stupid and reactionary bunch whose brains have not
moved ... Black reaction understands nothing ... its brain has not moved for
a thousand years. They think life is about getting something for nothing,
eating and sleeping ... sponging on others and a parasitic existence ... In the
Six points [of The White Revolution] there is an idea that is suitable for
everybody. What we are doing today is not behind other nations. If anything
it is more advanced ... But who is opposing it? Black reaction, stupid men
who don't understand and are ill-intentioned. The Red subversives have clear
decisions and, incidentally, I have less hatred towards them. They openly say
they want to hand over the country to foreigners, without lying and hypocrisy. But those who lie about being patriotic and in practice turn their backs
on the country are what I mean by black reaction ... it was they who formed
a small and ludicrous gathering from a handful of bearded, stupid bazaaris to
make noises ... they don't want to see this country develop ... the leader of
this miserable lot is the Egyptian Abdol Nasser ... they oppose reform because they cannot deceive anybody ... these men are one hundred times more
treacherous than the Tudeh Party.[24]

When he had finished the speech, the Shah abruptly ended the ceremony and nervously headed for his car. The following day photographs
appeared in all the leading newspapers, but the Shah's speech was heavily
edited on the orders of government and court officials. The undignified
language he had used was too much for his ministers.

If the Shah had intended to frighten off the mollahs, as his father had
done some thirty years before when he had driven to Qom and personally
punished Ayatollah Bafqi, then he had failed. On the day before the referendum the campaign for the boycott continued, although many preachers
were harassed or arrested. For its part, the government did its best to
encourage the population to turnout, and even school children as young
as ten were taken to say 'Yes'.[25]

Naturally, it was claimed at the time that the result was a resounding
endorsement of the reforms, although the actual turnout must have been
low, since the secular opposition had also called for a boycott. The Shah's

Western allies nevertheless took the result at face value. President Kennedy immediately sent him a telegram of congratulations and wished him well in guiding the Iranian nation towards progress and prosperity, while the Soviet media praised him as a modernising monarch.

Khomeini's next move was to urge passive resistance during the month of Ramadan to protest the arrest of dozens of mollahs and to expose the Shah's 'un-Islamic' actions. During Ramadan seminarians, eager to supplement their meagre stipends, usually travel to every corner of the land to preach, lead prayers and answer people's questions. Khomeini suggested that they effectively go on strike. He himself spent the month meditating, receiving visitors, and discussing future strategy.

On Eid-e Fetr, the festival that marks the end of Ramadan, Khomeini's home was for the first time the focus of attention for the many pilgrims who visited the city. From being one of many, he was suddenly a leading ayatollah whose views mattered. His name had reached every mosque and his photograph could be seen in many shops and homes. His home was packed with supporters, and for the first time since the referendum he began to preach. Emboldened by events, he advised the congregation to 'remain steadfast and resist ... do not fear these rotten and rusty bayonets, they will be broken soon.' The time had come, he added, for the government to learn its lesson and reconsider its policies.

The Shah was equally determined and on 14 March, while visiting Dezful, he once again vented his anger at the continued clerical agitation. Speaking to military personnel he said that his bloodless revolution was progressing fast. Referring to his clerical opponents as 'a numb and dispirited snake and lice who float in their own dirt', he threatened: 'If these sordid and vile elements with their reactionary friends do not awake from their sleep of ignorance, the fist of justice, like thunder, will be struck at their head in whatever cloth they are, perhaps to terminate their filthy and shameful life.'[26]

This threat of force was not lost on Khomeini, who, in an equally intransigent mood, told his students and followers to 'prepare themselves for death, imprisonment, compulsory drafting, maltreatment,' and for 'all the pain and tumult you will face in the defence of Islam and independence prepare yourself and persevere.'[27]

The Iranian New Year, the pre-Islamic festival of Nowruz celebrated on 21 March, was approaching. This is the most important holiday in the

Iranian calendar, a time of celebration that grips the country for two weeks. Determined to keep up the momentum of his campaign, Khomeini issued a public statement entitled 'The Clergy Do Not Celebrate This Year'. Using the style of a mourning notice he accused the 'tyrannical regime' of 'violating the sanctity of Islamic laws' and said that it was about 'to violate Qor'anic precepts and Muslim honour' by drafting eighteen-year-old girls into the army, forcing chaste young Muslims 'to the abyss of prostitution.'[28] At the time the Shah had no such plans, and indeed he vehemently denied the accusation, but in such a highly charged atmosphere few were prepared to believe him. Khomeini's statement was carried to the most distant parts of Iran and his call for the New Year celebrations to be abandoned was backed by other prominent clergymen.

In 1963 the second day of Nowruz – 22 March in the solar calendar – coincided with the anniversary of the death of the sixth Imam, Ja'far al-Sadeq, which, as with all Islamic anniversaries, is marked according to the lunar calendar. Ceremonies of remembrance were planned in which sermons would be delivered about the life and times of the Imam who had been imprisoned and, according to the Shi'i version of his story, killed in prison by the Caliph Harun al-Rashid (of *Thousand and One Nights'* fame). Stories of this kind are often skilfully used by preachers as parables in order to give the Imams contemporary relevance. On this particular Nowruz the Shah was portrayed as the Harun of his time, who imprisoned and tortured the defenders of the faith.

Throughout the night people gathered at the holy shrine in Qom followed the preacher in loud cries of *la'nat bar Harun* (may Harun be damned). The town's population was swollen both with ordinary pilgrims and a new kind of visitor who arrived by bus from Tehran and was generally young, well built, and dressed as a peasant or worker. These unusually robust 'peasants', mingled with the crowd and followed them to the shrines and to the homes of various ayatollahs. By dawn Khomeini's reception area and courtyard was filled with excited people who had come many miles to catch a glimpse of the man they believed had rekindled the spirit of the religious community. But as the first preacher began to speak of the sufferings of the sixth Imam under Harun's tyranny, an unusual number of *salavat* were heard. The *salavat*, or blessing, is an interjection made by the faithful when the name of the Prophet Mohammad is mentioned. The whole congregation cries loudly: 'Allahomma salle ala Mohammad va ale Mohammad' (O our God! grant blessing to Mohammad and his family).

The *salavat* is also asked for by preachers so that they can collect their thoughts when they run out of ideas, or if they want to change the subject, and it is used as a kind of applause for a speaker when he reaches the end of a thought. But in this instance it was a method of interruption used by intruders who had come to disrupt the congregation.

Soon Khomeini, who had remained in the inner part of his house, was informed of the intruders' presence. He walked into the courtyard to the enthusiastic cheers of the crowds and placed himself next to the pulpit so that he could be seen by everyone. Taking courage from Khomeini's presence, the preacher became more explicit and began attacking the un-Islamic policies of the Shah's regime. Again the intruders began to cry *salavats*. Witnessing this, Khomeini summoned Sheikh Sadeq Khalkhali, later to become the Islamic Republic's most notorious hanging judge, who took the microphone and relayed an ultimatum by Khomeini:'Attention please, His Holiness the Ayatollah says:"I warn those individuals who appear to have a mission to cause disorder and anarchy in this meeting, that if they act in a way that brings chaos and bad manner, preventing the speeches from reaching the people, I personally will make the necessary pronouncements from the shrine." A volatile and emotional man, Khalkhali raised his fist and shouted:'Every bastard, every treacherous infidel who has come here to disgrace the meeting should know that if they speak once more the Ayatollah will go to the shrine and tell the whole world how the clergy are treated in this country.' After Khalkhali's warning calm prevailed and speaker after speaker continued with attacks against the regime.[29]

The same scene was more or less repeated in the Hojjatieh School of Theology in which Ayatollah Shari'atmadari was holding court. There, people were moved to tears as the preacher, Haj Morteza Ansari, recited lines written by the poet Farrokhi Yazdi, murdered by the Shah's father:

> Mourners have no time for festive visits,
> O festive season leave Iran, we have no festive day.
> If a parrot recites felicitation in its cage,
> the inspired know it is only mocking.

Salavats filled the air and Shari'atmadari's aides, who were worried about his safety, immediately called upon a local athletic champion or *pahlavan*, who was some two metres tall, to sit close to the diminutive divine. The main event of the day, however, was to take place in the Feiziyeh School of Theology.

6

The Leader
Khomeini and the 1963 Uprising

At the Feiziyeh, Ayatollah Golpayegani was about to hold a special service for Ja'far al-Sadeq, the sixth Shi'i Imam and the founder of the Ja'fari school of jurisprudence. Large crowds of people, including those who had gathered at the homes of Khomeini and Shari'atmadari began to move towards the college. But as they neared Qom's main thoroughfare, they were suddenly confronted by troops. The First Division of the Signal Battalion of the elite Imperial Guard, all fully armed, had taken up positions on all sides.

Golpayegani, aware of the possibility of disruption, nevertheless decided to carry on with his service that was to take place in the spacious courtyard of the Feiziyeh. He himself entered the college after it had begun and found himself a place near the entrance to the main lecture hall. Sheikh Morteza Ansari Qomi was telling the crowd the story of the martyrdom of Imam Ja'far at the hands of the debauched caliph Harun, and, lest anyone should fail to understand the allegory, referring to the Qom theological centre as the 'university of Imam Sadeq' and the seminarians as 'soldiers of the sixth Imam'.

Suddenly a loud cry of *salavat* filled the air. Secret police agents, who had covertly joined the throng and were playing the part of *agents provocateurs* to the full, approached the pulpit, their voices amplified by the microphone and reverberating throughout the area. Ansari tried in vain to calm the situation, but a rather inexperienced talabeh tried to silence one of the intruders by punching him in the mouth. Retaliatory blows immediately rained down on him from every side, sending his turban flying into the air. Ansari attempted again to calm the several thousand-strong congregation by telling them that the disturbance was merely a fight over a cigarette and that it was now all over. But suddenly another cry of *salavat* burst over the crowd. At this the frustrated mollah drew his sermon to a close, came down from the pulpit and took his place next to Golpayegani.

With the preacher now out of the way, a well-built man grabbed the microphone and said: 'To the graceful soul of His Majesty, the late Reza Shah the great ... .' Suddenly the loudspeakers went dead. Nothing could have infuriated the mollahs more than hearing the name of Reza Shah. Another voice was heard crying 'Shut up!' and with this the war of words turned swiftly to violence. The intruders leapt on the crowd, but in the resulting chaos nobody seemed to know who they were attacking. The pilgrims, who were mostly peasants, moved towards the exit but the crowd was so huge that it made any movement very difficult. Feiziyeh's many seminarians, knowing they could not confront the security forces, raced up the stairs leading to the roof, and began to shower the Imperial Guard and the plain-clothes security men with bricks, stones and whatever else they could lay their hands on. This counter-attack was effective and the intruders temporarily retreated before the hail of missiles. But as they moved to the exit to take refuge in the eastern hall they were attacked by high school students who had come to the aid of the seminarians. One security agent had already been struck on the head by a brick and killed, and now his colleagues were losing the initiative. An order of shoot-to-kill was issued and the intruders regrouped, throwing aside their disguises. In the ensuing pitched battle many seminarians were thrown off the roof. Three of them fell to their death and many more were seriously injured. The security forces now went on the rampage. They smashed whatever they could lay their hands on, injured people, destroyed books, broke into rooms, and gathered all the turbans and cloaks they could find into the middle of the courtyards and set them alight. Amid the shooting and screaming that could still be heard around the Feiziyeh, stories began to circulate in the city that the Immortals, a crack unit of the Imperial Guards, had set fire to the Holy Qor'an and taken the wounded and the dead to nearby burial grounds.[1]

During the violence, Golpayegani and his entourage of about fifty men had been hidden by the seminarians in a room that had space for a dozen people at most. As the security forces systematically ransacked every room in the building they were soon discovered and Hojjat al-Islam Alavi, Golpayegani's son-in-law, mistaken for Golpayegani himself, was beaten so severely that his ribs were broken.

Eventually, by about seven in the evening, the skirmishes died down and people were allowed to leave the *madraseh*, Golpayegani among them. The security forces had won and, with the violation of their most sacred sanctuary, the clergy had tasted their first real humiliation. It seemed that the Shah's threat to muzzle his enemies with 'the thunderous fist of justice' had been fulfilled.

An atmosphere of fear hung about the city, and Khomeini's house was no exception. The crowd in his reception area sobbed loudly, visibly lamenting the victims of a skirmish which echoed the traditions of Shi'i martyrdom. Many had come from the Feiziyeh, bringing tales of the atrocities they had witnessed. Seeing Khomeini emerge from his retreat, his son Mostafa sealed off the entrance to the residence. Rumours that another assault was planned, this time on Khomeini's home, were sweeping Qom. But enraged by the regime's action, Khomeini had decided to visit the Feiziyeh to see the damage for himself. When his aides, who felt responsible for his safety, tried to deter him, he shouted at the top of his voice: 'Open the door, who told you to close the door? Who is Mostafa? Throw him out of here!'[2]

A young man in the crowd began to cry out, beating himself and jumping up and down as he pleaded with Khomeini not to go any further: 'Sir, I won't let you go, I won't let you go. There will be a blood-bath, people will be killed. I swear by God that I won't let you go!' Following such repeated pleas, Khomeini eventually retreated from the door and sat down, but he was far from calm. One of his aides thought it would be a good idea to make a speech to quieten the frightened and angry crowd, but a furious Khomeini refused permission and told him peremptorily to sit down.

Eventually, however, Khomeini realised that the crowd were genuinely afraid of what might happen. Collecting his thoughts, he spoke to them for twenty minutes, trying to make a virtue out of the disaster: 'Do not be worried and upset,' he began:

... cast out your fear and fright ... You have leaders who have withstood trag-edies and calamities with patience. What we are seeing today is nothing in comparison. Why are you afraid and worried? ... With this crime the regime has revealed itself as the successor of Genghis Khan and has made its defeat and destruction inevitable ... The son of Reza Khan has dug his own grave and disgraced himself.[3]

In the following weeks the government continued its propaganda cam-paign against the mollahs. The prime minister portrayed the incident at the Feiziyeh as a clash between, on the one hand, the supporters of land reform – the peasants – and on the other opponents of the reforms -the clergy and seminarians of Qom. Newspapers depicted them as reaction-aries and advised them to stay out of politics. The streets of Qom became the scene of an obscene war of words as amateur and over-enthusiastic security agents responded to crude anti-Shah slogans and posters pro-duced by the religious establishment. Posters appeared, allegedly published by the Women's Organisation led by the Shah's sister, Princess Ashraf, accusing Khomeini of, among other things, a lust for the female body. The language used on the posters would not have done credit to a women's organisation in a liberated society, let alone a traditional one. Anti-clerical posters also appeared in the name of the National Front, only to be dis-owned by the Front which accused the security police of fabricating them so as to drive a wedge between the religious and secular opposition forces.

In response, seminarians spent many hours of the day copying Kho-meini's statements by hand, advising the reader at the end that it was his duty to make several copies so that the truth would be known. Sometimes they would carry bundles of these hand-written statements and deliver them from door to door. They also drew parallels between the Feiziyeh events and the battle of Karbala, with all its emotional overtones. The calamity of martyrdom, always part of the Shi'i world-view, once more provided a symbolic link between modern political events and the roots of Shi'ism.

Khomeini now began to widen the scope of his opposition and raise new issues. He accused the regime, amongst other things, of 'allowing women to become judges, and giving preferential treatment to Baha'is who are really Israeli agents'. With no parliament in session and the leaders of the National Front still in jail after their arrest on the eve of the referen-dum, he also pushed his claim to leadership a step further. He now saw himself not only as the leader of the opposition, but also as the 'trustee of the people'. In one speech he proclaimed:

Now that a suitable system of redress no longer exists for the grievances of the people in Iran, and the country is being run in this mad manner, I, in the name of the nation, ask Mr Alam, the occupier of the prime minister's position, 'On what legal basis have you ... committed these crimes?' I have now prepared my heart for the bayonets of your agents, but not prepared it for your false claims and tyranny ... I will expose all your actions which are against the country's interests, when I see fit.[4]

'Iran's interest and glory' now entered the new political vocabulary of the clergy as a whole, widening the appeal of Khomeini among lay political activists. His earlier edict that *taqiyya*, dissimulation, was forbidden, and his defiant tone, showed his willingness to take enormous personal risks. His stature grew, and with it grew the heroic tales, stories and poems that were circulating about him. One of these stories, told over and over again, was that the Shah had sent a message to Khomeini saying that if he continued his behaviour he would put on his father's boots and come to Qom to sort him out, to which Khomeini was supposed to have responded: 'Your father's boots are too big for your feet.'[5]

Determined to cut the pro-Khomeini lobby down to size and show that he was still in control, the Shah tried another strategy. The chief of Qom's security police, Colonel Badi', the chief of police Colonel Partow and the governor of Qom were sent to see Khomeini. 'Tell the Aqa,' said Partow to Khomeini's aides, 'that we are His Majesty's emissary and we are to deliver a message.' The reply from Khomeini was: 'Since you want to see me on behalf of the Shah I cannot receive you.' Disappointed and furious, the officials went instead to Ayatollah Shari'atmadari, who was more accommodating. Their message was as follows: 'You will receive a telegram from Ayatollah Hakim in which he will invite you to leave Iran and go to Najaf. If you want to leave, the government will facilitate your journey. However, if you want to stay and create unrest over the telegram, commandos and whores will be set upon you; you will be killed, your honour will be defiled and your homes pillaged.' To reinforce the point they added: 'His Majesty's message is serious. It is not just a threat. We ask you to pass this message on to Ayatollah Khomeini.'[6]

Hakim, who was saddened and enraged by the Feiziyeh episode had decided that the best course was for the Qom clergy to migrate to Najaf –

a Shi'i tradition when the ulema were under pressure and wished to make a serious political point. His short telegram read:

Successive painful incidents and saddening tragedies to the illustrious ulema of Qom have injured the hearts of religious people and the faithful, and have been the source of deep sorrow to me. The revered ulema should collectively migrate to the high thresholds, the 'Atabat [Najaf and Karbala], so that I can pronounce my views about the government.

On hearing of this invitation, Khomeini met with the other clergy to discuss the proposal. They all knew full well that to leave would be easier than to return, and so they agreed that they would decline politely. Khomeini's reply to Hakim read as follows:

With unity we can defend Islam ... if we migrate, the great Islamic centre of Qom will be thrown into the abyss of blasphemy and Godlessness. Our dear brothers in faith would be the victims of torture and painful suffering. Major changes and developments would occur that would be a cause for concern ... For the time being we are ready to endure risks to our lives and remain in this burning fire to save this theological centre; and to issue orders for calm and silence, unless the tyrannical regime follows a path that forces us to express opinions and issue decrees, in which case we will take refuge in God Almighty.'

Three days later Ayatollahs Golpayegani and Shari'atmadari sent replies to Hakim along the same lines.[7]

The episode of Hakim's telegram helped maintain political tension, and within a week of Khomeini's reply the Shah embarked on another project which, for a short time, succeeded in frightening the clergy, in particular the younger ones. In the first half of April 1963, he ordered the conscription of seminarians, who until then had been exempt from military service, into the army. The 'arrests', in particular of activists were pursued with vigour, and many were sent to the barracks without even being given time to inform their wives, parents or teachers. Hundreds were taken in trucks, stripped of their religious attire and put into military uniform.

One of the first victims of this new policy of revenge was the twenty-nine-year-old Akbar Hashemi Rafsanjani, a loyal student of Khomeini's who would later become an important personality in the 1979 Revolution. On the morning of 11 April, Rafsanjani was on his way to post a quarterly journal he helped to edit in Qom, where he was living as a student. As he

was passing the police station a policeman appeared and arrested him –
provoking Khomeini to remark sarcastically when he heard of the incident: 'Why have they taken him? He is forty!'[8]

'Soon I was joined by others,' recalls Rafsanjani:

I was married with three children and carried my exemption papers with me,
but they were ignored. On the same afternoon I and twenty-five other seminarians were taken in a truck to Tehran and the next morning we found
ourselves in the Bagh-e Shah barracks. We began to learn useful things from
our military instructors and we also taught them a few useful things.[9]

The forced draft did nothing to quell the growing militancy of the clergy.
Families and friends of the seminarians began to visit the military barracks, bringing with them news of events in Qom and other cities and
copies of statements by Khomeini and other clerics hidden in their clothing. The new conscripts also began to congregate for prayer and to encourage the soldiers, who had previously not dared to show their religious
sentiments, to join them in the mourning of Hossein's martyrdom. It was
unheard of to see a soldier preaching to his friends in the barracks about a
tyrannical caliph, Yazid, who had ignored the religion of Mohammad and
of the martyred Hossein. The parade ground was suddenly adorned with
unaccustomed religio-political graffiti, such as 'long live Khomeini!' and
'death to the Shah!'.[10] In short, the mollahs began to influence their environment and not vice versa as the Shah may have intended. Through in-
termediaries the Shah offered to lift the conscription order under certain
conditions, but by then the issue had become such a good propaganda
weapon against him that the seminarians declined the opportunity to quit.
Meanwhile, Khomeini issued a message to reassure them:

Wherever you are, you are the soldiers of the Hidden Imam, and must carry
out your duty as a soldier. Your heavy responsibility is to enlighten and inform these soldiers you are dealing with. Follow military instructions with
persistence and seriousness. Strengthen yourselves physically and spiritually.[11]

As the fortieth day after the Feiziyeh tragedy, a traditional day of mourning, approached senior clerics, including Shari'atmadari, Mara'shi Najafi
and Khomeini began to issue statements condemning the actions which
had led up to the events. Khomeini's included a personal and calculated
challenge to the Shah: 'Wherever we go they say it was His Majesty's order, the crime of Feiziyeh was on his Majesty's orders.'[12] There followed a

list of anti-clerical actions which he claimed had been carried out on royal orders. 'Officials say that they have broken the law on the Shah's orders. If it is true, one should toll the bells for Islam, Iran and the law. If it is not correct and they falsely accuse the Shah of these inhumanities, why then does the Shah not defend himself, so that people know that it is the government who is to blame?' Khomeini went on to accuse the Israelis and the Jews of being behind the anti-Islamic and anti-clerical attacks of the regime and to appeal to Islamic governments, Arab and non-Arab, saying that the Iranian clergy, leaders of the nation and the army were opposed to relations with Israel and 'feel repugnant about it', dramatically concluding: 'Let the agents of Israel take my life.'

The result of these exhortations was that a whole host of meetings to commemorate the martyrs of Feiziyeh were held in mosques and theological schools throughout Iran. The clergy were already making good political use of a traditional religious and cultural practice that during the 1979 revolution proved to be of central importance in keeping the chain of revolutionary events moving. But although moderate ayatollahs had joined in the condemnation of the tragedy, it was the militant clergy, mainly associated with Khomeini, who had the upper hand among the mourners. The quietists did not like being led by the militants into a showdown with the regime. Some began to express misgivings in private and, realising that they were hostages to events, wanted to persuade the Shah to quietly drop his campaign. Aware of a widening gap between himself and other clerics, but as ever wanting to maintain the initiative, in one of his lectures Khomeini went on the attack against the quietists: 'Woe to this silent Najaf, Woe to this silent Qom!' This sentence more than any other was taken up by the young activists who preferred militancy.

Having failed to stem the rising tide of anti-regime feeling by other methods, the Shah finally sent a group of pro-court clerics to visit him privately and find out what he really wanted. In this meeting Khomeini sounded firm, but more reasonable than in his public statements. He gave the impression that he had no quarrel with the monarchy itself, but was only opposing the government bills and the referendum. Nevertheless, he issued a threat : 'The government should not think we have no answer to their bayonets, guns and tanks,' and, picking up his pen, he continued, 'They must know that with this very nib, I will make the bones of the army shake. At this point Khomeini himself, rather than the clergy as a body became the target of the regime's attacks. A court in Qom was instructed to issue a warrant for his arrest. The judge refused and was immediately dismissed, but his successor complied, issuing an order for Khomeini's appearance in court. Khomeini's son Mostafa, however, refused to receive the court official and so prevented the order being served on his father. 'You can go and tell the officials that I have prevented you from carrying out your duty,' said Mostafa.

The next move was more Machiavellian. Following accusations that Khomeini was in contact with the Egyptian government and had been receiving money from Nasser, a cleric took a man who claimed to be an Egyptian diplomat serving in Lebanon to see him. Khomeini received the man, talking to him about his views on Israel. The 'diplomat' said he was there 'on behalf of President Gamal Abdul Nasser to offer his thanks for your efforts against Israel and to extend to you his offer of help for whatever you need, money, weapons and so on. His aim is to help you on your way to victory.' Khomeini, however, could not be caught out: 'The current struggle is an internal matter for our country,' he replied.

To achieve our objective we do not need outside help or interference. I also extend my greetings to President Nasser. Please tell him if he feels duty-bound to help us in our campaign in Iran against Israel to broadcast our news and statements to the world. That is what you could do for us and we have no other expectations of you.'

Khomeini only later discovered that this man was an agent of the regime who had been sent to compromise him with 'evidence' of collusion with a foreign government.[13]

The Shah was growing impatient with Khomeini's obstinate opposition to his cherished 'White Revolution'. 'Unfortunately,' he told a meeting with members of the Lion's Club bitterly on 16 May 1963, '... many people will have to be punished; society must make this sacrifice ... our revolution is going to be stained with the blood of innocent people ... and of wretched, misguided people. Unfortunately, this is unavoidable. It will inevitably happen.' The Shah's predictions – or were they preconceived plans? – were to be fulfilled less than three weeks later.

It was almost Moharram, a month when the Shi'a immerse themselves in a frenzy of flagellation, chest-beating and weeping. The regime aimed to ensure that the preachers did not use this emotional occasion to attack the White Revolution. They asked all the trustees of the mosques and religious missions, or *hey'ats*, to report to the authorities and forbade the use of religious sermons for political purposes. At the same time Tehran's chief of police, Colonel Abdollah Vasiq, issued a confidential directive to all police stations in and around Tehran asking them to compile a file of all places that were to host mourning gatherings with the name of the patrons and preachers responsible. They were asked to obtain written guarantees not to allow their venues to be used for any other purpose but remembrance of Hossein. In addition a division of the Imperial Guard was sent to Qom for the month to prevent demonstrations and disorder.[13]

But Khomeini and his followers were not going to miss the chance to put the Shi'i zeal for tragedy and martyrdom to positive use. The death of Hossein, which had taken place in the wake of his rebellion against usurpers and tyrants, was something to be emulated. Khomeini issued a statement asking the preachers to 'ignore the police directive and continue to discuss tyranny and threats against Islam'. They should, he said, 'mention the danger of Israel and its agents' and compare the situation to that of the Umayyads when Hossein challenged the caliph and was slaughtered for it. He also told the cautious clergy: 'Silence in these days means support for the tyrannical regime and the enemies of Islam.'

For believers Moharram that year was full of adventure and excitement. The young frequented different mosques and *hey'ats*, listening to the speakers with pricked ears to see whether they were obeying the security police or Khomeini. Militant visiting preachers, who had gone from Qom to various towns and villages, were warmly welcomed by the *salavats* of the congregation and felt like celebrity showmen. Police and Savak reactions differed from town to town. Their orders were merely to report what was happening, but many were over-eager. Many young, outspoken seminarians were arrested and bused back to Qom, Mashhad or other towns. Some were imprisoned, others were beaten up.

In Mashhad, Ayatollah Qomi was the most outspoken of the clergy. He was less skilful than Khomeini but his abusive attacks on the Shah were attractive to many, in particular when his target was the Shah's personal lifestyle – his love of cabarets and nightclubs, his taste for wine and his love of dogs, which are considered unclean by Muslims. In Shiraz, Ayatollah Mahallati, with his deep understanding of the political situation and his shrewd use of religion against the regime, was the centre of attention. But the main centres of activity were Qom and Tehran. On each of the ten nights from 24 May to 2 June Khomeini visited a different mosque, or *hey'at*, taking with him a preacher to express his views. Wherever

he went he was greeted by rapturous crowds. But the peak of his campaign was to come on 3 June, when he planned, as the culmination of a
major demonstration organised by his students, to deliver an Ashura sermon that would send shock waves through the government. Agents had
reported his plans to the security commission set up by the Shah, and it
was now preparing for a showdown. At least 6,000 commandos, para-
troopers and special police forces were put at the disposal of the Tehran
police alone.

On the morning of Ashura, 3 June, Khomeini was listening to a sermon
at his home. As the preacher began comparing the Shah's anti-Islamic
posture to that of the hated Yazid, a man in the congregation stood up
and walked towards him. He introduced himself as Colonel Nasser
Moghaddam, a senior Savak official, and told Khomeini bluntly: 'His
Majesty has sent me to inform you that if you decide to deliver a sermon
in the Feiziyeh, our commandos will attack the school, setting it on fire
and shedding blood.' Without any change in his expression and without
hesitation Khomeini replied: 'We will also instruct our commandos to
chastise His Majesty's emissaries.'[14]

Attempts to dissuade Khomeini from delivering his sermon did not
end here. The government tried every possible non-violent means of stop-
ping him, to no avail. It was so worried that the crowd would attack government offices in Qom as soon as his sermon was over that it decided to
send a senior police officer, General Mohsen Mobasser, accompanied by
some 120 soldiers from the nearby Aliabad garrison. When they reached
Qom, Mobasser ordered his troops to drive around the city several times
in their trucks with their lights full on in a show of force. Mobasser was a
man with clear goals, a professional soldier who had gained considerable
military and intelligence experience during and after the coup of 1953. His
claim to fame was his involvement in the destruction of the military organisation of the Tudeh Party in the 1950s.

Mobasser's initial plan was to make a personal attempt to stop the
Ayatollah from preaching. However, the intermediary he found for this
purpose shocked him by voicing the opinion that the Shah's regime was
on the point of collapse and that a coup was imminent. Mobasser eventually plucked up enough courage to make a personal telephone call to Khomeini. He explained that he was making a personal initiative to dissuade
Khomeini from going to the Feiziyeh, emphasising that he was a soldier
whose duty was to restore law and order. 'You are a man of God,' he said,

'and I am sure you do not want to see innocent blood spilt.' Khomeini, however, remained adamant, insisting that: 'If I do not go I am not Khomeini.' Realising that there was little he could do, Mobasser begged him at least not to make any inflammatory statements and not to attack 'His Majesty'. Khomeini remained silent for a few moments before replying enigmatically, in what Mobasser described as his 'peasant accent', 'We shall see'.[15]

At about four in the afternoon, Khomeini set out for Feiziyeh as planned. Meanwhile Mobasser, nervous about what might happen, was attempting to remain calm, swallowing tranquillisers as he watched thousands of people create a corridor for their leader. As Mobasser later recalled, he had mused on the fact that during his twenty years of active service he had never seen the Shah accorded anything like such a welcome. The crowds had gathered around Khomeini's residence as well as in the streets and courtyards of the shrine and the theological schools surrounding it. As it was impossible for Khomeini to move on foot, a pale green Volkswagen 'Beetle' convertible was brought to bear him through the crowd. Many people were sure that the army commandos would mount an attack, and some even wrote their wills, leaving them with their families before joining the crowds.

As the car moved slowly forward, the chanting of the immense crowd singing Khomeini's praises, eulogising the martyrdom of Hossein and mourning the victims of the Nowruz attack filled the air. The crush was so great that the driver switched the engine off, allowing the little vehicle to be pushed along by the crowd as far as the door of the college. Khomeini dismounted and walked into the courtyard and towards the pulpit to cries of 'Blessings upon the Prophet and his household.' He ascended the tall pulpit, from where he was visible to all, and dramatically unfolded one round of his turban, pulling it up under his chin.

The organisers had supplied Feiziyeh and the neighbouring areas with a public address system, and had hidden batteries under the pulpit so that the system would continue to operate if there was a power cut. Before a thicket of microphones and thousands of the faithful burning to absorb his every word, Khomeini began his sermon. Thirteen hundred years ago Hossein had gone to the battle of Karbala to protect the faith, shouting: 'If the religion of Mohammad cannot be restored except with my blood, may the swords take me ... .' Psychologically, the crowd was ready to visualise itself playing a similar role at that historic moment in the middle of Ashura.

The very mention of the name 'Hossein' by Khomeini was enough to make people weep.

Khomeini then launched a bitter attack on the Shah, on Israel and on the United States, and replied to all the accusations levelled against him and the clergy. Admonishing the Shah not to listen to the enemies of Islam, he offered this advice:

O Mr Shah, dear Mr Shah, abandon these improper acts. I don't want people to offer thanks should your masters decide that you must leave. I don't want you to become like your father. When America, the Soviet Union and England attacked us [during the Second World War] people were happy that Pahlavi [the Shah's father, Reza Shah] went. Listen to my advice, listen to the clergy's advice, not to that of Israel. That would not help you. You wretched, miserable man, forty-five years of your life have passed. Isn't it time for you to think and reflect a little, to ponder about where all this is leading you, to learn a lesson from the experience of your father?

There followed a prophetic, account of the Shah's possible end:

You don't know whether the situation will change one day nor whether those who surround you will remain your friends. They are the friends of the dollar. They have no religion, no loyalty. They have hung all the responsibility around your neck. O miserable man!

While Khomeini was delivering his sermon, a chain of informers wrote down and passed on every sentence, for the local police did not have even a single tape recorder to put at General Mobasser's disposal. As Mobasser read Khomeini's words, his blood pressure rose bit by bit and he resorted to yet more tranquillisers. It was the most insulting speech ever made publicly against the Shah, and a further step towards Khomeini's rise to leadership. Some of Mobasser's colleagues wanted the turbulent ayatollah to be dragged down from the pulpit, there and then, so that he would be humiliated. But Prime Minister Alam was against such an approach, and the chief of police, General Nassiri, did not dare contact the Shah to ask permission lest his request was refused.

On this of all days, it was impossible to order the army to fire on the crowd that had assembled in Tehran, for the Shah would have been immediately compared with the tyrannical Yazid and passions further inflamed. So a pro-Shah group, led by two south Tehran gang-leaders, Nasser Jigaraki and Sha'ban Ja'fari 'Bimokh' (Sha'ban the Brainless), was sent to confront them. With shaven heads, they arrived in procession and were allowed to join the crowd in the school. Gang leaders, men for whom physical strength and loyalty meant a great deal, had been used before in street politics. Sha'ban the Brainless and other lesser known thugs had done the dirty job of roughing up people on behalf of the regime during the 1953 coup. However, Khomeini and his activists were to prove just as efficient manipulators of these leaders of these mafia-like gangs. One of them, Mehdi Araqi, a well-known figure in the Tehran bazaar, was by this time a firm supporter of Khomeini. An expert on south Tehran's gangland, he was aware that Tayyeb Hajji Reza'i, a long-time supporter of the Shah, was about to defect.[16]

Tayyeb's tale is an interesting reflection of the royal regime's heavy-handed inability to master the art of public relations, a weakness which was to bedevil the Shah in 1963 and eventually contribute to his undoing. After the 1953 coup, during which Tayyeb had been a key manipulator of the crowds who ousted Mosaddeq, he was rewarded for his services to the Shah with a monopoly over the banana hot-house in the grocers' bazaar. But in 1959, when Empress Farah had her first baby, the Crown Prince Reza, at a hospital in south Tehran, Tayyeb had been deeply insulted by Colonel Nassiri, who at the time was commander of the Imperial Guard. For people like Tayyeb it was a source of great pride that the Shah's first son was to be born in their midst, so when Nassiri put extra policemen on duty in the area surrounding the hospital they considered this an insult. Tayyeb protested. 'Move your policemen out' he said to Nassiri. 'Each one of my "lads" is a *feda'i* for the Shah.' Nassiri ignored him, and two days later when the Shah visited his newborn and the local gang leaders paid their respects to their monarch, Tayyeb protested in Nassiri's presence that the security arrangements were an insult to the boys (*bachehha*) of south Tehran. Nassiri, thus publicly humiliated, instructed the local police chief, Major Goltappeh, to teach Tayyeb a lesson.

Goltappeh started by delaying the delivery of bananas to Tayyeb. Tayyeb lost business, his financial situation deteriorated and he borrowed money but was unable to pay the interest on time. As a true macho he showered insults on his creditor, who complained to other local gang leaders. In a gangland skirmish Tayyeb was knifed. To add insult to injury he was promptly arrested when he left hospital two weeks later. Unable to contain himself he later confided to a friend: 'I am going to bring down the camel I have put on top of the hill.' By the summer of 1963 Tayyeb, supported by Araqi, was ready to throw in his lot with Khomeini.

Having secured the loyalty of two leading gang leaders, the pro-Khomeini leaders felt confident enough to let supporters of Sha'ban the Brainless and Nasser Jigaraki into the crowd, and a major confrontation was averted. The pro-Khomeini march started at about eight in the morning. Slogans compared the Feiziyeh killings with Hossein's martyrdom at Karbala. Praising Khomeini and attacking his 'bloodthirsty enemy', the crowd moved towards Baharestan Square near the Majles, then north-westward past the British Embassy towards Ferdowsi Square, where Araqi himself made a speech against the White Revolution. An estimated 100,000 took part in this march. By lunchtime they had passed Tehran University and once more headed south. Water and a variety of sherbets were served on the way, as the crowd's roar shook the air. When they reached the Shah's Marble Palace they began to shout: 'Death to the dictator, death to the dictator! God save you, Khomeini! Death to your bloodthirsty enemy!' Then they moved away towards the bazaar area, where they dispersed and announced that they would meet again on the following day in the Shah mosque in the bazaar. The next day, 4 June, the demonstrations and slogans were repeated. Students now joined in, and support for Dr Mosaddeq surfaced as his name was added to, and, in some cases, put before that of Khomeini. Later on that afternoon 5 to 600 people headed for the Golestan Palace, and at about six in the afternoon an order was issued for a crackdown. According to the police account itself, 122 people were arrested in Sepah Square in one swoop. All kinds of people were seized, ranging from a fifteen-year-old student to a forty-four-year-old estate agent. By evening hundreds of people had been rounded up in Tehran and other cities.[17]

7

Arrest and Imprisonment
The Emergence of a Political Ayatollah

Qom was full of activity in the dark hours of the morning of 5 June 1963, just two days after Khomeini delivered his momentous sermon. Commandos, Savak officers and soldiers joined the city's local security officers and moved towards the Yakhchal-e Qazi quarter where Khomeini lived. In overall command was Tehran's Savak chief, Colonel Mowlavi, who had been in charge of the Feiziyeh attack some three months earlier, and whom Khomeini had described as 'that vile individual whose name I will only mention when I have ordered his ears cut off'.

At about three in the morning when troops had taken up their positions outside Khomeini's home, Mowlavi ordered them to move in and within minutes they had completed a frenzied but fruitless search. Since Khomeini's inner house and outer reception room were both full of guests he was spending the night with his son. As dawn broke he came out into the courtyard to perform his ablutions, to prepare for the prayer. But he was interrupted by sudden cries from the alley. He called to his son: 'Get up Mostafa, it looks as if they have come.' Mostafa, half asleep on a simple mattress on the ground, watched his father dress.[1]

But as the noise from the street grew louder Mostafa jumped out of bed and went to the roof. What he saw stunned him. The little alley was packed with dark-suited security men and helmeted soldiers brandishing bayonets. Khomeini listened from behind the courtyard door to the voices of the security men who had come to take him away. They were beating the servants who had cared for his guests over the past twelve days. Unable to bear the howls of these tortured men, he opened the door and his loud and angry voice filled the air: 'I am Ruhollah Khomeini! Why are you hitting these men?' His summer *aba* was under his left arm while his right arm was raised in the air to reveal a fist clenched with anger. His furious voice repeatedly broke the silence: 'I am Ruhollah Khomeini. Why are you assaulting these poor people? What is this barbaric behaviour towards them? I am Ruhollah Khomeini. Are you not ashamed of yourselves? One of you could have come and told me: "Khomeini, come" – and I would have come.'[2]

Khomeini's unexpected appearance caused the security men to lose their nerve and they began to apologise in shaky voices. Politely they ushered him into the back seat of a black Volkswagen 'Beetle', a car often used by Savak to arrest people because it attracted little public attention. From the roof top Mostafa saw his father being taken away, and his first instinct was to jump on the car to prevent it from moving off. But his father chided him with a movement of his hand as one of the commandos took out his revolver and aimed it at Mostafa, shouting: 'If you move I will fire.' The helpless Mostafa could only cry out to the sleeping city: 'Oh people, they have taken Khomeini away,' but by this time the car was already on its way to Tehran.

Khomeini remained silent, not knowing what would happen to him. Years later he recalled: 'I saw that those in the car were very frightened. So I said to them: "It's me they want; why are you frightened?"' Light was spilling across the sky to herald sunrise and Khomeini had not performed his morning prayer. Anxious lest he miss it, he asked his captors: to 'Stop the car for a few minutes for the dawn prayer. You, too, must perform your prayers. You belong to the army of an Islamic country and you earn your salary from an Islamic budget so it is your duty to follow the rules and principles of Islam.' Ignoring him, the guards drove on and Khomeini lost his temper. Only after further protests did they stop for a few moments so that he could perform his ritual ablutions by the roadside (using earth in place of water). But he was forced to perform his prayer in the car, an act which in Islam is only acceptable in the most extreme circumstances.

Further along the road there is a salt lake which was popularly believed to be a graveyard for dangerous opponents of the Shah. 'When we reached the lake,' Khomeini recalled, 'one of them pointed towards it, and as soon as he did the car swerved off the road in the direction of the lake. I realised what he was suggesting but I was not at all afraid.' The car returned to the road and soon reached central Tehran, where it entered the garages of the Officers Club near the Foreign Ministry. Khomeini was kept in the Club until the evening, when he was transferred to the Qasr barracks.[3]

At about this time General Mobasser was resting at home after a difficult day when his telephone rang. It was his superior, Nassiri. 'Where are you, General?' the anguished Nassiri asked. 'I am ill,' replied Mobasser. 'This is a fine time to be ill,' replied an irritated Nassiri. Mobasser was startled by his panic. 'What has happened?' he asked. 'Come to the office right away and I will tell you,' replied Nassiri. Mobasser was soon in Nassiri's office. Telephones were ringing everywhere and the atmosphere was one of frenzy. Nassiri's first words were: 'Qom's police station is about to fall to rioters.' Mobasser asked him why. 'We had Khomeini arrested early this morning. Colonel Mowlavi went down and brought him in,' said Nassiri.[4]

There was little love lost between Nassiri and Mobasser, who considered his chief illiterate, whimsical, weak and servile. In Mobasser's opinion the Shah had made Nassiri a general not for his military ability but for his loyalty during the struggle to overthrow Mosaddeq. Mobasser felt insulted. He had passed out of the military academy and had dealt with the Tudeh Party, discovering and destroying its military cells. He had even written a book about communism in Iran, but the credit had gone to the post-coup military governor, General Teimur Bakhtiar. Mobasser hated to be pushed around by these yes-men. Nassiri had not allowed him to bring Khomeini in two days ago, but had instead sent Mowlavi, a noisy and deceitful Savak colonel, to make the arrest.

Nassiri now told Mobasser to go to Qom immediately and restore order there, but Mobasser replied furiously that he would not. 'Send Mowlavi to restore order,' he shouted. Nassiri raised his voice: 'I order you to go and you disobey?' Mobasser promptly undid his belt and put his revolver on Nassiri's desk. After a few very tense seconds, a red telephone rang. Nassiri stood up. 'Your servant, Sire. I kiss your hand, Sire.' His mood had completely changed. Mobasser realised it was the Shah, and heard him telling Nassiri: 'You useless, incapable lot! What have you done about Qom?'" Nassiri replied weakly: 'We have summoned General Mobasser,

Your Majesty, to go to Qom as we need to have a senior officer there.''It's a good choice. Don't delay,' replied the Shah. Nassiri put the receiver down, looked Mobasser straight in the eye, and with a cynical grin said: 'Are you going, General, or not?' Disheartened Mobasser had no choice but to say 'yes'. He got into his Mercedes and drove along the road towards Qom.

When he arrived in the city two hours later, crowds had filled the main streets and the shrine areas. Troops had already arrived, but the officer in charge was inexperienced and knew little about crowd control. The soldiers had been allowed into the streets and been pounced upon. A pitched battle had ensued in which twenty-eight people were killed by automatic gunfire. Now skirmishes and demonstrations were taking place at various points.

Mobasser lined up over 100 soldiers and ordered them to present arms, then kneel down as if ready to fire. From his Mercedes he shouted over the loudspeaker: 'I must warn you that, contrary to the stories circulating, our bullets are not made of cork. They are real. You can see that my troops are ready to fire. I give you fifteen minutes to disperse.' Having seen the blood of their friends spattered on the pavements of Qom a few minutes earlier, the terrified crowd began to edge back. For the next few hours tension was high between the battle-ready soldiers and the demonstrators but by mid-afternoon Mobasser had succeeded in restoring order. The day had been a major setback for the seminarians and supporters of Khomeini. They later claimed that hundreds of their colleagues were killed. Mobasser himself maintained that twenty-eight died and eighty were injured.[5]

Within minutes of Khomeini's arrest the Coalition of Islamic Societies had begun the work of alerting its supporters in Tehran. One messenger was sent to the gang leader Tayyeb, but he could not be found in his grocers' market stronghold. His son Asghar was informed instead and asked to close the market, arm his supporters with sticks and knives and take them to the centre of the city. Soon Tayyeb's supporters were rushing towards the nearest police station, which they attacked before moving on towards the northern end of the bazaar. As the number of protesters grew, they began to head for the Tehran Radio building and the royal palaces. Contemporary official documents, published after the 1979 Revolution, tell the story of that day clearly:

At about 9.15 am, a big crowd gathered at the Chahar Suq-e Bozorg in the

Bazaar shouting slogans in support of Khomeini ... At 9.20, some 300 people gathered at the Shah mosque in the bazaar. At 9.30 some 2,000 youths gathered at the Abbasabad Bazaar shouting 'Death or Khomeini' and moved towards the shoemakers' bazaar. Some 5,000 gathered at the Seyyed Azizollah mosque shouting 'Khomeini or Death'.[6]

These were by no means the only demonstrations. Police stations throughout the bazaar area of Tehran as well as Savak offices were attacked by the protesters. A number of government buildings in the centre of Tehran, including the Ministries of Justice, Interior, Information. Industry and Mines, Education and even the Golestan Palace were attacked and the Zurkhaneh ('house of strength') owned by Sha'ban Bimokh was set on fire. Some police stations ran out of bullets. Shooting continued all day, and hospitals were soon full of the dead and the injured. The crowd made several attempts to take over the Tehran Radio Station in Ark Square, but they were beaten back. In the afternoon demonstrations spread to other parts of Tehran to the east, west and further north including Tehran university. There were reports of a few pro-Mosaddeq slogans, but the majority were for Khomeini and against the Shah. One police report from northern Tehran spoke of 200 people gathered near the residence of Prime Minister Alam in Dezashib.[7] Gendarmes and commandos were sent to help the police. In the central areas of the city the soldiers were reluctant to open fire at first but eventually had to follow orders. Reports from all over Tehran and from some nearby townships indicated an uprising and that the rioting had spread to Mashhad, Qom, Isfahan and Shiraz. Dozens of Khomeini's leading supporters who were to hold important offices after the revolution were arrested throughout the country, including Morteza Motahhari, later chairman of the Revolutionary Council, Ali Khamene'i, later president of the Islamic Republic and Khomeini's successor as 'leader', Mohammad Javad Bahonar, later a prime minister and Sadeq Khalkhali.

When the cabinet met at 5 pm, chaired by Prime Minister Alam, it quickly became evident that the government had neither foreseen nor been prepared to cope with the day's bloody riots. As martial law was now a foregone conclusion the cabinet decided to announce a curfew from 10 pm to 5 am, effective from that evening. At the announcement the crowd dispersed, although it was some two hours before the soldiers took control of Tehran's streets. General Nassiri was made military governor of Tehran.[8]

Citing a law passed in 1910, the general declared that anyone who acted against the constitutional government would be punished by death. Arrests were widespread that evening. Tehran police files indicated that some 320 people from different backgrounds and age groups were taken in, including thirty leading clerics.[9]

Despite the imposition of martial law, on the following day, 6 June, thousands took to the streets in smaller groups. Tanks rolled through Tehran to guard government buildings. Soldiers in combat gear with shoot-to-kill orders gave the capital the air of a war-torn city. Shooting by the soldiers was in greater earnest than on the previous day, and this was the factor that helped the regime take control of the situation and stop the uprising. The heavy use of force led to rumours that the number of casualties was very high indeed. Police files indicate that only 380 people were killed or wounded, but the police figure does not include those who did not go to hospital for fear of arrest, or those who were taken to the morgue or were buried by the security forces. What the list of casualties kept by the police did indicate was that the demonstrators came from a cross-section of society: merchants, clergy, workers, craftsmen, students, peasants, women, and children as young as ten.[10]

The worst shooting took place near a village on the road to Tehran. Pishva, near Varamin, is a hillside village with two old plane trees and a shrine frequented by pilgrims. On the third day of the anniversary of the Imam Hossein's death there were still processions through the village streets. The news of Khomeini's arrest was announced on the loudspeakers of the shrine, where the mourners had gathered in a heightened emotional state. Some wore the white shrouds that indicated that they were prepared for death. The frenzied mood was further intensified as they began to beat their chests and shout slogans against the Shah and in support of Khomeini. On 5 June at 4.15 pm, 600 mourners waving huge black flags began their march from Varamin to Tehran shouting: 'Khomeini or death.'

They attacked the village police station, but when they reached the railway bridge near the village of Baqerabad on the road to Tehran, they were stopped by soldiers who ordered them to disperse and return home. The mourners refused. As if in a state of trance, they believed that if they retreated they would be traitors like those who had forsaken Hossein at Karbala thirteen centuries before. So they attacked the soldiers with whatever they had, injuring one of the commanding officers. The soldiers were then ordered to fire with machine-guns. Whether tens or hundreds were killed is not clear, but the casualties gave Varamin a place in the history of the uprising, and the tiny village of Pishva became the subject of much eulogy in religious literature.

The Shah was shaken by the experience and livid over the performance of his intelligence agencies. The Savak chief, General Pakravan, openly admitted that he had blundered by moving too late, while even the court minister, Hossein Ala, was privately critical of the government's approach as too harsh. Old court rivalries were also resurfacing, so Ala invited a group of elder statesmen on the afternoon of 6 June for consultation. They were the last generation of loyal ministers who had served the Shah in the past and were critical of his unrestrained policies. Knowing that the Shah was a weak man who had left many important decisions to his servile but trusted friend Alam, they criticised the government and decided that the best course of action to end the crisis would be for the Alam government to resign. An increasingly angry Shah summarily dismissed the group's opinions with the words: 'These elderly statesmen should be flushed down the lavatory.'[11]

The events surrounding 5 June gave the day a special importance. For the Shah's regime, completely taken off-guard by the events, they were an eye-opener to a potential religious threat. For the secular dissidents they represented an opportunity to re-evaluate their position. For the religious forces they constituted a new start under the militant leadership of a man who had a dynamic approach and who was able not only to play to the public but also to learn new tactics. The regime, with its White Revolution, had radicalised society, and the religious establishment, after an initial period of numbness, had now begun to search for an effective response.

Alam told the press that those who had been responsible for the riots were under arrest and would be court-martialled and shot. This made the clergy extremely anxious about the fate of Khomeini and the other detainees. Rumours began circulating that Khomeini would be the first to be dealt with in this fashion. Hearing such news, bazaars throughout the country closed in protest, and some fifty leading clerics from twenty cities rushed to Tehran to defend his life. Ayatollah Shari'atmadari took up residence at the shrine of Shah Abdolazim to the south of Tehran, where crowds of people visited him – on one day as many as 100,000. He would sit weeping under a tree in the courtyard, and his tears became contagious, so that soon all his visitors wept together. Ayatollah Milani, who tried to travel by plane from Mashhad, was forcibly turned back and had to delay his journey. Meanwhile, he sent a telegram from 'the prison of the home' to the prison in which Khomeini, Qomi and Mahallati were incarcerated. Indeed all the leading ayatollahs, including those in Najaf, joined the campaign to defend their arrested colleagues.

Eventually, it was decided to send an envoy to the Shah to negotiate their release. Again Ayatollah Kamalvand, who had met the Shah the year earlier to discuss the White Revolution referendum, was chosen. The meeting was frosty. Kamalvand argued that a *mojtahed* could not be tried, let alone executed, as the prime minister had threatened. He added that Khomeini's release would bring much-needed peace to the country. The Shah lectured his guest on the shortcomings of the clergy. Grinding his teeth, he told Kamalvand: 'I assure you that we are not going to kill Khomeini and turn him into a martyr. We are going to compromise and discredit him among the people.' In reality, the fact that the fate of Khomeini now dominated the situation was not at all to the Shah's liking, for short of physically destroying him, the Shah simply had no idea what to do with this man languishing in his prison. Once again it was Khomeini and not the ruler who was dictating the turn of events.

The hard-liners in the regime, led by Alam and Nassiri, wanted him tried and executed. The Shah himself and General Pakravan were still undecided and eventually came to the conclusion that a compromise was necessary. At Kamalvand's insistence the Shah eventually agreed that some news of Khomeini's whereabouts might reduce the tension, and gave permission for Ayatollah Khonsari, the senior Tehran cleric, to visit Khomeini in jail. The meeting, which took place in the presence of top-ranking security officials, was brief and restricted to conventional greetings, but it calmed the situation.

The bazaars in Tehran and other cities opened for business after two weeks, but life was still far from normal. Martial law was in effect, the clergy were still in Tehran and Khomeini's supporters were still active although mainly underground. For the Shah the whole thing was clear-cut. He recalled later that the rioting of 5 June 1963 was instigated by the agents of black reaction, led by a man who claimed to be a cleric. It was not at all clear where the man's family had come from. It was, however, clear that he had mysterious connections with foreign agents. Did not the 'treacherous, Godless, defunct Tudeh Party refer to Khomeini as ayatollah'?

In his book *The White Revolution*, the Shah charged the demonstrators with having attacked defenceless women, damaged buses carrying female pupils, destroyed libraries, demolished sports centres, plundered shops and thus left a 'glorious balance-sheet of this unholy alliance' between the destructive forces of the red (the Communists) and the black (the reactionaries). But it was on painting Khomeini as a foreign agent that the Shah's regime concentrated its effort.

Khomeini's opening of the anti-Israeli and pro-Palestinian issue, which was popular amongst Muslim activists, made him an easy target for the Shah's campaign. On 5 June, Savak Chief General Pakravan claimed that the rioters had been in touch with foreign agents. Two days later the Shah announced that: 'Among the detainees and injured there were many who said they had been given twenty-five rials [less than 20 pence] to say "long live so-and-so". Now we know where this money came from.'

Three days later, the martial law authorities announced that they had uncovered a treacherous and important spy network. A week later *Ettela'at* daily elaborated on the story for the first and last time saying that '... on 1 June, a certain Abdolqeis Jojo arrived from Lebanon and was found by alert customs officials to be carrying a million tomans. During interrogation he confessed that he was bringing this money from Gamal Abd al-Nasser for some specified people in Iran. Details of the affair will be announced to the public soon.' At the same time Savak investigators were working on Tayyeb Haj Reza'i and Haj Esma'il Reza'i, who had been arrested and were being personally 'looked after' by their old friend Nassiri.

Nassiri, who led the team responsible for concocting a file on Khomeini, wanted Tayyeb and his son to sign a short statement that read: 'Khomeini gave the money and I distributed twenty-five Rials to each person,' implying that thugs, low-paid workers and peasants had been bought for a day's wage. Tayyeb refused to sign. For days he and his friends were subjected to indiscriminate beatings and maltreatment until one of them, who was illiterate, signed the piece of paper.

Despite all his efforts, Nassiri failed to formulate a viable spy story, and so it was decided to work on Khomeini himself. But Khomeini's attitude to his interrogators was brusque, haughty and dismissive: 'You have no right to question me. Take your paper and pen, and leave this place. I do not want you to sit here.' Offers by the government to allow him to choose a lawyer were rejected with venom.

Next, psychological pressure was tried. For several nights Khomeini was kept awake by the screams of people appealing for mercy under torture.

Eventually, he protested to one of the officers: 'What is this barbarity and incivility you display in this place? Why are you torturing humans as in some uncivilised medieval era? Why do you not respect international rules and humane principles?' The officer, who was possibly not completely loyal to the regime, lowered his voice and told Khomeini apologetically: 'They are not torturing anybody here. It is just a tape being played nearby.'

After nineteen days, Khomeini was transferred to army barracks in Eshratabad and kept in a small cell. 'It was four and a half metres long and I walked for three times a day for half an hour as I habitually do.' The next day he was transferred to a small house within the barracks which had a tiny courtyard and a little pond. General Pakravan came to see him and apologised for the inconveniences he had suffered. 'You will excuse us. This place is not ready yet. We have no choice but to keep you here.' Khomeini replied: 'No, you wanted to show us that these places also exist.'[12]

The clergy waited anxiously to see what would become of Khomeini. Rumours were by now circulating that he would be sent into exile. Taking these rumours seriously, the three leading clerics, including Ayatollahs Shari'atmadari and Milani, issued statements condemning any thought of expulsion. Milani, a more political animal, was blunt: 'I, on behalf of the Iranian people, warn these criminals that the people will not tolerate the exile of Ayatollah Khomeini or any other cleric.'

By this time the moderates in the regime, led by the General Pakravan, had won the day in the dispute over what to do about Khomeini. The climb-down began when in early July Pakravan went to see Khomeini to tell him: 'I tried hard to find a connection between the Great Source of Emulation [Khomeini] and external powers. I even sent an Arab to see you [the man who, as we saw earlier, posed as an Egyptian diplomat], but I could not find the slightest connection between you and any foreigners.' Pakravan continued by expressing the Shah's anger and his desire for an apology from Khomeini:

His Majesty realises that the Source of Emulation has acted for purely religious reasons and not under foreign influence, and that he is not against the concept of monarchy. But His Majesty is wondering what he is to do in response to his Ashura speech in which he attacked the monarch and the monarchy. Your Holiness must agree that the speech was very strong. Whether a republic or a monarchy, a democracy or a dictatorship, it is unprecedented in the world for a head of state to be attacked so strongly.

Khomeini's instincts once again came to his aid. He gave the general an answer without compromising his position. As Pakravan finished his sentence Khomeini looked at the wall and said: 'There may have been some strong language in the speech, but the intention was to advise. That advice was necessary for the Shah. You should also advise the Shah.' Pakravan, a rather gentle man with a cultured background who generally avoided the corruption and rivalry of the Shah's court, could not help but laugh. After a few seconds of silence had elapsed he told Khomeini: 'Your Excellency will be free now. But I must tell Your Excellency that politics means lies, deceit, hypocrisy and cheating. That is our job. The Source of Emulation should not taint himself by getting involved in politics.' Khomeini retorted: 'From the very beginning we have never been involved in the kind of politics you have defined.'

An hour after this interview Khomeini was driven to a comfortable house in the northern Tehran suburb of Davudieh which belonged to Savak. The next day, clerical and lay supporters flocked to visit. A queue soon formed in front of the house, growing longer by the minute as people waited their turn to kiss Khomeini's hand and then leave. It was an emotional day even for Khomeini, a man not known for readily displaying his emotions. As the number of visitors increased, those in the courtyard grew impatient. Khomeini was asked to come to the window and he did so. The gathering cheered and waved wildly. Unable to restrain his true feelings any longer he sat down and suddenly shouted: 'What can I do with these feelings?' and burst into tears. Putting his hands into the pocket of his qaba, he brought out his handkerchief, weeping uncontrollably.

Having decided that it would be too risky to prosecute Khomeini, and that his continued imprisonment would make a martyr of him, the regime was none too happy about his continuing high profile. Within twenty-four hours soldiers were stationed around the house and visitors turned away. Khomeini had won his freedom for just one day. A few days later Khomeini, Qomi and Mahallati were told to find suitable accommodation for themselves. A bazaar merchant, Hajji Rowghani, offered his house in Qeitarieh in the north of Tehran, far away from the city centre and the bazaar. With security men both inside and outside the house, keeping everything under control, the containment of Khomeini was complete.

Meanwhile discontent continued to seethe below the surface and, in order to give the Shah's government a semblance of normality, parliamentary elections were announced for 5 October. But only the two officially sanctioned parties, Mardom and the newly formed Iran Novin, were permitted to contest them. Predictably they were denounced by the Islamic movement as an illegal farce. The publication and distribution of anti-Shah leaflets and underground newspapers continued throughout the election campaign. It was from this time that Savak gained a new notoriety as the nemesis of the dissident clergy. Although liberal and left-wing opponents of the Shah had already visited the dreaded Savak interrogation chambers, up to this point the clerics and seminarians had not. But it was now clear to the authorities that any sign of weakness would only embolden Khomeini's supporters. So Savak, originally designed to deal with the communist threat, now turned its attention to the agitation in the seminaries. Harassment became the norm. Seminarians and young priests would often be stopped and searched on buses and trains. Spies were planted among them. Every effort was made to halt the increasing number of statements being distributed around the country.

The seminarians responded with devices of their own. They discarded their clerical garb, shaved or trimmed their beards, and even took to wearing ties to evade detection. They would rise before dawn to distribute leaflets to houses, but to ensure even speedier delivery they often gave leaflets to shopkeepers in the form of waste paper in which tea, turmeric, pepper and other goods could be wrapped.

If the conflict between the two sides, already locked in earnest combat, took an even more serious turn with the trial and execution of the former gang leaders Tayyeb Haj Reza'i and Esma'il Reza'i for their role in the 5 June Uprising. Memorial services held for Tayyeb in mosques and theological centres added to the tension. He had become a religious martyr, and in accordance with the general Shi'i tendency to replay the Karbala tragedy, every element of the Karbala paradigm had to be recreated. Khomeini was to follow in the footsteps of Hossein, Qom was Karbala, the Feiziyeh was the place of martyrdom, the Shah was Yazid and Tayyeb was Horr, a leading commander of Yazid who joined Hossein in AD 680 and was subsequently martyred.

Yet despite the emotional tension, maintained through this and other events, the combination of propaganda and suppression was gradually working in the regime's favour. Among the clergy divisions began to surface over the wisdom of staging further confrontations while a change of government set the stage for a solution. On 8 March, just two weeks before the anniversary of the Feiziyeh attack, the Shah appointed a new prime minister, Hassan Ali Mansur leader of the Iran Novin Party. Confident that the clergy had been effectively defeated, Mansur felt that he could be magnanimous towards them. He spoke of reconciliation with the clergy and wasted no time in contacting Khomeini. Within a month he had secured the Shah's agreement to let Khomeini return to Qom. Late at night on Tuesday 7 April 1964, ten months after his arrest, Khomeini was driven to his home. The militant clergy had sustained a temporary defeat, but the crisis had established Khomeini as their undisputed leader.

Khomeini's homecoming was treated as a major festival. The Feiziyeh School organised three days of celebrations, the bazaar was lit up, and the town assumed a holiday mood. Tall and neatly dressed in his clerical garb, Khomeini's charisma was crystallised in his calm and deceptively inattentive gaze. His home became a place of pilgrimage for thousands of well-wishers from all over Iran, who were happy to merely achieve a glimpse of this awesome figure. Old men of learning, who had never taken any ayatollah seriously, preferring to remain quiet in their isolation lest they be affected by worldly desires, rushed to see him. The fact that he managed to come out of the prison of 'Pharaoh' alive had given him the enigmatic quality of a Moses. Even the government treated Khomeini differently. Just one day after his release the Minister of the Interior, Javad Sadr, travelled to Qom to convey the best wishes of the new prime minister. Sadr was appalled by the dark, narrow, muddy alley leading to Khomeini's home. When he left he immediately ordered it to be asphalted and street lighting installed.

Sadr's gesture did not, however, mollify Khomeini who was determined to continue his fight. Qom's theological students had welcomed him with a 'resolution' which they read out in his presence. They demanded that he should work towards a reorganisation of the theological colleges, for the imposition of the whole body of Islamic law – including those elements left out of the *Towzih al-Masa'el*, such as holy war, enjoining the good and forbidding the evil, death by stoning, and the amputation of hands – and for the 1906 Constitution to be observed in its entirety, allowing for the creation of a council of five leading clerics with the power to veto all legislation. They demanded the abolition of all anti-Islamic laws, the dissolution of the present 'illegal' parliament, an end to the influence of 'the agents of imperialism and Zionism' in the country, the implementation of social justice and the creation of a prosperous Iran under the

banner of Shi'ism, a ban on alcohol and drugs, control of the media, a halt
to the spread of corruption through the theatre and cinema, an amnesty
for political prisoners, and the welfare of the families of the martyrs of 5
June. Although the seminarians stopped short of advocating the overthrow
of the monarchy, this was a blueprint for an Islamic state – one that sounded
very much like the Feda'iyan-e Islam's political programme – which set
the tone for the next round of confrontation.

It is not clear whether Khomeini had been consulted about this resolution. Although its content was certainly in line with his thinking, he may
well have disapproved of its timing, as he was making a great effort to
appeal to a wider public and, by attempting to sidestep the image of a
'reactionary mollah' stamped on him by the Shah, to exert more influence
over secular university students.

Khomeini's growing appeal to young secular activists was the result of
the vacuum in which such dissidents now found themselves. With Mosaddeq under permanent house arrest at his village of Ahmadabad the secular opposition no longer had a charismatic leader. At the same time, Khomeini had shattered the view that the clergy were the collaborators of an
American-installed Shah. He for a time had the whole political arena to
himself and his emphasis shifted from more strictly religious topics to the
social, political and cultural aspects of Islam. Political and economic independence, unemployment, corruption, health and education became his
key themes. A strong anti-Israeli tone gave his statements a sharper edge,
not only because people sympathised with the plight of the homeless Pal-
estinians, but because the Shah was seen as an ally of Israel.

A day after Khomeini's release, the newspaper *Ettela'at* published a commentary thought to have been officially inspired. Under the headline 'Holy
Unity for Holy Objectives' it reported: 'It is a great pleasure to know that
the clergy have now joined the people in support of the Revolution of the
Shah and the People.'[13]

On Friday 10 April 1964 many Tehranis travelled to Qom to hear Khomeini make his first public pronouncement after his release and his first
for ten months. His speech that day, along with the Feiziyeh resolutions
pronounced two days earlier, shattered the government's illusions, especially those of the new prime minister. Colonel Mowlavi was once again
dispatched to Qom to find out who had been behind the resolution which
had already been disowned by most senior clerics. But when he enquired
at Khomeini's home he was told: 'When you tell us who wrote the article

in *Ettela'at*, we will express our opinion on this issue.'[14]

The duel between Khomeini and a now outraged Shah recommenced immediately as the Shah reverted to his old offensive position, labelling the clergy reactionary and anachronistic. These summer months of 1964 also saw increasing tension between Khomeini and some of his rival ayatollahs. Aware that his confrontation with the Shah could only be successful if he retained the support of his fellow clerics, Khomeini at first tried in public to maintain an attitude of self-effacing deference towards Shari'atmadari and Golpayegani, thanking them for their support at the time of his arrest and for securing his release. The weekly meetings which these elders of Shi'ism had held regularly before Khomeini's arrest were also resumed after his release. But despite these efforts the cracks could not be papered over. For example, Khomeini tried but failed to persuade the others to join him in issuing a statement on the first anniversary of his arrest on 5 June and the killings that followed. Thus, when demonstrations to commemorate the anniversary did break out in Tehran, support among the people was confined to those directly loyal to Khomeini, making it easier for the security forces to disperse the crowds relatively quickly.

In danger of being isolated Khomeini had to outflank his clerical opponents. This he did by seeking out the secular dissidents – nationalists, liberals, and Marxists. And the issue with which he found his mark was the 'capitulations'.

In the autumn of 1964 the government forced a bill through parliament extending diplomatic immunity to American military personnel, placing them outside the jurisdiction of Iranian courts for any civil or criminal act perpetrated by them. This was a time when the military bond between Iran and the United States was growing closer, bringing with it an increasing number of military technicians and advisers. In the circumstances it was perhaps natural that the United States should insist on handling civil disputes or criminal transgressions involving its own personnel. Such legal arrangements are not unusual in situations where the troops of one country are stationed on the territory of another. But in an Iran which saw itself as only recently freed of British domination, and where Khomeini found it increasingly advantageous to play the 'foreign devil' card so as to woo the secular opponents of the regime, he had to seize the opportunity.

News of the new law had been kept secret, but the text of the discussions was leaked to Khomeini via one of his students. When he read it he confided to his companions: 'They can no longer call us reactionary. The point is that we are fighting against America. All the world's freedom-fighters will support us on this issue. We must use it as a weapon to attack the regime so that the whole nation will realise that this Shah is an American agent and this is an American plot.' Khomeini had spotted a stick with which to beat the regime, and he picked it up with alacrity. Once more he went on the offensive.

On the birthday of the Prophet's daughter Fatemeh – which in 1964 fell on 27 October – many believers make a pilgrimage to Qom and the houses of prominent clergy overflow with supporters and seminarians who gather to hear their customary sermon. On this occasion, Khomeini's home was by far the most crowded. At about 8.30 am he appeared before the crowd and ominously pronounced the Qor'anic dictum reserved for occasions of mourning: 'We belong to God and to Him we shall return.'

I cannot express the sorrow I feel in my heart. My heart is constricted. Since the day I heard of the latest developments affecting Iran, I have barely slept: I am profoundly disturbed, and my heart is constricted. With sorrowful heart, I count the days until death shall come and deliver me.

Iran no longer has any festival to celebrate: they have turned our festival into mourning. They have sold us, they have sold our independence: but still they light up the city and dance.

If I were in their place, I would forbid all these lights: I would give orders that black flags be raised over the bazaars and houses, that black awnings be hung! Our dignity has been trampled underfoot: the dignity of Iran has been destroyed. The dignity of the Iranian army has been trampled underfoot!

A law has been put before the Majles according to which we are to accede to the Vienna Convention, and a provision has been added to it that all American military advisers, together with their families, technical and administrative officials, and servants – in short, anyone in any way connected to them – are to enjoy legal immunity with respect to any crime they may commit in Iran.

If some American's servant, some American's cook, assassinates your *marja'* in the middle of the bazaar, or runs over him, the Iranian police do not have the right to apprehend him! Iranian courts do not have the right to judge him! The dossier must be sent to America, so that our masters there can decide what is to be done!

First, the previous government approved this measure without telling anyone, and now the present government just recently introduced a bill in the

Senate and settled the whole matter in a single session without breathing a word to anyone. A few days ago, the bill was taken to the lower house of the Majles and there were discussions, with a few deputies voicing their opposition, but the bill was passed anyhow. They passed it without any shame, and the government shamelessly defended this scandalous measure. They have reduced the Iranian people to a level lower than that of an American dog. If someone runs over a dog, belonging to an American, he will be prosecuted. Even if the Shah himself were to run over a dog belonging to an American, he would be prosecuted. But if an American cook runs over the Shah, the head of state, no one will have the right to interfere with him.

Why? Because they wanted a loan and America demanded this in return. The government has sold our independence, reduced us to the level of a colony, and made the Muslim nation of Iran appear more backward than savages in the eyes of the world!

What are we to do in the face of this disaster? What are our religious scholars to do? To what country should they present their appeal:

Other people imagine that it is the Iranian nation that has abased itself in this way. They do not know that it is the Iranian government, the Iranian Majles – the Majles that has nothing to do with the people. What can a Majles that is elected at bayonet point have to do with the people? The Iranian nation did not elect these deputies. Many of the high-ranking ulema and *maraje'* ordered a boycott of the elections, and the people obeyed them and did not vote. But then came the power of the bayonet, and these deputies were seated in the Majles.

They have seen that the influence of the religious leaders prevents them from doing whatever they want, so now they wish to destroy that influence! … If the religious leaders have influence, they will not permit this nation to be the slaves of Britain one day, and America the next.

If the religious leaders have influence, they will not permit Israel to take over the Iranian economy: they will not permit Israeli goods to be sold in Iran – in fact, to be sold duty-free!

If the religious leader have influence, they will not permit such misuse to be made of the public treasury.

If the religious leaders have influence, they will not permit girls and boys to wrestle together, as recently happened in Shiraz.

If the religious leaders have influence, they will not permit people's innocent daughters to be under young men at school: they will not permit women to teach at boy's schools and men to teach at girls' schools, with all the resulting corruption.

If the religious leaders have influence, they strike this government in the mouth, they will strike this Majles in the mouth and chase these deputies out of both its houses!.

If the religious leaders have influence, they will not permit some agent of America to carry out these scandalous deeds: they will throw him out of Iran.

So the influence of the religious leaders is harmful to the nation? No, it is harmful to you, harmful to you traitors, not to influence, you cannot do everything you want to do, commit all the crimes you want, so you want, so you wish to destroy their influence. You thought you could cause dissension among the religious leaders with your intrigues, but you will be dead before your dream can come true. You will never be able to do it. The religious leaders are united."

I esteem all the religious leaders. Once again, I kiss the hand of all the religious leader. If I kissed the hands of the *maraje'* in the past, today I kiss the hands of the seminarians, I kiss the hands of the simple grocer.

Gentlemen, I warn you of danger!

Iranian army, I warn you of danger!

Iranian politicians, I warn you of danger!

Iranian merchants, I warn you of danger!

Ulama of Iran, *maraje'* of Islam, I warn you of danger!

Scholars, students! Centres of religious learning! Najaf, Qom. Mashhad, Tehran, Shiraz , I warn you of danger!

The danger is coming to light now, but there are other things that are being kept hidden from us, In the Majles they said, 'Keep these matters secret!' Evidently they are dreaming up further plans for us. What greater evil are they about to inflict upon us? Tell me, what could be worse than slavery? What could be worse than abasement? What else do they want of you? What are they planning?

What use to you are the American soldiers and military advisers? If this country is occupied by America, then what is all this noise you make about progress? If these advisers are to be your servants, then why do you treat them like something superior to masters? If they are servants, why not treat them as such? If they are your employees, then why not treat them as any other government treats its employees? If our country is now occupied by the United States, then tell us outright and throw us out of this country!

This Majles that makes empty noises about independence and revolution, that says: 'We have undergone a White Revolution!'

I don't know where this White Revolution is that they are making so much fuss about. God knows that I am aware of (and my awareness causes me pain) the remote villages and provinces, of the hunger of our people and the disordered state of our agrarian population ... If an American runs over me with his car, no one will have the right to say anything to him!

Those gentlemen who say we must hold our tongues and not utter a sound – do they still say the same thing on this occasion? Are we to keep silent again and not say a word? Are we to keep silent while they are selling us? Are we to keep silent while they sell our independence?

By God, whoever does not cry out in protest is a sinner! By God, whoever does not express his outrage commits a major sin!

Leader of Islam, come to the aid of Islam!

Ulama of Najaf, come to the aid of Islam!

Ulama of Qom, come to the aid of Islam! Islam is destroyed!

Muslim peoples! Leaders of the Muslim peoples! Presidents and kings of the Muslim peoples! Come to our aid! Shah of Iran, Save yourself!

Are we to be trampled underfoot by the boots of America simply because we are a weak nation and have no dollars? America is worse than Britain, Britain is worse than America. The Soviet Union is worse than both of them. They are all worse and more unclean than each other.

But today it is America that we are concerned with.

Let the American President know that in the eyes of the Iranian people, he is the most repulsive member of the human race today because of the injustice he has imposed on our Muslim nation. Today the Qor'an has become his enemy, the Iranian nation has become his enemy. Let the American government know that its name has been ruined and disgraced in Iran.

Those wretched deputies in the Majles begged the government to ask 'our friends' the Americans not to make such impositions on us, not to insist that we sell ourselves, not to turn Iran into a colony. But did anyone listen?

There is one article in the Vienna Convention they did not mention at all – Article 32. I don't know what article that is: in fact, the chairman of the Majles himself doesn't know. The deputies also don't know what that article is: nonetheless, they went ahead and approved and signed the bill. They passed it, even though some people said, 'We don't know what is in Article 32.' Maybe those who objected did not sign the bill, They are not quite so bad as the others, those who certainly did sign. They are a herd of illiterates.

One after another, our statesmen and leading politicians have been set aside. Our patriotic statesmen are given nothing to do. The army should know that it will also be treated the same way: its leaders will be set aside, one by one. What self-respect will remain for the army when an American errand boy or cook has priority over one of our generals? If I were in the army, I would resign. If I were a deputy in the Majles, I would resign, I would not agree to be disgraced.

American cooks, mechanics, technical and administrative officials, together with their families, are to enjoy legal immunity, but the ulema of Islam, the preachers and servants of Islam, are to live banished or imprisoned ... .

All of our troubles today are caused by America and Israel. Israel itself derives from America: these deputies and ministers that have been imposed upon us derive from America-they are all agents of America, for if they were not, they would rise up in protest.

I am now thoroughly agitated, and my memory is not working so well, I cannot remember precisely when, but in one of the earlier Majleses, where Seyyed Hassan Modarres was a deputy, the government of the day put pressure on the Majles to accept the Russian demand.

According to an American historian, a religious leader with stick in hand (the late Modarres) came up to the tribune and said: 'Now that we are to be destroyed, why should we sign the warrant for our own destruction?' The Majles took courage from his act of opposition, rejected the ultimatum, and Russia was unable to do anything!

That is the conduct of a true religious leader: a thin, emaciated man, a mere heap of bones, rejects the ultimatum and demand of a powerful state like Russia. If there were a single religious leader in the Majles today, he would not permit these things to happen. It is for this reason that they wish to destroy the influence of the religious leaders, in order to attain their aims and desires!

There is so much to be said, there are so many instances of corruption in this country, that I am unable in my state at the moment to present to you even what I know. It is your duty, however, to communicate these matters to your colleagues. The ulema must enlighten the people, and they in turn must raise their voices in protest to the Majles and the government and say, 'Why did you do this? Why have you sold us? We did not elect you to be our representatives, and even if we had done so, you would forfeit your posts now on account of this act of treachery.'

This is high treason! O God, they have committed treason against this country. O God, this government has committed treason against the Qor'an.

All the members of both houses who gave their agreement to this affair are traitors. Those old men in the Senate are traitors, and all those in the lower house who voted in favour of this affair are traitors. They are not our representatives. The whole world must know that they are not the representatives of Iran. Or, suppose they are: now I dismiss them. They are dismissed from their posts and all the bills they have passed up until now are invalid.

According to the very text of the law, according to Article 2 of the Supplementary Constitutional Law, no law is valid unless the *mojtaheds* exercise a supervisory role in the Majles, From the beginning of the constitutional period down to the present, has any *mojtahed* ever exercised supervision? If there were five *mojtaheds* in this Majles, or even one single religious leader of lesser rank, they would get a punch in the mouth: he would not allow this bill to be enacted, he would make the Majles collapse.

As for those deputies who apparently opposed this affair, I wish to ask them in protest: If you were genuinely opposed, why did you not pour soil on your heads? Why did not rise up and seize that wretch by the collar? Does 'opposition' mean simply to sit there and say, 'we are not in agreement,' and then continue your flattery as usual? You must create an uproar, right there in the Majles. You must not permit there to be such a Majles. Is it enough to say simply, "I am opposed," when the bill passes nevertheless?

We do not regard as law what they claim to have passed. We do not regard this Majles as a Majles. We do not regard this government as a government. They are traitors, guilty of high treason!

O God, remedy the affairs of the Moslems! O God, bestow dignity on this sacred religion of Islam! O God, destroy those individuals who are traitors to this land, who are traitors to Islam, who are traitors to the Qor'an.

And peace be upon you, and also God's mercy.[15]

In the tense week that followed the government-controlled press attacked the clergy while trying desperately to find a plausible justification for giving Americans extra-territorial rights. Even in the Majles a sizeable minority had expressed its concern, causing Prime Minister Mansur to flounder as he tried to explain away the capitulation law. The government was cornered. Khomeini's shrewd exploitation of the Shah's American link had found its mark. But more important, by homing in on an issue that affected Iran's sovereignty he had become a political leader, the first time that a teaching *marja'* had achieved such a position.

The outcome was inevitable: on 4 November 1964, Khomeini was arrested again and this time driven straight to Tehran airport where a Savak official handed him a passport and told him: 'You are now going to Turkey and your family will join you soon.' Tehran Radio broadcast a brief statement: 'Since Mr Khomeini's behaviour and his agitation are against the interests of the people and the security, sovereignty and independence of the country, he has been sent into exile.'

8

In the Den of Snakes
Exile in Turkey and Iraq

They took me straight to the airport. The plane was ready. When I boarded, I saw they had prepared a place for me by covering it with blankets. It was a transport plane. They told me there were no passenger planes available and they wanted to deport me as quickly as possible. I told them that the truth was quite the reverse, that they were flying me out in a transport plane so that I would not be among other people.[1]

On board the Hercules transport plane of the Imperial Iranian Air Force, Khomeini appeared calm and composed. He was accompanied only by Colonel Afzali, his Savak minder. As soon as the plane took off Khomeini struck up a conversation. 'Do you know,' he asked Afzali, 'that I am being exiled for defending the integrity of the army and the independence of my homeland?'. 'As long as we need America, we will have to make some concessions to it,' obliged Afzali. 'You mean we should even put our honour at their disposal?' Khomeini retorted. Afzali said nothing, shook his head and later reported the conversation to his superiors in Tehran.[2]

The steward came to offer tea. Khomeini must have imagined that anyone who worked for the Imperial Iranian Air Force was an unbeliever and thus religiously unclean for he asked the Colonel whether the steward was a Muslim. The steward did not wait for Afzali. Offended, he replied: 'Of course I am a Muslim. I am from a religious family.'[3] Khomeini accepted the tea. After a while Afzali suggested that he might like to see the plane's cockpit. Unexpectedly Khomeini took this opportunity to familiarise himself with a feat of modern engineering and spent the remainder of the three and a half hour journey cross-questioning the pilot and co-pilot about the plane.

On touch-down at Ankara airport, Turkish security officials met Khomeini and Colonel Afzali and drove them to their hotel. For Khomeini there could not have been a greater wrench. He had been imprisoned, under house arrest, and lonely before. But he was now in a strange land whose political ethos, the secularism of Kemal Atatürk, he hated. In fact he had fought all his life to prevent Iran from becoming another Turkey. Was he depressed in room 514 of the Bulvar Palace Hotel? Did he feel sad, miss his wife, his personal belongings, the low table he worked on in his small room at home, surrounded by leather-bound books and papers? The letter he wrote that afternoon to his son Mostafa shows that, however deeply perturbed, he remained composed.

'I arrived this morning at Ankara,' he wrote. 'The weather here is better than in Qom. Do not worry about me.' He sent his regards to his relatives and asked his son to tell them to be patient and not to call for help. At several points he advised Mostafa, who was bad tempered, to be on his best behaviour with his mother, younger brother Ahmad and his sisters and told him that he had refused an offer for his family to join him in Turkey. He had no idea that Mostafa had been arrested and was also under threat of exile and asked him to send clothing, including an *aba*, shirts and a towel, a prayer book and some textbooks to work on. Concerned about his family's financial situation, he told Mostafa to get money from 'Mr so-and-so', not mentioning the name so as to avoid revealing his identity to Savak.[4] A day later, Khomeini was moved to a house to avoid the attentions of journalists who had quickly learned of his exile.

Colonel Afzali reported to his superior in Tehran that on the second day of his stay Khomeini felt better and was 'now spending most of his time relaxing, reading the Qor'an, praying and eating. Occasionally he notes down some Turkish words. But he should not be left alone.' By the third day Khomeini was unwilling to remain indoors, and insisted that his guards take him to see Ankara. To humiliate Khomeini, and perhaps to dissuade him from making too many public appearances, he was banned from wearing his clerical attire. His protests were to no avail.[5] In his next letter home, written five days after his arrival, Khomeini cancelled his request for shirts and a towel and, unusually for a man who never paid much attention to food, he wrote: 'Send me also some dried fruits, pistachio nuts and gaz (nougat).' Reporting that he had been very tired, he said he needed rest but nevertheless asked for more books to fill his time. He again reminded Mostafa to be kind to his mother and the family, adding that he was soon to be sent to Bursa which he had been told was a religious city.[6]

Once in Bursa Khomeini again wrote asking Mostafa to send clothes and a winter aba. He must have been thinking of the possibility of death in exile, for he instructed Mostafa to pay someone, as is the religious custom, to perform two or three years of daily prayer and ten years of fasting for him after his death for his possible spiritual lapses. He reiterated that his will remained unchanged 'The house belongs to your mother and the books are yours.'[7]

In Bursa, much to the annoyance of his Savak bodyguards, Khomeini came to like his Turkish hosts rather too much. Savak documents indicate that the Turks were doing their utmost to treat their guest kindly. In his letters and conversations with visitors Khomeini repeatedly spoke of the hospitality of his Turkish minder, Ali Bey – the Persian-speaking Colonel Ali Cetiner of Turkish Military Intelligence.

When Khomeini arrived in Bursa he was met by Ali Bey, who recalled:

I went to greet him at the airport. He was rather tall. He was sixty-three, with a white beard and thick, dark eyebrows. He was a quiet, gentle and good-tempered old man. As I had been unable to find a safe place for him, and was unprepared, I took him to our home. He could live with us if need be. Later, if it was appropriate, I was to rent a separate place for him.'[8]

For Ali's wife, Melahat, the picture was slightly different. When she first met Khomeini, she recalls:

Ali had told me that a great Iranian leader would be coming to stay. He had been sent into exile by the Shah, but it was to be a secret that he would be staying in Bursa, so for the time being he would live at our place. This was government business, so we were to do whatever was necessary. As a 'great leader' had been mentioned, I thought he would be a modern type of person. I was anxious to receive him as graciously as possible. On the day of his arrival I started the preparations early. I tidied the house and prepared his room. I furnished it with a new bed and bought new sheets. As he was a religious figure, I put a Qor'an at his bedside.

The cultural clash between a secular middle class military family in Turkey and a man who wanted to overturn the secular order in Iran becomes starker. Melahat went to the hairdressers. She wanted, she said, to look 'prim and proper' for him. While Ali went to the airport to meet Khomeini Melahat cooked an evening meal and got herself ready:

I dressed myself up. I was young at the time. I put on my best dress and waited for our guests. They arrived, a whole group of them, after dark. The Iranians who had accompanied him to Turkey were also there. One of the Iranians was a colonel. In all the confusion Khomeini and I were not introduced. I saw him from a distance. He was tall, with a white beard, and seemed healthy. He had a turban on his head. He wore a long dress, rather like a nightdress, and over that a robe. He constantly looked straight ahead and he appeared sad. He was a gentle-looking, calm old man. I was not able to see to him much, and began to set the table. At one point the man with the beard [Khomeini] began to shout. I rushed out of the kitchen to see what had happened. Khomeini was speaking in Persian and I could not understand what they were saying. But the colonel had gone all red because he was being scolded.

Ali asked the colonel, who spoke Turkish, why Khomeini was upset. 'Because there is no ewer,' replied Afzali. 'We will get a ewer tomorrow, tell him not to worry,' interjected Melahat.

At this point Khomeini noticed me. He looked me over steadily and raised his eyebrows. Then he frowned and began shouting. The colonel again replied in a low voice and then turned to us with sadness in his voice: 'He says he does not want a woman in the house. He says the woman with the uncovered head should leave.' I was shocked and angry. 'Colonel,' I replied, 'I am not his housekeeper here. I am the lady of the house. I could not leave my house even if I wanted to. The government has ordered us to look after him and to treat him as our guest. We are going to live together in this house. But if he insists, I will cover my head immediately and wear a long dress.' The colonel turned to Khomeini again. Shortly afterwards the old man appeared to calm down. I rushed to the bedroom and put on a long nightdress. I covered my head and then I came out again. During his entire stay in Bursa, whenever I was in his presence I wore a long dress down to my ankles and covered my head. This pleased him very much.

That first night we all sat down to dinner, my two sons, my daughter and the Iranian colonel. My wife had prepared a long table. Khomeini sat at the head of the table. The Iranian colonel and I flanked him on either side. Next to me sat my two sons Tanju and Tulga, followed by my daughter Payan. She was in middle school at the time and was about twelve years old. Food was served. Khomeini was staring in front of him and would not start his meal. 'Father,' I said, 'please start.'. He did not say a thing. He did not even look up. We were amazed. I asked the Iranian colonel if perhaps he did not like the food. 'The colonel turned to Khomeini and they exchanged a few words. Khomeini was angry, speaking in a loud voice. Then, all of a sudden, he made a fist and pointed his finger like a spear at my daughter. His eyes were wide with rage. 'Giz,' he said in Turkish. He knew a few words of Turkish. 'Kiz' or 'girl' was one of them. But he could not pronounce 'kiz' properly so he said 'giz'. My daughter was terrified. We were shocked. We did not know what to do or to say. Khomeini was angry because my daughter had sat at the table without covering her head. She sat frozen in her seat for a time, her eyes wide open. Then she ran crying to her mother in the kitchen. That evening she refused to show herself to Khomeini and she did not return to the table. After my daughter left the table he appeared to relax. He began to eat as if nothing had happened. I can never forget this incident. That is no way to treat a child.

Ali Cetiner's observations of that evening provide an interesting insight:

Khomeini's whole life was based on image, I believe this was also part of his image. It was part of his cunning. Later, we noticed that he was very careful to preserve an image, and did everything to conform to that image. If the Iranian colonel had not been there, I think he would not have reacted to my daughter in the way he did. In fact later he got used to her. My daughter [continued to] dress in an ordinary way like everyone else. She did not cover her head and lived her life normally in the house. Khomeini did not say anything [again].

Melahat Cetiner's relations with Khomeini soon improved, and it was not long before a tolerable modus vivendi was established:

After the way he had behaved towards my daughter and myself, I decided not to sit with him at the same table for meals. For two nights my daughter and I ate our meals in the kitchen. He had offended me with his shouting and had made my daughter cry. But he was a very sensitive person. He was deeply moved by the fact that shortly after he had shouted at me I had put on a dress down to my ankles and covered my head. The next day I set the table and served the food. Then I took my daughter and went to the kitchen. But he refused to eat unless we came to join him at the table. He sat staring at his plate. Ali asked him, through the Iranian colonel, why he would not eat. Apparently he turned and said: 'Let the hanim [lady] come too.' They called us in. My daughter and I felt obliged to join them so as not to appear rude. As soon as I sat down to the table he began eating his food, smacking his mouth and chewing with his mouth open. He slurped the soup and belched at the table. He was like that in the beginning. But he was very clever. In time he changed. He would watch our behaviour and act accordingly. He began to imitate us. Soon he was eating silently without smacking his mouth or belching. He was fond of sweets. He would receive colourful aromatic sweets from Iran which he would offer to me as well. He also liked little bits and pieces such as nuts. He was not a glutton like his son Mostafa. He would cook Azeri [from Azarbaijan] dishes for himself. But his favourite was a kind of pilau rice which the Iranians call 'chilau'. This was made from a special, long-grained rice. His visitors from Iran would bring it. That was his favourite dish, followed by kebabs and meat dishes generally. He would never show his feelings. For example, he detested Atatürk. But because he knew that we loved [Atatürk] deeply, he did not say anything. Only once did he call Atatürk a 'troublemaker'.

While in Bursa, Khomeini as a rule never discussed politics. He tried to give the impression that he was not interested in the subject. Perhaps he was putting into practice a view summed up by one of his students: 'Imam Khomeini believes that while one is captive in the claws of the enemy, one should fool the enemy without compromising one's position, status, beliefs and ideology, in order to secure one's freedom. It is irrational to shout slogans and thus put yourself in a difficult predicament while in prison or exile.'[9]

Melahat was getting to know Khomeini better:

He told us that throughout his life he had never stood up for a woman. But he would stand up when I entered the room. He had also never looked a woman in the face. Later, he began to look me in the face as well. He would chat to me amicably and smile. He was a nice old man and very polite. Soon he picked up enough Turkish to get by as well.

In Bursa, Khomeini was not allowed to meet people, and his contacts with other people were kept to a minimum. He stayed with the Cetiners for three months. Later, new accommodation was arranged nearby, but the Cetiners were with him almost every day. Ali provided for all his needs, his maintenance and his strolls, and was solely responsible for Khomeini's welfare, safety and actions. They treated him like a father. To the Cetiners, Khomeini appeared calm and collected, he was not an excitable person. He did not like to talk much either. Yet his apparent calm, deep down he was restless. He would sit at home all day and pace about. One day Ali said to him:

Father, you are bored at home, why don't I take you out? There are many historic mosques in Bursa. I will show them to you. But you cannot go out [dressed] like that, it is forbidden in our country.' I had strict instructions from Ankara that he was not to be allowed out in his turban and robes, which were like a symbol of power for him. He saw himself as a powerful figure in that outfit. 'No,' he said, 'I refuse to wear trousers.' Also, having worn robes since his childhood it had become part of his person. So I did not insist too much and waited. Some more time passed. One day I turned to him and said: 'Father, let me get you some trousers and a jacket and take you out.' He did not object but nodded his head to indicate 'Yes.' So I went out and bought him a jacket and trousers and gave them to him. He wore the trousers but refused to put on the jacket. Instead, in the summer he wore a raincoat and in winter an overcoat. In summer he would go out without anything to cover his head, and in winter he would wrap woollen scarves around it.

According to my instructions, I was to take a photograph of him without his turban and robes. The first mosque we planned to visit was the Ulucami [the grand mosque]. At the time, Khomeini's arrival had been kept secret from everybody, including the governor and police chief of Bursa. No one knew who he was. So I could not get someone else to take the photo. My son Tanju was, at the time, at middle school. I gave him a camera and said: 'We shall enter the mosque through the west entrance and come out from the east side. You hide somewhere around there and take a picture when we come out.' But Khomeini spotted Tanju as we were coming out. He was very angry. He went pale with rage and froze. 'Is anything the matter Father?' I asked. 'Let us go back home,' he said angrily. Then he pointed to Tanju. 'Tanju,' he said forcefully. I tried to calm him down. 'Father,' I said, 'He was only trying to take a photo as a memento. But if you object, we will destroy them.'

I called Tanju over, took the camera and removed the film. He [Khomeini] was visibly relieved. He was terrified of having his photograph taken. He was afraid that photos of him in that outfit would be sent to Iran. For a long time he lived in fear of this. But later he got used to the idea. He would even ask for his photograph to be taken. I expect that pictures of him in normal outfit are still there in the state archives. In fact these photos showing Khomeini without a turban were published in Iran after the 1979 Revolution.[10]

For the Cetiners, with whom Khomeini spent eleven months, it was difficult to believe the amount of money sent by his followers.

When he arrived from Iran he did not have a penny on him. But when he left Turkey in November 1965 he was a millionaire, even by the standards of those days. He was given the money by visitors from Iran. Khomeini left Turkey with a fortune and went to Iraq.[11]

On 3 January 1965, two months after Khomeini went to Bursa, he was joined by his son Mostafa. A well-built man and often overweight, Mostafa had brought nuts and coffee and other items his father had requested from Iran, including a few books. When Mostafa arrived Khomeini's first question to the poor young man was: 'Did you come or did they bring you?' Mostafa was surprised by the question but replied that he had been arrested and exiled. Khomeini sighed with relief, adding that had he come of his own free will he would have told him to leave immediately. Mostafa was often bored with his life in Bursa and the Cetiners found it difficult to cope with him.

Pressured by the clergy, the Shah agreed to let a group of mollahs visit Khomeini in the summer of 1965. Khomeini was taken to Istanbul in his Western clothes. Seeing him without his robes his visitors wept for a while. But once they had calmed down they asked Cetiner to take them with Khomeini to the seaside. Cetiner described what happened on the municipal beach in Florya. None of them had a swimming costume.

We bought some as we entered the beach. Khomeini did not want one, saying that he would not swim. We all went up to the beach cafeteria. Khomeini gazed around at the women. He looked at the beach, then he turned his back to them and sat down. He neither offered any criticism, nor made any comment, preferring to remain silent and disinterested. We left the cafeteria together with the mollahs on their way to a swim. We each went to a cabin to change. Coming out I saw Khomeini's son Mostafa heading for the water in his long underpants. The other mollahs had put on swimsuits. But Mostafa was wearing his long white underpants. Suddenly we were surrounded by boos and hisses. Everyone, men, women and children, was booing Mostafa. I was deeply embarrassed and rushed to his side. 'What do you think you are doing?' I asked. 'You can't go in like that. Look, everyone is booing you.' He was laughing. He did not give a damn, but in the end I convinced him to change into a swimsuit.

The visiting mollahs were eyeing the women on the beach and sighing. Mostafa could not look at anything else either. Then one of the mollahs pointed at the women and said:'Are these women Muslims?''Yes,' I said. They all laughed. 'They cannot be Muslims,' said one of them. When I said: 'You are Muslim, but you are also swimming,' they replied:'Yes, but we are men.' I did not dwell on the subject and that was the end of it. Khomeini did not swim that day, neither did he comment on the men and women on the beach and swimming in the sea.

A few days later we went to Kumla. Khomeini did swim that day. We would often take Khomeini for picnics at the seaside in Kumla. It was July and the beach was teeming. His son put on his swimsuit and joined us in the water. Khomeini was sitting in the shade, watching the people on the beach. He called me over and said that he wanted to take a swim, but that he would not wear a swimsuit. He asked me for a *peshtemal* [a kind of loin cloth to wrap around the waist]. Where would we find a *peshtemal* there? We brought him a towel. He wrapped himself in that and went into the water. He stayed there for some time, obviously enjoying himself. He told me that he had been in the sea for the first time in his life in Turkey.

But for Khomeini life in his Turkish exile was not just consumed by day-to-day trivialities. With his books around him, and plenty of free time on his hands, he set to work on his writings. It was here in Bursa that Khomeini wrote his *Tahrir al-Wasilah*, a commentary on a traditional theological text which also covered socio-political issues abandoned by his contemporaries, such as holy war and 'ordering the good and forbidding the evil'. A substantial book, it raised his status as a jurist. Khomeini returned to the question of Islamic government with vigour, taking it up from where he had left off in *Kashf al-Asrar*. Here Khomeini states that the Imam, or the leader of the Muslim community, true to the Islamic spirit of intervention in the ordering of people's lives, has the right to fix prices and generally interfere in the regulation of commerce if he feels it is in the interest of Islamic society – functions that religious scholars would normally regard as the preserve of the temporal authorities. He also tackles many political issues in terms of foreign policy, aiming to prevent the Muslim community from falling under the influence of foreigners.[12]

In a way the most interesting aspect of Khomeini's writings in Bursa was his introduction of concepts into the body of Islamic law that were new to the clergy and that must have been inspired by his journey to Turkey and contact with a world which was unfamiliar to him. He thus began to pronounce on issues as diverse as artificial insemination, sex changes and praying in aeroplanes. While other clerics reflect questions asked by their followers, Khomeini must have been one of the few ayatollahs to see his own experience having some impact on the development of *feqh*.

In the early 1960s relations between Turkey and Iran were cordial. There was co-operation between the Central Treaty Organisation (CENTO) and the RCD (the organisation for Regional Co-operation and Development), and both countries enjoyed the benefits of Western protection. However, under the surface there was plenty of scope for mistrust and rivalry. The Turks were often bemused by what they perceived to be the Shah's arrogance in styling himself the 'Emperor of the East'. The Iranians on the other hand, conscious of Turkey's historical and cultural links with the West, were keen to overcome their image as the backward Eastern neighbour. The wariness with which these countries have always regarded each other in the twentieth century came into sharper focus in the 1960s when oil-rich Iran was making its dash for modernisation while a stagnant Turkey was wrestling with its economic and political difficulties.

It is in this setting that we see Savak officials perturbed by the courtesy extended to Khomeini by the Turks. A Savak report of 18 January 1965 shows how anxious they were that the Turks might exploit his apparent affection for them. 'Ayatollah Khomeini is being exploited by the Turkish authorities,' said the report. 'Extreme hospitality and visits to developed areas in Bursa, Ankara and Istanbul arranged for Khomeini have made him over enthusiastic about Turkey. His Turkish minder, who speaks fluent Persian, presents Turkey to him as a completely Islamic country which supports other Islamic countries. Consequently the Turkish minder, without attacking Iran directly, makes it appear an anti-Islamic state.'[13]

Later in this report Savak's fears are crystallised in the following terms: 'Although relations between Iran and Turkey are cordial, were they to deteriorate for some reason a person like Khomeini could play an important role in propaganda and agitation among the Iranian people in Turkey's favour.'

Savak's conclusion was that since the Iranian government was paying for Khomeini's stay in Turkey they should have their own minder present in order to neutralise this 'Turkish influence' over him and to ensure that 'Khomeini understands that he owes his comfort to his own country.'[14]

Meanwhile, there was great pressure on the government in Iran to end Khomeini's exile. Agitation by his supporters, demands by leading clerics, letters from international human rights organisations and the United Nations kept his name alive. Eventually in October 1965, following a long discussion between the Shah and his advisers, Khomeini was permitted to go to the holy Shi'i city of Najaf in Iraq. The regime in Iran, justifiably perhaps, believed that there he would be eclipsed by the towering figures of long established ayatollahs and that his name would sink into oblivion.

This journey from Turkey, which was to change Khomeini's fortune, was not without its last moment of human sentiment. 'The day Khomeini left,' says Ali Cetiner, 'we bought each other presents. It was a fond farewell.' For Mrs Cetiner and Khomeini it was not that easy either. 'We all went to the airport to see him off. Khomeini appeared sad. He was in low spirits. He was overcome with emotion. So was I. We both cried. He was wiping away his tears as he boarded the plane.'

Khomeini arrived in Baghdad with Mostafa on Tuesday 6 October 1965. To their surprise there was no one at the airport to collect them. After waiting for a while in the airport lounge, Mostafa decided that they would have to look after themselves. So they took a taxi to Kazemein, one of the Shi'i holy places which lies to the west of Baghdad and is almost part of the city. Khomeini, much to Mostafa's amusement, haggled with the taxi-driver over the fare.[15] Although the large sums of money that had been sent to him while he was in Turkey were for his 'treasury', this was what would nowadays be called a 'legitimate' expense; he cannot have been short of cash, and yet he was always careful with money to the point of sometimes appearing mean.

In Kazemein the travellers found themselves a room in a cheap hotel next to the golden domes of the shrines. Khomeini may well have felt a certain disappointment that he was no longer a pampered guest of Turkish security; but he was at least free to wander in the streets and after a short rest he took the opportunity to visit the shrines. In his life as a leading mollah this was the only time he went out incognito. But the anonymity was to be short-lived. Mostafa began to call Najaf to inform friends of their arrival in Iraq. The hotel manager overheard the conversation and it suddenly dawned on him that the man he was playing host to was none other than the famous Grand Ayatollah Khomeini. So he arranged for father and son to stay in his own home.

As news of Khomeini's presence spread, visitors arrived from every theological school in Iraq to welcome him and on the second day of his stay the Iraqi government sent a senior minister to pay its respects.[16] It was very important for Khomeini's supporters in Iraq to ensure that he received as much publicity as possible, for he had a difficult task ahead of him in Najaf, the city he called 'a den of snakes' where he planned to settle.[17]

By Thursday (8 October 1965) Khomeini was once again the centre of attention. Hundreds of supporters accompanied him on a visit to Samarra, a city full of sentimental significance for him. It was in Samarra that the Hidden Imam of the Shi'a, the Mahdi, had gone in to occultation in AD 874. Samarra had also been the seat of one of Khomeini's heroes, Mirza Hassan Shirazi, whose edict lending support to rebellious merchants of the bazaar had made him an historic 'anti-imperialist' figure. And it was in Samarra that his father had studied as a young man. In a reception held in his honour at the school his father had attended, Khomeini was eulogised not only by Shi'i but also Sunni clerical speakers who compared his militant campaign in defence of Islam with those of Shirazi and the romantic 19th-century Pan-Islamist, Seyyed Jamaleddin al-Afghani.

Khomeini's next stop was Karbala, where students who had travelled from as far away as Qom and Najaf had organised a grand welcome. As was the custom among Iranians, the traveller was met some miles from the city, in the village of Mossayyeb, where hundreds of mollahs and seminarians showered him with flowers and then accompanied him on the last stage of the journey. A procession of some forty vehicles followed Khomeini's car to Karbala. As he prepared to enter the city of Hossein, where the notion of martyrdom as a fundamental aspect of Shi'ism came into being, Khomeini was surely apprehensive. He remained as cautious as ever, still uncertain of the sort of reception he would receive from the grand ayatollahs of Najaf, who not only opposed the politicisation of religion, but also saw in Khomeini a major rival who had already gained control over religious centres in Iran.

In this city, the symbol of self-sacrifice and the fight against tyranny,

Khomeini avoided the temptation to make political points and strictly forbade his supporters from making any political gestures. He was particularly annoyed to discover that they had distributed his photograph in the bazaar, for this could have antagonised the other clerics.

Khomeini's 'good behaviour' was noted with some surprise by the Iranian Consul-General in Iraq who, in a cable to Tehran, wrote: 'Since his arrival Mr Khomeini seems to be trying to preserve order and tranquillity (sic) amongst his supporters to prevent criticism. He has not given them the slightest opportunity to show their emotions.'[18] Indeed so determined was Khomeini to keep a low profile – politically at least – that when a seminarian asked him whether he knew that 'two clerics [Ayatollahs Zanjani and Mostanbet] have sent greetings to the Shah on the silver jubilee of his accession to the throne,' he was rebuked for gossiping and told to mind his own business.[19]

After a week in Karbala, Khomeini's supporters organised yet another ceremonial entry into Najaf, the real power centre of the clerical establishment. On 14 November 1965, at about 4 pm, Khomeini arrived in front of Imam Ali's shrine in Najaf. It was his first visit to the 'den of snakes', not as a seminarian, as he would have wished, but as an exiled cleric plagued by the animosity of the Shi'i clergy of Iraq who viewed him as a potential rival and a threat. 'This Seyyed has created havoc in Qom. We must be careful not to let him do the same in Najaf,'[20] one of them is reported to have remarked when Khomeini took up residence in a rented house prepared for him by his supporters.

As soon as he was settled, two of Najaf's most important clerics, Grand Ayatollah Kho'i and Grand Ayatollah Mahmud Shahrudi, visited his home along with many others to welcome him. However, the most senior of them all, Grand Ayatollah Mohsen Hakim, waited until the second day, which was taken by Khomeini's supporters as a sign of disrespect. Hakim's first frosty meeting with the turbulent mollah of Qom lasted only five minutes. Their relationship was always to be fraught with tension.

On his fourth night in Najaf Khomeini paid the customary return visit to Hakim. When, in the usual small-talk, the question of Hakim's ill-health was mentioned, Khomeini brusquely suggested that he go for a 'breath of fresh air' to Iran to see for himself what was happening. During Borujerdi's lifetime, he continued, he and his clerical colleagues had given Hakim the benefit of the doubt. 'As far as you are concerned,' he told the Iraqi cleric, 'I have the feeling that you are not being informed of the atrocities of the Iranian regime. Otherwise, you would not have remained silent.'[21]

This led to a debate on the role of the clergy, Khomeini arguing the case of the militant Imam Hossein who chose martyrdom in the face of Yazid's tyranny, and Hakim the case of Hossein's elder brother, the more pragmatic Imam Hassan, who remained silent during the rule of Yazid's shrewd father Mo'awiya. Their conversation reportedly went as follows and is worth relating in detail.

'Now that you are here,' said a doubtful Hakim, 'it is not worth my while going to Iran. What can one do? What would such a trip achieve?'

Khomeini had no doubts: 'It definitely would achieve results. How could it not be effective if the ulema were united? With our uprising we can put an end to some dangerous measures being taken by the government.'

Hakim continued distant and noncommittal: 'If it was plausible and a rational approach could be worked out, it might bear fruit.'

KHOMEINI: 'It would definitely be effective, as was demonstrated by the uprising. We also want to achieve results through rational means. Irrational measures are definitely out of the question. Our objective is to follow actions initiated by the ulema and the wise.'

HAKIM: 'If we took drastic measures people would not follow us. The people lie and follow their whims. They won't die for religion.'

KHOMEINI: 'How could people possibly lie? People gave their lives, were tortured, gaoled, banished and had their property looted. How could the average man in the street who bared his chest to bullets tell lies?'

HAKIM: 'They would not follow us. They are in pursuit of their worldly desires.'

KHOMEINI: 'As I mentioned, people showed their honesty and courage in the June uprising [of 15 Khordad].'

HAKIM: 'If we staged an uprising and people suffered there would be chaos and people would curse us.'

KHOMEINI: 'When we staged the uprising it only raised the esteem in which we are held. We received nothing but respect and submission and the people kissed our hands [in gratitude]. Those who failed to join the uprising were denounced and held in contempt. When I was in exile in Turkey, I once visited a village whose name has slipped my memory. People there told me that when Atatürk was engaged in anti-religious activities, the Turkish ulema united in acting against his decisions. [So,] Atatürk laid siege to the village and killed forty of them. I was really ashamed of myself, thinking that these people who were Sunnis sensed a threat to Islam and rose to confront it, forty of them offering their lives as a result. But the Shi'i ulema, in the face of such a threat against our faith, have hardly suffered a bruise. It is really shaming.'

HAKIM: 'What should be done? We must balance our actions against the result. There is no point in sending people to their deaths.'

KHOMEINI:'Anti-religious measures fall into two categories. For example, Reza Khan engaged in such action without connecting it with religion. So, our action in confronting him was the forbidding of the evil. But the present Shah justifies his anti-Islamic actions by the Qor'an. It is a heresy which threatens the foundation of Islam and therefore cannot be tolerated. We must sacrifice our lives. Let history note that when religion was in danger a number of Shi'i ulema stood up to defend it and a group of them were killed.'

HAKIM:'What is the point of [merely] being mentioned in history? It [standing up for religion] must achieve something.'

KHOMEINI:'How could it not achieve results? Did not the uprising of Hossein serve history? Are we not benefiting greatly from his uprising?'

HAKIM:'What do they have to say about Imam Hassan? He did not stage an uprising!'

KHOMEINI: 'If Imam Hassan had as many followers as you have he would have led an uprising. He initially stood up [for his religion] but failed because his followers had sold themselves out to the enemy. But you have followers in all Islamic countries.'

HAKIM:'I do not see anybody who would follow us if we took action.'

KHOMEINI:'You order an uprising and I will be the first to follow you.'

Hakim smiled and remained silent.[22]

This conversation has to be seen against the background not only of Hakim's polite attempts to parry his visitor's militant – and for a newcomer, unusually pugnacious – remarks, but also the live and let live relationship that had since the inception of the modern state of Iraq in the 1920s prevailed between the Shi'i hierarchy and successive governments of very different political hues.[23] The Iraqi clergy were, of course, threatened in the same way as the Iranian by the secularisation of government and society. But historically, their position within the state was very different from that of the Iranian clergy. Iraq had in the past been part of the vast Ottoman Empire whose official creed was Sunni Islam and the ulema who resided in the holy places, many of whom were from other parts of the Shi'i world, had a very different and far more distant relationship with political authority than their Iranian counterpart. In Iran Shi'ism was the state religion and the ulema were central to society and politics. Furthermore, although the modern state of Iraq was governed by a Sunni minority – with the Shi'a and Kurds forming the majority of the population, outside the holy cities the bulk of the Shi'a population was made up of peasants. The urban social constituency that might have supported a claim on the part of the Shi'a for a greater stake in the political order simply did not exist. Against this background it is hardly surprising that Khomeini and Hakim found it extremely hard to understand one another and that al-Hakim's only major political act had been to issue a *fatwa* in 1960 forbidding the Shi'a from joining the Communist Party.

Even after Abdol Salam's bloody *coup d'état* in 1963, in which tens of thousands of people were slaughtered in the space of a week, this mutual circumspection was observed, as it was under Abdol Rahman Aref who succeeded to the presidency after his brother was killed in a helicopter crash in 1966. Only after General Ahmad Hassan al-Bakr came to power in yet another military *coup* in 1968, three years after Khomeini's arrival in Iraq, did relationships begin to sour.

The new attitude of hostility seems to have been triggered partly by the much stronger authoritarian tendencies of the Ba'th under al-Bakr, and partly by two events that followed very closely on one another. The first was the Ba'th regime's attempt to eliminate the clergy's educational autonomy in theological centres and to restrict the activities of the Da'wa Party. The Da'wa was formed in Najaf in 1958 by young clerics such as Baqer al-Sadr and Mahdi al-Hakim to revive Islamic ideas among the youth and 'to fight atheism' – probably both communism and Ba'thism. The party seems at this stage to have been a rather small affair and not to have involved the upper echelons of the religious hierarchy. As it was permitted to operate without much restriction, its influence grew among the Shi'i intellectuals and slum-dwellers of Baghdad. This worried the Ba'th regime enough to form a special department in the security services to deal with the Shi'i opposition groups and the Da'wa was forced to go underground. The second was the outbreak of a boundary dispute between Iran and Iraq in 1969.

Relationships between the two countries had swung from hostility to cooperation throughout the 1960s. But in February 1969 Iran had demanded a revision of the 1937 treaty that demarcated the boundary between the two countries along the Shatt al-Arab waterway. When the Iraqis refused, Iran unilaterally abrogated the treaty. In retaliation, Iraq began to deport Iraqis of Iranian origin or those still holding Iranian passports – which, of course, included many of the Shi'i clergy.

Although pressed, Ayatollah Hakim refused to take a public stand in defence of his government. Within weeks, in the summer of 1969 the Ba'thist regime unleashed a campaign of repression against the Shi'i clergy. A theological college in Najaf was closed, strict censorship was imposed on religious publications, for the first time in Iraqi history the sale of alcohol was permitted in the holy cities, and religious endowments were confiscated.[24] Relations between Ayatollah Hakim and the Ba'thists soon deteriorated further as the media accused him of being a foreign agent because of his support for the Iranian Shi'a. Pressure on theological centres, and arrests and maltreatment of seminarians and clerics subsequently became so frequent that Hakim left Najaf for Baghdad in protest, thus allowing himself to be neutralised by the government's tactics. He died on 2 June 1970 in a Baghdad hospital, a humiliated old man.

By this time Khomeini had shrewdly decided to stand completely aloof from both Iraqi politics and the religious politics of the holy cities. For the Iraqis, he was potentially a valuable weapon. He could, if necessary, make trouble for the Shah who for some time had been giving considerable logistical and financial support to Iraqi Kurdish separatists. Within a week of the start of the Shatt al-Arab affair, Khomeini received a visit from an Iraqi government delegation which included some security officials. He was in open meeting when the delegation arrived asking to speak to him privately. Khomeini immediately realised that they wanted to discuss relations with Iran and refused, insisting that he would not interfere in the matter and that he had nothing to say in private. 'How could you say you do not interfere while Iran has aggressed against Muslim Iraq?' they are said to have retorted. 'The least we expect from you is to denounce these actions and give your support to us as we are, like you, the enemy of the Iranian regime.' Khomeini replied in Persian, but before doing so asked for his words, which were usually roughly translated in order to avoid causing offence, to be translated directly:

First, our differences with the government of Iran are matters of principle and ideology that will not go away. Your differences are seasonal and ephemeral. Second, what has the Iranian regime done that you have not?

They have brutally suppressed people. You have also behaved as tyrants in the last few days with the Iranians. You have expelled them barbarically, even insulted the ulema, and I am told that your agents in the city of Kazemein have pulled Iranians out of bathrooms and disgracefully thrown them into cars and had them taken to the border.

The officials denied that any such action had taken place. But Khomeini continued until finally they left in a huff declaring that 'your support is not needed.'[25]

Khomeini's criticism of the Iraqi regime for expelling and maltreating people of Iranian origin was never, however, publicly stated.[26] Survival in the hostile environment of Iraq was for him the name of the game. Despite his opposition to the Ba'thist approach, he continued to receive officials whenever they came to see him. Asked by a student why he did not stand against the Iraqi regime in the same way as he had stood against the Shah, Khomeini replied: 'In Iran we were supported and helped by the people. In Iraq now we are foreign and alone. The Iraqi people are not familiar with us, nor do they have any contact with us. Cutting off contact would serve no purpose. Despite this we will not allow them to exploit these meetings and we make sure always to receive them publicly and not in private.'[27]

Despite such considerations, relations between Khomeini and the Iraqi government deteriorated. At the theological school in Najaf persecution reached such a degree that some of the students began to emigrate. Khomeini viewed this trend as a major threat to the existence of the theological centre itself. He asked the students not to leave, and had their stipends increased from two to three dinars a month, to be taken out of his own funds. He continued to raise their stipends until his last days in Najaf, when he was paying 50 Iraqi dinars to each student. This demonstrates the major increase in the amount of money Khomeini was receiving from his supporters in Iran.

Realising the tension between the Iraqi regime and Khomeini, Savak officials decided to ask him whether he would be willing to consider travelling either to Iran or Pakistan. After much discussion and consultation, however, it was decided that neither option was appropriate. Eventually, on 31 August 1969, the following telegram was sent from Savak to the Iranian embassy in Baghdad, instructing them in a curious cipher not to contact Khomeini in Najaf:

His Excellency Kayqobad [General Nassiri] has graciously decided that the return of the Saltshaker [Khomeini] to the Moon [Iran] and his departure for Banana [Pakistan] is not appropriate. It is best that he remain in the Candlestick [Iraq].[28]

Within the holy cities Khomeini seems to have made some attempt to establish a 'political presence' but to have found the Iraqi Shi'a unreceptive and to have retreated disillusioned. Najaf, like Qom and Mashhad, was a centre of intrigue and gossip at the best of times. Religio-political rivalry is as intense among the Shi'i clergy as in any political party and sometimes borders on the childish, with grand ayatollahs refusing to speak to each other. With their lines of loyalty that resemble those directed by tribal chieftains rather than spiritual elders, the great Shi'i religious centres have always looked like a confederacy of fiefdoms.

It is not surprising that, faced with the need to establish himself anew in this system, Khomeini yearned for his old seat of power. In Qom he knew everybody by name, knew their strengths and weaknesses, and could use his influence to activate them, organise them and challenge the authority of other mollahs. His tactic in Qom had been to inform the junior clergy, his former students and his supporters, of his actions, activate his network of sympathisers in the bazaar, and through pressure and encouragement ensure that the other clerics acquiesced.

This method of operating was obviously not viable in Najaf. Given the relatively peaceable relationship between the holy cities and the Iraqi government over the first five years of Khomeini's stay, his ability to move Hakim from his conservative position or the bulk of the clerical community – many of whom, in addition, did not want to upset their relationships with the Iranian establishment – was restricted.

His disappointment and his uncertainty over his own future and that of the clergy in Iran were evident in the early years. 'This old man who is spending the last moments of his life ... ' was how he introduced himself when asking young people never to give up hope and to acquire self-discipline as well as knowledge.[29] His frustration with the Najaf clergy is also evident in a remark made to a student: 'I do not know what sin I have committed to be confined to Najaf in the few remaining days of my life.'

He added:

Whatever I do I face obstacles from the mollahs of Najaf. If I stand up to the Ba'th Party, they shout that I want to uproot the Najaf theological centre! If

I remain silent, they will accuse me of collusion! If I use the language of counsel with the Ba'thists they say: 'why are not you using the same language with the Shah?' Even if I do something that is in the personal interests of these gentlemen, they will still continue to oppose and undermine me.[30]

Nevertheless, in his inimitable way Khomeini gave the Najaf clergy the benefit of his advice. It was, he announced in one sermon, their duty to introduce Islamic law, rules and codes to the educated youth by writing and talking about Islam through modern means of communications such as newspapers and the radio.

He also made an attempt to rally young seminarians. Recalling the success among the young of his lectures on ethics in Iran, he exhorted students in Najaf to pay attention to their personal ethical code instead of the wheelings and dealings of the clerical factions. 'You will have to shoulder great responsibilities in later life,' he told them:

If you become the cleric of a town, the responsibility of that town rests on your shoulders. If, God willing, you become the clerical leader of a country, you must shoulder the responsibility of that country. If you become the source of emulation for a community, you carry the responsibility of that community. That is why you should purify yourself now and strengthen your morality. If one is not purified in his youth it is difficult to change himself in old age when the spirit is weak and the forces of evil are strong.[31]

For the most part, however, he turned his attention to trends and events outside Iraq – even trying, perhaps, to cast himself as a modern-day, though much more traditional, version of the peripatetic Seyyed Jamaleddin al-Afghani. He would now, rather frequently, express his general views on the moral degeneration and political emasculation of the world of Islam, and in particular its sleepy theological centres. His thinking became more international. His brief sojourn in Turkey, and now his life in Iraq, had given him an understanding of the complexities of the Islamic world. In his sermons he targeted Muslim presidents, kings and governments with appeals to accept that Islam differed from Christianity, 'which only deals with relations between Man and God'. 'Islam,' he declared, 'has a plan for government, for life. Islam has ruled for five centuries, and it is the duty of Muslim rulers to return to it, and practise it once again.'[32] They [foreigners] will not let Egypt, Iran, Iraq and Turkey become united,' he said in another appeal for unity. 'But the duty of Muslim leaders is, while preserving their borders, to unite their thoughts ... Had they been united, who would have dreamt it possible for a bunch of Jewish thieves to take Palestine while the Islamic countries slept? How could the [British] have reached India to take our beloved Kashmir?' Realising in Najaf the value of the media, he advised: 'Islamic rulers must have a radio programme for the introduction of Islam in which the clergy can tell the truth about Islam.'[33]

Another new interest was his fast-developing relationships with Iranian student bodies abroad. Here was a window of opportunity for him in those dark days. The number of Iranians who settled, often for as much as a decade, to read for degrees in Europe and America had increased steadily throughout the 1960s, and took off in a big way from the early 1970s. As the sums of foreign exchange at the disposal of the Iranian government grew, and scholarships became more plentiful, the social background of these students also became more varied. Furthermore, free of the restraints of family and of the stifling and repressive political atmosphere in which they had grown up, politics was a major preoccupation and pastime for these young people.

Most of the student bodies were, in varying degrees, leftist. Within these groups there were debates on how far their opposition to the Shah justified promoting Khomeini. Most, however, had little idea of the detailed, for them obscure, interpretation of the role of the clergy in society that formed the basis of Khomeini's political stance. His overall political position was the main attraction. He managed to become a *cause célèbre* among young people, although their own outlook on life was light years away from his, because he had dared to confront the Shah – something the secular constitutionalists of the National Front had failed to do. In his turn Khomeini regarded these groups as no more than a chorus whose anti-Shah sentiments could be mobilised whenever the occasion demanded.

Khomeini's main attention was devoted to religious groups associated with the National Front that were based in the United States, Canada, France, Germany and Britain, and it was these groups which ensured, until the time of the 1979 Revolution, that his pronouncements were properly circulated among Iranians studying abroad. Key figures in this wing of the student opposition included a student of sociology in Paris, Abolhassan Bani Sadr, the son of an ayatollah from Hamadan, a friend of Khomeini's with whom he would sometimes stay to escape Qom's unpleasant summer; Ebrahim Yazdi, an American-educated physician with a bazaari background and strong links to Bazargan's Freedom Movement who was to become foreign minister when Mehdi Bazargan was made prime minister in 1979; Sadeq Qotbzadeh, a peripatetic student activist who was to become the first head of radio and television appointed by Khomeini and later foreign minister, and Sadeq Tabataba'i whose grandfather was one of Khomeini's teachers. Tabataba'i was the nephew of Imam Musa Sadr of Lebanon, and his sister became Khomeini's daughter-in-law.

Khomeini was extremely sensitive about keeping in touch with these students, and rumours in Iran that he once failed to receive one of their representatives brought about a swift statement of denial:

This kind of rumour may have been spread by the regime to cause anxiety among the students and create divisions between them and me. It is better if the students themselves rectify this misunderstanding, since the regime exploits these matters.[34]

Most important of all, throughout his stay in Iraq, Khomeini kept in touch with his supporters in Iran. For one thing, he was anxious that in his absence from Qom the fervour he had created amongst the seminarians there should not evaporate. In a letter to his student and friend Ayatollah Montazeri (later Khomeini's nominated successor), he expressed this concern:

I fear that in my absence, if it continues, the learned gentlemen may waver. My hope is that I might [again] be amongst the learned, virtuous clergy of Qom, who have shown their loyalty [to me], so that I might share their happiness and sadness. I would like to be among them as soon as I am free from the restrictions which have been placed on my liberty.[35]

Similar sentiments were expressed by him in a letter to Ayatollah Mara'shi Najafi, who was also in Qom.[36]

But if the Shah and Savak had hoped that a long period of exile would separate Khomeini from his constituency they were mistaken. Despite government pressure, his devotees continued to collect substantial sums in alms on his behalf. He had established channels in the Tehran bazaar through which donations were sent to him via Lebanon, Kuwait and Syria, In addition, his Pakistani, Afghan and Indian students in Najaf played a role in attracting religious alms from their own countries.

Savak documents published after the revolution indicate how deeply worried the Iranian regime was, not merely about the way Khomeini might use the funds at his disposal, but over the popularity and support they reflected. Savak's Third Bureau, headed by Nasser Moghaddam, thus began a concerted campaign to prevent money going to Najaf and issued a directive calling for Khomeini to be kept under close observation. Its agents were instructed as follows:

To detail the precise extent of Khomeini's contacts with the outside world, to delegate agents to collect information on his anti-state activities, to assess the amount of money which was sent to him and ways of preventing it from reaching its destination, to strengthen government support as well as that of his enemies, to counter his possible opposition activities, to investigate those who were strengthening him financially or otherwise, to create difficulties through Iranian networks in Iraq, to discover his contacts with foreign agents and use it as propaganda against him and, finally, to find out the names of those who were supported by him.[37]

Savak apparently tried to plant agents among Khomeini's immediate entourage. The strategy, according to members of Khomeini's inner circle at this time, failed because Khomeini kept most of his secrets to himself and dealt with all important issues personally. Nevertheless, clerical rivalry helped the Third Bureau to set up a vast network of paid clerics in Najaf to inform on him and occasionally engage in some malicious rumour-mongering.

Hakim's death in 1970 might have been the occasion for Khomeini to make his presence felt in Najaf. In religious terms Hakim had been a towering figure – the most widely followed marja' in the Shi'i world after Borujerdi. Naturally, potential successors were hoping to attract his followers. As soon as he died, the usual competition among the clergy and their followers over who would be the next marja'-e amm began. In normal circumstances Khomeini would have let the matter take its course, as he did after Borujerdi's death in 1960 when he was only 58 and well aware that there were other senior ayatollahs, including some of his own teachers, more qualified than him to assume the position. He had, while Hakim was alive, grudgingly accepted his seniority. Now there was no ayatollah he felt he could recognise as the head of the Shi'i community. The two most likely candidates were Ayatollah Kho'i in Najaf, who was well-established there as a leading teacher of principles of jurisprudence, and Ayatollah Shari'atmadari in Qom. There were also other, second line contenders in

Iran – Grand Ayatollah Ahmad Khonsari, Grand Ayatollah Golpayegani and Grand Ayatollah Mara'shi Najafi.

The Shah, who after the death of Ayatollah Borujerdi sent a telegram to Ayatollah Hakim implicitly recognising his position as *marja'*, now sent two telegrams – to Shari'atmadari and to Khonsari. Savak also took an active interest in ensuring that Khomeini would not emerge as the key figure after Hakim. Conservative mollahs, especially in Iraq, were guiding the faithful towards other *marja's* such as Kho'i. In Iraq itself, the most likely source of support for Khomeini – the young Ayatollah Mohammad Baqer Sadr, a theorist of militant Islam closely connected to the Da'wa Party, and the Da'wa party itself, gave their support to the apolitical Kho'i.

Khomeini disapproved of all these men and feared that the outcome of the competition for leadership would be a new *modus vivendi* between the senior clergy of Iran and the Shah. Indeed, both his entourage in Najaf and his supporters among the university students in Europe and North America issued separate statements accusing Shari'atmadari and Khonsari of compromise with the Shah's regime. But despite his disapproval of his two conservative rivals, and his fears for the future, Khomeini knew that any open disagreement would weaken the clergy as a whole and benefit no one. His supporters among the Iranian clergy had prepared the ground for his campaign by immediately, after Hakim's death, issuing a statement in the form of a telegram to Khomeini praising his leadership of the Islamic community. They were waiting for his decision before they continued. But Khomeini, at least on the face of it, was unwilling to go ahead. He decided to distinguish himself by his absence. It was a very difficult time for him:

He did not sleep that night. He spent his time praying and contemplating. At dawn, after he had said his prayers, he called in one of his aides and said: 'tell my friends that I do not want them to get involved, do not campaign on my behalf in the contest that will take place in the theological centres.'[38]

A week later Khomeini wrote a letter to his son Ahmad in Qom repeating the advice.[39]

Just after the painful episode of Ayatollah Hakim's humiliation at the hands of the Ba'thists, between 21 January and 8 February 1970, Khomeini delivered a series of lectures on the Islamic state in which he elaborated an idea which, less than a decade later, would begin to change the face of Iranian society. He seems to have chosen his moment with some care. He took the treatment of Hakim as yet another sign of the weakness of the Shi'i religious institution in the rapidly secularising societies of the Middle East, and the need for internal reform. It was also easier for him, with the old quiescent grand ayatollah out of the picture, to air his views more freely. A clash with the Ba'thist regime could be avoided by delivering the lectures in Persian.

Khomeini's ideas on Islamic government had emerged slowly over the years in a number of books. He had dealt with the issue of the *faqih's* rule in the context of more a general discussion of the jurist's authority in his five-volume *Ketab al-Bai'* (Book of Sale), a treatise on commercial contracts and law which he had written over fifteen years but finished and published in Najaf. He was aware of the explosive nature of the discussion and so he had left the task of providing a more popular, but at the same time more elaborate, exposition until the time was ripe.

His immediate audience for his 1970 lectures was made up of young students, many of whom had left the seminaries at Qom, Mashhad and Isfahan to work with him. But his words were meant for a much wider group: the clergy as a body and, through them, all Muslims. To reach this mass audience Khomeini simplified and popularised the doctrine on which he based his blueprint of the Islamic state: the *velayat-e faqih*, which has been variously translated into English as 'the viceregency of the theologian', 'the governance of the jurist' or 'the guardianship of the jurisconsult'. Khomeini's theory of the *velayat-e faqih* was a re-interpretation of the Shi'i doctrine that the perfect Islamic state could only be brought into being on the return of the Hidden Imam; in the meantime, responsibility for the day-to-day political affairs of the community should rest with the state. Qualified *mojtaheds*, that is learned jurists, are in some versions of the orthodox doctrine given wide-ranging jurisdiction over legal and moral affairs. But Khomeini, beginning from the premise that the Qor'an and the *sunna* contain all the law and ordinances man needs 'to attain happiness and the perfection of his state', and that law is 'actually the ruler', argues that God would not have created the law – the *shari'a* – had he not wanted to enforce it. God's will was to establish a just society on earth. That intention did not end with the disappearance of the Twelfth Imam and it had been the intention of both the Prophet himself and Imam Ali that God's law should be enforced by religious scholars, the *fuqaha*, – those most qualified to interpret the law – until the Hidden Imam returned. By discussing the absolute authority of the *faqih* in the administration of the state and the implementation of the laws of God without giving him a supernatural status of the Imam, Khomeini tried to make the whole notion more acceptable to the Muslim community as a whole. In this sense, he was attempting to offer a model of Islamic government that was acceptable to Shi'is and Sunnis alike.[40]

Using his mastery of the art of rhetoric and polemic, Khomeini began his lectures by presenting a survey of 'the hopelessness and impotence of the world of Islam'. He referred to the way Muslims, with the help of servile and corrupt rulers, had been wronged by Jews, Christians, imperialism and colonialism. Criticising the clergy for indulging in scholastic and pedantic points on topics such as menstruation and outward cleanliness, he sought to drum political consciousness into his listeners, who, he said, were to assume future responsibility for the introduction of Islamic laws and systems. He urged his audience to work towards the establishment of an Islamic state in which the clergy would assume responsibility for executive, legislative and judicial affairs. Indeed he pronounced the goal as a religious duty. Realising that he would be attacked, as on previous occasions, by the conservative clergy for mixing religion and politics, he dealt explicitly with his own predicament:

Whenever a man has risen to prominence they have killed, imprisoned or exiled him, and have tried to accuse him of being political. This mollah is political. The Prophet was a political person. This evil propaganda [the need for the clergy to remain outside politics] was spread by agents of imperialism to cause you to shun politics, to prevent you from intervening in the affairs of society, and struggling against treacherous governments and their anti-nationalistic and anti-Islamic policies. They want to do whatever they please without anybody trying to stop them.[41]

Overall, the twelve lectures on Islamic government were divided into three main topics: the necessity of Islamic government, the form of Islamic government and a programme for the establishment of Islamic government. On the necessity for an Islamic government Khomeini argued that Islamic laws are not limited with respect to time or place. They are permanent and must be enacted until the end of the time. They were not revealed merely for the time of the Prophet, only to be abandoned thereafter, with retribution and the penal code of Islam no longer to be enacted, or the taxes prescribed by Islam no longer collected, and the defence of the lands of Islam suspended.⁴² On the form of Islamic government, Khomeini writes:

Islamic government is neither tyrannical nor absolute, but constitutional. It is not constitutional in the sense that the rulers are subject to a certain set of conditions in governing and administering the country, conditions that are set forth in the Qor'an and *sunna* [traditions of the Prophet]. It can be described as the rule of divine law over men.

Khomeini goes on to clarify the last point:

The fundamental difference between Islamic government and constitutional monarchies and republics is this: whereas the representatives of the people or the monarch in such regimes engage in legislation, in Islam the legislative power and competence to establish laws belongs exclusively to God Almighty.⁴³

In the Islamic state:

… a simple planning body takes the place of the legislative assembly that is one of three branches of government. This body draws up programmes for the different ministries in the light of the ordinances of Islam and thereby determines how public service are to be provided across the country.⁴⁴

Naturally, in a system in which the people's representatives cannot legislate:

… the *faqihs*, as the trustees of the prophets' would emerge to implement the divine laws. Therefore, the role of the people is to choose the *faqihs* with the guidance of the clergy themselves.

Finally, on the programme for the establishment of Islamic government, Khomeini is at his most passionate. Long term planning, propagation, education and organisation are the key words for the struggle he proposes. He offers a survey of the Islamic countries dominated by imperialists or corrupt and incompetent rulers. But the most important target of his attack are the clerics he describes as pseudo-saints and about whom he gives some useful advice to the people:

Try to awaken them. We must say to them 'can you not see the danger? Do you not see that the Israelis are attacking, killing, and destroying and the British and Americans are helping them? You sit there watching, but you must wake up!'

And on the ulema who had joined the Shah's state apparatus:

God knows what misfortunes Islam has suffered from its inception down to the present day at the hands of these evil ulema![45] Our youth must strip them of turbans. I am not saying they should be killed; they do not deserve to be killed. But take off their turbans! They do not need to be beaten much; just remove their turbans.[46]

In his final lecture, Khomeini was very explicit about what he wanted from his students:

Act so that your deeds, conduct, character, and aversion to worldly ambition will have an uplifting effect on the people. They will imitate your model and you will become models for them and soldiers of God. Only thus can you make Islam and Islamic government known to the people.

Khomeini then summarises the implication of his lectures in four short, sharp points:

Let us overthrow tyrannical governments by (i) severing all relations with governmental institutions; (ii) refusing to cooperate with them; (iii) refraining from any action that might be construed as aiding them, and (iv) creating new judicial, financial, economic, cultural and political institutions.[47]

In *The Islamic State*, Khomeini relocated the *velayat-e faqih* from its position as a sub-chapter of jurisprudence and attached it to the principle of imamate or leadership of the community. He was, however, not merely concerned to theorise about an Islamic state led by the clergy, but to set one up. For this, committed, disciplined mollahs with high moral values were needed and Khomeini believed that it was as important to train young hearts and minds in ethics as it was to train the brain in jurisprudence. So towards the end of 1972, he followed up the political programme he had outlined with a call to his students to purify themselves in preparation for the struggle that lay ahead of them and the responsibilities that would fall on their shoulders should the struggle bear fruit. These lectures, published as *Jehad-e Akbar*, 'The Struggle against the Appetitive Soul or the Supreme Jehad', were delivered as believers prepared themselves spiritually for the Ramadan fast. Khomeini's text was a litany that is recited by the Shi'a during Sha'ban, the month that falls before Ramadan in the religious calendar. Part of this litany was particularly close to his heart and he often recited it at the end of his sermons or at the close of public meetings:

O God, grant me total separation from other-than-You and attachment to You and brighten the vision of our hearts and the light looking upon you, so they may pierce the veil of light and attain the fountainhead of magnificence, and our spirits may be suspended from the splendour of your sanctuary.[48]

In *Jehad-e Akbar* he offered a mystical interpretation of the Sha'ban litany which called believers to holiness through action. To him the litany was a bridge to God's presence: a call to defiance of the material world, to an offensive against personal desires and to a pro-active campaign for purification, decision and strength of will. He also used it to reinterpret the orthodox Shi'i view of *esmat*, the quality of infallibility. In the mainstream view *esmat* is a divine gift given only to fourteen infallible beings – the Prophet and his daughter Fatemeh and the twelve Imams who were prevented from sin by divine action. Infallibility, he told his audience, is nothing but perfect faith. He added that 'the meaning of infallibility for prophets and saints is not that their hand is held by Gabriel – [although] of course if Gabriel had held the hand of Shemr [who killed Imam Hossein] it would have been impossible for him to commit a sin.' The Infallibles, he goes on to say, having been created from pure substance, have attained presence through 'asceticism, the acquisition of illumination and their virtuous disposition.'[49]

Khomeini's purpose in dealing with the thorny issue of infallibility in *Jehad-e Akbar* was to challenge the fatalism, quietism and inaction of his fellow clergy. Many of the quietist clergy go along with the popular image of the *ma'sumin* or Infallibles – an image in which they have no human features, no will of their own and are not subject to physical human limitations such as death but are instead 'either poisoned or killed'. For Khomeini, on the other hand, infallibility is acquired by faith, certitude and action. His reading could also be seen as an attempt to lay claim to the status of an Imam, in the spiritual and political role manifested in the Prophet and Imam Ali – the only two Infallibles who were actually in charge of the Islamic order in their own time.

Both *Jehad-e Akbar* and *Velayat-e Faqih* were widely, but clandestinely distributed in Iran during the first half of the 1970s, often together. They were laboriously typed under the supervision of Khomeini's students and sent to Mecca from whence pilgrims took them to Iran on their return journey. A mini printed format of *Velayat-e Faqih*, 12 by 8 centimetres, was even produced so the book could be easily smuggled through customs, and in Iran its clandestine distribution was made easier by the use on some editions of the title 'A Letter from Imam Musavi Kashef al-Ghita'.[50] The tapes of the lectures were also distributed and over the next five years or so these played a vital role in spreading Khomeini's message throughout the traditional sectors of society, whether literate or illiterate. For many religious Iranians Khomeini's voice became a familiar, recognisable source of inspiration.

Khomeini's theory of the Islamic state attracted much praise from supporters and vigorous criticism from his opponents. His major and most dangerous critic in Najaf – and by far his most authoritative and influential critic in the Shi'i world – was the Grand Ayatollah Kho'i. Commentators have pointed to a great many flaws in Khomeini's reasoning, but the two reasons that Kho'i cited for his opposition to the theory of *velayat-e faqih* are shared by most other orthodox critics. First, Kho'i believed that the authority of *faqih* – which in mainstream Shi'i theory was limited to the guardianship of widows and orphans – could not be extended by human beings to the political sphere. Secondly, Kho'i argued that in the absence of the Hidden Imam, the authority of jurisprudents was not the preserve of one or a few *faqihs*.

Ayatollah Kho'i, who had a massive following, not only in Iraq and Lebanon, but also in Iran itself, maintained his opposition to Khomeini until the end. In December 1978, when Khomeini was actively trying to overthrow the Shah, Empress Farah visited Najaf accompanied by Saddam Hussein to plead for Kho'i's help. The Ayatollah gave her a ring as a gift for the Shah. The inscription on it read 'God's power is superior to theirs'. He believed, as he said on another occasion, that 'the Iranians have gone mad to oppose the Shah.'

Not surprisingly, Khomeini harboured a deep resentment of Kho'i. Once he had left Najaf and was no longer bound by its rules of caution, he let fly against his rival several times. He would refer to Kho'i as 'Mr Well-known' (Aqa-ye Sarshenas). On one occasion, he was told that, upon hearing of the deaths among those who joined in the street demonstrations against the Shah, Kho'i had remarked: 'it shows they are donkeys. Human beings do not stand in the street facing the machineguns.' Khomeini's sarcastic rejoinder went as follows: 'While our young people were killed in the streets he sent a ring for the health of Mohammad Reza (the Shah). These people, as Imam Ali himself has said, devote their entire attention, like animals, to their fodder, their whole life is spent filling their stomachs.'[51]

By forcing conservatives like Ayatollah Kho'i to react to his lectures, within a very short span of time Khomeini achieved, perhaps inadvertently, at least one of the goals he had in mind when he attempted to theorise the concept of an Islamic government: namely the politicisation of the clergy.

9

Waiting in the Wings
Iran Prepares for Revolution

By the time Khomeini was flown to Turkey on a cold November day in 1964 to begin his long years of exile most of the opposition forces that had taken shape in the brief years of freedom between the abdication of Reza Shah and the *coup d'etat* of 1953 were effectively silenced. The Tudeh Party, which went underground after the *coup*, had been savagely dealt with in a series of roundups between 1953 and 1958.[1] The leadership of the Second National Front had been imprisoned on the eve of the White Revolution referendum after it had called a meeting under its slogan 'reform yes, dictatorship no!' At around the same time, Mehdi Bazargan and Mahmud Taleqani, along with nine of their colleagues in the religiously-oriented Freedom Movement of Iran, were arrested and sentenced to long terms of incarceration. The National Front never recovered as an effective political organisation, despite an attempt by its student wing to mount demonstrations in support of free elections to the 21st parliament in the autumn of 1963, and a swiftly suppressed bid to form a Third National Front in the Spring of 1964. Some of the rank and file of the Freedom Movement similarly tried to keep it going, but failed in the face of the regime's pressure.[2]

Khomeini's exile did not, however, put an immediate end to his own follower's zeal. On 21 January 1965, some two months after Khomeini was flown to Turkey, Prime Minister Mansur was sprayed with bullets as he made his way to the parliament building in central Tehran. He died in hospital two days later. The killing was carried out by the Coalition of Islamic Societies, the bazaar-based organisation that had been established at Khomeini's behest during the 1963 uprising.[3] Just after his departure, and the arrest of a number of loyal clerics who continued to preach in his support, an armed wing was added to the Coalition. It was largely made up of former members of the Feda'iyan-e Islam. Apparently supported by the clerics Khomeini had nominated to guide the Coalition in his absence, who included Morteza Motahhari, Beheshti, Mowla'i and Anvari, the organisation had drawn up a long list of people it intended to assassinate, including the Shah himself, thirteen leading figures in his government – General Ayadi, his powerful special physician, former prime minister Eqbal, General Nassiri who by now was the head of Savak, eleven civil servants, and newspaper editors who had attacked the clergy and Khomeini.[4] Its first target, however, was Mansur, for whose 'execution' an edict was obtained from the most political ayatollah resident in Iran at the time, Hadi Milani of Mashhad.[5]

Mansur's assassin, Mohammad Bokhara'i, was caught and as a result of his interrogation his accomplices and many leading members of the Coalition were arrested. Four were executed, including Bokhara'i, and twelve were imprisoned. This was the biggest blow so far sustained by Khomeini's supporters, for many of those arrested – such as Hashemi Rafsanjani and Mohammad Beheshti, perhaps the two most important of Khomeini's post-revolutionary strongmen, and Morteza Motahhari, who later became an intellectual powerhouse of the Islamic movement – were people on whom Khomeini had to depend if his brand of opposition to the regime was to continue.[6]

Yet another religious group, the Islamic Nations Party, was discovered later in 1965. It had been established earlier that year by Mohammad Kazem Bojnurdi, the son of a grand ayatollah who had lived in Iraq for many years and had been influenced by pan-Islamism. Its members were idealistic, inexperienced young men to the left of the Islamic movement who had copied the organisational structure of left-wing Arab nationalist and Nasserist groups but differed from them in their emphasis on Islam and its goal of unity. Bojnurdi was, through Khomeini's movement, able to recruit dozens of people as political agitators to lead what he hoped would be the armed struggle of the peasants' uprising.[7] The authorities learnt of the group while they were training for an armed attack on specified government targets on 16 October 1965, but did not move against it until the following January, when some sixty-nine members were rounded up and interrogated. Bojnurdi was condemned to death, but under pressure from the clergy his sentence was commuted to life imprisonment. He was released at the time of the revolution and later became governor of Isfahan province and a member of the central committee of the Islamic Republican Party.

Less than four months after Mansur's killing the Shah had himself been the target of a failed assassination attempt by one of his own guard plotted by a group of left-wing intellectuals recently returned from their studies in Europe. If there had ever been a chance that after his victory over the opposition to his White Revolution he might have considered a dialogue with his opponents, these incidents persuaded him that repression was the safer course. Throughout the 1960s and until the very eve of the 1979 revolution he made no attempt – and increasingly felt no need – to establish a dialogue of any sort, even with the moderate secularists who were critical of his regime. And although elections were religiously held every four years to his rubber stamp Majles, no one, not least the Shah himself, took them seriously. The Iranian people were for a decade and a half effectively excluded from formal politics and the political system was dangerously deprived of any sort of safety valve.

Instead the cultured and intelligent General Hassan Pakravan was dismissed in 1965 as head of Savak on the grounds that he had failed to suppress the religious opposition and was replaced by the sycophantic and ruthless General Ne'matollah Nassiri. Under Nassiri, who retained his post until he was belatedly removed by the Shah in 1978 because he had become such a hate figure, Savak was provided with a huge budget and given free rein to infiltrate not only potential groups of dissenters with its agents, but every social institution. Members of the secular opposition were systematically monitored and intimidated, and in the bazaars and theological colleges there was hardly a Khomeini supporter who was not warned, summoned and very often beaten. Savak became a ruthless and brutal machine, a *cause célèbre* which ultimately served Khomeini's purposes well by creating political martyrs and functioning as a focal point for opposition to the regime.

The illusion of security created by this repressive system was reinforced in the late 1960s and the first half of the 1970s by an unprecedented economic boom. Even before the huge oil price rise that came in the aftermath of the Arab–Israeli war of 1973, the economy was developing rapidly and the state was spending more and more on the creation of a modern infrastructure – social as well as economic. From 1974, when the country's sudden fourfold increase in oil revenue enabled the Shah to press full speed ahead to what he called 'the gateway to a great civilisation', the social and economic changes already set in motion by the growth of the late 1960s quickened – for many at an unbearable pace. The frantic spending of oil revenues brought with it an uncontrolled consumer boom which in turn led to inflation, bottlenecks and shortages, what amounted to a mass exodus from the villages to the shanty towns that surrounded the major cities, huge inequalities in income distribution, and a massive influx of Westerners and Asians as well as migrants from neighbouring countries.

On the international stage too the Shah's power and prestige grew over this period – though at the price of locking Iran into an alliance with the United States that to many of his subjects appeared to be nothing less than a new form of colonialism. After 1973, Iran, already important to the country's military-industrial complex, became the most important buyer in the world of American arms. Huge sums were spent, and in the Persian Gulf the enhanced capacity of Iran's armed forces was used as a surrogate American presence. In addition to his image as an American stooge, on the regional stage the Shah's cordial relationships with Israel, which provided Savak with its advisers, and his hostility to the Palestinian cause, further undermined his legitimacy among progressive young people and the religious community.

Culturally the Shah fared no better in the eyes of the population. It was not merely a question of the bombardment of the country with Western cultural products and the spread of lifestyles which, to the large number of villagers who in these years flooded the margins of Iranian cities, seemed alien and wicked. Regime propaganda, on radio and television and in the press, was all-pervasive and increasingly cast in a rhetoric that portrayed the Shah as the successor of the glorious pre-Islamic empires of the Achaeminids and the Sassanids. Iran's Islamic heritage, and the people's religious values, appeared to be of little consequence to a political elite that was, by the early 1970s, deeply out of touch. The 'imperial ideology' the Shah's regime tried to sell lacked all substance, found few committed takers and only managed to create greater alienation.

The celebrations of the 2,500th year of the Iranian monarchy, staged in

Persepolis in October 1971, were the epitome of all that separated the Shah and the small elite surrounding him from the rest of the Iranian people. The ceremonies were financed and conducted on a grand scale – but where they were involved at all, ordinary people were used as mere props. A huge tent city was set up to house foreign heads of state at the foot of the plateau on which the ruins of Persepolis stand. It was designed in France, manufactured in the most costly materials and filled with the most luxurious furnishings, all imported. The Shah's guests ate French foods and drank French wines. The high point of the proceedings was a ceremony held at the tomb of Cyrus the Great, the founder of the Persian empire, where the Shah reassured his predecessor that he could sleep in peace 'for we are awake!'

For all the boasts that Iran had become 'an island of stability in an increasingly volatile region and world', the Persepolis celebrations took place against the backdrop of a massive security operation prompted by the sudden outbreak earlier in 1971 of urban guerilla activity in the country. In February, members of a leftist Cuban-style guerilla organisation known as the Feda'iyan-e Khalq (Warriors of the People) had taken over a gendarmerie post at the village of Siahkal in Gilan. They were quickly captured with the help of villagers and, together with other members of the organisation discovered by Savak, were executed a month later. In August of the same year, on the eve of the celebrations, the authorities, alerted by an ex-communist turned informer, rounded up sixty-nine members of a second, hitherto unknown, guerilla organisation, the Mojahedin-e Khalq-e Iran (The Holy Warriors of the Iranian People) which had planned to blow up Tehran's main power station and disrupt the festivities in the capital. Eleven of the organisation's founders and members of its central committee were executed in April and May 1972. The others were condemned to long prison sentences.[8]

Both these organisations were formed in great secrecy in the mid-1960s by small clusters of young people who reacted to the regime's suppression of conventional political activity in the wake of the 1963 uprising by preparing to take up arms. The Feda'iyan, a militantly Guevarist organisation, originated in an alliance between a group established in late 1963 by Bijan Jazani, a left wing member of the student organisation of the National Front, and a second group formed in 1967 by Mas'ud Ahmadzadeh who also came from a National Front background. The Mojahedin was established by young people previously associated with the religious wing of the National Front and, in particular, Bazargan and Taleqani's Freedom Movement. Its nucleus began to take shape in secret in 1965. Its founders, impressed by the logic of Marxism, attempted to show that the true Islam of Mohammad, Ali and Hossein was as revolutionary as Marxism without abandoning the spiritual dimension of life. Since they based their ideology on selected sources within Islam, and interpreted it to suit their claims, they soon distanced themselves from those they considered reactionary.

The Mojahedin survived the capture of their leadership. Admired at the time for their organisation, courage and determination, over the following years they were able to recruit extensively among young religious people from middle and lower middle class provincial backgrounds. They also moved increasingly to the left and in 1975 a faction of them declared that they had completely dropped Islam in favour of Marxism-Leninism, causing a major split and a considerable weakening of the organisation's political capability.

Throughout the period between 1972 and the onset of the revolutionary movement in 1978, both the Fedayi'an and the Mojahedin carried out hit-and-run guerilla operations. Impressive though these may have been in face of the might of the Shah's security apparatus, the guerilla organisations might have been no more than a thorn in the flesh of the regime were it not for the chord they struck among young people, especially the rapidly growing body of university students who, according to ideological tendency, saw in one or another of them an inspirational vanguard in the fight for justice.

By 1971 the university students were part of a growing undercurrent of cultural resistance which had begun to challenge the legitimacy of the Shah's regime. Since the establishment of secular universities in the 1930s, and at a greater speed after the Second World War, most educated Iranians – including some in key positions in the state bureaucracy and other spheres of public life – were influenced by left-wing literature. Indeed the intellectual influence of Marxism was so pervasive that even the White Revolution was presented to the public in a Marxist language by former members of the Tudeh Party who had gone over to the regime. People of this kind saw the Shah as an Eastern bloc dictator using revolutionary language to justify his drive for development. On the opposing side, dissenting poets, novelists and journalists from a variety of left-leaning political backgrounds explored the limits of censorship, using allegorical language to express their criticism. They in this way developed an exceptionally rich literature of dissent. But since they could not engage in open discourse, the normal process by which ideas are developed, criticised assimilated or rejected in a free society, and then passed on to a wider audience, was closed to them.

But the expansion of university and state secondary education had, by this time, drawn into the ranks of the educated many more people from a traditional, often provincial or lower middle class background. Many from this group were uncomfortable with the philosophical materialism of the leftists or the agnostic humanism of a considerable part of the intelligentsia's discourse. But the traditional clerical leadership did not have much to offer them either. For this reason, the religious cultural scene came to be dominated in the late 1960s and early 1970s by those Muslim writers, preachers, and activists who had attempted to arm themselves with a knowledge of Western culture and to produce a synthesis of some of its elements with Islam. Indeed, even the more traditional preachers were obliged to change their discourse in order to be taken seriously by young people bombarded daily with soap operas and crude versions of Western culture. It was not unusual to hear them quoting from the pulpit authors such as Gustave Le Bon, Maurice Maeterlinck, Thomas Carlyle and others to prove a point on Islam and the existence of God, or invoking Western writers, scholars and philosophers to refute atheist materialism.

In this process, men like Ayatollah Mahmud Taleqani, Mehdi Bazargan, Allameh Mohammad Hossein Tabataba'i, Morteza Motahhari, Mohammad Taqi Shari'ati, his son Ali Shari'ati, Mohammad Hossein Beheshti, Ali Golzadeh Ghafuri, Nasser Makarem Shirazi and Mohammad Reza Hakimi led the way in introducing new ideas to address questions posed by seminarians and university students alike. They used the modern Persian language quite different from the traditional clergy, whose wooden style was heavily influenced by old Arabic words and sentence structures. The writer Jalal Al-e Ahmad, although not exactly in this camp, also encouraged young people to join the new Islamic wave through his essays and books, which included *Gharbzadegi* (Westoxication), a polemic against the Iranian enchantment with all things Western. As a former communist and a leading dissident intellectual, Al-e Ahmad was taken by the activist young as a symbol and expression of their own frustration.

In the late 1950s and early 1960s, the efforts of Mehdi Bazargan and Mahmud Taleqani had been particularly effective in clearing away many of the anachronisms which, they argued, had attached themselves to Islam through the introversion and reaction of the orthodox religious leadership and which they feared would enhance the attraction of the Tudeh Party's materialism for the young. The two men, who had known each other since childhood and remained lifelong friends, continued in this period to exercise wide influence.

Bazargan, who was a key figure in the 1979 Revolution and became the first prime minister of the Islamic Republic, was the son of a pious merchant. Born in 1907, he was educated in modern schools; but his father ensured that he also received a good religious education. He was a clever student, and in 1928 won a scholarship to study engineering in France. After his return to Iran he became a professor of thermodynamics at Tehran University. By contrast Mahmud Taleqani, the son of a provincial clergyman who had settled in Tehran, had a conventionally religious education at the Feiziyeh seminary, which he entered in 1923 at the age of eleven. For a time he also studied in Najaf where he received an *ejazeh-ye ejtehad*. From 1939 he moved back to Tehran and there founded the Islamic Society which held discussion groups on the interpretation of the Qor'an for lay Muslims, an important innovation in those days. Bazargan published his first article, 'Religion in Europe' in the Islamic Society's journal, *Daneshamuz*.

Although their impact was limited in terms of the wider political and intellectual scene,[9] throughout the 1940s Taleqani and Bazargan actively promoted their cause in lectures – notably to the Muslim Students Association – sermons and writing, and in Taleqani's case on the radio. In 1943 Bazargan published the first of a number of books in which he attempted to show that the principles and tradition of Islam are compatible with the scientific modernism of the twentieth century. A gentle dreamer, his project sometimes led him to odd conclusions. He compared, for example, the reading of the morning papers by Westerners with the Muslim's daily prayer, a neat analogy, even if far-fetched. Taleqani began in this period to formulate the ideas on Islam and property ownership that were later to be developed in a book under the same title in which he argued that Islam properly interpreted supported a socialist system.

Like other more modern and liberal minded elements among the activist Muslims of their generation, Bazargan and Taleqani entered politics in the late 1940s as supporters of Mosaddeq's National Front. Bazargan, who until that time had dismissed politics as a childish game, was in 1951 appointed by Mosaddeq as the first chairman of the newly nationalised National Iranian Oil Company. Imprisoned for five months in 1955, in 1960 he joined with Taleqani and Dr Yadollah Sahabi to found the Freedom Movement of Iran. This landed the three men in prison several times in the 1960s and 1970s.

The Freedom Movement remained linked to the National Front until the latter was suppressed. Its programme was constitutionalist, that is it upheld the 1906 Constitution 'as an integral whole', and Mosaddeqist in that it believed that the independence of the country was vital to the creation of a democratic order.[10] But it also proclaimed the religious commitment of its members:

We are Muslims ... our entry into politics ... is prompted by our national duty and religious obligations. We do not consider religion and politics separate, and regard serving the people [as] ... an act of worship ... We are Muslims in the sense that we believed in the principles of justice, equality, sincerity, and other social and humane duties before they were proclaimed by the French Revolution and the Charter of the United Nations.[11]

The Freedom Movement's commitment to Islam as the basis of its political principles and its belief that there was no essential difference between these and the principles of the enlightenment was to bring it into sympathetic alliance with Khomeini's 1963 uprising – much to the dismay of secular segments of the National Front. This cordial relationship with Khomeini's camp was indeed maintained up to, and for a short time after, the revolution both in Iran, where many of its members felt they had much in common with the more enlightened of Khomeini's own followers, and abroad, where its student wing was carefully courted by Khomeini himself. The Freedom Movement, though never a large organisation, thus came to serve during the 1979 Revolution as a vital bridge between the secular and religious forces. But equally, the democratic beliefs of many of its leading members subsequently brought the two allies into conflict.

Another cleric who, in addition to Taleqani, became a major figure in the modernist tendency was Morteza Motahhari. Born in 1919 to a clerical family, as a young seminarian in Qom, Motahhari attended Khomeini's classes in *akhlaq* (Islamic ethics), which he described as being in reality lessons in the theoretical and practical approaches to mysticism. He later studied metaphysics with Allameh Tabataba'i as well as jurisprudence with Khomeini. He was especially attracted by philosophy, theoretical mysticism and theology. Subsequently, he himself became a well known teacher in Qom. In 1952 he moved to Tehran where, two years later, he began teaching in the Theology Faculty of Tehran University. Later he became deeply involved with the Coalition of Islamic Societies which formed the nucleus of the movement that was to eventually bring the 1979 Revolution.

In making his move out of the confines of the traditional seminary and into the very different intellectual environment of Tehran and its university, Motahhari found himself faced not only with new intellectual challenges, but also with the need to understand and come to terms with the problems of living a life in accordance with the demands of Islam in the rapidly changing Iranian urban setting. He was able to see these problems from a wide variety of social angles as a result of his numerous activities outside the university, for he also maintained contact with, and continuously increased his standing in, the more traditional religious world.

Indeed it was this traditional background which marked Motahhari off from many other Iranians who tried to forge a modern Islamic ideology. While others were often criticised by the traditionalists for mixing Islam with innovations, and for misunderstanding or even misrepresenting Islam either deliberately or through insufficient knowledge of the Islamic sciences, this charge could not be levelled against Motahhari. He was, on the other hand, often taken to task by certain radical elements in the Islamic movement who found his approach too cautious. Nevertheless, he was accorded great respect by practically all the teachers and students in the religious centres and was able to inspire readers of the many books he wrote for a lay audience as a committed and socially aware Muslim with a traditional education who could make an intellectually appropriate and exciting response to modern secularising tendencies.

Motahhari was avid in his pursuit of new ideas in philosophy and other modern sciences, and his wide-ranging scholarship is reflected in his writings, which include works on philosophy, law, theology, history and literature. But he was selective about what he accepted – agreeing with ideas and arguments from other intellectual traditions which he considered to be true and sincere, and vigorously rejecting others which were less to his taste, or which he thought were muddle-headed or purposefully deceiving.

One great advantage he had whenever he entered the polemic between secularists, traditionalists and the in-betweens was his expertise in the field of *tafsir*, the interpretation of, or commentary on, the Qor'an. No utterance seemed to be possible in this debate without an argument based in some way on a verse from the Qor'an. Communists would try to show that the Qor'an was the first manifesto, others that Islam and socialism were synonymous and that Islam was a truly revolutionary ideology in the sense that it worked through the masses. Not only were such manifestly political claims made from all sides, but others, in a somewhat older tradition, tried to show that the Qor'an had anticipated nineteenth-century evolutionary theory, relativity, quantum mechanics, black holes and so on. In a less direct way, these too were political statements, for the clergy were threatened by scientism as much as by politicism. Both these attacks demanded a response, but few were able to give it.

The correct interpretation of the Qor'an was for this reason a constant theme in Motahhari's writings. Fortunately for his purposes, the new interpretations tended to be superficial, and it was often sufficient simply to show that they rested on an inadequate understanding of Arabic. But these demolition jobs were also intended to show that what was needed for a correct understanding of the Qor'an was not so much the ability to wield the tomes of the authorities on *tafsir* and the vast store of Shi'i traditions, as a well-trained analytic technique. Indeed Motahhari believed that the need to quote traditions to support an exegesis of the Qor'an was a leftover from the days when traditionalism held a tight grip in the Shi'i schools, and he felt very strongly that anti-rationalist tendencies were un-Islamic. In this sense he was a thinker who could be as critical of certain kinds of traditionalism as of those modernist interpretations he considered superficial.

Motahhari's most important work was *Divine Justice* in which he tackled the age-old problems of theodicy, of good and evil, and how to understand the apparent injustices of a divinely created universe. But a large part of his writing is devoted to what may broadly be called 'ideological concerns'. Here an important inspiration for him was the work of Allameh Tabataba'i, one of the leading Shi'i philosophers of his age, who had written a lengthy reply to the objections against Islamic philosophy made by Marxists and other secular intellectuals – *The Foundations of Metaphysics and the Method of Realism*. Subsequently Motahhari wrote a voluminous annotation of this work in which he expanded the more general arguments of his teacher Khomeini, pointing out specific genealogies for ideas from Western philosophy, which, while not always entirely accurate, showed a concern to explain the origins of these ideas as rational productions of the human mind under particular circumstances.[12]

Motahhari's longest book on a social issue was his *The Rational Order of the Rights of Women in Islam*, in which he argued that the concepts of equality and identity were quite distinct, and that while Islamic law was not based on an identity of rights between men and women, because men and women were biologically and hence socially different, it was based on an equality of rights. This idea of the difference between equality and identity, which he would call a philosophical distinction, and hence one which could be applied in all kinds of situations, was crucial in his understanding of the nature of society as a whole. It has since become a prime target of criticism from secular feminists.

In 1967, soon after he was released from prison, Motahhari became involved, together with a number of wealthy laymen, in the creation of a religious centre known as Hosseiniyeh Ershad. The centre had its origins in The Monthly Talks Society, a group of religious modernists, mostly linked to the Freedom Movement, which between 1960 and 1963 had organised a series of lectures at the house of Ja'far Kharrazi, a prominent bazaar merchant.[13] The aim of the lecture programme, to which Motahhari and Taleqani made the largest contribution, had been 'to shake up the religious community, to put an end to the lethargy that had characterised it and to attempt to make Islam relevant to social, economic and political problems of the day.'[14] The Centre was in practise more a focus for reform minded clergy and lay religious intellectuals than a popular draw. But three subsequently influential books resulted from its activity – its own proceedings, which covered a range of topics and were published in three volumes, Taleqani's *Islam and Ownership*, and a volume of essays entitled *A Discussion on the Marja'iyat and Clergy* to which members of the Centre, along with a wider group of intellectual clergy, made contributions.

Hosseiniyeh Ershad was a far more ambitious venture. Its backers put up very large sums to purchase a prime site of land in northern Tehran on the Shemiran road and to erect a fine building with a marble façade and a blue dome which housed a library, a mosque and a large lecture hall. They were determined that their new venture should attract the middle classes and young people who had been educated in the secular system.

The original lecture programme at Ershad largely reflected Motahhari's interests and connections. It included lay figures in the modernist movement such as Mohammad Taqi Shari'ati, Kazem Sami, Habibollah

Peiman and Fakhreddin Hejazi – but not Bazargan or Taleqani whose involvement would at the time have represented too much of a political risk[15] – as well as a handful of 'intellectual' clerics, many of whom later played a prominent role in the institution. However, far and away the most popular speaker at Ershard was Ali Shari'ati, who began lecturing there in 1969 and continued until the centre was closed down by Savak in 1972. Although he was recruited by Motahhari himself, who was at first greatly impressed by the young man's abilities, Shari'ati's stupendous success led eventually to Motahhari's withdrawal from the institution – by some accounts because he came to envy the younger man, by others because he could not accept the militant and anti-clerical interpretation of Islam Shari'ati developed in the course of his lectures.[16]

Ali Shari'ati's background differed sharply from that of Motahhari, and he was a very different thinker. His father Mohammad Taqi was a cleric, but of an unconventional sort who put aside his turban for an independent intellectual life. He taught in state schools in Khorasan and ran his own religious discussion groups in which the ideas of modern thinkers, Iranian, Arab and European, were discussed. An ardent supporter of Mosaddeq's National Front, Mohammad Taqi spent much of his adult life campaigning for a progressive Islam, which could meet the demands of the modern world and offer an alternative to the seductive materialism of the Tudeh Party.[17]

Ali, who was born and brought up in the environment created by his father's activities, at first became a teacher in a small school on the outskirts of Mashhad. During this time – the early 1950s – he translated a book on Abu Zarr by an Egyptian novelist. Abu Zarr, a companion of Imam Ali famous for his opposition to the opulence of the early caliphs and his isolated life of utter simplicity, had became a role model among Islamic socialists and the work Shari'ati translated made the claim that he had been the world's first socialist. The young Shari'ati also became a member of a small political grouping known initially as the Movement of God-Worshipping Socialists and later as The League for the Freedom of the Iranian People. The group, which maintained that Islam's social and economic doctrines were those of scientific socialism based on monotheism,[18] became part of the Mosaddeq's National Front, and during the movement to nationalise oil Ali was deeply involved in its activities.

In 1955, Shari'ati began to study Persian literature at the University of Mashhad and in 1959 he went to Paris on a government scholarship to work for a doctorate. This was the time of the Algerian Revolution, and he became immersed in Third World politics, publishing and contributing to dissident Persian periodicals for which translated short pieces by Sartre, Fanon and Che Guevara, studied with two of the leading figures of French Orientalism, Louis Massignon[19] and Henry Corbin, and attended courses taught by the eminent sociologist George Gurvitch.[20] After he returned to Iran, Shari'ati taught for a short time at Mashhad University before moving to Ershad as, in effect, its speaker in residence.

Shari'ati's approach to relating Islam to modern politics was totally different from either Khomeini's, or Motahhari's. While Khomeini was trying to stimulate the quietist ulema and the theology students of Qom and other cities by reviving the potential of traditional Islam, Shari'ati was persuading the university students and the modern educated active opposition to enlist in his radical version of the religion. In his main book, *Eslamshenasi*, published in 1969, he argued that Islam in its original form was a prescription for an egalitarian and democratic society, that historically monarchs on the one hand and the clergy of institutionalised Shi'ism on the other had created a false version of the religion that obstructed people's right to know and to pursue the perfect society it prescribed, and that it was the duty of the true Muslim to oppose both these authorities.

Shari'ati was a mesmerising speaker whose fusion of Islam and various elements of Western thought, especially Marxism, and whose insistence on the religion's revolutionary and liberating potential struck a deep chord among young idealists. Ershad's large lecture hall was frequently unable to accommodate the audiences that flocked to listen him, and loud speakers had to be set up so that people left in the courtyard – and even on the pavement – could hear his lectures.[21] His books, mostly transcripts of these and lectures he had delivered at the University of Mashhad, sold in untold quantities – more, it is said, than any other works in the history of Iranian publishing.[22] Shari'ati's magnetic polemic, delivered in razor sharp thrusts against the iniquities of the time, served to galvanise an increasingly educated youth whose social origins lay in the bazaari and lower middle classes. While their parents looked to the Khomeini generation of clerics, or people like Bazargan and Motahhari, for inspiration and emulation, the young followed the Hosseiniyeh discourses.

Ershad was closed down by the security forces in November 1972, about eighteen months after Shari'ati had begun his lectures. The authorities had suddenly, it seems, recognised his impact and they were even more concerned because the institution had become a fertile recruiting ground for the Mojahedin-e Khalq. Shari'ati had little or no contact with the organisation and was not their ideologue; but the regime believed that this was the case. Shari'ati himself was forced into hiding and finally surrendered to Savak in the Autumn of 1973 after his aged father and his brother-in-law were taken into custody. He was released from prison in March 1975 and two years later left Iran to live in exile in England where he died of a sudden heart attack soon after his arrival.

In spite of this culture of dissent, and the intermittent guerrilla activity, until the middle of the 1970s the Shah was in a very strong position. In March 1975, however, he made a major blunder, as he admitted later, by establishing an all-embracing one-party system in the country. His so-called 'two party democracy' with its 'loyal' opposition had served little purpose. It was neither an outlet for dissent nor a vehicle through which loyalty to the regime could be encouraged. The Shah's new party, the Rastakhiz or Resurgence Party, was meant to mobilise the population to give the regime a political base. 'My aim,' said the Shah, 'was to enable all social and industrial groups to express their views and constructive criticisms with freedom – but unfortunately this experiment failed.'[23]

The Rastakhiz project did not just fail, but played an important part in destabilising the political system. For one thing, the Shah demanded that the whole adult population should join the party. If an individual did not want to join, he or she could, said the Shah, leave the country. In the end, the Shah's order was not systematically pursued and there was only one 'official' case of 'voluntary exile', of someone who – according to the government press, which ran pictures of a middle-aged man with a decidedly down-and-out look about him receiving his passport from suitably disapproving officials – had chosen to emigrate to the Soviet Union. Nevertheless, in the weeks that followed the fanfare of the Rastakhiz inauguration, people came to believe that, whatever their feelings for the regime, they needed to register in order to secure their future. Such pressure threatened to undermine the one safety-valve the state, inadvertently perhaps, had in place: the tacit understanding that, as long as they did not actively challenge the status quo, people's professional and personal life would be secure. Neither Mohammad Reza Shah himself, nor his father before him, had ever demanded that citizens should demonstrate loyalty and commitment of the kind usually associated with twentieth-century totalitarian states. Secondly, in 1976 party officials, wanting to make their mark, enthusiastically took up the Shah's declaration of war on profiteers which was launched in a cack-handed attempt to deal with the spiralling inflation which by that time gripped the economy. The business community, from the humblest of shopkeepers to wealthy traditional bazaar merchants and leading industrialists, became the target of a campaign against 'over-pricing' (geranforushi). Many were briefly imprisoned and sent home with shaven heads, many more were fined and some were consigned to jail for longer periods. Finally, the rhetoric of Rastakhiz and its attempts to develop an explicit 'ideology' to underpin the Shah's rule did much to intensify the sense, especially among the religious community, of a creeping cultural fascism. A particularly provocative move was the Shah's decision in the same year that the Islamic calendar did not really reflect Iran's state of civilisation. Overnight, he changed the calendar, which although solar (the Islamic calendar is lunar) counted the years from the hejra, the Prophet's flight from Mecca to Medina, to a new one based on the establishment of the Persian Empire by Cyrus the Great which brought the year from 1355 to 2535.

From his place of exile in Najaf Khomeini responded to the advent of Rastakhiz with a long fatwa. The creation of the party, he said, was the Shah's admission of the failure of his 'White Revolution' or, as Khomeini put it, 'his damned black revolution'.[24] The party was opposed to Islam, the constitution and international norms and to join it was forbidden.[25] He produced another follow up statement three months later on 7 June, the twelfth anniversary of the 15 Khordad uprising[26] and a third just over a year later in September 1976, in which he forbade the faithful from using the 'imperial' calendar.[27]

This little spate of fatwas was unusual because throughout the ferment of the 1970s Khomeini had addressed very few statements to his followers, or to the general public in Iran. Indeed to most people, especially those too young to remember the events of 1962, although he was often invoked as a symbol of opposition to the Shah, he had become a distant figure whose politics were dimly understood, even by the more religiously inclined. Nor did he himself have any time at all for the political currents that attracted this group – those versions of Islamic modernism represented by the Mojahedin, Shari'ati, or even Taleqani. He had, as early as 1968 when 'left' Islamic ideas were first beginning to take hold in Iran, declared them 'corrupting'.[28] For the most part, however, in the years before the revolution he upheld a discrete silence on the issue, making his views clear to limited individuals and circles, and yet managing to maintain the general impression that he could be a figurehead for all forms of Islamic radicalism.

Khomeini's dealings with the Mojahedin-e Khalq provide an eloquent illustration of this posture. In their early years, the Mojahedin openly admired him: 'The person of the Ayatollah,' said one of the organisation's pamphlets, 'is the symbolic figure of the people's epic. He is no longer an unknown religious leader. He is a famous hero and the symbol of the Iranian struggle.'[29] Furthermore, the Mojahedin shared their most important social constituency with Khomeini, drawing material support from the bazaar and their personnel from families who, if not always bazaari, shared its culture. Even some of Khomeini's clerical supporters, notably Hashemi Rafsanjani and Mahmud Do'a'i, were at one stage or another Mojahedin sympathisers.

Khomeini never attacked the organisation in public although he was careful to maintain his distance from it. Early in 1972, at the time when the captured leadership of the group was on trial, with the help of Do'a'i, who was at the time serving as Khomeini's aide, members of the organisation visited him in Najaf hoping to win his support. Over seven interviews, each lasting for an hour, Khomeini cross-questioned them about their beliefs. According to an account of these meetings published much later – towards the end of 1980 – by the Mojahedin participants, the two sides found that they had almost nothing in common. Khomeini was vehement in his condemnation of the Mojahedin's anti-clericalism, even their denunciation of the apolitical and pro-regime clergy who were so often a target of his own polemic, demanding that they withdraw such attacks from their books.[30] He was also, he told them, against armed struggle: 'You believe in armed struggle,' says an account of this meeting written by a member of Khomeini's camp, '[but] I do not believe in armed struggle. The time is not right and it will not succeed.'[31] The regime, Khomeini added, would only fall when the clergy as a whole joined the opposition.[32] He refused the request for political support but gave permission for the families of Mojahedin political prisoners to be helped from his funds.[33] A second meeting with Mojahedin representatives in 1974 seems to have ended in the same fashion.[34]

Khomeini adopted a similar, but somewhat less wary, approach to the

work and influence of Ali Shari'ati. Shari'ati's biographer cites evidence
that around 1970, and again in 1972, Khomeini was approached by clerics
who wanted to elicit a condemnation of Shari'ati's writings. But on both
occasions he refused to be drawn into the fray and responded that they
were not unIslamic. On the second occasion he added that he was not
about to approve Shari'ati's works, but that Shari'ati had many supporters
and that he was 'doing a service'.[35] In early 1977 his attitude was still distant
but ostensibly tolerant: 'I have read Shari'ati's books,' he said to an aide.
'He should not have said what he did. It is too early. I have sent him a
message telling him that it is not now the right time for these things.'[36] A
little later, after Shari'ati's sudden death, Khomeini was visited by Ebrahim Yazdi of the North American Islamic Students Association. Yazdi
wanted Khomeini to respond to a letter of condolence from the Association and to endorse the students' feelings by describing their hero as a
martyr. Khomeini, however, refused and wrote a brief letter that merely
acknowledged the 'loss' of Dr Shari'ati.[37] Deeply upset, Yazdi left Najaf
without the reply. His action prompted a gentle rebuke: 'I have a message
for Dr Yazdi,' Khomeini said to an aide who was on his way to Beirut to
attend a fortieth day mourning ceremony for Shari'ati. 'He may be there.'
Then, in a friendly tone, he added that if the aide did see Yazdi he should
say 'why did he get so angry and leave my message on Shari'ati's death
behind? Have I not got the right to my own views? Tell him he can add
any other word to my message. But he cannot use that word [i.e. martyr].'[38]

Soon after this incident, however, Khomeini received a detailed letter
from Motahhari voicing his concern about ideological trends in the student community which prompted him to shift to an openly hostile position. In his letter, Motahhari reflected on the influence exercised by the
combination of Shari'ati, the Mojahedin and Marxist groups in the universities of Iran and even among seminarians, some of whom were very
close to Khomeini himself:

Marxist ideas are making an inroad onto the Islamic thinking. The Mojahedin are becoming a sect of their own and deny the authority of the clergy, yet
some of our friends defend them. I have always criticised the clergy. But I
believe we should reform and keep it. All these groups have joined hand in
criticising the clergy. You should make sure that some members of your office are not undermining the clergy. The pro-Shari'ati groups are trying to
turn him into an idol. Shari'ati's least sin was his attempt to undermine and

defame the clergy among the people.[39]

At this Khomeini, demonstrating extraordinary confidence in Motahhari's advice and analysis of the complex religious, political and social scene in Iran, responded unambiguously: 'I despise these treacherous grouplets, whether communist or Marxist, or deviant from the Shi'i faith under whatever name or title, and I consider them traitors to the country, to Islam and Shi'ism.'[40]

Khomeini's own network had a much lower public profile than the modernists. But the group of clerics and students who were closest to him during the 1963 uprising and the Coalition of Islamic Societies proved remarkably loyal. They remained in close touch with him and managed to maintain their activities, both under and above ground, despite the repression suffered by other political groups.

One of the principle means by which they survived, and even flourished, during these years was through the creation of private Islamic primary and secondary schools for boys and girls. This strategy had been decided upon by the Coalition of Islamic Societies after the arrest in 1966 of its political and military wing and was managed on behalf of the Coalition by Mohammad Javad Bahonar, Mohammad Ali Raja'i and Jalaleddin Farsi.[41] The schools founded by Coalition members – as well as others that were independently owned and run by modernists such as Bazargan – taught the same curriculum as those in the state system but placed great emphasis on religious education. The government regarded them, as well as the charitable associations and religious discussion groups that flourished alongside them, as a harmless way to channel religious activity and as a way of countering the influence of the seemingly far more dangerous Marxist and leftist influence of the secular-oriented intelligentsia on the young. They were therefore very largely left alone.

Yet they were a subversive influence and in the 1970s they became part of the cultural struggle against the Shah and gradually and methodically challenged the authority of his regime. Whatever propaganda the Shah's officials produced to portray the superhuman qualities of 'His Majesty the Shadow of God', the religious schools more than matched it. Instead of the celebrations held at the state schools on the Shah's birthday, the religious schools celebrated the birthday of the twelfth Shi'i Imam by unfolding massive banners congratulating the Islamic people on the birthday of 'His Majesty the Guardian of the Age'. And their pupils were taught that 'Her Majesty' was Fatemeh, the daughter of the prophet Mohammad and the wife of the first Shi'i Imam Ali, not the Empress Farah.

Another tactic was to rewrite Islamic history. Clerics, including Bahonar, Mohammad Beheshti, and Ali Golzadeh-Ghafuri, were employed by Ministry of Education to write religious textbooks for the schools and would turn them into works of Islamic indoctrination. In one of these books, for example, Bahonar and Golzadeh-Ghafuri provided a blueprint for the creation of an Islamic government. 'Islamic society,' they argued, '... is not an accidental, but an intentional society ... which is neither individualistic nor communal, but a mixture of both.' They put forward views on the Islamic system which were not dissimilar to those of the post-revolutionary Islamic constitution. 'To create a just social system,' they maintained, 'the following elements are necessary: law, leadership, faith in the executive and the [religious] law, and the permanent supervision of the executive to prevent it from deviation and dictatorial tendencies.'[42]

The kind of language and culture that was promoted by the more modern wing of the militant clergy put them in an advantageous position. For as long as their projects could be defined as 'religious', 'social' or 'cultural', their activity went unimpeded by the regime and, where it concealed covert political propaganda or organisation, undiscovered. However, when the same, or similar ideas were put in a more overtly popular and political language by militant clerics of the more traditional kind, it made them vulnerable. Surveillance, arrest, torture and imprisonment were widely practised with the clergy of this kind who maintained their contacts with Khomeini, collected and helped transmit funds to him, and from time to time used the pulpit to attack state policy. Ali Khamene'i, Mahdavi Kani, Musavi Ardebili, Montazeri, and Hashemi Rafsanjani were all sentenced to spells of imprisonment or internal exile in the early 1970s. Two members of this relatively small, but in terms of later developments in the period of the revolution, significant group who died, possibly under torture, in prison were Hossein Ghaffari on 27 December 1974 and Gholam Reza Sa'idi on 10 June 1970.

Throughout the 1970s Khomeini's most trusted link to this group and to his followers in the bazaar was Morteza Motahhari.[43] Khomeini had appointed Motahhari as his representative in 1968 in a *fatwa* that read as follows: 'Motahhari is authorised to collect the sacred *sahm-e Imam* and to spend half of it on the advancement and consolidation of religion and to send the other half to me in order to spend on theological centres.'[44] Since

Montazeri and the other more senior clerics in his circle were often in prison or internal exile, Khomeini had, as time went by, gradually delegated most of his affairs to Motahhari[45] who over the years had paid several visits to Najaf. His final trip in 1976 was crucial.

The previous year had seen some revival of political activity both above and underground. In June 1975, on the twelfth anniversary of Khomeini's 1963 uprising, pro-Khomeini groups had surprised the security forces and staged a major demonstration in Qom which the local police could not cope with. Paramilitary forces had to be brought in leading, according to a denunciation issued by Khomeini, to forty-five deaths and 300 arrests.[46] In addition, the split in the Mojahedin-e Khalq was beginning – despite Khomeini's apparent opposition to armed struggle – to spawn a number of guerilla organisations whose membership was drawn from more traditionalist quarters and which were able to attract some of the bazaar money that had previously gone to the Mojahedin. These groups were closely connected to and assisted by the Coalition of Islamic Societies. Indeed the Coalition claims that from 1970 it had begun preparations to take up arms under the supervision of Andarzgu, a bazaari who assumed many names and remained on the run for many years until he was shot dead in the streets of Tehran in 1978, Sadeq Eslami, Mohammad Ali Raja'i and Mohsen Rafiqdust.[47] Some of these groups received training in guerilla camps set up by Amal and the PLO in Lebanon, and after the 1979 Revolution seven of them emerged from the shadows to form an organisation known as the Mojahedin of the Islamic Revolution (Omir).

These developments had lead to wide-ranging discussions in Khomeini's camp on how to unite all militant clerics and all Muslim activists in a country-wide organisation. The discussions involved Beheshti and Bahonar, who travelled to Mashhad to deliberate with Khamene'i, Va'ez-e Tabasi and Hashemi-Nejad. Other clerical participants had been Meshkini, Jannati, Hojjati Kermani, Movahhedi Kermani, Taheri Khorramabadi, Rabbani Amlashi, Emami Kashani and Musavi Kho'iniha. Montazeri and Rafsanjani were also secretly contacted in their prison cells and their opinion sought. The lay activists involved included Hassan Ayat, Asgar Owladi, Mehdi Araqi, Sadeq Eslami and Andarzgu.

Motahhari, whose purpose in his trip was to inform the ayatollah of these discussions, returned from Najaf with messages giving his go-ahead for the formation of an organisation that later came to be known as the Society of Militant Clergy.[48] 'The roots of this perverse tree are rotten.'

Khomeini declared, 'We have to cut them off with collective action.'[49] Khomeini's permission was also obtained at this point to spend religious revenues for 'the printing and publication of political-Islamic books which expresses the Islamic truth and the opinions of the grand religious authorities on opposing and fighting the tyrants, colonialists; and for enlightening people and bringing about an Islamic intellectual revolution'.[50]

Motahhari was put in charge of the newly revived movement, thus becoming, as Ali Khamene'i put it, 'one of the architects of the Islamic system.'[51] His principle lieutenants were Beheshti, Bahonar, Mofattah and, of course, the Coalition of Islamic Societies' activists. Communications improved and old networks throughout Iran revived. By 1977, in Tehran alone, the association had formed eight branches which set up bases in local mosques to organise debates, distribute leaflets, recruit local youth, organise strikes, distribute Khomeini's tapes and statements, supervise demonstrations and provide their localities with food and fuel during the hard winter days of the revolution. These groups formed the basis of what later became the revolutionary committees.

10

Khomeini in Paris
The End of an Empire

By the time Jimmy Carter took office as President of the United States in January 1977, deteriorating domestic conditions in Iran had given new life to dissidents of every hue. Now Iranians kept their ears carefully cocked to developments in the America. They watched political changes there with hope or anxiety depending on their attitude to the Shah. They knew that Republican administrations were generally less critical of his autocratic rule, while Democratic presidents were inclined to press for reform. The Republican administration of 1952 helped to overthrow Mosaddeq, while President Kennedy was seen as the influence behind the Shah's decision to make the reformist, Ali Amini, prime minister in 1961. Even Khomeini's son Ahmad, displaying the typical Iranian trait of looking for external causes of internal developments, thought it significant that his father was sent into exile on the night Lyndon Johnson became President of the United States. The advent of Jimmy Carter thus raised expectations among Iranians that with him in office there would be change.

The Carter administration indeed appeared to be making human rights issues a cornerstone of its foreign policy. It had set up an Office for Human Rights in the State Department and very early on in 1977 Cyrus Vance, the Secretary of State, had politely reminded the Shah that human rights played an important role in Carter's policy. It was only a reminder.[1] Nevertheless, whether as a result of American pressure, or because it seemed to offer a way of calming domestic unrest, the Shah began to speak of liberalisation and even, slowly, to release political prisoners. Remembering how Kennedy's administration had forced various reforms in 1962, some leaders of the pre-1965 Mosaddeqist opposition calculated that the Carter Administration would stand by them. In June they sent an open letter to the Shah calling upon him to 'observe the principles of the constitution and of the Universal Declaration of Human Rights, abolish the one-party system, allow freedom of the press and freedom of association, release all political prisoners, allow the return of political exiles and establish a government based on the representation of the majority.' The letter was drafted by Mehdi Bazargan, but a dispute between the Freedom Movement and the secular leaders of the National Front over whether it should bear the signature of 'personalities' alone or include other, less prominent, activists meant that in the end it was signed only by the secularists: Shahpur Bakhtiar, Karim Sanjabi and Dariush Foruhar.[2] Bazargan, a humble and rather shrewd man, was side-lined.

The Shah simply ignored the letter. Instead of responding to such demands by considering the creation of channels through which voices of moderation could be properly represented he opted for a cosmetic change: on 7 August he replaced his long-serving prime minister Amir Abbas Hoveida with an apparently more energetic man, Jamshid Amuzegar the general-secretary of the Rastakhiz Party. No one for a moment believed that the appointment would solve anything – especially in view of the fact that, for all the talk of liberalisation, Ayatollah Taleqani had a week or two earlier been arrested on charges of subversion.

All the same the change represented the first crack in the solid wall of 'stability' and continuity in the Pahlavi regime and further encouraged the dissenters. Throughout the summer the National Front, the Freedom Movement, members of the writers' and lawyers' associations and intellectuals of all persuasions had been getting bolder, sending more open letters to the Shah and the prime minister decrying the absence of constitutional and civil liberties and forming committees for the defence of these principles. The Writers' Association now took a bolder step, gathering for a series of a poetry reading nights at the Goethe Institute put on by courtesy of the sympathetic German cultural attaché. On the last night of the readings, armed soldiers waited outside in the heavy rain while writers and poets of all kinds spoke of 'dark nights of suppression' and voiced political criticism of a kind that had not been heard in public for many years. They left unhindered by the wet, and no doubt deeply bemused, soldiers who had been ordered not to use force unless violence broke out. The readings were thus repeated although the second series, held at the Arya Mehr Industrial University, was persecuted and harassed by Savak.

Khomeini, watching from abroad, began to feel that some kind of social revolution had started in Iran and knew that, despite these secular beginnings, religion could play an important role in it. He delivered a sermon in which he emphasised the balance needed between this and the other world, quoting a *hadith* in which the Prophet had said: 'My brother Moses was blind in the right eye [he was so worldly], and my brother Jesus was blind in the left eye [he was other-worldly], but I [Mohammad] have two eyes [I combine both the spiritual and the material world].'[3] Khomeini also believed, like other members of the opposition, that the Americans were planning to do something about the Shah's regime. 'We are now waiting to see whether the present American government is sacrificing its honour and that of the American people,' he said, 'to material interest in exploiting Iran, or by taking its support away from these dirty elements [the Pahlavi regime] to regain honour and integrity for its government.'

Soon afterwards, on Sunday 23 October 1977, Khomeini's elder son Mostafa died quite suddenly – and, or so people were led to believe, in mysterious circumstances. Several weeks earlier, while on a visit to Syria and Lebanon, Mostafa had been contacted by two visitors from Iran. They discussed recent events with him and arranged to meet him in Najaf, to which Mostafa soon returned. There, at about ten o'clock one night, a friend informed him that he had guests. Nobody was to see these 'guests' again. The next day Mostafa was found dead, apparently of a heart attack. When Khomeini was told the news of his son's death he simply repeated a Qor'anic verse: 'We belong to God and to him we shall return.'[4]

The event gave Khomeini media prominence once more, exactly thirteen years after the start of his exile. When the news reached Qom the same day, people flocked to offer their condolences to his brother Morteza Pasandideh and the rest of the family. Loudspeakers in Qom began to broadcast Qor'anic verses and commemorative services were hastily arranged. On 26 October, a large notice was printed in the newspapers in which anyone who wished was invited to a major service at a central Tehran

mosque, the Masjed-e Ark. The organisers, Morteza Motahhari and Mohammad Reza Mahdavi Kani, succeeded in persuading both religious and
secular groups to attend the event at which, after a long period of taboo,
praise for Khomeini was freely voiced. Supporters went a step further,
calling Mostafa a 'martyr' who had been murdered by Savak. Responding
to telegrams and letters of condolence, Khomeini took the opportunity to
depersonalise and widen the issue. In a message of thanks to the Iranian
people, he said: 'We are facing a great calamity and should not mention
personal tragedies.' He warned them to stay united and 'not to be fooled
by the recent relaxation of press censorship ... The aim of this apparent
relaxation is to cleanse the Shah of his crimes.'[5]

Khomeini's name was once again mentioned in services, and demonstrations took place in Qom in his support, calling for his return. He referred to the death of his son as 'God's hidden providence', and did not
hesitate to exploit the incident to support his anti-Shah campaign. His
camp was by this time reactivating and openly expanding its network which
internally covered a variety of institutions, offices, and urban and rural
centres and externally extended to Iraq, Syria, Lebanon, Kuwait and into
sectors of the Iranian students' movements in Western countries.

As the Shah prepared for a state visit to America on 15 November, the
whole spectrum of opposition to his rule had slowly emerged from its
long hibernation and was making ready to use the occasion to ensure that
the whole world would be briefed on the monarch's violations of human
rights and civil liberties. Noisy demonstrations outside the White House,
organised by the Confederation of Iranian Students, reflected the views
of many Iranians in the United States, while the picture on Iranian television of the Shah crying from the tear-gas spilling on the White House
lawns further tarnished his image at home. Simultaneously, in Tehran and
other cities, students held demonstrations demanding that the Shah 'put
President Carter's human rights programme into effect immediately.' These
demonstrations on the whole passed off peacefully with few arrests. But
just after the Shah's return, on 22 November, a meeting of about 1,000
National Front supporters, held in a garden just outside Tehran owned by
a veteren member of the Front, met a far more vicious response. The meeting was convened to discuss the formation of a united anti-government
coalition, but within minutes of its opening it was broken up by Savak
thugs who beat up and injured many of the participants. The Shah could,
if the eyes of the world were on him, just about tolerate talk – but not the

prospect of even peaceful organised opposition.

The impact of this incident on secular dissenters was compounded by the implicit rebuff delivered by President Carter on a New Year's Eve visit to Tehran. A month earlier, on 27 November, twenty-nine opposition personalities had declared the establishment of an Iranian Committee for the Defence of Freedom and Human Rights had written to the United Nations asking for its help to establish freedom and democracy and copied their statement to the President. But at the state reception organised for the occasion, the Shah and Carter toasted each other with champagne – in front of cameras that were broadcasting the proceedings live to the nation – and Carter declared his 'close personal friendship' for the Shah, describing Iran as 'an island of stability ... a great tribute to the respect, admiration and love of your people for you.'[6]

As Carter spoke these words, the incident that was to trigger the great popular upsurge that would sweep the Shah aside and give Khomeini decisive leadership of the revolution was just days away. Somehow believing that the huge social and cultural changes that had occurred in Iran since the early 1960s meant that it could safely attack the outdated obscurantism of the Khomeinists, on 6 January 1978 the Ministry of Court published an article, apparently approved by the Shah, in the afternoon daily Ettela'at under the title 'Black and Red Imperialism.' Written under the pseudonym Ahmad Rashidi-Motlaq, the article was part fact and part opinion, but above all it was full of personal insults against Khomeini. As soon as the newspaper reached Qom, people rushed into the streets to demonstrate. The next day lectures at the Qom seminary were cancelled. Demonstrators began to shout 'Long live Khomeini!' and 'Death to Pahlavi Rule!' By singling out Khomeini, the regime had forced the other ayatollahs in Qom, Shari'atmadari, Golpayegani and Mara'shi Najafi, to come out in strong condemnation of the article. In a meeting addressing the protesters Golpayegani did not mince his words: 'They are lying when they claim that we agree with their policies.' Shari'atmadari was as usual milder, but even he declared: 'What you are doing is sacred, as you are defending the position of the religious leadership and the clergy.'[7]

In a clash with the security forces in Qom, at least six demonstrators were killed. The deaths unleashed powerful emotions. Khomeini issued another strongly worded statement in which he reviewed the past fifty years of the Pahlavi monarchy, putting more pressure on moderates such as Shari'atmadari by declaring that: 'Only false clerics can agree with the

Shah.' This episode was a godsend for those who wanted to raise the political temperature: the Shah had inadvertently come to their aid. An unstoppable chain reaction began, based on the Muslim cycle of mourning on the seventh and fortieth day after a death. Tabriz was the next city to witness disturbances on the fortieth day after the Qom killing and there were further deaths. Then it was the turn of Yazd to rise on the fortieth day of the Tabriz shootings. The Shah was, as usual, compared with the hated Yazid. Khomeini was encouraged. In an interview with *Le Monde*, he took the opposition inside Iran by surprise by declaring that the Pahlavi dynasty must be overthrown, adding that the ideal would be the establishment of an Islamic state.[8]

Throughout the early part of 1978, the Shah vacillated between concessions and crack-downs, but whatever the Shah did, Khomeini, now pursuing maximalist goals, capitalised on it. In an attempt to stay the flood of protest, several former ministers and even some high ranking Savak officials were accused of corruption and violence and became victims of an imperial purge which demoralised the security forces. When in August a fire in a cinema in Abadan led to the deaths of 477 people, the regime and the opposition blamed each other. But people were by this time only prepared to believe accounts that held the regime responsible and panic reigned. It was now Prime Minister Amuzegar's turn to be jettisoned.

The Shah appointed Ja'far Sharif Emami as the next prime minister. Sharif Emami had served as speaker of the Senate and head of the Pahlavi Foundation and he was the only elder statesman the Shah trusted to come to his rescue. He had been prime minister once before in the late 1950s and early 1960s when he had been unable to act independently. But this time he had far more authority, and because he came from a clerical background it was thought that he could appeal to the moderate religious leaders for help. But although in principle willing, the moderates were afraid of Khomeini and his supporters who by this time had the upper hand. Khomeini's headquarters in Najaf were regularly distributing his messages, usually recorded on tape cassettes, while the Coalition of Islamic Societies was active once again under the leadership of Motahhari and Beheshti. Sharif Emami began to reverse some of the Shah's policies, beginning by closing the casinos which belonged to the wealthy Pahlavi Foundation, abolishing the 'imperial' calendar and declaring that, in accordance with the constitution, all political parties had a right to be active. These measures were, however, too little too late and the bloodshed continued.

On 6 September, on the festival ending the Ramadan fast, thousands
of people participated in a demonstration in Tehran in which, for the first
time, activists from the Coalition of Islamic Societies added to the secularist slogan 'Liberty and Independence!' the phrase 'Islamic rule' (*hokumat-
e Islami*). At this point also Khomeini distanced himself from the left wing
and appealed to the army to join the peoples' movement.[9] A nervous Shah
decided to crack down and further marches were banned. But the demonstrations continued for two more days, attracting on 7 September an estimated half million. Despite informal warnings that severe action might
be taken against the demonstrators, on 8 September a smaller crowd gathered in the eastern part of Tehran and without prior notice martial law
was declared. A warrant was issued for the arrest of a number of secular
leaders, who were briefly detained, and soldiers were ordered to shoot on
demonstrators who had gathered in Jaleh Square. The ensuing bloodshed
earned that day the title of 'Black Friday', discredited the government and
closed off any possibility of a compromise between regime and opposition.

The political situation began to deteriorate further as – though his illness was still publicly unknown – the Shah's cancer grew worse and he
was left with no adviser to trust. As a result he began to rely heavily on the
advice of the American and British ambassadors, even at one stage asking
the advice of the Soviet ambassador! But the Americans were also in a
state of disarray. Some members of the Carter administration were in favour of a crackdown, while others wanted to accommodate the moderate
opposition. The President was as indecisive as the Shah himself. Khomeini moved a stage further in his campaign and ordered students and
seminarians to join the movement and woo the army. He also advised
them to distance themselves from those who were trying to reach a compromise with the regime.[10] He knew that if he continued to attack the
Shah directly and demand his overthrow he would be accepted as the
undisputed leader of the anti-Shah movement. In early November even
the Soviet Union, delighted by Khomeini's anti-American rhetoric,
switched its support to the opposition.

The Iranian authorities put pressure on Iraq to restrict Khomeini's activity, as he had increasingly become the main barrier to any compromise
with opposition forces. Meanwhile, the Iraqis had begun leaning on
Khomeini; but he had already decided to leave Najaf rather than tone
down his anti-Shah statements.

In the Autumn of 1978, the Kuwaiti Embassy in Baghdad was presented with a passport in the name of Ruhollah Mostafavi, who had been 'invited to Kuwait by a well known cleric'. It issued a visa without realising that the person in question was Ayatollah Khomeini, the Shah's arch enemy. However, when the Kuwaiti authorities on the border were confronted with Khomeini and his entourage, they refused to let him enter the country. Khomeini later recalled:

The Iraqi government, pressurised by the Shah, could not tolerate my activities [the goal of which was] to serve Islam and Muslims. That is why I had no choice but to leave that country and go to Kuwait. Although I had a visa for Kuwait, I was not allowed in. I was left with no choice but to go to France to ponder on which Islamic country to go to. However, during my temporary stay in France I decided that if I ever felt restricted while carrying out my duties, I would leave since it does not matter where I go as God's earth is bountiful.[11]

Accompanied by his son Ahmad, Ebrahim Yazdi who had flown from the United States to Iraq, and a few friends, the seventy-six-year-old cleric arrived in Paris on 12 October. He could not speak French, and he had little understanding of, or sympathy with, the Western way of life. Ever since his youth Khomeini had been brought up to view foreign influences as a source of malaise in the Islamic world. In his first published work, *Kashf al-Asrar*, he amplified this sentiment, but when in the 1960s Jalal Al-e Ahmad wrote his book *Westoxication*, Khomeini found new ammunition with which to attack those who had been mesmerised by Western culture, albeit a soap-opera version of it. Unfortunately, Khomeini did not have the chance to see much of the French way of life for himself. From the moment he set foot on French soil, he was never left alone. He was taken to Bani Sadr's home and immediately admirers and sycophants of all kinds began to descend upon the small fourth-floor flat in Cachan on the outskirts of Paris. The neighbours soon complained about the noise and the police passed on these complaints to Khomeini's aides. As a result a more spacious house with a garden was found for him in the nearby village of Neauphle-le-Château. Khomeini himself was not sure what to do or where to go. 'Beirut is out of the question for family reasons. What about Syria?' Khomeini asked one of his supporters. 'Is it appropriate to go there? Has it direct telephone links with Iran?' In fact, it did not.[12]

Recalling his journey to France, Khomeini told a gathering after the revolution:

When I entered Paris friends were very kind to me, including Mr Habibi, Mr Bani Sadr, Mr Qotbzadeh and Mr Yazdi. To begin with, the French government was a bit cautious. But then they were kind to us and we could publicise our views extensively, much more so than we expected, and the news concerning us and our demands was even reported by the media in America itself ... every day groups of Iranians came to see us, and this strengthened and helped to promote our objectives.[13]

The modest villa where Khomeini lived with his aides – old and new – was run like a royal court. Bani Sadr, Qotbzadeh, Yazdi, Khomeini's son-in-law Eshraqi, and Ahmad, his only remaining son, were his viziers. For Western correspondents, hundreds of whom began to gather in this tiny village, he was and remains an enigmatic figure. He was not used to small-talk, whether in Persian or in any other language, or to the formalities of introduction. Unless they were dignitaries or grand ayatollahs, the old patriarch would remain cross-legged, without getting up to greet his visitors. He was accustomed to people coming to him, kissing his hand and telling him their problems or making their requests as he listened attentively. He would then express his opinion briefly. Correspondents trained to meet their interviewee and hold a warm-up session to obtain some background before making their recording had a frustrating time. For one thing, Khomeini only accepted interviews if written questions were submitted the previous day. For another, he often refused to answer subsidiary questions, and was not pleased to redo an interview if a technical fault with broadcasting equipment made this necessary. A correspondent who went to interview him when he first arrived in Paris noted:

This tremendous presence from some remote century made no effort to welcome us, or at least me, and hardly gave us a glance. He sat on a pile of cushions in a corner of a small living room, eyes lowered, and harangued my colleague's tape recorder. There can't have been more than four or five of us in the room, I think. I saw him often later, though never in so small a group, in the departure lounge at Orly airport the night we flew back to Tehran and at prayers in Tehran. It falls to a journalist, if he or she is lucky, to see at close quarters some of the people who leave their stamp on history. Of them all, I have never met anyone who made so great an impression as this man to whom the nuances and compromises of the twentieth century were, it seemed, of as little lasting significance as the snow that fell that winter of 1978.'⁴

Opposite Khomeini's home there was another house with an open garden in the middle of which grew an apple tree. As the number of visitors and pressmen multiplied, this house was also put at Khomeini's disposal and Khomeini would often receive them sitting on a carpet under the tree. Later on, as winter approached and the number of visitors swelled even further, a tent was set up by the apple tree.

Khomeini received important people in his own villa, but would go to the tent just before mid-day to make a speech and lead the prayer. One day, when the ever-punctual Khomeini took a long time to emerge from the lavatory, his wife became increasingly worried about him. After about a quarter of an hour he appeared, sleeves rolled up and bucket in hand. His astonished wife asked him what he had been doing and rushed to help him wash himself when he calmly announced:'The people who come to use the lavatory are my guests. It is my duty to help you keep this place clean.'¹⁵

Ahmad speaks of his father's behaviour towards his family in Paris as friendly and simple, dealing with any topic in private just as he would in public.

He argued with the children, played with them, talked to them and made them laugh. Financially, he was, as always, cautious both with his own and with other people's money. In France he was showered with money, even more so than in Iraq, by wealthy Iranian merchants and rich Shi'a from various parts of the world who were newly converted to his cause. But he would monitor how much the family spent. At breakfast-time, when the table was laid on the floor, he would place himself near the samovar and serve the family.

Like most Iranians, he had the habit of taking his shoes off at the front door. On one occasion in Paris, when his shoes were wet, he would put them on something to dry them, usually a foreign newspaper. One day, someone spread an old Iranian newspaper over the threshold. Khomeini refused to leave his shoes on it, asking Tahereh Dabbagh, an Islamic activist who was staying with the family:'It seems that these papers are Iranian?''Yes, Haj Aqa,' replied Dabbagh, 'but these pages have only advertisements.'Still,' continued Khomeini, 'they may have the name of Ali or Mohammad on them.'¹⁶

It is part of popular religious belief that one should not touch, or act disrespectfully towards, the names of the Imams, the Prophet or God.

And Khomeini was greatly attached to popular religion. In Najaf, for example, he made a point of going to the shrine of Ali every night to say his prayers and supplications. One night it was very stormy and Mostafa pointed out that he could legitimately perform his prayers at home. 'Mostafa, please don't take away my simple faith,' came the reply.[17]

In Paris Khomeini imposed a gruelling routine on himself. He would go to bed at about eleven. At three in morning he was often overheard examining his papers, as he did not have time to do so during the day. He read letters and translations of foreign press reports prepared for him the previous day, then said his prayers. He would have breakfast at seven and then until nine he would deal with news from Iran. Between nine and ten he dealt with personal affairs. From ten to twelve he prayed and ate lunch and at two he took a one-hour siesta. At three he resumed dealing with the news and the affairs of the nehzat, the 'movement' (as the word 'revolution' had not yet gained currency). At five he would perform the evening prayer, and at nine he would have dinner and then listen to recordings of the day's broadcasts in Persian of foreign radio stations, particularly the BBC.

He still walked regularly, as he had done throughout his life, both inside his house and in the countryside of Neauphle-le-Château. As he was provided with permanent police protection he was never alone. One night, however, he did manage to escape their notice and walk through the village. The police soon discovered his absence and, according to one of his aides, swiftly put an end to these surreptitious outings.

A cold December day on which there were some 400 journalists waiting for Khomeini to come out of his house typifies the atmosphere that prevailed at Neauphle-le-Château during these weeks. Khomeini had only to cross the street which was about 10 metres wide, but the police had cordoned off the area and the traffic had come to a standstill. He emerged to cheers of Allahu akbar ('God is great'). Tall and elegant in his winter attire, he smiled briefly at his son-in-law, Eshraqi, and stood looking through the gate which he had to enter at the other side. He began to walk, his eyes fixed on the ground. His presence was overwhelming. He was unwilling to share his world of emotion with outsiders. Even when the group of admirers began to sing 'Khomeini, O Imam', he paid them little attention, merely smiling slightly.

Bani Sadr stood in the street with the mien of someone who took himself too seriously, occasionally exchanging a few words with inquisitive journalists. Ebrahim Yazdi, a shrewd American-educated physician who was thought to be always up to something, was taking journalists to one side and briefing them about the 'Imam's movement'. The gregarious Qotbzadeh on the other hand mingled with everybody, laughing, joking and exchanging pleasantries.

Although they came from a similar background – all were Islamic modernists and Qotbzadeh and Bani Sadr had National Front leanings – these three 'viziers' were very different personalities. Bani Sadr saw himself as an ideologue and acted like one. He would often ramble on to the press about how he had dissuaded Khomeini from establishing the 'governance of the jurisprudent', a concept that the Ayatollah nevertheless continued to cherish. Yazdi's chief concern was with organisation and to gather support from students and visiting Iranians. Qotbzadeh was simply happy to be close to Khomeini, occasionally acting like a jester in a medieval court whose job it was to make the caliph laugh.

All three were all trying to present Khomeini to the outside world as they perceived him on a personal level. When they translated his interviews for the Western press, they often softened the sharper edges to make Khomeini's words more palatable. They were also in charge of translating the Western press for Khomeini, to keep him informed of world opinion of his movement. They were essential to him in the alien environment of Paris and under the illusion that, through their linguistic skills and understanding of the West, they had him under their control. But they sometimes overstepped the mark, presenting themselves as Khomeini's sole spokesmen. Such insolence aroused the anger – and jealousy – of the people who had cared for him through his long years of exile who did not want him to be hijacked by outsiders. The resulting bickering and backbiting among his entourage was a constant source of irritation to Khomeini. In one instance, while expressing some of his particularly controversial views, he publicly announced that he had no spokesman. Someone took down his words in bold letters and pinned them up in several prominent positions in and on the buildings. 'When Yazdi saw the notice on the wall he asked me what it was. I told him he could see what it was,' a Khomeini supporter relates. 'He went away and after a few minutes the notice had gone. It was then re-written and mounted on the wall again.'[18]

People from different periods of Khomeini's long life travelled to Paris to see him. They included his close students and trusted friends such as ayatollahs Montazeri and Motahhari, who remained only briefly as they were needed more urgently in Iran to organise the movement and keep morale high. Among his supporters from the early 1960s, visitors included Mehdi Araqi, a bazaari who had been jailed for years for his involvement in the assassination of Mansur and for being a prime mover in organising the uprising in June 1963. There was also Asadollah Lajevardi, who later earned notoriety as governor of Evin prison as the revolutionary prosecutor and was assassinated in 1998. Some visitors, such as Sheikh Ali Asghar Morvarid, were Khomeini's students from Qom. Others, like Ali Akbar Mohtashami, later ambassador to Damascus and interior minister, and Hojjat al-Islam Musavi Kho'iniha, later state prosecutor, belonged to his Najaf days.

Others were Sheikh Sadeq Khalkhali, an old student of Khomeini, later nicknamed the 'hanging judge', a self-publicist with a grotesque sense of humour, and Mohammad Montazeri, Ayatollah Montazeri's son who died in an explosion in Tehran in 1981. Among the younger generation of laymen virtually every faction and tendency within the Islamic groups was represented. Ahmad Khomeini, as the non-partisan representative of his father, was friendly with all groups and was particularly close to Ali Mohammad Saduqi, whose father was a life long friend of Khomeini, and Mohammad Khatami who in 1997 became President of Iran. At the same time he was close to Yazdi, Qotbzadeh, Sadeq Tabataba'i, Ahmad's brother-in-law, and Hassan Habibi who prepared the first draft of the constitution and later became minister and vice-president.

As Khomeini's aides awaited indications of the regime's collapse the Shah continued to vacillate between the carrot and the stick until the 'Black Friday' killings spread the opposition throughout the country. It was no longer merely the big cities which were in open revolt. Khomeini's cassettes and statements were circulated deep into the countryside. Demonstrations, marches and mourning for the movement's martyrs were now regular features in Iranian villages. Such mobilisation of the rural masses in which young and old, men and women, participated was a completely new phenomenon. Mollahs sent by car to the remotest villages to spread Khomeini's word and preach revolt wore civilian attire, and in the spirit of the time felt themselves part of a veritable 'cloak and dagger' operation.

While left wing and Mosaddeqist groups had more influence in the industrial and urban areas in organising strikes and demonstrations, the countryside was totally Khomeini's. Financed by the merchants, helped by the young and led by the clergy, villagers were brought to the towns to demonstrate, and they were soon doing so of their own accord.'When the city bakers were on strike we baked bread in our own oven, took it to the city and gave it to the people,' said a village woman who took part in demonstrations in the nearby town.

All this turmoil meant that the security forces were stretched to the limit. From mid-October, for example, the authorities in Neishabur, an ancient but small town in the north-east, were short of security personnel. 'The clergy had planned a meeting of the townspeople either by distributing leaflets or [issuing] threats' read a document of the county security meeting. 'As we see today there are clergy and students [present] from other places [and] the meeting may lead to violence. We will have to ask for a fully armoured company of soldiers and officers to come here as soon as possible, to prevent sabotage and to arrest the non-local leaders of the agitators.' But no forces were sent. The security meeting at Neishabur was stunned to hear that there were not enough troops to spare in Mashhad.

At the next meeting, officials were saying: 'The families of the security forces are frightened by threats they have received from opponents [of the regime],' admitting that they had too little manpower at their disposal 'to protect the classified areas'. Again they asked Mashhad for help but again none was forthcoming.

Still unable to decide on an effective way out, in November the Shah replaced his 'conciliatory' prime minister, Sharif Emami, with the military government of General Azhari while naïvely informing the nation that 'I have heard the message of your revolution.' The main aim of General Azhari's military government was to restore the oil industry to a state of semi-normality, to restore order and to give the Shah a breathing space. But the ailing monarch's confused approach to the crisis made his task difficult. As a strict curfew was imposed on some areas, people were encouraged by Khomeini's supporters to go onto their roof-tops and shout *Allahu akbar* at night.

While emphasising the principles of Islam, Khomeini at this point spoke of a 'progressive Islam' in which even a woman could become president and in which 'Islamic rules of retribution would not be applied unless sufficient preparations had been made to implement Islamic justice in its totality.'[19] He did not discuss the *velayat-e faqih*, 'guardianship of the jurisprudent', and was careful to sidestep in public the issue of the nature of an Islamic state. He confined his statements on the Islamic content of the future political system of Iran to the need for the clergy to play a supervisory role – which was interpreted by most people to mean the position that clergy were supposed to exercise under the 1906 constitution.

Iranian intellectuals, whose elitism – conscious or not – together with government-imposed censorship, prevented them from communicating with the masses, faced a very difficult choice in this particular period. Those among them who were sympathetic to a particular political party more or less blindly followed events and accepted party policy. The more thoughtful among them, who concluded that Khomeini's real intention was a thorough-going Islamic state, were left in a position in which they had to remain silent. None of them, however, could possibly contemplate being seen to support the Shah and his regime.

Indeed it was not until January 1979, when the revolutionary crisis peaked, that some intellectuals began to express their misgivings about the possibility of a clerically-led regime. Among these was Dr Mostafa Rahimi, a moderate secularist and long-standing critic of the Shah, who wrote an open letter to Khomeini entitled 'Why I disagree with Islamic government'; but lone voices like his were easily drowned amid the gathering revolutionary clamour.

In Khomeini's camp there were only two more goals to be achieved: the departure of the Shah and his own return.[20] The first objective was brought closer on 10 and 11 December 1978, the two important religious days of Tasu'a and Ashura, 9 and 10 Moharram, when millions of people up and down the country marched peacefully through city streets demanding the removal of the Shah and the return of Khomeini. The presence in the Tehran crowd of Ayatollah Taleqani, freshly returned from banishment to the provinces, gave the mourners an additional incentive to attend. Some estimates put the number of marchers throughout Iran at an astonishing 17 million, and in Tehran itself at 2 to 3 million. Khomeini delivered a message the next day to the Iranian nation thanking them for their peaceful march, and told other states to take notice of this 'referendum'.[21]

The confused state of policy-making in Washington continued to work in Khomeini's favour. President Carter's statement on 7 December, in which he said that it was 'up to the people of Iran to decide' the Shah's fate was music to the revolutionaries' ears. But for the Shah it was an ill-judged and ill-timed intervention. Meanwhile, National Security Adviser Zbigniew Brzezinski, who was in touch with Ardeshir Zahedi, the Iranian ambassador to Washington, was encouraging the Shah to pursue a tough line, while Cyrus Vance was advising him to find a peaceful settlement.

Amidst all this confusion time was running out for the Shah. The Tasu'a and Ashura marches had deeply shocked him. The next day he received the American ambassador and informed him that, contrary to what he had been told, Khomeini commanded enormous power and all banners and slogans proclaimed him as the country's leader.

The Shah was wavering between forming a national coalition government, setting up a regency council and leaving the country, or forming a military junta to crack down the opposition and restore order. In the end, under pressure to make up his mind, he opted for a convoluted strategy which had some elements of all these options. He entered into negotiation with opposition leaders to form a government. The only one among them who agreed was Dr Shahpur Bakhtiar. But the main question was the role of the military and its fate. The Shah, who was also the commander-in-chief of the armed forces, had always kept the military leaders out of politics, but Khomeini kept on wooing the younger officers by appealing to their religious zeal and patriotism.

Meanwhile, Khomeini doggedly pursued his own agenda with a three-point plan of action, which he quietly circulated among his candidates for a revolutionary council and provisional government. His determination to set up new Islamic institutions, parallel to existing bodies, in this way found a bolder focus. Unveiling his plan to the public on 10 January 1979, he claimed that: 'according to religious right and based on the vote of confidence by an absolute majority of the people in me, a council called the Islamic Revolutionary Council has been formed. Its members will be introduced at the earliest possible opportunity.'

As was revealed later, the membership of this council consisted of Khomeini's students and pro-Bazargan personalities with two dissident retired generals. Its main responsibility was to consider and discuss the conditions for the formation of a transitional government at the first opportune moment. The new government would be assigned to carry out the following tasks: (i) the formation of a constituent assembly, to be elected by the people, to ratify the new constitution; (ii) the holding of a referendum on the regulations of the constituent assembly and on the new constitution and (iii) the transfer of power to the newly elected representatives of the people.[22]

In a public message Khomeini promised that the Islamic Republic would ensure freedom, independence and social justice. He chided the Shah for entertaining any thoughts of staging a *coup d'état* in the last days of his rule with the help of a few 'treacherous' army officers, but assured the people that the majority of the army supported his movement and that the Shah's departure would not change that. Hearing this, Bakhtiar replied: 'The Shah's departure will bring heavy pressure on his government but the Islamic Revolutionary Council is unable to sweep his government away.'[23]

On 16 January an ailing and sad Shah left the country, never to return. Khomeini was performing his dawn prayer when Tahereh Dabbagh broke the news: 'The brothers say that the Shah has left the country and Radio Tehran has broadcast the news.' Khomeini remained calm and composed, merely saying 'What else?', and that was the end of the conversation.

Since Khomeini continued to put pressure on the government, Bakhtiar's only chance of survival was to buy time by threatening a military coup and to meanwhile attempt to come to terms with Khomeini. For a brief period there was division in the Khomeini camp, but once Khomeini had been persuaded by his hard-liners to reject an accommodation with Bakhtiar it was completely ruled out. Bakhtiar's next move, and indeed that of the Americans, was to delay Khomeini's return. But after several days, on 1 February 1979, Khomeini was back in Iran greeted by millions of Iranians as the leader of the revolution.

11

Revolution
The Return of the Imam

The old man who was spirited away from Tehran airport in the autumn of 1964 returned to his country triumphantly on 1 February 1979 as the undisputed leader of one of the major revolutionary movements in modern history. Leaving the airport in 1964 he had asked his minder, a Savak colonel, whether he knew that he was being exiled because he had defended the honour of his homeland. Now, as he entered Iranian airspace, he was asked what emotions he felt after nearly fifteen years of exile. 'None!' he replied bluntly. For a man who felt himself permanently imbued with the love of God, a homeland did not mean much. For mystics and puritanical Muslims it is the 'Dar al-Islam', the House of Islam, not the *patria*, which is all-important. For those politically practised Iranians who hoped to find in him a mainstream nationalist leader, Khomeini's reply was a warning; but in the frenzy to come their's was but a faint voice.

To the masses Khomeini was no ordinary man. He had become an ideal, a living symbol of hope for millions who desperately wanted a leader who would personify their aspirations, restore their spirituality and who would bring freedom, independence and justice. For the average man and woman it was almost as if the Hidden Imam of the Shi'a, their Messiah, had reappeared, albeit not in Mecca as tradition would have it, but on an

Air France charter flight from a city long associated by the faithful with little else but sin. Yet in Paris, carefully protected by his entourage, Khomeini had hardly taken in much about the society around him. His worldview was set to the reincarnation of a society that has not been in existence since the death of the Prophet in the seventh century. A skilled practitioner of clerical politics, a master tactician who succeeded in bringing disparate opposition groups together, and a supreme strategist of revolution, Khomeini's only goal was the recreation of an idealised past. But those in Iran who awaited his return were looking above all for a better future – and not necessarily only in spiritual terms.

It was in this expectation that throughout Iran young and old exchanged sweets and swept the dusty alleys of their remote villages as they told each other that 'Aqa' (Mr, Sir, holy man) was about to arrive. In Tehran the coalition of forces awaiting Khomeini wanted to define a host of vague issues, but above all they wanted him to rid the country of the remnants of what was soon to be the *ancien régime*.

When the plane landed at 9.30 am local time a 'welcoming committee' set up by the secret Islamic Revolutionary Council moved quickly to take charge of Khomeini. Ayatollah Motahhari, its chairman, Morteza Pasandideh, Khomeini's elder brother and several other leading dignitaries boarded the jumbo jet to greet the old man. Their aides spent the best part of half an hour trying to keep at bay those not considered to be Islamic revolutionaries and to prevent them from being photographed with Khomeini as he descended from the aircraft. Several personalities were asked to leave. Even close Paris companions such as Yazdi, Qotbzadeh and Bani Sadr were lost among the sea of turbans that surrounded Khomeini and spirited him away. 'It seemed', remarked Bani Sadr wryly, 'that the duty of the intellectuals was to bring Khomeini to Tehran and hand him over to the mollahs.'[1]

The atmosphere was frenzied. As soon as Khomeini stepped off the plane, flanked by fawning admirers and helped by a steward, the cry of *Allahu Akbar* went up. The chant 'Khomeini, O Imam', which had become standard revolutionary ritual in Neauphle-le-Château, was sung by schoolchildren to welcome him, almost drowned by shouts of 'Khomeini, O Imam, we salute you, peace be upon you.' A personality cult was in the making; overnight Khomeini had been transformed into a semi-divine figure. He was no longer a grand ayatollah and deputy of the Imam, one who represents the Hidden Imam, but simply 'The Imam'. In Arabic the term 'Imam' is used to describe a leader or prayer leader, but in Shi'i Iran, where the title was reserved for the twelve infallible leaders of the early Shi'a, among ordinary people it carried awe-inspiring connotations. In encouraging its use, some of Khomeini's supporters clearly wanted to exploit popular religious feelings and to imply that he was the long-awaited Hidden Imam. The senior traditional clergy never accepted this title. As for the revolutionary clergy, the more scrupulous among them believed that they were merely adopting a practice which had developed among Arab Shi'a who in recent decades had begun to refer to religious leaders who had gained some political prominence, such as Musa Sadr in Lebanon, as imams. As time went by the title was institutionalised – and yet it has never in Iran been applied to anyone but Khomeini.

In the airport building, Khomeini delivered a short speech, thanking people for 'their sentiments', which he declared to be 'a heavy burden on my shoulders'. His priorities were clear: 'I thank the clergy who have sacrificed so much in this affair. I thank the students who suffered tragedies. I thank the merchants and traders who suffered. I thank the young of the bazaar, the universities and the theological colleges who offered their blood ... .' He noted that although the Shah, whom he referred to as 'the former Shah', had gone, the remnants of his regime still existed, so the people had to remain united if they were to succeed.[2]

Outside the people of Tehran had staged an all-night vigil forming the longest human chain the city had ever witnessed, stretching several miles to the Behesht-e Zahra cemetery where Khomeini was to pay his respects to the martyrs of the revolution. In the difficult and hazardous drive through the crowds Khomeini was guarded by hard core Islamic activists – volunteers and members of the popular committees set up during the strikes to look after the poor and the needy. Mohsen Rafiqdust – later the minister for the Revolutionary Guards and head of the Foundation for the Oppressed – drove his car, a American-made Blazer station-wagon, and Khomeini constantly asked his son Ahmad the names of the streets, for the Tehran he had known was quite different from the city to which he had returned. But eventually the sheer size of the crowd, estimated at several million, made it impossible for him to continue and a helicopter of the Imperial Air Force had to come to the rescue.

When he arrived at Behesht-e Zahra to offer prayers for those killed in the revolutionary struggle, Khomeini spoke in the familiar tone of his 1964 sermons at the Feiziyeh. His voice was strong and his characteristic monotone unchanged. The two Pahlavi rulers, he told the crowd and the mass of microphones that surrounded him, had both been usurpers of power who had governed without popular consent. In any case, he declared: 'Our forefathers did not have the right to appoint anybody to rule us. Were our fathers our guardians that they should have appointed someone over us?' His main message, however, was addressed to government officials, members of parliament and the Shah's last prime minister, Dr Shahpur Bakhtiar, all of whom he described as illegitimate remnants of the monarchy which should be uprooted. Realising that the army was the only force in the country with the power to abort his revolution, he invited its commanders to join the nation, and warned them against remaining under the direction of American and foreign advisers: 'Oh Mr Field-Marshal, Oh Mr Major-General, do you not want to be independent? Do you want to remain a servant? Come back to the warm bosom of the nation.'[3]

Khomeini set up his temporary headquarters at the Refah School, an Islamist high school for girls close to the parliament building where the still-secret Revolutionary Council held its meetings.[4] With the remaining power of the old regime now divided between the commanders of an uncertain army and a shaky prime minister's office, this modest building replaced the Shah's palace as the focus of political activity. People began to arrive there in droves to pledge their allegiance to Khomeini. The telephones never stopped ringing with offers of blood for the injured and medicine, food and blankets for the struggle.

Khomeini's flight from Paris to Tehran was for many of his followers like the Prophet Mohammad's flight from Mecca to Medina in AD 622. In the new vocabulary developed by the Islamists, Khomeini was 'prophet-like', the man who 'brought to an end the age of ignorance and introduced the light of Islam'. We do not know whether Khomeini thought of himself in this way. Had he done so, he would never have admitted it. But there are apt parallels – and telling differences – between the concrete political tasks faced by Khomeini the man and Mohammad the Prophet after their respective historical flights. In Medina Mohammad's priority was to create a political order out of a fusion of religion and tribalism; in Tehran Khomeini had to create a political order from a fusion of religion, radicalism and liberal constitutionalism. Mohammad's first action in Medina was to establish his authority within the community or *umma*; Khomeini's task was to establish his rule in a society infinitely more sophisticated and complex. In Mecca the verses of the Qor'an revealed to

Mohammad were of hope and promise; in Medina he became a ruler who proclaimed laws, issued decrees, and punished unbelievers and infidels. Khomeini in Najaf and Paris offered a vague utopia designed to maintain the unity of a wide spectrum of leftists, liberal democrats and Islamist opposition groups. In Tehran he was gradually to reveal a more divisive agenda which he executed systematically.

Once in Iran, Khomeini's tone began to change, though at first in quite subtle ways. He knew that he must prepare himself to take over the apparatus of the state very quickly. Organisation was necessary – but so too was strategy, for he still had to establish his own position without alienating those who had helped the revolution. His first act was to appoint a provisional prime minister and, within two days of his arrival, possible candidates for the post were discussed with members of the Revolutionary Council. It was quickly agreed that the best man for the job was the leader of the Freedom Movement of Iran, Mehdi Bazargan, an Islamic modernist whose democratic credentials were widely accepted.

Characteristically, Bazargan was at first reluctant to accept the responsibility offered to him. 'The Revolutionary Council wanted an immediate and positive answer from me,' he recalls. 'This was so that they could issue a statement, face Dr Bakhtiar with a *fait accompli*, and forestall any opposition. I did not want to accept and I told them to let me study [the offer] and consult. When they put pressure on me to finalise the matter that same night, write a decree and announce it, I got annoyed. Ayatollah Khomeini smiled and said we should leave it until the morning.'[5] The next day Bazargan acquiesced; but, an honest man, he warned Khomeini and the other members of the Revolutionary Council that he was a gradualist who did not like to rush things. He reminded them of his background, and his commitments to democracy and moderation. In that tense period, when the army could have started a blood-bath, his appointment was to play a major role in ensuring a smooth transition of power.

On 5 February 1979, Khomeini held his first ever press conference in Iran to announce Bazargan's appointment. He sat in front of the international media flanked by Bazargan and a youthful looking Hashemi Rafsanjani, who read the Imam's decree. The text stressed that Bazargan was chosen as prime minister of the provisional government 'regardless of his party political affiliations'. He was charged with preparing a referendum on changing the country's political system to an Islamic Republic which would pave the way for the election of a Constituent Assembly to ratify a new constitution and elect the delegates for a new parliament. Bazargan got up to speak. Wearing a tight, short jacket and wide tie he showed his sense of humour even in such serious company: 'With this frail body, my shortcomings and my defects, as a rule I should have not accepted this position and such responsibility.' Khomeini then began to speak, elaborating on the decree and in effect pronouncing a religious edict:

As a man who, through the guardianship [velayat] that I have from the holy lawgiver [the Prophet], I hereby pronounce Bazargan as the Ruler, and since I have appointed him, he must be obeyed. The nation must obey him. This is not an ordinary government. It is a government based on the shari'a. Opposing this government means opposing the shari'a of Islam and revolting against the shari'a, and revolt against the government of the shari'a has its punishment in our law ... it is a heavy punishment in Islamic jurisprudence. Revolt against God's government is a revolt against God. Revolt against God is blasphemy.'[6]

With this pronouncement Khomeini set the tone of the new regime. Having emerged from arbitrary imperial rule, Iran was, it seemed, set to experience a new autocracy, divinely inspired. From Khomeini's edict would flow the arbitrary arrests, the executions, the floggings, the confiscations of property and the abrogation of women's rights which would bedevil the new regime and begin to erode its legitimacy.

Khomeini's words also included a reference to the concept of the velayat-e faqih (guardianship of the jurisconsult) which went largely unnoticed at the time. After the rejection by the leading Shi'i clerics of his theory, elaborated in the 1969 lectures he delivered in Najaf, he had remained silent on the issue. Now, for the first time in nearly ten years, he claimed his legitimacy from it and gave an indication of the nature of the theocratic government he aimed at – a system which was a world apart from all that Bazargan had struggled for. The secular elements in the revolutionary coalition seem to have missed, or perhaps ignored, this hint of what was to come.

While the direction in which Khomeini was heading was lost on most Iranians, the country now had two governments. Dr Bakhtiar had refused to merge his own with that of Bazargan, although he had conceded that he would tolerate the 'shadow' government as long as it remained just that. Khomeini's decree had, however, made it abundantly clear that this was not the intention. Almost immediately, resignations from members of parliament and government officials poured into Bakhtiar's office. Simultaneously, Khomeini received numerous declarations of support. On 7 February, two days after his press conference, large rallies were organised in Tehran and other cities to demonstrate support for Bazargan's premiership. Bakhtiar, for his part, chose the next day to stage a counter-demonstration in support of the 1906 Constitution. It was not a success; no more than a few thousand people took part, further exposing his lost cause. Most of the Shah's erstwhile supporters among the middle classes, sensing the way the wind was blowing, had evaporated into silence or exile. Most of the liberal and nationalist opposition, who in other circumstances would have been a natural constituency for Bakhtiar, had thrown in their lot with Khomeini, believing that he would bring genuine democracy to the country and that there must be a clean break with the past.

Events were moving very fast indeed and it seemed that nothing short of a military *coup d'état* could prevent the complete destruction of the old regime. The moderate army chief of staff General Gharebaghi maintained constant contact with both Bakhtiar and Bazargan, while the American Embassy, anxious to ensure a smooth transition of power, used its considerable influence in the military to support the position of the moderates. But the revolutionaries feared that pro-Shah elements could still assert themselves.

In fact it was a division within the armed forces that triggered the final act of revolution. On 8 February hundreds of air force technicians descended upon the Refah School to pledge an oath of allegiance to Khomeini. The next day, in formation at their bases, they gave formal salute to the Imam. This was too much for the Imperial Guard, whose elite unit, the 'Immortals', attacked air force bases around Tehran, at Doshan Tappeh and Farahabad, later that day. In response, units of the People's Feda'iyan and Mojahedin-e Khalq guerrillas rushed to the scene to support the technicians and the fighting quickly spread to the rest of Tehran. Throughout the city police stations and army barracks were attacked by guerrilla organisations and revolutionary crowds. Arsenals were systematically looted.

Bakhtiar made an attempt to resist the inevitable. In the early afternoon of 10 February Tehran's military governor announced that a curfew would be imposed on the city from 4.30 pm to 5 am the next morning. 'It was a plan,' Bakhtiar recalled later, 'according to which any person breaking martial law or curfew regulations could be arrested on the spot, and roughly so, since too gentle an approach was not appropriate.'[7] But with the capital's population armed and mobilised it was too little too late. Khomeini seized his chance and promptly instructed his followers to ignore the curfew. He added that he would proclaim a *jihad* against any army units which did not surrender. Cars with loudspeakers announced his decision throughout the city, bringing crowds onto the streets. Guerrilla units attacked the barracks of the Immortals, and took over American military buildings, the Evin prison, the television and radio station and numerous government offices. By the next morning the Supreme Council of the Armed Forces had decided that nothing more could be done and at 1.15 pm Tehran Radio broadcast the following statement:

In view of recent developments in the country the Supreme Military Council was convened at 10.20 am on the 22 Bahman 1357 [11 February 1979] and, in order to prevent further disorder and bloodshed, decided unanimously to declare itself neutral in the current political disputes and ordered all military personnel to return to base.

Sporadic fighting continued that afternoon and throughout the night, but the revolution – and Khomeini – had triumphed. 'This is Tehran – the true voice of the people of Iran, the voice of the revolution,' shouted an excited announcer. 'Attention! Attention! Here is the latest pronouncement from the Grand Ayatollah Imam Khomeini, leader of the Iranian People's Movement':

In the name of God the Merciful, the Compassionate. Heroic Muslim people of Iran, first I would ask you not to allow rioting and unrest to take place. I would remind you that our revolution has not yet achieved complete victory over the enemy and I would request you, my dear brothers and sisters, to cooperate with the interim revolutionary Islamic government.

A subsequent message from Bazargan, who was described by Tehran Radio as the 'Prime Minister of the people of Iran', reflected a rather different approach and set of priorities:

I congratulate you, the struggling Muslim people of Iran, on the attainment today of another victory along the tortuous way towards your revolution ... The armed forces have declared their neutrality. It is necessary for you, dear fellow countrymen, to exercise patience and give the government a breathing-space so that in due course, with equity and clear-sightedness, the country's affairs can be put in good order and the positions and duties of the various authorities assigned. It is clear that not only will agitation and disturbance and hastiness prevent things returning to normal, but, God forbid, they will actually make the situation worse than it was and cause more suffering.

For a little while the moderating influence of liberals amongst the Islamic revolutionaries, such as Bazargan and Taleqani, prevailed over the hotheads. Khomeini too, despite his militant temperament, was clearly concerned to bring the forces he had unleashed under control. Although he continued to speak of the need for vigilance and for action to complete the revolution, during these early days he issued appeals to the population to prevent chaos and arson, to preserve Iran's artistic, scientific, and industrial heritage, not to lay waste public or private property belonging to the enemy, to be kind and compassionate to captives as Islamic tradition requires, and to refrain from arbitrary punishment of officials of the Shah's regime.

But the voice of moderation was drowned by a clamour for blood. Thousands who had dared to challenge the Shah's autocratic style of leadership, or had simply criticised the regime and suffered humiliation, or had lost members of their families through execution or torture, wanted revenge. Pressure from these groups mounted, along with demands from extreme elements in the secular left and Islamic radicals that all leading members of the Shah's regime should be executed. Sensing that he might lose control over the forces he had unleashed, Khomeini showed that he too could be ruthless. He very rapidly acceded to summary trials and executions to avenge the 'martyrs of the revolution'[8] and put an old supporter, Sheikh Sadeq Khalkhali, who soon earned the nickname 'judge blood', in charge. A classroom in the Refah School was converted into a makeshift courtroom and executions began on the roof of the school on the evening of 15 February when four leading generals, including the ex-Savak chief General Nassiri, were shot.

The executions at the school continued non-stop for several weeks, drawing horrified protests from Bazargan, most other members of the provisional government, and from international organisations. The protests succeeded in bringing an end to executions for about three weeks from mid-March; but during April they began again with the execution of the Shah's longest serving prime minister, Amir Abbas Hoveida. Hoveida was well-known to Khomeini. In 1967, while still in Iraq, Khomeini had sent the premier an open letter threatening him with 'the people's rage' and giving a full account of what he considered to be Hoveida's crimes: 'friend-ship with Israel, subservience to the United States, undermining Islam and the clergy, destroying the economy' among many others. Human rights lawyers, with the help of Bazargan's government, tried to organise a proper trial for Hoveida, but were outmanoeuvred. Khalkhali later disclosed that he knew of the forces trying to obtain Hoveida's release and that, to save the situation, 'revolutionary forces' requested the Imam to send him to the prison in which Hoveida was being held:

In early April, I went to Qasr prison. At about two in the afternoon I told them to bring Hoveida. He was given *baqali polo* [broad beans and rice, a favourite Iranian meal] for lunch. I ordered the prison doors to be closed, then I put all the phones inside the fridge and locked them so that no news would leak out. At 2.30 pm Hoveida was ushered to the place of the accused ... He talked for about two and half hours. He said 'I was prime minister in a system and I was powerless. The system should be blamed for mistakes and shortcomings, not the individual.' I replied that he was prime minister for thirteen years. 'Many things occurred against the interest of Iran and in fa-vour of imperialism. You gave free oil to the Americans in Vietnam and you supplied Israel with oil products and food during the war with the Arabs.'⁹

Khalkhali accused Hoveida of a long list of 'crimes' and finally told him to make his closing defence. Hoveida's pleas that he be permitted to write the history of Iran in the past twenty-five years, and that he needed time to prepare a proper defence, went unheeded. He was told to write his will. When he asked to see Ahmad Khomeini, Khalkhali told him that Ah-mad did not interfere in judicial affairs. That afternoon, on 7 April 1979, Hoveida was executed by firing squad. Within a short period over 200 of the Shah's senior officials followed Hoveida to their graves.

Protests over the waves of summary executions poured in from inter-national human rights bodies; but Khomeini was not going to shed tears even if a 'criminal' had not been properly tried. In a reply to the human rights lobby he made his views quite plain:

Criminals should not be tried. The trial of a criminal is against human rights. Human rights demand that we should have killed them in the first place when it became known that they were criminals ... They criticise us because we are executing the brutes. As soon as former Savak chief Nasiri's identity was established he had to be killed. Despite the fact that he deserved summary execution, he was kept for a few days and was tried. Doesn't the human rights lobby think that criminals must be killed for the sake of human rights, in order to ensure the rights of man and those whom these people killed, tortured and destroyed? Nevertheless we are trying them and we have tried them. Our belief is that criminals should not be tried and must be killed.[10]

This was just the beginning of Khomeini's quarrel with international bodies.

From the very first day of the revolution, Bazargan had wanted to establish the rule of law and respect for human rights, an important demand among many of those who had opposed the Shah. But Khomeini, while he spoke of controlling the revolutionary forces, was more concerned to further his own agenda, which had 'not yet achieved victory'. During those heady days Bazargan seemed out of place. His overtures to the non-communist left, and his non-revolutionary, gradualist and legalistic style, admirable as they might have been under normal circumstances, did nothing but attract mistrust and disappointment from the young generation of Islamic radicals who were burning with revolutionary enthusiasm. It also aroused the hostility of the young radical leftists gathered mainly under the banner of the People's Feda'iyan. Bazargan's public declaration, just a day before the collapse of the old regime, stunned these groups: 'I am not a bulldozer like Khomeini, I am a fragile automobile and I need a proper road on which to travel. You must pave the way for me.' Bazargan's soft approach towards the United States, and his hatred of the Tudeh Party, aroused many misgivings.

But the fact that his own world-view was poles apart from that of Bazargan did not matter to Khomeini, at least in the short term. He recognised the difficulty of dismantling a secular regime and replacing it with the rule of God overnight, so at first he was content to view Bazargan as a facilitator – an intermediary between the reality of the present and the dream of the future. He recognised that the potential threat to an Islamic future from the military, the nationalists, the liberals and the leftists was a real one, especially since these elements aroused a more sympathetic resonance in the West. It was important that these potential threats be neutralised, but equally important that these groups not be provoked into coalescing against him. Bazargan was the ideal vehicle. His impeccable Islamic credentials gave the new government a clear-cut Islamic colouring, while his equally impeccable credentials as a former colleague of Mosaddeq and a member of the National Front provided comfort to the secularists. However, as Khomeini's confidence grew, so Bazargan found himself increasingly at odds with the pace of the revolution and with its leader, who was now enjoying his role as the supreme ruler of the country.

To achieve the full-blooded Islamic rule he wanted, Khomeini was from the start well aware that he could not rely on the Western-educated or even the liberal Muslims. He saw himself as an architect raising a grand monument in the name of Islam out of the ashes of decadence and foreign domination. He did not have to go too far to find the right men to help him. His loyal and unquestioning followers and students were at hand to translate his wishes into reality – revolutionary activists from the student organisations, the traders of the bazaar who had financed his movement and the Coalition of Islamic Societies which in turn led them.

From the time that Khomeini's return to Iran was certain the Coalition and the small circle of clerics who were close to it and to Khomeini – Beheshti, Mofattah, Musavi Ardebili, Khamene'i, Rafsanjani and Bahonar – had begun to organise in order to secure his hegemony in the post-revolutionary period. The Coalition was everywhere. It played a role in the committee that welcomed Khomeini; Rafiqdust, a long-standing and prominent member of the organisation, had been his driver on the journey from the airport to Behesht-e Zahra; it had a very large hand in organising the logistics of, and keeping order in, the huge street demonstration that lined the route, and it owned the school that became Khomeini's headquarters.[11] Within days of Khomeini's arrival it had, with the help of Beheshti, gathered all those who accepted his leadership unconditionally – the bazaaris, seven Islamic guerrilla organisations which had just united under the umbrella name of the Mojahedin of the Islamic Revolution (Omir), and a large segment of the politically active clergy – under the banner of the Islamic Republican Party. Plans had existed for well over a year to form such a party and the matter had been discussed with Khomeini in Najaf in 1977 and again in Paris. But the project had been delayed in the period before the Shah's departure because no-one could decide whether the party should be underground or openly active.[12]

In subsequent weeks the Islamic Republican Party evolved under Beheshti's supervision as a tightly organised authoritarian instrument. The assumption was that it would have some sort of say in the government, if not actually take control. In the event it did not succeed in this; but from the beginning of the revolution until its dissolution in 1987 it played a vital role as Khomeini's task force, the vehicle through which opponents, or even undesirable allies, were outmanoeuvred and the supremacy of the clergy in government was ensured. And it operated on every level of society, from government offices to almost all city quarters, as well as in some villages.

In the street it wielded power through organised gangs of strong-arm thugs known as the Hezbollah, the Party of God who were, it later emerged, supervised by a young protegée of Khomeini, Hojjat al-Islam Hadi Ghaffari. The Hezbollah attacked demonstrators who challenged Khomeini's position, the offices of newspapers critical of the direction in which the post-revolutionary government was moving, and the premises of opposition organisations. In the early months of the revolution a pretence was maintained that the Hezbollah represented the spontaneous will of the people and that Khomeini and the Revolutionary Council had nothing to do with them and could not control them.[13] But although they never became a formal part of the structures of state, as time went by their status as the IRP's shock troops was openly admitted. 'The Hezbollahis,' *The Guardian* reported in July 1981 at a time when the struggle between the Khomeinists and the opposition forces reached its height, 'are at their most striking in cavalry formation, riding in great armadas through the streets on their motor bikes, traditional Shi'ite black flags and banners held aloft, and sometimes preceded by a mollah in a bullet-proof Mercedes.'[14]

Also allied with the IRP, though in a somewhat looser fashion, were the *komitehs* which sprang up throughout country during the revolution. These were organised from the mosques by the Coalition and the Jame'eh-ye Ruhaniyat-e Mobarez, the Society of Militant Clergy, and they were able to flourish because they were based on the social structure of the religious community. During the last months of 1977 they had played a large role in mobilising ordinary people behind Khomeini's banner and had distributed food and clothing to the needy. After the revolution they were armed and saw it as their main task to keep order and security and to act as the new regime's eyes and ears. As such they were responsible for many arbitrary arrests, executions and confiscations of property. At Khomeini's behest they were purged in the summer of 1979 both to eradicate the influence of the leftist guerilla movements that had infiltrated them and were eventually absorbed into the police force.

A fourth organisation, the paramilitary Islamic Revolutionary Guards Corps, whose purpose would be 'to protect the revolution from destructive forces and counter-revolutionaries' was created within weeks of Khomeini's return to Iran and on his direct instructions. The Guard was responsible to the Revolutionary Council and had its own budget. It was initially put under the general supervision of Ayatollah Hassan Lahuti. Hashemi Rafsanjani was drafted in to supervise training, in which he was helped by Mustafa Chamran, an Islamic activist who had received guerilla and military training with the Shi'i Amal Party in Lebanon. Its first commanders were drawn from the Mojahedin of the Islamic Revolution – Behzad Nabavi, Ali Shamkhani and Mohsen Reza'i – and from the remnants of the Islamic Nations Party – Javad Mansuri, Abbas Duzduzani and Abbas Zamani. Kazem Bojnurdi, the founder of the Islamic Nations Party, was also offered a command but he opted instead to work on his project for a 'Great Islamic Encyclopaedia'.[15] Recruits, about 4,000 in the first instance, and a massive 25,000 by the end on 1979,[16] were carefully monitored to ensure that young men from 'communist' or 'eclectic' (People's Mojahedin) backgrounds did not infiltrate the corps. From the moment they entered, they were thoroughly schooled in loyalty to Khomeini and his principles.

The Islamic Republican Party's first job was to make certain that the referendum planned for March would yield the desired result. This was not difficult since it had already been agreed in Paris between Dr Sanjabi, the leader of the National Front, and Khomeini that the choice should be between a monarchy and a republic and that the designation 'Islamic' should be used. But what that meant exactly was left vague and Khomeini had allowed people to read their own meaning into it. There was, therefore, much discussion in the press about the nature of the republic the country should adopt, whatever the formal title: a 'democratic republic', the option favoured by the non-Islamic leftists and the secular liberals and democrats, or the 'Islamic democratic republic' favoured by some of the more mild-mannered clergy and the more moderate and Western-oriented elements of the Islamic movement. Khomeini and the mainstream of his radical followers meanwhile maintained a discrete silence on the form of Islamic government they favoured.

The almost universal enthusiasm for the revolution and the question that was put to the people, and supported by most elements of the coalition of forces that had brought the revolution about, meant that the endorsement Khomeini wanted was a foregone conclusion. Nevertheless, eager to maintain the momentum, he relentlessly preached the need for participation and energetically mobilised his forces. He ordered the theological colleges to close during the referendum campaign and instructed mollahs to visit the four corners of Iran to ensure a 'yes' vote. He urged women to participate actively in the referendum, thus acknowledging their role in the revolution. The fact that, in doing so, they would be putting their social and economic rights at the mercy of priests who, interpreting the laws of the *shari'a*, had in 1963 opposed votes for women, was not a point to be dwelt upon. On 1 March, a month before the referendum was scheduled to take place, he warned the people:

Though freedom has been achieved, the roots of imperialism and Zionism have not yet been severed. To achieve real independence we have to remove all forms of American influence, whether economic, political, military or cultural ... Soon a referendum will be held. I am going to vote for an Islamic republic, and I expect the people to do the same. Those who are opposed are free to vote accordingly.[17]

But, within weeks of the revolution, it was already quite clear that, whatever the form of the words, 'those who are opposed' could expect to suffer damaging consequences. Not surprisingly, on 30 and 31 March, 97 per cent of the electorate, including most of the secularist political organisations, voted 'yes' to an Islamic Republic whose actual form had never been spelt out for them.

At the beginning of March Khomeini had left Tehran to return, for the first time in fifteen years, to his family home in Qom. Ostensibly, he intended with the move to withdraw from a direct role in government; but in practise the centre of decision making simply shifted with him. For the nine months or so that he remained in residence there, the tiny city was no longer just the religious centre of Iran; it became the seat of political authority and, in effect, the capital of the new caliph of Islam. Politicians streamed across the dusty desert from Tehran to consult with him over important decisions or to promote the interests of one or another faction. And hundreds of ordinary people made pilgrimages, increasingly organised for security reasons, to attend the public audiences which, in the oldest tradition of the ideal Islamic ruler, he held almost daily.

In the early phase of the revolution these sessions usually involved a eulogy delivered by the spokesperson of the visiting group and a sermon on revolutionary virtues from Khomeini. But occasionally, and with increasing frequency in the tense, later months of 1979, the advice he offered to his audience was more concrete. For example, as tensions rose between left-wing groups and his supporters on university campuses in Tehran, a group of religious Tehran University students complained to him about the activities of left wingers who had gained the upper hand and who had turned the campus into an armed stronghold for themselves. Khomeini, who had until then been taking a softer line on the question of student politics, suddenly raised his voice: 'How is it that you have sat idle and allowed a handful of communists to take control of the university? Are you less than them? Challenge them, argue with them, stand up to them and express yourselves.' After giving this advice, he began to tell them a story – probably apocryphal – of an official in his home town of Khomein under Reza Shah who had dared to insult the clergy by naming his two dogs 'Sheikh' and 'Seyyed'. Khomeini's elder brother, Morteza Pasandideh, wrote to him asking him to go to Tehran to see the leading clerical politician Modarres, who at the time was a member of parliament. Khomeini asked Modarres to use his influence and arrange the transfer of that particular official. 'Modarres said: "Kill him,"' Khomeini recalled. 'I asked him how. He said: "I give you written permission to kill him."'[18] When Khomeini objected that it was not possible, Modarres responded with a jibe about the well-known problem of highway banditry in Khomein: 'How is it that you can rob the caravans passing by Khomein, yet cannot kill one person?' For Khomeini the moral of the story lay in Modarres' final words: 'You hit first and let others complain. Don't be the victim and don't complain.' In this way Khomeini encouraged the students to take the law into their own hands. It was one way of controlling the growing opposition to his rule.

Khomeini also kept in close touch with his adoring wider public when he moved to Qom, the millions for whom he was simply the 'Aqa', the man who epitomised their intense religious sentiments. When the power of the microphone, the television camera and photography became clear to this once camera-shy old man, he capitalised on what these technological aids could produce. Khomeini was the first ruler of Iran to use television and other forms of mass communication to address, specifically, the ordinary people. Before the cameras and microphones he treated heads of state and humble workers equally. And with the exception of Iranian officials and selected guests, he generally denied his prominent visitors any privacy.

The first distinguished guest to learn this lesson was the then Soviet ambassador Vladimir Vinogradov. A veteran diplomat, Vinogradov visited

Khomeini in Qom in June 1979 only to hear a vigorous condemnation of
Nur Mohammad Taraki's communist regime in Afghanistan as unrepre-
sentative. When Vinogradov began to point out that there were counter-
revolutionary elements in Afghanistan, Khomeini told him: 'It seems that
you do not know much about the situation in Afghanistan.' The meeting
was cool and terse – not at all what Vinogradov, who was expecting to
establish dialogue with a potential new ally, had hoped for. And it was
broadcast word for word on the radio. Vinogradov was annoyed; he had
been trapped into a role in Khomeini's very public political and diplomatic signal that the Soviet Union could expect no friendship from Islamic Iran. He did not pay a repeat visit to the Ayatollah.

The business of maintaining morale, or carrying out the ceremonial
duties of a de facto head of state were not, however, the only, or the most
important matters to engage Khomeini's time and energy in this period.
To him the revolution was far from complete. He wanted an Islamic Republic not just in name but in practice. 'Western laws,' he announced on
the day he returned to Qom, 'must be abolished and replaced with Islamic
law. We will uproot all Western cultural influence and will set up a just
Islamic government.'[19] Steadily pursuing this purpose, with the referendum was out of the way he started to criticise Bazargan's gradual approach
to change. He also, without consulting Bazargan, issued a barrage of orders which caused problems and protests in Tehran. Among them was an
instruction to female employees of the government to dress in accordance
with the Islamic code.

Simultaneously, Bazargan's position was undermined from all sides by
the increasing number of Khomeinist representatives within government
departments throughout the country. By the late spring, the determination of the Revolutionary Council and the Islamic Republican Party to
exclude other elements from power was already beginning to show. The
country once again had two governments: an official one led by Bazargan
and an unofficial, but far more powerful one, led by Khomeini, the Revolutionary Council and supporting organisations. Bazargan, as he put it
himself, had become 'a knife without a blade'.[20] Khomeini at times tried to
maintain the semblance of support for his prime minister; but the reality
was that his move to Qom meant that the liberals in Tehran had less access to him than his lifelong supporters and friends in the theological centres, and his own agenda pushed him to oppose many of Bazargan's wishes.

Towards the end of April Khomeini's apprehension of the direction in which things might move if a tight reign were not kept on opposition activities was reinforced by a series of assassinations carried out by a shadowy anti-clerical Islamist group which called itself Forqan. The first of these was of General Gharani, who after the revolution had been appointed chief-of-staff of the army but had since retired a disillusioned man. Forqan subsequently claimed credit for six more assassinations of Khomeini supporters. All were a considerable loss. But by far the most devastating was the killing of Morteza Motahhari on 1 May, an act which not only removed a man who was the Chairman of the Revolutionary Council and Khomeini's closest advisor among the clergy, but also severed the most important link between Khomeini's clerical circle and lay politicians such as Bazargan.[21] Khomeini, broken-hearted by the loss of the man he called my 'dearest son', 'the fruit of my life', showed open and uncharacteristic emotion. Throughout the service of remembrance held for Motahhari at the Feiziyeh school, he sat clutching his handkerchief, sobbing and sometimes crying out loudly for his friend.

Bazargan was not alone in his opposition to the growing power of the Islamic Republican Party. Very early on, cracks had begun to appear within the religious establishment, let alone between the religious establishment and the secularists. On 17 April Ayatollah Taleqani, whose sons had been arrested as members of a leftist guerilla organisation, issued a joint statement with Karim Sanjabi, who had just resigned from Bazargan's cabinet in protest at the arrest, denouncing the return to despotism and dictatorship. Leading clergy such as Ayatollah Shari'atmadari, Ayatollah Qomi of Mashhad, and many others were also critical of the IRP and the revolutionary courts, accusing them of making a mockery of Islam and using religion to their political advantage. Many lawyers, writers, professionals of all kinds and minority leaders also joined the battle over human rights and democracy.

The most divisive of all the issues to arise at this time, and the key to the whole direction of the revolution, was the form the new constitution was to take and the arrangements for convening the Constituent Assembly that would approve it. While Khomeini was in Paris a draft constitution had been drawn up by a group liberal Islamists. The draft was kept under wraps while it was refined, first by a small commission of civil jurists appointed by the Revolutionary Council and chaired by Hassan Habibi, and then by a larger commission chaired by Bazargan's Freedom Movement colleague, Yadollah Sahabi, which included secularist politicians from Bazargan's cabinet. The final document made no mention *velayat-e faqih* and it confined the role of religious jurists to a Guardian Council which could only intervene to declare legislation incompatible with the *shari'a* at the request of specified officials. It had, nevertheless, according to a Freedom Movement's account, been carefully read and approved by Khomeini.[22] And indeed, three days after it was published on 14 June, the Ayatollah publicly declared that the draft was, for the government, 'correct'.[23]

Yet by then Khomeini had already started to denounce the supporters of a 'Democratic Islamic Republic', whose ideas were enshrined in the draft, and who included Bazargan, as 'enemies of Islam'. He had also taken the first steps in a campaign launched by his lieutenants in the IRP to ensure that the new constitution would incorporate the notion of the *velayat-e faqih*. Just after the referendum, Bazargan's Minister of the Interior had announced that arrangements were in progress for elections to the promised Constituent Assembly which was to have nearly 300 members. But, much to the dismay of Bazargan and his colleagues, by the middle of May Khomeini and the clerical members of the Revolutionary Council had already decided, without consulting them, that a much smaller body – an 'Assembly of Experts' with seventy members – should consider the constitution. The change was contested over the next weeks but finally ratified at the beginning of July by a decree of the Revolutionary Council announcing that elections to the Assembly of Experts would take place on 3 August.[24] The difference was significant. With fewer candidates standing for membership in the assembly from much larger constituencies it would be easier to rig the elections – and the likelihood of dissenting voices in the Assembly could be reduced to almost nothing.

Khomeini and his followers had begun their campaign for a thorough-going Islamic state in almost the same breath as they declared their support for the draft constitution. On 15 June, targeting the liberal and left-wing groups who were still advocating a Constituent Assembly, Khomeini menacingly declared them to be 'counter-revolutionaries' against Islam, 'communists' or 'misguided people … unable to realise that the switch … served to establish the order of the Qor'an.'[25] Speaking candidly for the first time he said that he was against the idea of a Constituent Assembly because 'our desire is to create an Islamic constitution' for which no 'Westernised jurists' are needed, only 'noble members of the clergy' and laymen who are 'knowers of Islam.'[26] His favourite student, Ayatollah Montazeri quickly followed his lead, stating that he believed the new republic should have a 'pure Islamic constitution ... far removed from every Western principle'.[27] A campaign was thus launched to popularise the idea of the *velayat-e faqih*, the rule of the jurisprudent, which, until that moment most Iranians, whatever their level of education, had never heard of, let alone considered as an option for the political system that would replace the monarchy. One after another members of the clergy joined the bandwagon to advocate a form of government that many Shi'i jurists regarded as highly unorthodox.

The IRP meanwhile began a vicious campaign against the opposition. Its principle targets were two organisations: Ayatollah Shari'atmadari's Muslim People's Republican Party and the National Democratic Front of Iran. For the time being, however, direct confrontation with the MPRP was avoided. The National Democratic Front was a new organization formed at the beginning of March, at a time when all shades of secular opinion outside the guerilla movements were beginning to sense the direction of Khomeini's political strategy. It was a broad coalition which aimed to provide a political home for those groups and individuals frustrated by the close alliance of the old National Front's leadership with Bazargan's government and the reluctance of the Tudeh party and some other elements to criticise Khomeini because they believed him to be a committed anti-imperialist. With its appeal to the heritage of Mosaddeq, and its vigorous defence of democratic rights, the Front attracted a great deal of support. It was launched at a meeting attended by around a million people which was held to commemorate the twelfth anniversary of Mosaddeq's death at Ahmadabad – a village some 60 miles from Tehran where the famous statesman had lived under house arrest. Through the summer of 1979 the Front organised demonstrations over a range of issues, including a campaign for a free press which focused on the fate of the daily *Ayandegan* whose staff's stubborn insistence on the right to free expression had angered Khomeini, and a meeting held on 22 June in support of a Constituent Assembly. All these drew large crowds into the streets and all were ferociously attacked by gangs of Hezbollahi toughs.

But the Front and other opposition organisations could do nothing to loosen the grip of the Islamic Republican Party on the course of events, especially the carefully orchestrated elections to the Assembly of Experts which the Muslim People's Republican Party and many of the secularist organisations boycotted in protest. Vote-rigging, violence against undesirable candidates and the dissemination of false information were all used to produce an Assembly overwhelmingly dominated by clergy loyal to Khomeini and a handful of laymen who followed 'the Imam's line'. Among the few moderates from the Islamic camp who managed to win seats were Ayatollah Taleqani, Abolhassan Bani Sadr and Ezatollah Sahabi, a leading figure in Bazargan's Freedom Movement. One of the two known secular politicians to succeed, Abdolrahman Qasemlu, the leader of the Kurdish Democratic Party of Iran, could not attend because a warrant for his arrest had already been issued by Ayatollah Ahmad Azari Qomi, the revolutionary prosecutor of Tehran.[28]

On 10 August, two days before the Assembly opened, the delegates travelled to Qom to pay their respects to Khomeini whose address instructed them ' ... to make sure that our constitution is within the framework of the law of the *shari'a*. If any one or all the members negate the *shari'a* they are not our representatives.' He also made his attitude to opposition elements, secular or religious, crystal clear. Those who campaigned against the Assembly of Experts and in defence of *Ayandegan* had, he proclaimed, abused the freedom given to them by the Islamic Republic:

... the 'clog-wearer and the turbaned' have given you a chance. After each revolution several thousand of these corrupt elements are executed in public and burnt and the story is over. They are not allowed to publish newspapers. After so long the October Revolution still has no newspaper, except [the newspaper the state] wants. We will close all parties except the one, or a few which act in a proper manner ... We all made mistakes. We thought we were dealing with human beings. It is evident we are not. We are dealing with wild animals. We will not tolerate them any more.[29]

Yet only a year earlier, while in Paris, Khomeini had assured a Western journalist that 'an Islamic Republic is a democratic state in the true sense of the word ... everyone ... can voice their own opinion ... and the Islamic state will respond with logic to all the arguments put forward.'[30]

Khomeini's angry denunciations of the opposition had ensured that the growing tension on the streets would come to a head. Three days before the Assembly of Experts began its deliberations on 12 August – a day enshrined in the national memory as 28 Mordad, the anniversary of the CIA coup against Mosaddeq and the popular democratic movement that supported him – the National Democratic Front had scheduled a mass demonstration to protest the closure of *Ayandegan* and other violations of the freedom of the opposition press. The demonstration was viciously attacked by Hezbollah thugs. The next day, 10 August, the revolutionary prosecutor of Tehran issued a warrant for the arrest of Hedayat Matin Daftari, one of the Front's leading figures, whose property was confiscated. Soon afterwards he issued orders for the closure of twenty-six major newspapers and magazines. Meanwhile the Hezbollah attacked the offices of the People's Feda'iyan and the Revolutionary Guards made an attempted assault on the offices of the Mojahedin-e Khalq. Peaceful resistance to Khomeini's brand of Islamisation became, from this point onwards, virtually impossible.

The Assembly completed its work two months later, on 11 November, in an atmosphere of even higher drama than that which had surrounded its inauguration. Just a week earlier Bazargan and his government had resigned over an issue that finally put his premier beyond the pale for Khomeini: Iran's relations with the United States. Khomeini had always been suspicious of American intentions towards the revolution. He could never quite accept that an America which, over the past generation, had invested so much political, military and commercial capital in building up and maintaining Iran as a staunch ally in the Middle East would swallow the 'loss' of its ally with equanimity. As it happens, contacts between American officials and Khomeini's circle in the weeks leading up to the revolution had been close, and in the weeks and months that followed relations between the United States and the new Iranian government had been correct and workmanlike. For example, when, days after the revolution, hotheads invaded the American embassy for the first time, Bazargan's government, backed by Khomeini, had responded swiftly to expel the intruders. But Khomeini was convinced that the apparent American acquiescence in the change of regime in Tehran merely reflected a desire to play for time until new plots could be hatched to restore America's influence. Thus, when the cancer-ridden Shah was allowed into the United States for medical treatment on 22 October 1979, following an unseemly cold shouldering by his other erstwhile Western friends, Khomeini fumed at what he considered to be a provocative act. To him this was evidence of American plotting. His statements became increasingly belligerent, and he railed against the machinations of 'the Great Satan'.

In this tense atmosphere Bazargan travelled to Algeria to participate in celebrations marking the anniversary of the Algerian Revolution. Also in Algeria was President Carter's National Security Adviser, Zbigniew Brzezinski. Their fateful meeting on 1 November was to prove Bazargan's undoing and was exploited to alter the course of contemporary Iranian history. The two men were photographed shaking hands, and the Iranian media, which was firmly controlled by radicals of all colourings, went to town to alert the nation of the return of American influence. For the IRP and the Islamic radicals who sought to undermine Bazargan and attack the liberals at every turn, the meeting was a godsend.

Inspired by Khomeini's increasingly anti-American rhetoric and by the IRP's belligerence towards Bazargan, on 4 November 1979 radical students charged over the walls of the American embassy in Tehran, occupied the building and the grounds, and took 90 hostages. The 'hostage crisis' was to last 444 days. Though women and black Marine guards were soon released, the remaining 52 diplomats became an icon of Iranian radicalism for fifteen months. The immediate result of the attack was that Bazargan offered his resignation, on 6 November. Unable to muster the support of Khomeini, or of the Revolutionary Council, for the eviction of the students, he recognised that he was impotent.

When Khomeini heard of Bazargan's resignation, he summoned the three leading members of the Revolutionary Council – Beheshti, Musavi Ardebili and Bahonar – to Qom. The trio spent their time in the car on the two-hour journey discussing various scenarios. How had Khomeini reacted to the resignation? And if he were to accept it, who would take over? For them the issue was problematic because the general view was that, despite his victory over the constitution, Khomeini would be reluctant to let go of Bazargan and would not even contemplate allowing the Revolutionary Council, by this time decisively dominated by clerics, to take over executive affairs. To their surprise, as soon as they were ushered into his presence he announced that he would accept the resignation. When they asked what should be done next his response was brief and decisive: 'Nothing. You go and run the country, the people will carry on with their own duties.'[32] The next day he issued the Council with instructions to prepare for a constitutional referendum, and for presidential and parliamentary elections.[33]

Reflecting on the momentous events of 1979 and his own role in them Bazargan later wrote:

Under the circumstances, Khomeini was still fighting the Bakhtiar government and the hard-line generals in the army. He was also negotiating, through his aides, with the Americans to ensure a smooth and bloodless hand-over of power. To achieve this, as well as to avoid a civil war which might have led to the takeover of revolutionary leadership by the radicals and left wingers, Khomeini's choice [of premier] was indeed limited. But it was evident that the marriage between the two wings of the Islamic movement [clerical and non-clerical] was a marriage of convenience that would not last long.[34]

Forgetting this hugely important service to the cause of the *velayat-e faqih*, however innocently performed, the Ayatollah was later to say that he regretted his appointment of Bazargan:

We made a mistake, we did not act in a revolutionary way. We were two groups. One came from the school of theology, the other came from the outside. We did not have the revolutionary experience, they did not have the revolutionary spirit. That is why from the beginning we appointed the provisional government. We made a mistake. We should have appointed a young and resolute candidate, and not an impotent one. But at that time we did not have anybody, we did not know whom to choose, [so] we chose Bazargan, and it was a mistake.[35]

However, in the heated political climate of the time, concerned that Bazargan's supporters, or the anti-clerical parties, might take to the streets in his name Khomeini, ever the politician, paid a low-key tribute to him. 'Mr Bazargan,' he said, in an address to students from Isfahan University, 'is respected by everyone. ... He was a little tired and preferred to stay on the sidelines for a while.'[36]

But in fact, with Bazargan's departure, revolution had triumphed over reform and an honest politician had been hounded from his post. Bazargan, a rare fusion of piety, liberalism and patriotism returned to his old role as Iran's longest-standing opposition leader.

12

The Ruler
Creating an Islamic Republic

Less than a year after the revolution Khomeini was on the verge of realising his great dream – the abolition of secular institutions and the creation of a government based on the *shari'a* of the kind his hero, Sheikh Fazlollah Nuri, had favoured at the beginning of the twentieth century. In Qom he frequently visited the tomb of Sheikh Fazlollah to pray for his soul and for the success of the project he shared with the dead warrior of Islam.[1] Sheikh Fazlollah was hanged after the civil war that followed the 1906 Constitutional Revolution for his defence of absolutism[2] and his fate became a major theme in Khomeini's polemic against his secular foes: 'They want to sideline the clergy just as they did after the Constitutional period. They killed Nuri and diverted the path of the nation. They have now the same plan; they have killed Motahhari and perhaps it is my turn tomorrow.'[3]

Another activist, the first to devise a detailed, rather simplistic, blueprint for an Islamic government in Iran, was the charismatic Navvab Safavi whose ideas may have been influenced by Khomeini's *Kashf al-Asrar*. Navvab resorted to violence in his attempt to impose Islam on society and lost his life in the process. Afterwards it was to Khomeini, as an emerging political cleric, that Navvab's loyalists had turned in the early 1960s. Khomeini, for his own part, needed Navvab's supporters when he was looking for foot-soldiers.

After the revolution Khomeini was under pressure from the followers of Navvab Safavi to implement the rule of Islam in its entirety, immediately. They wanted the wholesale introduction of Islamic legal and social codes including a ban on music, alcohol, the cinema, usury, women working outside the home and compulsory veiling. But life had taught Khomeini to look before leaping and the failure of Nuri and of Navvab Safavi was constantly on his mind. He wanted to make use of secularists – whether left, right or nationalist – and then part ways with them at a time of his own choosing. The Feda'iyan of Islam may have been close to his heart and made up a large part of his entourage. But he was careful about how much he conceded to them. To Khomeini the social and cultural issues that concerned these men, the desire to impose on everyone what was in effect the religious culture of the urban lower middle classes, were of far less importance than the creation of a state whose institutions enshrined the clergy's right to rule. And the danger was that the whole enterprise might collapse unless there was a compromise on social and cultural issues, at least until such time as the population, which had become accustomed to the social, if not political freedoms of the Shah's era, could be forced to accept the situation. His major social measures in the early stages of the revolution were to enforce Islamic dress on women, the abiding symbol of an Islamic society, and to ban alcohol; but in other areas he moved more cautiously, for example banning unacceptable films but not films as such, unacceptable music but not music as such.

Many of the secularists who had been incorporated into Bazargan's government had resigned as it became increasingly evident that the clergy were exercising determined domination over the reins of power and Bazargan had attempted to resign several times. Now that Khomeini had strengthened his hand and fortified his regime by allowing time for his trusted students to be trained for the top jobs, to inject the apparatus of state with loyal clergy at every level and to set up new institutions, he was in a much stronger position.

Khomeini's display of confidence when he finally accepted Bazargan's resignation thus came from the knowledge that his drive for Islamic government had been taken an important step further. The Assembly of Experts had by this time produced a constitution that secured his position as ruler and laid the foundation for a theocracy and for a legal system based on Islamic jurisprudence.

The new constitution reflected the attitudes of two different groups of Khomeini loyalists in the Assembly: those who wanted Islamic rule with the Qor'an as its 'constitution', untainted by the Western concept of democracy and division of powers and responsibility, and those who believed that Islamic rule could be made more palatable by giving it a semi-democratic structure. The result of this mix was the creation of a peculiar political formula, a blueprint for a populist theocracy, that ensured a working anarchy.

The hastily arranged document stipulated that 'sovereignty belongs to God' and put God's viceregent, the *vali-ye faqih*, in the role of God's agents. It thus centralised the polity in the actual or theoretical person of the *vali-ye faqih* or jurisconsult. In addition, it gave him wide-ranging specific powers: the authority to declare war and peace, to appoint military leaders, to confirm the president and to choose the highest-ranking judicial officials. On paper the new constitution also allowed popular participation on almost every level of the political process and a theoretical division between the three branches of government – the executive, the legislature and the judiciary. But equally, since the *faqih* – or his representatives, that is the clergy – could exercise rights of veto at every level, the notions of participation and the division of powers were potentially meaningless.

Khomeini was, of course, to be the first *vali-ye faqih*. But in view of his advanced age the constitution laid down arrangements for the selection of his successors. The *velayat* or leadership was to be appointed by an Assembly of Experts whose role may be compared with that of the Catholic 'College of Cardinals', an arrangement that is regarded by some as an innovation in Shi'ism whose religious leaders traditionally emerged by popular acclaim, based on the opinion of the faithful and, in practice, the second-rank ulema who were consulted by the people. The Assembly of Experts would sit at least twice a year to advise, reprimand and, if need be, replace the leadership. Its members would be elected directly by the people every eight years – although from candidates approved by the Council of Guardians.

Khomeini was not entirely happy with the document finally endorsed by the Assembly of Experts, which he rightly believed to be contaminated by Western ideas. It was not the apparently modern notion of elections that disturbed him. From his point of view, the structure of authority in the new political system was crystal clear: the Guardianship of the Jurisprudent was divine rule, and 'the people's participation was their vote of allegiance' (the old Islamic concept of *bay'a*) rather than their choice.[4] Yet in his view, reports Yusef Sane'i, one of his students, 'the Assembly of Experts was afraid of the intellectuals otherwise they would have given more power to the *faqih* such as the right to "appoint" rather than to "confirm" the president.'[5]

He nevertheless decided that, for the moment at least, it was good enough. His personal charisma and the veto he could exercise over virtually any decision meant that in matters that were vital to him he could overrule the formal structures of power – just as, in practice, those who had his confidence would be able to exercise more influence than those who held positions in the formal state structure. But more important, although by this time the Hezbollah had effectively driven the National Democratic Front, the main focus of secularist opposition during the summer of 1979, from the political arena, Khomeini was faced with a tidal wave of revolt over the constitution, which was to be put to the people in a referendum scheduled for 3 December. The armed left-wing guerilla movements, principally the People's Mojahedin and the People's Feda'iyan, the ethnic minorities and Shari'atmadari's influential Muslim People's Republican Party were all vehemently opposed to it.

He was able to defuse the guerilla movements temporarily by manipulating the hostage crisis. For several days following the occupation of the American Embassy, Khomeini had remained uncharacteristically silent. This was clearly a period fraught with danger. If he immediately backed the Islamic radicals in public and then the liberals managed to organise support against the excesses of the radicals, or the Americans presented Iran with a decisive ultimatum, he might have to face a humiliating climbdown. As things stood it seemed prudent to allow some days to pass before he committed himself. For all his fiery rhetoric, Khomeini was at heart a deeply pragmatic man whose every move was planned. Taken by surprise by the affair of the embassy, he needed time to gather his thoughts and assess the potential advantages and disadvantages of any pronouncement by him for or against the move.

Within days it became clear that the domestic forces opposing the radicals were not strong or united enough to mount any kind of move against them. On the international front it was equally clear that, for all the expressions of outrage emanating from Washington and the capitals of Europe, no agreement existed within the West on an appropriate response. The West had blinked, and Khomeini was quick to exploit its weakness;

it was now safe to back the radical students openly.

Khomeini's support for the attack on the American embassy took two forms – actions and words. Firstly he sanctioned the entry into the embassy of Hojjat al-Islam Mohammad Musavi Kho'iniha as prayer leader and spiritual guide to the 'students following the Imam's line' as they now called themselves. Kho'iniha was a close friend of Ahmad Khomeini and one of Khomeini's radical students who was also on the directorate of Iranian radio and television. His association with the embassy takeover gave the students an air of legitimacy sufficient to prevent them from being labelled as communists. 'It was the presence of Mr Kho'iniha that enabled us to resist,' said one of the student leaders 'The Leader of the revolution must have realised our vulnerability, as he sent us a private message in the early hours of the first night which gave us enormous moral support to resist all threats.' What is even more significant is that the position taken by the students was described as a position 'taken by the Leader [Khomeini] and expressed by the students'.[6] They as a result had free rein to publicise their early demand, which was the exchange of the Shah, who was in a New York clinic, for the hostages.

The publicity given to the American embassy hostage crisis by the world media gave Khomeini a new buoyancy and assertiveness, setting the stage for a major confrontation with the Carter administration. 'The Americans can't do a damn thing,' he pronounced to the Students Following the Imam's Line and the rest of his young supporters. 'The speculation about American military intervention is nonsense. How can America militarily intervene in this country? It is not possible. The whole world is watching. Can America stand up to the world and intervene here? America would not dare.'[7]

By supporting the takeover openly, Khomeini was able to associate America with the opponents of the 'guardianship of jurisconsult' (velayat-e faqih) who he damned with the claim that America, instead of intervening by force was trying to infiltrate the country through the pen.[8] He was also easily able to distract the attention of the leftist guerilla organisations who were still enthusiastic in their belief that the priority was to support Khomeini's anti-imperialist stand. In short, Khomeini viewed the occupation of the American embassy in terms of his domestic policy. As he explained to the foreign minister Bani Sadr:

This action has many benefits. The Americans do not want to see the Islamic

Republic taking root. We keep the hostages, finish our internal work, then release them. This has united our people. Our opponents do not dare act against us. We can put the constitution to the people's vote without difficulty, and carry out presidential and parliamentary elections. When we have finished all these jobs we can let the hostages go.[9]

When Bani Sadr suggested that hostage-taking undermined the legitimacy and credibility of the revolution, Khomeini's response was characteristically inflexible: 'They cannot destroy the legitimacy of the revolution. Taking hostages has increased our credibility. Don't you hear the news of demonstrations in support of us in other countries? While the hostages are in our possession they will not dare do anything.' Bani Sadr recalls: 'When I told him that the United States was prepared to ignore the lives of fifty-two people so as to achieve its objective in Iran, Khomeini curtly replied:"This is all nonsense. We must be hard. We will reach our objectives and we will get many concessions." When Bani Sadr tried again to argue against the hazards of hostage-taking, Khomeini's response was: 'I am tired now, I must go.'[10]

Khomeini had never been particularly interested in discussion and dialogue. He was an introvert; his dialogue was with himself rather than with others, and his approach was intuitive. He could listen to someone attentively for a long time if need be; but when he made up his mind about an issue his patience ran out very quickly. Bani Sadr, who within months was to fall out with his former mentor, can be expected to be critical. Nevertheless as one of the people closest to Khomeini his observations do carry some weight. Bani Sadr alleges that the reason Khomeini did not want to get involved in discussion was that he felt 'it would damage his authority of leadership and dignity'. He recalls Khomeini's reaction in some prior conversations:

When he heard something that he felt he should comment on, he expressed his views. If he heard approval for his views or a complimentary view, then Khomeini would smile, perhaps allowing the conversation to continue for one or two more minutes. If he was confronted with an opposing view, his face would become stern and he would look down. This meant that he was no longer willing to listen or talk, and that the conversation had ended. If one persisted, then Khomeini would either say that he was tired and leave the room, or brusquely say: 'I don't want to hear any more'.[11]

The hostage crisis was a watershed in Khomeini's life. Not only was he now the leader of the revolution in Iran, but the 'Imam of the Islamic Community of the World' and the 'Hope of the World Oppressed'. The cautious, pragmatic politician who had masterminded a coalition with left-wingers, intellectuals, nationalists and liberals to overthrow the Shah now began to talk and behave like a modern revolutionary single-mindedly pursuing a dogma. For Khomeini, the Qor'anic vocabulary was no longer sufficient to express the tumult generated by events. He began to use the vocabulary he had learnt from the West against it. Imperialism, liberalism, democracy were negative words. Yet at the same time 'revolution', a concept which originated in the West and had been imported by Western-educated Iranians into Persian, was transformed into an anti-Western word with an Iranian and religious colouring.[12] It became a sacred word, sometimes more important than Islam. 'Acting in a revolutionary manner' was approved by Khomeini, even if it was argued to be anti-Islamic by rival clerics. In this climate and in this state of mind, Khomeini abandoned his earlier policy of acting as a moderating influence on the hardline revolutionaries. Khomeini came to regard the domestic fallout of the occupation of the American embassy on 4 November 1979 and the crisis it provoked as 'the second Islamic Revolution'.

With the left, for the time being at least, neutralised after the hostage-taking the glare of radical revenge and revolutionary terror was turned on Khomeini's clerical opponents and the secular forces who rallied behind them. The clerical opposition to his move towards a fully theocratic state came mainly from Ayatollahs Reza Zanjani, Qomi and Shari'atmadari. Of these three, the old, rather gentle Grand Ayatollah Shari'atmadari was by far the most important.

Shari'atmadari had lost much prestige with young revolutionaries because of his mild approach to the Shah's regime. Nevertheless, he commanded a large following throughout the country, particularly in his native Azarbaijan where many recognised him as their *marja'-e taqlid*. Furthermore, as time went by and the undemocratic thrust of Khomeini's politics became clearer, many of those who opposed him for one reason or another, including some secular leftists, knew they had an ideal vehicle in this benign man.

Shari'atmadari and the MPRP had, throughout the summer of 1979, campaigned openly against Khomeini's brand of Islam and his methods. Khomeini had personally avoided direct confrontation with them during this period although the inevitable war of words and some clashes between the supporters of the two ayatollahs had broken out. But the challenge had been serious enough to prompt private action. On 18 June 1979, a rare conclave, arranged through the mediation of other eminent ayatollahs took place at the home of Khomeini's senior colleague, the apolitical Grand Ayatollah Golpayegani. Besides the austere bespectacled Golpayegani himself the meeting included Grand Ayatollah Mara'shi Najafi, a relaxed man blessed with casual manner who was more interested in scholarly pursuits than in the intrigues of theological circles, and of course Khomeini and Shari'atmadari. The four men were the leading Shi'i divines residing in Iran and their meeting was symbolic of the new relationship that had emerged between the institution of the *marja'iyat* and a *marja'* who had in effect become a ruler.

Sitting cross-legged under whirring fans, sipping small glasses of tea, the four grandees got down to business. Golpayegani opened the conversation with a reference to the tense atmosphere that had developed in Qom: 'This is going to harm Islam the clergy and all of us.' But his attempt to bring about a reconciliation in the interests of Islam itself merely provided Khomeini with an opportunity to present – implicitly – his final ultimatum to Shari'atmadari. He sat in his place grimly, armed with documents and files taken from various archives of the Shah's bureaucracy. From these he read passages that, to him at least, showed how in the past Shari'atmadari had not only failed to support him but had 'co-operated' with the Shah's regime. In the sombre atmosphere Khomeini managed to generate, the mediating ayatollahs were unable to make any progress.

Shari'atmadari was undeterred, and while the constitution was being discussed in the Assembly of Experts, he aired his misgivings about its undemocratic nature in the strongest possible terms. To him the principle of the *velayat-e faqih* could be applied only in cases where the *shari'a* had not provided an authorised agent, and then only when it was a matter of dealing with unavoidable issues.[13] Power and sovereignty were, he believed, rooted in the people and the Assembly of Experts had no authority – theological or otherwise – to approve any principle that would call into question the sovereignty of the people.[14] Each week while the Assembly was in session the Muslim People's Republican Party held meetings at which its members discussed their criticisms of the concept of the *velayat-e faqih* which were summarised for the public in the party's weekly newspaper *Khalq-e Mosalman*.[15] When the Assembly concluded its proceedings the party declared that it would boycott the 3 December referendum unless certain modifications were made to the text of the constitution, while Shari'atmadari publicly announced his refusal to participate unless the article on the *velayat-e faqih* was modified.[16]

But Shari'atmadari was no match for Khomeini, despite the fact that it was obviously difficult for Khomeini to condemn statements of a fellow *marja'* in the same way that he had undermined the challenges of the secular opposition.[17] A violent campaign was launched against him immediately after the referendum. It began with a threatening demonstration outside his house in Qom where a large crowd chanted slogans in favour of the new constitution. The incident enraged the population of the large north-western city of Tabriz, the capital of Iranian Azarbaijan, who looked upon Shari'atmadari, himself a Tabrizi, as their spiritual guide. The Azarbaijanis were further antagonised when the ayatollah's picture was shown on the television superimposed with the appeasing declaration of another clergyman whose name, conveniently for Khomeini's strong-armed men, was also 'Shari'atmadari'. Shari'atmadari's supporters rushed to occupy the radio and television station and threatened insurrection. The disturbance was in fact short-lived, and yet it was significant. On the one hand, it displayed the depth of feeling among broad segments of the population over the great political issues of the day and a diversity of ideas on government, even among the ulema. But on the other hand, it made Khomeini all the more determined to impose his Islamic system of government – by force if necessary.

Khomeini himself condemned the attack on Shari'atmadari's home and, referring to incidents in which his own portrait had been torn up in Tabriz and slogans shouted against him, had emphatically told his supporters: 'If anyone should abuse my name, or tear up my picture or beat me up, it is absolutely forbidden to react. We are in a dire situation.'[18] But within days a campaign was launched to blacken the MPRP as an organisation penetrated by 'anti-Islamic foreign agents'. It was easy to advance spurious 'proof' of the charge because, unable to use the domestic media, Shari'atmadari and his followers had to advance their case as much as they could through foreign airwaves and newspapers.

On Thursday 6 December 1979 Khomeini went to see Shari'atmadari at his home to deliver what appears to have been an ultimatum. What went on in their meeting has not been disclosed, but the tone can be gauged from Khomeini's subsequent message to the people of Azarbaijan: 'we have forbidden bloodshed, otherwise these rotten elements could not have carried out these actions. Were we to ask people [to act], the people of Azarbaijan themselves would put things in order.'[19] Surprised by Khomeini's harsh tone, Shari'atmadari retorted that the MPRP was an independent party. There were, he went on to say, differences of opinion between himself and Khomeini, but only of opinion and if Khomeini's officials did not agree with his, they could ignore the matter.[20] In a separate statement, in reply to a telegram from a leading cleric who had wanted him to dissolve MPRP, he said 'there is no need for founding members to dissolve political parties, since the government will gradually dissolve all parties labelling them as anti-Islamic, Zionist or American, so you should not worry about it.'[21]

Unlike Khomeini, Shari'atmadari had never been a militant fighter and his inability to give effective voice to his valid objections to the draft constitution weakened his position. He also had a badly organised political platform in the MPRP. At first he resisted the pressure and the party continued to organise huge demonstrations in Tabriz – reportedly some of them attracted a million people into the streets – demanding that the Ayatollah give them the order for holy war. Adverse to blood-letting, Shari'atmadari in the end decided to dissolve the party temporarily. But his supporters continued their demonstrations in Qom attacking shops belonging to supporters of Khomeini and marching on Khomeini's home. The incident amounted to an anti-Khomeini riot, and a serious challenge. But Shari'atmadari dissociated himself from it and the Tabriz uprising was rapidly put down.[22] Later in January many of Shari'atmadari's aides were arrested and he was put under virtual house arrest in Qom.

The December referendum returned a massive endorsement of the new constitution. But the turnout had been much lower than that for the March referendum, and many opposition groups and professional associations concerned with civil rights had abstained from voting. The opposition's accusations that Khomeini was trying to impose the rule of the turban and the substantial support it could still rally, meant that caution remained necessary if Khomeini was to legitimise his concept of the Islamic state among the modern, educated and secular forces in Iranian society as well as his own constituency. He therefore banned clerics from nominating themselves as candidates for the presidential election, scheduled to take place at the beginning of 1980. Other major potential candidates, too, either refused to run for office, or were disqualified for various reasons – usually for their beliefs and 'social attitudes'.

At first Khomeini's favoured candidate was the Islamic Republican Party nominee Jalaleddin Farsi, a leading figure in the Coalition of Islamic Societies who had close links with the Feda'iyan-e Islam. However, rather late in the day it was discovered that Farsi was born of an Afghan father and was not eligible to stand according to Article 115 of the constitution, which stipulated that candidates for the presidency had to be both of Iranian origin and nationality. It was too late for the IRP to produce another credible candidate and, with Farsi out of the running, Abolhassan Bani Sadr, Khomeini's adviser in Paris and a man popularly viewed as one of his 'favourite sons', became the front runner. Perceived by the electorate to be the closest to Khomeini among the candidates, Bani Sadr defeated his main rivals, the lacklustre Islamic modernist Hassan Habibi and the secularist Admiral Ahmad Madani, by a wide margin to become the first president in Iranian history.

He received Khomeini's confirmation on 4 February 1980. 'I will say one word to Mr Bani Sadr,' Khomeini had rather ominously remarked in a statement supposedly confirming his one-time adviser's victory, 'whatever office man achieves, it will be taken away from him one day, on an unspecified day. One must take care not to become too proud with high office. I ask Mr Bani Sadr not to change because of the office.'[23] In a statement issued the same day he added 'my confirmation depends on his adherence to the law of Islam and the constitution … I ask everyone … to support him as long as he acts according to the principles of Islam and supports the poor and the downtrodden and avoids quasi-*taghuti* [devilish *viz.*, in Khomeini's lexicon, secular] behaviour.'[24]

Bani Sadr's victory raised high expectations. For one thing, people felt confident that, for the first time in modern Iranian history, they had voted for a political leader in a relatively free election. For another, while he propagated his own utopian theories of Islam, Bani Sadr had been a member of the secular National Front and his politics differed substantially from those of the IRP. But his moment of glory was short-lived. Confusion over the constitutional role of the president became a source of difficulty for him, especially when he began to look around for his prime minister, while the powerful IRP, led by shrewd mollahs, from the beginning worked to undermine his position. Nor did Bani Sadr, even in the short-term, benefit from the support he might have expected from Khomeini given the latter's apparently neutral stance during the election and his delegation to the president, just a few weeks later, of his own powers as commander-in-chief of the armed forces.

Khomeini had also taken an important first step towards limiting Bani Sadr's power by immediately after the presidential election exercising one of his important constitutional prerogatives and appointing the IRP leader, Ayatollah Mohammad Beheshti, as chief justice of the supreme court. Beheshti had emerged as a central figure in the complex process of negotiating the peaceful transfer of power to Khomeini and establishing the institutions that supported and defended his position. As leader of the IRP he exercised important influence over the machinery of revolutionary terror, which he had used over the past months in a controlled, calculated manner. And, above all, he had been the main brain behind the formulation of the constitution. Khomeini's move ensured that Bani Sadr and other elements in the revolutionary movement who wanted a secular judiciary could exercise no influence over reforms in this sphere, and put his most able lieutenant in a position to preside over the Islamisation of the law, a process that was central to the construction of his Islamic state.

But it was not merely in the judiciary that Bani Sadr was to be excluded. Galvanised by its failure to make good in the presidential election, in the two-round elections for the first Islamic Parliament held in March and May 1980, the Islamic Republican Party mobilised its network among the clergy, the komitehs and the revolutionary guard. This time, clerical candidates were not only permitted, but, in an exhortation to the population to 'vote for only good Muslims', received Khomeini's explicit blessing. Meanwhile, the Hezbollah attacked the rallies and the offices of opposition parties who had fielded candidates – very largely the Mojahedin-e Khalq. Amid widespread accusations of malpractice – including one from Khomeini's brother, Morteza Pasandideh, who warned that violations of the kind that had been witnessed at the polls would alienate the people from the Islamic Republic[25] – the IRP succeeded in capturing about 85 seats. But its real strength was far greater. Parliament was dominated by the clergy, the Mojahedin won no seats at all, while Bani Sadr could command no more than a handful of supporters among the deputies.

As soon as it opened, the new parliament launched a long, debilitating confrontation with Bani Sadr over the selection of a prime minister who, under the constitution, was to be nominated by the president but approved by parliament. Unable himself to come up with a candidate acceptable to Beheshti and his IRP, Bani Sadr nevertheless refused to contemplate anyone suggested by parliament. The struggle dragged on for weeks until in August

Khomeini's intervention forced him to accept the IRP's candidate, Mohammad Ali Raja'i. Raja'i, an ex-school teacher from a poor family, had been an active member of the Coalition of Islamic Societies who worked closely with Beheshti, Farsi and Rafsanjani in setting up private Islamic schools and was very close to Mohammad Javad Bahonar who later became his prime minister. Bani Sadr publicly described Raja'i as 'incompetent' and refused to approve his cabinet list. The wrangle over the cabinet dragged on until well after the outbreak of the Iran–Iraq war on 22 September.

The IRP's drive for hegemony was conducted on numerous fronts during these and the following months. It was largely unimpeded by Khomeini, although he managed most of the time to keep his distance from the day-to-day details of the political fray. Despite repeated calls for unity in the face of Iraq's invasion, the political conflict between Bani Sadr and the clergy gained its own momentum. It affected all aspects of political life, including the conduct of the war. For the regular army was commanded by Bani Sadr, while the Revolutionary Guards took orders from his clerical rivals. Differences between traditionalists and modernists, which came to a head in June 1981 with the impeachment of Bani Sadr, had been building up since the early days of the revolution. In the debate between these two groups, the dominant theme was 'faith' versus 'expertise'. The modernists argued that the main criterion for deciding who should run the country and who should be appointed to important posts in the ministries and armed forces must be technical qualifications – expertise. The Islamists, however, stressed the importance of doctrinal or ideological commitment. That is, to use the terminology that developed after the revolution, a *maktabi* – one who is committed to the 'right path', a conformist who accepts the *velayat-e faqih*.

Under Bani Sadr this debate took clear shape, with the president becoming a focal point for all those who thought the mollahs should withdraw to their mosques and leave the running of the country to the 'experts', meaning the professional politicians and the technocrats. But for Khomeini himself, 'expertise without ideological commitment' was not only 'useless' but also 'dangerous'.[26] Indeed, as time went on, he became increasingly vehement on the subject. For example, on 27 May 1981, in a speech on the first anniversary of the opening of Majlis, aware of the groundswell of derision and opposition towards *maktabis*, he said:

As soon as they hear the word *maktabi*, the gentlemen poke fun at it. *Maktabi* means Islamic. To poke fun at it is to poke fun at Islam. If [a man] does so with conviction, he is an apostate which means his wife no longer is his and his property should be given to his heirs and he should be killed.'[27]

With such ideological backing, and with IRP members in virtual control of the state bureaucracy, the modernists had little chance of resisting the purges which swept government ministries from the second half of 1980, replacing their old personnel with people acceptable to the new order.

The Iraqi invasion in September 1980 gave Khomeini a new opportunity to call for unity and Bani Sadr a new lease of life. For Khomeini the sudden bombing of Tehran airport and Iraq's subsequent capture of large areas of western Iran, including the country's largest port and the centres of its oil industry, did not, on the surface, seem to be a big shock. His public reaction was to quieten the situation: 'A thief has come, thrown a pebble and fled back to his home and God willing will not be able to re-peat his action,'[28] he said as the population of Tehran reeled in shock at the sound of bombs on the airport. Underneath this calm appearance, however, Khomeini was genuinely worried. Iran's defences were in poor shape. The armed forces were dependent on America for the spare parts they needed to bring their military hardware up to scratch and, with the hostage crisis still unresolved, there was little hope of finding supplies there or in Western Europe. All three regular forces – the army, the air force and the navy – had also been weakened by repeated purges of their most highly trained cadres, the men who knew how to work the equipment.[29] There was a distinct danger that the Islamic Republic may collapse.

In the months preceding the outbreak of war, seeing himself as the leader of the Islamic Revolution, Khomeini had called on Muslims throughout the world to unite, suggesting that nationalism – an ideology that, after all, originated in the West – was the cause of their divisions. With the beginning of the war, he once again emphasised the need for Islamic unity and refused to compromise with Saddam Hossein, whom he regarded as an infidel. Comparing the Iran–Iraq War with the Prophet Mohammad's war against the infidels, he called on the Shi'i population of Iraq to overthrow Saddam. And yet, at the same time, he used Iranian patriotic sentiments to mobilise the population, calling on the 'Iranian nation' to unite and defeat the invader, though of course adding that this was for the sake of Islam.

For a time, a sense of purpose dominated the political scene in Iran, and appeals were made to all factions to come to the aid of the country and Islam. Khomeini, who by this time had left Qom to take up residence in the village of Jamaran in the northern part of Tehran, ordered the president and his clerical opponents in the Islamic Republican Party to leave their political warfare behind them and moved to strengthen Bani Sadr's position by appointing him chairman of the Supreme Defence Council in addition to commander-in-chief of the armed forces.

Bani Sadr responded by attempting to boost the morale of the army and strengthen its position. One of his first moves was to free air force pilots and military commanders who had been arrested on suspicion of involvement in a July 1980 military coup, and to install some in key positions within the military command and in the presidential office. But, finding the atmosphere at the military headquarters at the front more congenial, he spent nearly all his time in the south of the country, abandoning Tehran to his enemies who were determined not to abandon their own crusade. Once more he faced day-to-day obstruction from the IRP and had to resort to a very public campaign against them through his newspaper, Enqelab-e Islami (The Islamic Revolution). The IRP, however, held all the decisive instruments of power, including the radio and television. By the Spring of 1981 the conflict between the party and Bani Sadr had, despite the dangerous military situation, turned into a major media campaign.

A voracious consumer of the media, Khomeini followed it all in detail. Besides listening to Tehran Radio and foreign radio stations, he watched television and read most newspapers. In addition to Bani Sadr's Enqelab-e Islami and the IRP's Jomhuri-ye Islami, he was an avid reader of the opposition press: Bazargan's Mizan with its features and readers' letters criticising various social aspects of the revolution,[30] the Mojahedin's Mojahed; Ommat, edited by Dr Habibollah Peiman who led a group of left wing Muslims; Peikar, the newspaper of the defected Marxist wing of the Mojahedin, and the Tudeh Party's Mardom were all part of his daily reading matter and he would frequently present his aides with cuttings and requests for further analysis and investigation. He thus had a wide insight into the various political divisions which existed in Iran. The editorial board of Enqelab-e Islami, which at the height of the tension between the IRP and Bani Sadr, and after much wrangling with Khomeini's office, obtained an audience with him were surprised by his first hand knowledge of the editorials and other columns in the paper.[31]

Just before the Iranian New Year, in March 1981, Khomeini tried to heal the rift between the president and the IRP. The occasion was the aftermath of a large rally held by Bani Sadr on 5 March on the campus of Tehran University to commemorate the death of Mosaddeq. The rally was protected by members of the People's Mojahedin who had disarmed Hezbollahi thugs sent to attack the demonstrators and found IRP membership cards in their pockets.[32] The two sides were summoned to Khomeini's presence and told to appoint arbitrators in order to sink their differences. But Bani Sadr refused to recognise the prime minister, or to acknowledge the legitimacy of the IRP's command over the key institutions of the state.[33] The next day Khomeini issued a decree banning speeches and newspaper articles that might contribute to the friction until the end of the war.

Although the decree was apparently neutral and binding on both parties, and although it confirmed Bani Sadr in his position as commander-in-chief of the armed forces, it in effect disarmed him. He had to either fall silent and settle down to the role of a figurehead president in a political arena in which the IRP made all the running, or resign and take his place on the sidelines of politics as Bazargan had done before him. But Bani Sadr was strongly influenced by the results of weekly public opinion polls taken by his aides, which invariably placed him at the top of the popularity chart. He and his close aides were sustained by the belief that he commanded the loyalty of nearly 95 per cent of the population. Indeed his aides insisted that he was, in fact, more popular than Khomeini himself. His newspaper, Enqelab-e Islami, which was widely read after it began to publish material aimed at boosting anti-IRP morale, definitely gave that impression.

In general terms this was almost certainly an illusion. But, like Shari'atmadari, the president had become the rallying point for all doubters and dissidents. Chief among his supporters were the People's Mojahedin, who Bani Sadr had once dismissed as 'eclectics', but whose support he now gratefully welcomed.

Despite their ideological differences the Mojahedin had, over the first phase of the revolution, coexisted with Khomeini. But as time went by, and all organisations other than those which actively supported the regime were attacked, they were thrown into increasing confrontation. Khomeini, who had always been quietly suspicious of the movement and its ideology, had referred to them in scathing terms just before the March

1980 parliamentary elections as 'eclectics' (*elteqati*) who were contaminated
with the 'Western plague' and were trying to mix Islam and Marxism. He
was later to add the terms *monafeqin* (hypocrites) and *kafer* (unbelievers)
to the lexicon he used to describe them.[34]

After the revolution and the release of their leading members from
prison, the Mojahedin had retained and built upon the underground guerilla experience they had acquired under the Shah. They could also rally
very considerable support; indeed it is estimated that, even on the official
count, and despite all the malpractice, they received as much as 20 per
cent of the vote in the elections to the first Islamic parliament.[35] Their
principle social base was among the young educated members of religiously-
inclined middle and lower middle class families who rejected the conservatism of their parent's generation. But once the National Democratic Front
and Shari'atmadari's party were destroyed, many secularist dissenters from
all walks of life supported them in preference to Marxist groups such as
the Feda'iyan-e Khalq. After the elections, and up to the overthrow of
Bani Sadr in mid-1981, the Mojahedin conducted a vigorous campaign
against the government on all fronts and became increasingly involved in
demonstrations and street clashes with the Hezbollah. Khomeini was repeatedly drawn into the confrontation and by the end of 1980 the organisation's leadership had virtually been driven underground.

In the wake of Khomeini's March decree, the Mojahedin and Bani Sadr
continued their joint struggle against the IRP. But after a demonstration
in Tehran on 27 April, which drew 150,000, the chief prosecutor banned
the Mojahedin from demonstrating.[36] Increasingly beleaguered, Bani Sadr
started to challenge Khomeini's own authority. His miscalculations were
to become apparent in May and June 1981. On 8 June he made a fatal move
in a speech at the Shiraz air force base in which he called for resistance to
dictatorship. This was tantamount to threatening an uprising. Some of
his enthusiastic supporters went as far as encouraging him to take over
with the help of the army and sympathisers he was reported to have in the
Revolutionary Guard. On the very same day, Khomeini countered by telling an audience that the law of the land was for all. It had to be respected
by all, and if it was not accepted by a minority it did not mean that they
were entitled to come out and protest against it. Opposition to the law
through street demonstrations was, he said ominously, a dictatorial act.
Those who tried to break the law were dictators trying to infiltrate into
society and put forward their plans in the guise of Islam or democracy.[37]

In response, Bani Sadr accused Khomeini of destroying the country by refusing to allow a competent government to introduce modern and democratic policies, and preferring an impotent administration. He further suggested that it was actually the IRP and its authoritarian and corrupt leaders who threatened Islam, the nation and Khomeini himself.[38]

On 10 June, Khomeini stripped Bani Sadr of his title of commander-in-chief of the armed forces. The Majles, in turn, moved to impeach him while the Mojahedin rallied to support him. On the surface, this must have seemed an opportune time to strike back and either overthrow Khomeini or weaken him so much that he would have to compromise. The combination of an armed guerrilla movement and an elected president was tempting. On 20 June, the day of the Majles's impeachment vote, the Mojahedin, supported by all opposition groups except the Tudeh Party and the majority faction of the Feda'iyan-e Khalq, called on the people to take to the streets and march against dictatorship. It was the most direct challenge to Khomeini since the revolution, and an unmistakable attempt to overthrow the religious establishment. The authorities reacted swiftly and violently, sending Revolutionary Guards and Muslim toughs out into the streets to prevent the demonstrations at all costs. According to the Mojahedin, 500,000 people took to the streets of Tehran on 20 June and one million in the country as a whole; according to some others the Tehran demonstrators numbered no more than 100,000, including Marxist guerrilla groups. Hezbollahis armed with chains and sticks succeeded in breaking up the crowd near the central Ferdowsi Square. Serious fighting then ensued between the guerrillas and the Revolutionary Guards who opened fire on the crowd. Up to twenty people died, including several Revolutionary Guards, and more than a thousand were arrested. Some of the Mojahedin casualties were the victims of summary executions carried out on the spot.

On 21 June, the Majles voted 177 to 1, with 11 abstentions, to impeach the president, and on the following day Khomeini dismissed him from his post. But that was not enough to settle the issue. Sporadic Mojahedin demonstrations continued while Bani Sadr, from a secret hideout, issued further calls for a mass uprising. The authorities reacted with unprecedented violence, including further summary executions in the streets. In a week of clashes, more than fifty opponents of the religious leadership were killed in the streets and prisons. The chances of the Mojahedin overthrowing Khomeini or seriously crippling the establishment were small, but there were indications that IRP leaders – who had never commanded the kind of popularity that Bani Sadr enjoyed – were so nervous that they overreacted to the challenge. The large number of executions and killings backfired, creating a new wave of sympathy for the Mojahedin.

On 28 June 1981, a large bomb destroyed the IRP headquarters in southeast Tehran where party leaders were holding urgent discussions. Among over seventy people[39] killed in the explosion were Ayatollah Beheshti and other key functionaries, including cabinet ministers and nearly two dozen members of parliament.[40] A devastating blow had been dealt against Khomeini and it stunned not only the establishment but the whole country.

Panic broke out among officials in the Imam's office over how to inform him of the tragedy; but the anxiety, as it turned out, was misplaced. Khomeini had heard the news on a foreign radio station and by the time his aides ventured into his presence he was completely composed. When, the next day, Rafsanjani and Ahmad Khomeini went to visit the old man, it was he who consoled them and turned to business as usual. The Majles, he instructed them, should resume its proceedings to secure the appointment of a new chief justice to replace Beheshti and new government ministers to replace those who had died.[41]

It was never established who was behind the bombing. Officials at first pointed the finger of accusation at both former Savak agents and the Mojahedin. But in his first public reaction to the event, Khomeini made his own view of who was responsible very clear. He referred to Beheshti as 'the wronged martyr' (shahid-e mazlum – the term used to refer to Imam Hossein) because, as he put it, 'he was accused of many things and made out to be many things which he was not.' 'This calamitous incident,' he continued, was 'committed by the agents of America, and by those who, if one reads their Epistemology, one knows have no belief in any of the principles of Islam. They were martyred by them.'[42] He meant the Mojahedin and his reference was to one of the group's major ideological tracts, Ketab-e Shenakht (Epistemology).

The Mojahedin never publicly attempted to claim or to disclaim responsibility for the bombing although they have described it as 'natural and necessary reaction to the regime's atrocities.' They were nevertheless generally perceived as the culprits and the bombing was used as a pretext to wage an all-out war against them, against left-wing groups and against the National Front which had already been accused by Khomeini of

apostasy for its opposition to the introduction of *sharia* (Islamic) laws.
Executions of opposition figures in prison, which had begun after the 20
June demonstration when Sa'id Soltanpur, an openly critical poet and
writer, was suddenly taken from his prison cell and shot, were stepped up.
The Mojahedin responded in kind and in the weeks that followed many
other leading officials and clergy in Tehran and other major cities were
wounded or killed. On 6 July Hojjat al-Islam Shari'ati-Fard in Gilan, on 4
August Dr Hassan Ayat in Tehran, on 11 September Ayatollah Madani in
Tabriz, on 29 September Hojjat al-Islam A. K. Hashemi-Nejad in Mashhad and many lesser officials. Khomeini's response was to

congratulate the Islamic nation and their relatives for having offered such
martyrs ... These blind people, who presume that the Islamic Republic would
collapse with the absence of few people, have no understanding of Islam and
faith. We are sorry to have lost these precious people but we have others
queuing up to fill their places.[43]

In the aftermath of the explosion thousands were imprisoned, and at
least 100 were executed within two weeks. By late August there had been
900 executions and, according to Amnesty International, the total by the
end of 1981 reached over 2,500.[44] The executions continued until January.
The authorities' overreaction worsened the crisis and was seen by many as
unnecessary. It was nevertheless predictable. More disconcerting, even to
his close associates, was Khomeini's calm determination to sustain the
terror as a means of enabling the Islamic Republic to weather the crisis.
His opponents' miscalculations, on the other hand, facilitated the task.
On 30 August, mysterious bombers struck again, this time killing Mohammad Ali Raja'i, who had been elected on 24 July to replace Bani Sadr
as president, and Mohammad Javad Bahonar, now his prime minister.

A week later it was announced that a member of the Mojahedin, Mas'ud
Kashmiri, was responsible for planting the bomb. Kashmiri worked un-
der cover as one of the prime minister's security officials and at one stage
he was the secretary to the National Security Council. While Bahonar
and Raja'i were in a meeting he left the room leaving his suitcase behind.
According to Ahmad Khomeini, some time before this incident, on 22
August, when Raja'i took his entire cabinet to introduce them to the Imam,
Kashmiri had attempted to take his suitcase into Khomeini's office:

Kashmiri was with Raja'i and Bahonar when they came to see the Imam. We did not allow him to bring his suitcase with him. They both felt let down, arguing that he is the secretary to the state security council and is just carrying documents.[45]

Had Kashmiri been successful he would have been able to target tens of people including Khomeini and all members of the government.

Khomeini reacted with characteristic aplomb:

Any martyr from us and from you is in the interest of Islam and against their interest. We are not afraid. Had they acted with wisdom, he [Bani Sadr] would have still been president and could have pushed towards the West and all would have prayed towards the West. But God prevented that and they could not act with self-restraint.[46]

Unlike Beheshti, Raja'i commanded sympathy and affection among ordinary people, and the reaction against the Mojahedin was intense. Within weeks of the 20 June, and before the election of Raja'i, Rajavi and Bani Sadr had escaped in an air force plane to Paris.

Nevertheless, in a nationwide broadcast Khomeini added further fuel to the campaign against the Mojahedin and other opposition groups by announcing that the religious duty of all individuals would be to keep an eye on their neighbours. The appeal drew a wide response. Opposition hideouts were disclosed one after another. Many were arrested on the flimsiest grounds. Brothers began to spy on brothers. There was even an example of a religious mother who handed over her own son to the authorities and watched his execution. Those who were detained suffered not only from the cruelty of prison, but also from visits by their own parents and relatives advising them to repent and get out. A religious judge was to order the execution of his own son. The great wheel of terror did not differentiate between kith and kin. It brutalised the whole society.

The assassinations of leading officials and active supporters of the regime by the Mojahedin were to continue for the next year or two. The killing was reactive on both sides. Assassinations avenged executions, triggering in their turn waves of dark vengeance in the prisons. Numerous members of the regime lost their lives, while over the months executions of Mojahedin supporters and leftists rose to several thousands – no one knows the exact figure.

The threat posed by the Mojahedin began to wane from early 1982 when their commander Musa Khiabani was killed and his hideout destroyed.

But it was not for another year that the challenge mounted from inside the country by this and other guerilla organisations was essentially defused. In the effort to bring the situation under control the authorities set up a repressive machinery that would prove difficult to dismantle. The main danger to the government then came to lie in its own behaviour and the effects of the repression on the general public.

13

The Warrior and his Theocracy
Khomeini Defies the World

On the 20 October 1981, Hojjat al-Islam Ali Khamene'i took over as the third president of the Islamic republic. His election marked a turning point for Khomeini, who had previously discouraged the clergy from ambitions which might draw the accusation that he was trying to create a theocracy. But the removal of Bani Sadr and the killing of Beheshti, Raja'i, Bahonar and tens of politicians and clergy had shaken the foundation of the republic and brought about an air of instability. Stunned by the carnage, Khomeini now made it clear that he wanted the clergy to become more, not less involved in the political scene: 'I have brought them up. I brought up Beheshti, Khamene'i and Rafsanjani. I know they don't want to monopolise power. They are not monopolistic. Of course they want the monopoly of Islam. The Prophet of Islam says there is only one God. Is this monopoly? If it is, then all prophets were monopolistic and God is monopolistic.'[1]

Khamene'i was another member of the inner circle of clergy who had been at Khomeini's side since the 15 Khordad uprising. He was also a personal favourite and Khomeini would sometimes refer to him in public using his first name followed by 'Aqa', master, a form of respectful endearment reserved in Iran for family and close friends. 'I suggest that Ali Aqa

Khamene'i should go to the university,' he said to students complaining in the early months of the revolution about the extension of leftist influence on the campuses. 'Go to him and tell him that I have asked him to [take on the task] and fill Motahhari's place. He is very good, he is learned, he speaks well.'[2] His high regard for Khamene'i's eloquence and oratory led Khomeini to appoint him in January 1980 as the Friday Prayer leader of Tehran and to describe him on that occasion as 'a man of good reputation and worthy of knowledge and action.'[3] This rare combination of 'knowledge' and 'action', but more importantly, enthusiasm, and his obedience to his master, made Khamene'i, only 41, a man Khomeini could trust. Indeed over the ten years of Khomeini's rule he received Khamene'i in his different capacities nearly 150 times – more than any other official.

Khamene'i came from a clerical family which originated in Azarbaijan; but he was brought up in Mashhad. He had spent time in jail and internal exile during the 1960s and 1970s and was highly regarded in theological circles. A frequenter of literary societies, he spoke Persian eloquently, was the author of a number of books and had translated works by Islamic thinkers including one by Seyyed Qotb, a leading ideologue of the Muslim Brotherhood in Egypt. Soon after the war with Iraq began, Khamene'i became the Imam's special representative in the Supreme Defence Council. He was later made deputy defence minister and for a while put in charge of the Revolutionary Guards. After Beheshti's death he was made general secretary of the Islamic Republican Party. Miraculously, he escaped the various attempts to bomb the clerical leadership into oblivion, a feat which in some quarters earned him the title of 'the living martyr' and, after one particularly close shave, a fulsome note from Khomeini: 'I congratulate you my dear Khamene'i. A selfless soldier and a caring guide in the arena of the revolution, who has served the people at the battle front wearing military fatigues and behind the front wearing clerical attire.'[4]

Khomeini, as the tone of his exchanges with his new turbaned officials indicated, was clearly more at home with them than he had been with Bazargan or Bani Sadr, even during the short-lived honeymoons with both. When in January 1982 Khamene'i and his prime minister and cabinet went to greet Khomeini on the occasion of the Prophet's birthday, he was full of compliments:

Not since the inception of government the world over, has there ever been such an amiable gathering. We are all together. We all talk about our problems and together we pay attention to them. I hope we can save the deprived from the misery they have suffered in the course of history and offer them prosperity in this and next world.[5]

For liberal Muslims such as Mehdi Bazargan, who for years had fought the Shah to establish a democratic system based on a tolerant Islam, the turn of events brought bitter disappointment. For them, the path Khomeini had taken was totally different from the one he had advocated in Paris where he had painted a picture of a democratic system which would act like the Prophet Mohammad's ten years of government in Medina and the five years of the Shi'i Imam Ali's in Kufa. Above all Bazargan was concerned that there was no more dialogue. In his view, Khomeini had turned the slogan 'we are all together' on its head and was effectively saying 'you are all with me'.[6]

Khomeini's personal role in the gradual transformation of the clergy into a 'clerical regency' – as Bazargan, using the French term, called the new theocracy[7] – was significant. He actively encouraged mollahs to come forward and take over key positions in the government and the civil service: 'Islam is a religio-political faith (*din-e ebadi-siasi*). Its worship contains politics and its political affairs contain worship.'[8] Even learned *mojtaheds*, some of whom were reluctant to move out of the seminaries because involvement in executive matters might have affected their chances of becoming a *marja'* were urged to join the political fray: 'time and place are two elements in *ejtehad*. *Mojtaheds* must be well versed in current issues. It is not acceptable to the youth, or even to ordinary people, for a *mojtahed* to say he has no opinion on political issues.'[9] Important decision-making jobs were entrusted to the clergy as not only secularists, but also religious intellectuals and non-political professionals who were not in tune with the theocracy were pushed out. In a speech to the Council of Guardians in 1983, Khomeini stated that he had been wrong to assume that after the victory of the revolution there would be politicians competent to take responsibility and act according to Islam. He had frequently promised, he said, that religious personalities were to be only a temporary presence in government and that after the revolution they would confine themselves to their religious duties. But now he realised that there were very few people who had the type of competence he sought.

[The fact that] I have said something does not mean that I should be bound by my word. I am saying that for as long as we have not implemented all

Islamic rules and have no competent people to do the job, the clergy should stay in their positions. It is below the dignity of a clergyman to be a president or to occupy other posts. He does it because it is a duty. We have to implement Islam and should not fear anyone.[10]

The network set up by the clergy throughout Iran was all-embracing. From the village mollah to the top leaders in Qom or Tehran, there were contacts on all kinds of issues – religious, security, judicial, economic and political. The population's own contact with mollahs was, before the revolution, a private matter, largely confined to requests for spiritual help and guidance. But after the revolution, and certainly by 1983, the bureaucracy and the official world in general was so extensively dominated by the clergy that everyone had to deal with them on a day-to-day basis, whether they liked it or not. Mollahs were no longer just in mosques and *madrasehs*, but in revolutionary courts, committees, education departments, universities, tax offices, the local governor's office, factories – any institution you may care to mention. Mosques, on the other hand, were centres for the recruitment of war volunteers and for dispensing ration cards and other perks among the families of revolutionary and war victims. The imperial regime never had so much presence in the country, nor such a vast network of representatives.

The near civil war at home in mid-1981 had slowed the effort to drive the Iraqi army from Iranian territory to a virtual standstill. With Bani Sadr's departure, however, better co-operation could be achieved between the army and the Revolutionary Guards. As the internal strife subsided, the focus shifted to the war, and to the task of liberating Iranian territories. 'Mr Bani Sadr was eloquent,' Khomeini said in a pep talk to the armed forces, 'but it was you who were doing the job. If you achieve victory once or twice, then no one will say that the changes have affected your morale.'[11] They obliged. In the autumn new offensives were launched against the Iraqi forces which had occupied large swathes of Iranian territory in the south-west of the country. The year-long Iraqi siege of Abadan, the site of Iran's key oil installations was broken in September. Over the next six months Iranian forces notched up a string of victories, large and small, which climaxed in the re-capture in May 1982 of Khorramshahr, the country's major port. The triumph was announced on Tehran radio at about 4 pm local time while Khomeini was on one of his 30-minute daily walks in

Jamaran accompanied by his son Ahmad and one of his grandchildren. As usual, he was listening to his pocket-size short-wave radio.[12] It was an emotional moment. Khamene'i, Rafsanjani and Prime Minister Musavi hurried to offer their congratulations and Khomeini delivered an up-beat address to the Iranian people:

You should not become proud with victory. I should advise ... our neighbours that we have your good at heart providing you do not follow the United States and treat us according to the holy Qor'an. Our nation and government are talking from a position of power. You can be certain that people like Hosni Mobarak of Egypt and Hossein of Jordan and their other criminal colleagues will be of no benefit to you.[13]

Hard in the heels of the re-capture of Khorramshahr, Israel invaded Lebanon and Saddam promised to withdraw his remaining troops from Iran 'in order to fight the Israelis'. By now deeply worried by Iran's rhetoric, he and his backers among the Arab states were keen that the Iranians should follow suit and negotiate an end to the conflict. Khomeini wavered. 'The Imam wanted to stop the war after the liberation of Khorramshahr,' says Ahmad. 'But those in charge ... said we should advance to the Shatt al-Arab bank so that we would be in a position to demand reparations. The Imam was against it. He replied that "if you continue the war and do not succeed, this war will never end. Now is the best time to end the war."'[14] If this is true, it did not take long for Khomeini to change his mind. In the middle of July, Iranian forces launched the first of a series of offensives that took the war into Iraq. The gains by the end of 1982 were small; but they were significant enough to encourage Iran to dig in and believe that victory over Saddam Hossein was a real possibility.

These thrusts into Iraqi territory employed the 'human wave' tactic for which Iranian offensives became famous, or notorious, depending on how you looked at it. 'Human waves' were attacks led by thousands of Basij volunteers who cleared minefields by walking over them, and to draw the enemy's fire. The Basij, which was formed after the revolution as a civil defence force, but in practice became a grass-roots intelligence organisation, was largely made up of young boys aged between ten and sixteen and, during the war, unemployed old men, some in their eighties. The boy soldiers were mostly volunteers from peasant, working class and lower middle class families[15] who got caught up in the excited atmosphere of a mobilisation effort in which mollahs, past masters at the art of extracting the last drop of emotion from people, called upon religious and patriotic feelings and the Shi'i love of martyrdom. The young were targeted through visits to the schools and a intensive media campaign. 'On the television,' in the words of one volunteer, 'they would show a young boy dressed as a soldier, carrying a gun and wearing the red headband of the Basij. He would say how wonderful it was to be a soldier for Islam, fighting for freedom against the Iraqis. Then he would curse the Iraqis and all Arabs, saying they were not good Muslims. Next he would tell us to join him and come to the war.'[13]

At first the response to these calls was overwhelming. Countless boys left their homes and schools, some with, some without their parent's consent. They were sent onto the battlefield with little training and scant equipment. Inevitably, many were killed or captured. One, who was taken prisoner by the Iraqis when he was thirteen, describes his experience:

After only a month's training at a camp near Khorramshahr I was sent to the front. When we arrived we all assembled in a field where there must have been thousands of us, young boys, some younger than me, and old men as well. The commander told us we were going to attack an Iraqi position northeast of Basra which guarded the road to Qurna, to try to capture the road.

The following morning we set off at 4.00 am in army trucks, and I had been given a gun and two hand grenades. At the camp we'd been taught to use a Kalashnikov ... The sun was beginning to come up as we started walking towards the Iraqi lines, and boy, was I scared! ... When we got to the top of a hill, we started running down the other side towards the enemy position. I wasn't afraid any more. We all shouted 'Allah-u-Akbar' [God is great] as we ran, and I could see the soldiers in front of us – a line of helmets – then they started firing. People dropped all around me, but I kept running and shouting, kept going while many were being killed. By the time I reached the trenches, I'd thrown my grenades and somehow had lost my gun, but I don't remember how. Then I was hit in the leg and fell over and lay for a long time right in front of the lines.[14]

From the liberation of Khorramshahr the war dragged on for another five years sapping the strength of both countries. It was for the most part a war of attrition on the ground, compared by many observers for the scale of human carnage and limited territorial gains it involved with the First World War. But as time went by, two other theatres of conflict developed. Unable to decisively repulse Iran's 'human waves', in 1984 Iraq began to use its superior weaponry in a vain attempt to force Iran to the negotiating table. In the Persian Gulf it deployed its navy, equipped with French Super-Etendard missiles, to launch the so-called tanker war. On land it fired Soviet-made Scud missiles at Iranian cities along the Western border. On the battle front it used chemical weapons. Iran, however, pressed on and in February 1986, against all odds, succeeded in capturing the Faw peninsular, much to the horror of the neighbouring Arab states. It was the beginning of the end.

Once he had taken the decision to continue, for Khomeini the war became 'God's hidden gift'. He saw it as something that would ensure the survival of the clergy and enable them to consolidate the revolution. An Islamic state had been created, but not an Islamic society. More time was needed and people had to be kept in a state of high alert. Khomeini was also persuaded that the revolution would not be allowed to survive if it remained within Iranian borders. He began to see himself as the acclaimed leader and liberator of oppressed Muslims from both the Eastern bloc and from Western powers represented by Zionism. 'We do not want to occupy Iraq. Our aim is to rid Iraq of its tyrannical rulers and to liberate Jerusalem.'[18] Ahmad later articulated this thinking:

The war gave us an opportunity to tell the world about the power of the revolution, the power of the Imam and our cultural and ideological values in relation to Western values. For eight years our news was headline news throughout the world. Every missile we sent to Iraq carried with it the Imam's thoughts to the world. It was the Imam's line of communication to every single Muslim. It led to the creation of resistance cells among the Muslims.[19]

The war, from this perspective, was Islamic propaganda writ large.

From 1982 Khomeini pursued his crusade regardless of the burden it imposed on the country, and regardless of its progress. He defied all those inside and outside the country who continually pleaded with him to agree to end the war. 'We carry out our [religious] duties,' he would often reply to domestic critics, 'and are not responsible for the result.'[20] Foreign condemnation of his intransigence was likewise brushed off with statements such as: 'These international bodies never ask this man who talks of peace why he attacked [Iran].'[21]

The exact costs to the country of this unyielding approach may never be known. Estimates of war related deaths stand at between 180,000 to 300,000.[22] The loss of life among men aged 18 to 30-years-old was especially high; a whole generation of young and potentially productive citizens was reduced.[23] Iranian officials put the damages of the war, including loss of oil revenue and agricultural output, damage to villages, towns, the cost of compensation or pensions for the dependants of nearly a million killed or maimed and of dealing with a million and a half refugees at us$300 billion.[24] The social and psychological and physical scars of the war on the survivors were also beyond calculation.

By the time the decision to continue the war was taken, the regime had more or less destroyed the armed opposition although assassinations by the Mojahedin continued intermittently throughout 1982. A leftist guerilla group, the Sarbedaran, had launched armed attacks on a number of fronts in September 1981 and had even managed to briefly take over Amol on the Caspian coast. But they had been quickly defeated. In the Spring a sustained security operation had destroyed most of the surviving cells and safe houses of the two main guerilla organisations. It had also uncovered a plot to assassinate Khomeini which involved the former foreign minister Sadeq Qotbzadeh, one of Khomeini's three Paris viziers. Qotbzadeh and up to seventy army officers accused of conspiring with him were executed six months later.

In the course of his interrogation Qotbzadeh had confessed that Ayatollah Shari'atmadari knew of the *coup* plan and had given it his blessing. Khomeini's reaction was swift and ruthless. Echoing the worst of the Stalinist show trials, Shari'atmadari, whose son was threatened with execution as a co-conspirator, was forced to make a public repentance on television and to plead with Khomeini for forgiveness. He was subsequently 'defrocked' – a happening totally without precedent in Shi'i Islam and deeply shocking. Strictly speaking it is impossible to defrock a source of emulation since no one appoints him in the first place. He is simply recognised as such by his followers. Nevertheless, it was an act of humiliation, one far deeper than that inflicted on Khomeini himself when he was forced to wear 'civilian' clothes in Turkey. Coupled with his house arrest it effectively cut off Shari'atmadari from his constituency. It also represented an unprecedented intervention of political authority into the very heart of the Shi'i religious institution, one all the more surprising given that Khomeini had, throughout his adult life, claimed his respect for its integrity. With this dramatic move Khomeini had made a statement about his political relationship to the senior clergy. To them he had, besides abusing a venerable religious leader, destroyed the sanctity of religion. But they were, as intended, silenced. Four years later, when Shari'atmadari died and was buried without public ceremony, Grand Ayatollah Golpayegani was so scandalised that he wrote to Khomeini to say what had happened between him and Shari'atmadari was up to God and history to judge; Shari'atmadari, as a senior clergyman, deserved better treatment.[25] Other grand ayatollahs, however, still preferred to keep a low profile and not to rock the Islamic boat.

Although Khomeini was in firm command of the machinery of the Islamic Republic, he was not involved in the day-to-day running of the government and could, in the traditional style of Muslim caliphs, act as a court of appeal for officials and ordinary people alike. From the beginning of the revolution he had regularly, often five times or more a week, held audiences for groups from one organisation or another and he maintained this practice until the illnesses and disappointments that plagued him in the last months of his life put a stop to them.

Even at the height of the terror and counter-terror of 1981 and 1982, people would be taken to the mosque that was just a few paces from his Jamaran home. Security checks on the congregation were severe. Everyone who entered the mosque was searched from head to toe, men and women alike. Audio and video equipment had to be left with the guards twenty-four hours in advance. But the checks did nothing to dampen the highly charged atmosphere that surrounded these occasions. Housewives and high officials alike would often burst into tears as soon as Khomeini opened his mouth, or into laughter when he told an entertaining story.

The meeting would usually begin with a petition or a speech by the spokesman of a visiting group, or a complaint about government shortcomings. What was said in these petitions was only occasionally reported. But it is possible to conclude from Khomeini's responses that people spoke to him of economic shortages, their grievances against officials, the prolongation of the war, or the arbitrary behaviour of local committees. For example, in a reference to food rationing, shortages and other economic troubles, Khomeini repeated his maxim that revolution was not about material well-being: 'the counter-revolutionaries are trying to dishearten the Muslim people of Iran by spreading rumours about shortages of commodities. This is meant to strike a blow against your honour. They think that you have lost your dear ones and your young ones for material things and that you have served Islam simply for the purpose of filling your stom-achs.'[26] Such calls to revolutionary virtue may not have provided much of a solution. But at least people felt that the Imam was listening to them, a point he often stressed: 'You said that I am not informed; but this is said by those who want to imply that I am an ill-informed man and therefore what I say cannot be correct. I am not an ill-informed man. You came and sat and told me all you wanted.'[27] Individuals and groups come and see me and give me petitions. I personally see and read the newspapers, a sum-mary of what the papers write and a summary of what is happening in the country.[28]

His remarks and his sermons in the latter part of 1982 indicate that Khomeini was well aware of the pressures that were building up in society as a result of the war effort, widespread corruption and the atmosphere of terror created by the drive against the opposition. On 15 December 1982, he moved to defuse the situation with an eight-point decree in which he effectively instructed the courts to ensure that people's rights and the due process of Islamic law would in future be safeguarded. He instructed the prime minister and the chief justice of the Supreme Court to prohibit unlawful entry into people's private premises, the arbitrary confiscation of their property and unlawful detentions. He also insisted that 'people's rights in the courts are to be observed, judges must be competent, and the judi-ciary must be Islamic and independent'[29] – rights which were supposedly guaranteed by the constitution but which had simply been ignored. Spe-cial councils were also established to investigate complaints against the authorities.

Khomeini's decree signalled the official end of the crisis touched off by the June 1981 confrontation. More importantly, it was a message to the middle classes that there would be a return to normality and they could coexist with the Islamic regime as long as they observed the Islamic code of conduct in public. The universities, closed in 1980, began to reopen. The Hezbollah, unleashed to uproot the opposition, was brought under control. But it was some time before the authorities could bring the re-pressive machinery that had been erected in late 1981, under a semblance of control.

The promise of social peace did not, however, mean greater tolerance of those parties outside the religious establishment which had not already been suppressed, such as the Freedom Movement of Iran, the Hojjatieh

Society and the Tudeh Party. When they were needed they were welcomed. Now they were perceived as nuisances and were suppressed. Bazargan's Freedom Movement, with its limited influence amongst the enlightened and patriotic segment of society, was never formally banned, possibly because of the role it had played in the revolution. Nevertheless, it suffered much intensified criticism from the political factions around Khomeini or from the state media, periodic closures of its offices, physical attacks on its meetings, restrictions on its activities and occasional arrests of its leaders and sympathisers. The communist Tudeh Party which, because it was backed by the USSR, might have been a major threat, was a different story. Much to the disgust of the rest of the opposition, the Tudeh Party had, from the beginning of the revolution, supported Khomeini's Islamic government as an anti-imperialist regime. It had backed and advised the Islamic Republican Party in its unsuccessful drive to set itself up as the single ideological party of the state modelled on the ruling communist parties of the Eastern bloc, and helped to undermine its main independent socialist rival, the Feda'iyan-e Khalq by causing a split in its ranks. Culturally the Tudeh had wielded great influence on the post-revolutionary Islamic scene and was, at least in part, responsible for the adoption of a bipolar vision and class-based vocabulary by the IRP and even by Khomeini himself. With their particular talent for rhetoric, the political mollahs had embellished the Tudeh's lexicon and words such as 'capitalist', 'world-devouring America' and 'bloodsucking imperialist' soon gained currency in their discourse. To be a 'liberal' was a sin, 'revolution' was sacred.

The Tudeh's close links to the Soviet Union meant that once the decision was taken to carry the war into Iraqi territory, in line with their masters they began to criticise Khomeini's war policy. A rude awakening followed. In February 1983, the Tudeh leaders were suddenly branded as agents of a foreign power and all, including the party's general secretary Nureddin Kianuri, were arrested. Kianuri and the party's ideologue Ehsan Tabari confessed on television to spying for the Soviet Union. They and the rest of the party's leadership were spared; but many of its active members were imprisoned or put to death. The party disappeared virtually overnight as a factor in Iranian politics.

At the other extreme of the political spectrum the Hojjatieh Society, a traditionalist, free-market religious group whose anti-Baha'i and anti-communist activities were endorsed by some in the regime, also came under attack.[30] Their impeccable religious credentials and good organisation had enabled members of the society to become influential after the revolution, often filling the gap created in the administration by the purges, particularly in education. Some post-revolutionary cabinet ministers were even thought to have had close associations with the society. But the Hojjatieh were in a peculiar position. They were firm believers in the orthodox Shi'i doctrine that Islamic government must await the return of the Hidden Imam. In other words, they opposed the idea of the *velayat-e faqih* and before the revolution had been openly critical of Khomeini's position. Afterwards, fearing that the country faced what was to them the even greater danger of a leftist takeover, they had joined forces with him and, at the behest of their leader Sheikh Mahmud Halabi, had voted for the *velayat-e faqih* in the December 1979 referendum.[31] However, after it became clear that the war would continue, the Hojjatieh renewed its criticism of the new order. Although its attacks were always muted, Khomeini's increasing intolerance of any kind of dissent, the Hojjatieh's secretive character, and the resentment generated by the success of some of their members, made them vulnerable. With the Tudeh Party out of the way, Khomeini renewed his attack on the Hojjatieh and what it stood for:

Those who believe that we should allow sins to increase until the Twelfth Imam reappears should modify and reconsider their position ... Those who grumble about the predicament of the faith under the Islamic Republic and say that this Islam is useless are saying that the Shah's Islam was correct ... If you believe in your country get rid of this factionalism and join the wave that is carrying the nation forward otherwise it will break you.[32]

On the same day, 12 July 1983, the Hojjatieh announced its own dissolution. However, it remained strong and retained its networks.

The exclusion of all non-clerical parties from the political arena brought to the fore differences between the ruling clergy themselves over a range of issues: foreign policy, theology, economic policy, and cultural and social affairs. The conventional political divisions of right, left and centre were here multiplied by sometimes cross-cutting theological orientations to create a complex, shifting range of factions whose conflicts were often extremely acrimonious. The main lines of this division can very roughly be depicted as traditionalist, reformist and radical.

The traditionalists were in favour of observing what could be achieved through established theological reasoning and rules with the minimum of change. Theologically they were the followers of the Grand Ayatollahs Kho'i, Golpayegani and Mara'shi Najafi. On the economy and social affairs, they believed in minimum state interference; they also held that the clergy should have only a supervisory role in judicial and legislative matters, and none at all in executive affairs. They supported the political leadership of Khomeini, but they did not all accept his concept of Islamic government. The reformists, most of whom were Khomeini's own students, believed in the traditions of Shi'ism but wanted to make them practical for modern times. Theologically and politically, they followed Khomeini, but socially they tended to be more relaxed. For instance, within the parameters of the Islamic code of behaviour they promoted the education of women and their participation in the social sphere. They also supported a mixed economy. The radicals wanted social justice, even if it involved changing or abandoning traditional Shi'i theological reasoning. They often justified their action through selective verses of the Qor'an, the *hadith* and Imam Ali's 'Path of Eloquence', the *Nahj al-Balaghah*. Third Worldist, Islamic socialist and populist, they wanted to export the revolution to other Muslim countries. In the political arena, the radicals were represented within the younger generation of theologians, the Revolutionary Guards, the Reconstruction Crusades, the remnants of the students who took over the American embassy, and in the universities and the Majles.

From 1984 the conflict between these factions became most evident in relationships between the government, parliament and the Guardian Council. Elections to the second Islamic parliament were held in the Spring of 1984. By this time the rules governing the eligibility of candidates were so tight that in practise only those who declared their allegiance to the *velayat-e faqih* could stand.[33] Predictably, the clergy were even more dominant in the new Majles than they had been in the first. But the majority of MPs belonged to the radical and reformist factions which were also after this time dominant in the cabinet of Prime Minister Mir Hossein Musavi. On the other hand, the twelve-man Guardian Council, the committee of jurisconsults charged with examining legislation to ensure that it was compatible with the laws of Islam and the Constitution, was dominated by conservatives.

Throughout the 1980s the main bone of contention between the various factions was the economy. Social and economic justice had been a central popular demand in the revolution and was indeed enshrined in the constitution. But beyond confiscating the property of the Pahlavi family and other associates of the *ancien regime*, and the nationalisation of banks and factories belonging to those who had fled the country, very little had been accomplished. Meanwhile, the economy, deprived of new investment, of the skills that had kept it going in the past, and squeezed by the war effort, had begun to decline. However, attempts by the Musavi government to introduce reform or interventionist economic measures, such as a government monopoly on foreign trade, consistently met with conservative and bazaari resistance. Just about every piece of legislation on such issues that was passed by parliament was rejected by the Guardian Council.

For the most part Khomeini appeared to take no particular side in this argument. In the economic sphere, as well as in politics, he relied on trial and error. In all probability he was also quite genuinely of two minds over economic issues. On the one hand, his insistence that under Islamic government all legislation should be derived from the *shari'a* meant that his views on the sanctity of private property did not, in the end, diverge much from those of the Guardian Council. He had never explicitly promised economic reform, only that the corruption and mismanagement of the Pahlavi era would be brought to an end. Furthermore, he had to avoid alienating his constituency in the bazaar and particularly the Coalition of Islamic Societies whose members were ranged with the conservatives. On the other hand, Khomeini the populist politician had also made rash and simplistic promises to the dispossessed – that the government would provide homes for the poor throughout the country, or that everyone would have free water and electricity. With the war effort in full swing in the middle years of the decade, he could not afford to alienate ordinary people, let alone the large element among the activist clergy who believed in a policy of thoroughgoing state intervention or a mixed economy.

Although the watchword of the regime during this period was 'one voice', when it came to disputes among the clergy, and the expression of views of which he did not necessarily approve, Khomeini's threshold of tolerance was rather high. He allowed them far more room for manoeuvre than he would have given to lay politicians and, some would say, he even encouraged debate. He generally respected the independent reasoning of those he considered to be *mojtaheds* and he rarely intervened until he had made up his mind. A particularly interesting example here is a debate which raged for some time in the Islamic Republic, and is still current, over 'traditional' and 'dynamic' jurisprudence known respectively as *feqh-e sonnati* and *feqh-e puya*. Although this was a 'free-standing' issue it became, in the mid-1980s, closely identified with the disputes between the government, the Majles and the Council of Guardians with the radicals and the reformists promoting 'dynamic' *feqh* as a means of finding Islamic justification for legislation that was often frankly modern in both form and content.

Khomeini remained silent on the matter. Then his reasoning, his sense of history and his belief in ensuring the interests and the supremacy of the clergy brought him down on the side of traditional *feqh*. At the same time, however, he told the traditionalists to take into account the issue of time and place (*zaman va makan*) and 'secondary rulings' (a term used for rulings that temporarily modify Islamic precepts). Another example of a thorny issue was music, which led to a running battle in the media, the Majles, the theological centres and the mosques. The radicals, who had the control of the state radio and television, were broadcasting music against the traditionalists' wishes. In this case Khomeini stepped in to redefine the views of both sides by saying that if music edifies believers and enhances their revolutionary and Islamic feelings, then it is not forbidden.[34] Despite his ideological conservatism, there was in Khomeini a rebel with a vision which at times made him act as a radical in the sphere of politics.

If Khomeini's caution helped reduce the potential for violent upheaval among the clergy, the resulting lack of decisive leadership over policy added to the paralysis created by parliament's inability to legislate. Furthermore, the conflict between the conservatives and the radicals went to the very heart of Khomeini's conception of an Islamic state, in which the *shari'a* was supposed to be the cornerstone. Matters came to a head in December 1987 when Khomeini authorised the government to punish hoarders without going to court and then to introduce a bill cutting off essential services from companies which did not pay their taxes, or their employees' insurance, or observe the laws that protected workers.[35] When the Guardian Council challenged him directly, in a public exchange of letters over the legitimacy of according such powers to the executive, Khomeini came out with a decree which in effect declared that the Islamic government of Iran is the continuation of prophecy and Islamic rule pioneered by the Prophet.

Although Khomeini did not directly claim the same status as the Prophet and the imams, he nevertheless clearly believed that he had the same responsibility for running the government. In other words, he declared that Islamic government was supreme and all other aspects of Islam were subordinate to its interests. From now on religion would serve the

Islamic state rather than vice-versa.

In an attempt to interpret Khomeini's views on the subject of the re-sponsibilities and powers of government, President Ali Khamene'i, in a Friday Prayer sermon delivered on 1 January 1988 at Tehran University, made a statement suggesting that Khomeini had meant that the govern-ment should act within the rules of Islam. In a curt response Khomeini issued a corrective which included the historic statement that 'Islamic gov-ernment, which stems from the absolute *velayat* of the Prophet Moham-mad, is one of the primary injunctions in Islam, taking precedence over all subsidiary precepts, even praying, fasting, and performing the Haj. The government may even unilaterally annul the legally-binding agreements it has made with the people when these agreements are against the interests of the Islamic state.' In Khomeini's view such an absolute authority could even abrogate the constitution. It seemed that the *faqih* was now able to change, or at least revoke, legal rulings which had been firmly enshrined as part of Islamic law, for the sake of a higher principle – the preservation of the government of Islam. It was an unprecedented move.

Having admonished Khamene'i for misrepresenting his views, Kho-meini quickly issued a reassurance that he still had confidence in him. In so doing he sent a strong signal to the conservative camp that the survival of the Islamic regime enjoyed a higher priority than keeping the balance between the factions. As a gesture of submission, the secretary of the Coun-cil of Guardians, Ayatollah Lotfollah Safi Golpayegani, the son-in-law of Grand Ayatollah Golpayegani, immediately went to see Khomeini to as-sure him that the Council members, as his appointees, had no quarrel with his ruling and that they merely wished to carry out their responsi-bilities. Nevertheless, Safi resigned over the issue and returned to his teach-ing in Qom. Musavi's government, on the other hand, congratulated itself on winning from Khomeini what it had wanted for a long time, a clear victory over the Council of Guardians.

The Council was not, however, going to give in on all issues. For exam-ple, it interpreted the Ayatollah's support for Musavi's government as ap-plying not only to the executive but to all branches of the government, that is the state. Thus it saw itself as having given in only in areas where Khomeini had made specific pronouncements.

To pre-empt further conflict, Ahmad Khomeini, Hashemi Rafsanjani, Musavi Ardebili and Khamene'i wrote to consult Khomeini about the recurrence of disagreement between the Majles and the Council of Guardians and to complain about the length of time it took to make government bills into law. Khomeini responded by ordering the formation of a new body, given the cumbersome name 'The Council for Assessing the Interests of the System' (Majma'-e Tashkhis-e Maslahat-e Nezam), to be chaired by the president. In deciding that this thirteen-man Council should be made up of six theologians from the Council of Guardians, six officials from the executive and legislative branches of government plus his own representative, Khomeini was clearly attempting to avoid the possibility that it may further alienate the conservative clergy and create more division between the reformists and conservatives.

To many the new edict seemed to be the ultimate arbitrary act of the despot. Hashemi Rafsanjani, the speaker of the Majles, probably sensed this when, a few days later he said: 'All those who talk about absolute power and dictatorship are wrong.' In his opinion, critics had failed to understand and see the democratic system that had been set up by the *velayat-e faqih*, whose powers derived from the population. In Islamic Iran, he declared, 'by the grace of the *vali-ye faqih*, people live in a democratic environment and are ruled by a healthy style of government of the people by the people.'[36]

A key issue if the Islamic state was to be preserved beyond Khomeini's lifetime was the succession. As soon as the armed rebellion of the early 1980s was suppressed, Khomeini had ordered elections for an Assembly of Experts to consider candidates for the post of successor and to make a choice. The Assembly held its first meeting in Tehran in July 1983 when it was firmly told by Khomeini that its selection should be 'for the sake of God and for God alone.' He added a warning that the future leader or leaders would have to keep a careful 'watch for infiltrators in your offices, who could cause tragedies.'[37]

The constitution bound the Assembly either to select an individual similar to Khomeini himself – that is a leading theologian (*marja'*), a recognised revolutionary and an efficient administrator – or, in the absence of such an individual, to appoint a council of three to five jurists. It was not an easy task. Khomeini's exceptional career was a major hindrance; there was no other jurist in the land who could lay claim to all his qualifications, especially on the political front. Yet they were qualifications without which the republic's future would be jeopardised. The fact that it took the Assembly over two years to reach a decision indicates how difficult it was to agree on the matter.

The eventual choice, announced in November 1985, was a man Khomeini habitually referred to as 'the fruit of my life', Ayatollah Hossein Ali
Montazeri. An uncommon commoner among the top mollahs, Montazeri
was born in 1922 into a poor peasant family from the small town of
Najafabad near Isfahan, a family which did not even claim descent from
the house of the Prophet. Like other members of Khomeini's inner circle
Montazeri had been his student and had remained loyal to him throughout his years in exile. A committed activist, from 1966 until the revolution
he spent a great deal of his time in prison or in exile. He was a man of
outstanding learning and a militant jurist with an impeccable track record
of piety and courage.

Among Khomeini's followers Montazeri was regarded as the most senior revolutionary cleric after the Imam, and became Tehran's first post-
revolutionary Friday prayer-leader. He later served as the president of the
Assembly of Experts which drafted the constitution in the autumn of
1979. Nevertheless, compared to men like Motahhari, Beheshti or Hashemi
Rafsanjani, on the political stage he played a rather minor role. His local
Najafabadi accent, village simplicity and sincerity led many to look upon
him as a benign, soft-spoken religious leader who had neither a keen interest, nor much belief in, power politics. But this very same background
and his sufferings during his imprisonment under the Shah, were to make
him genuinely sympathetic to political detainees and the underprivileged,
endearing him both to revolutionaries and to ordinary people. He was, so
far as foreign affairs were concerned, a fiery, anti-American radical and a
firm believer in the export of the revolution and the world Islamic movement. But on the domestic stage, his down-to-earth style, constant criticism of injustices, corruption, red tape and drug abuse, as well as his tolerant approach to moderate opposition leaders such as Bazargan, were signs
of an independence of mind which angered his foes and did not necessarily please his friends or allies.

Politicians in Tehran took it for granted that Montazeri could be easily
manipulated. His appointment as Khomeini's successor thus revived, and
indeed intensified, the discord among the clerics. As soon as the news of
the appointment was confirmed by Rafsanjani, the supporters of the conservative ayatollahs demonstrated against the self-effacing Montazeri, who
prevented his supporters from staging a counter-demonstration, saying
that he did not want to be the future leader. As deputy chairman of the

Assembly of Experts, Rafsanjani had supported Montazeri's nomination for the future leadership in order to keep the conservative ayatollahs out of the running. Yet on various issues his differences with Montazeri were as deep as those of the conservatives.

For all their professed sentimental attachment to each other, from the beginning of 1981 when Khomeini took up residence in Tehran, he and Montazeri had seen little of each other. It was Hashemi Rafsanjani, not Montazeri, or President Khamene'i, or Prime Minister Musavi, upon whom, after the death of Beheshti, Khomeini had come to rely most for political advice. A witty and soft-spoken politician, Rafsanjani saw himself as a patriot and a reformer and tried to advance a pragmatic interpretation of Islam, the revolution and Khomeini's thinking. Formally his position was subordinate to that of the president and the prime minister. However, his access to Khomeini, based on his long-standing friendship with Khomeini's son and facilitated by the fact that, at Khomeini's request, he and his family had moved to a mansion in Jamaran, was exceptional.[38] This close personal relationship, his hard work, his consummate skill at networking and his clever wheeling and dealing soon made him the dominant figure on the political scene, a fact that was recognised abroad. Indeed, when he visited China and Japan in June 1985, Rafsanjani was received like a head of state.

It was during this visit to Japan that Rafsanjani received a message from President Reagan thanking him for his help in bringing the hijacking earlier in the month of a TWA jet by the Lebanese Hezbollah to a rapid and peaceful end. The message marked the beginning of a new phase in Iran's relationship with America. Rafsanjani, through his ability to bypass Musavi's government, now dominated foreign policy. Musavi was furious, but to no avail; it was Rafsanjani who had Khomeini's ear.

To pursue the war Iran desperately needed the military equipment denied her by an American trade embargo which had been in force since the hostage crisis. A series of complex secret negotiations, in which Israel was the principle intermediary, began for the purchase of arms in exchange for Iranian help in freeing American hostages captured in Lebanon. These culminated in a secret visit to Tehran in May 1986 by Robert McFarlane, who from 1983–85 was the American National Security Adviser. Inevitably, news of the visit got around and alarmed the radicals, who could not stomach any rapprochement with the West, especially the United States.

One of the most extreme of the radical mollahs was Mehdi Hashemi, the brother of Ayatollah Montazeri's son-in-law Hadi Hashemi. Hashemi had been head of the Revolutionary Guards' Office for World Islamic Liberation Movements, an organisation devoted to the export of the revolution. Though this was not a programme that was officially frowned upon, Hashemi acted quasi-autonomously in his dealings with the Lebanese Hezbollah and with the Afghan Mojahedin, and his activities brought him into constant conflict with the Foreign Ministry and Khomeini's office. In particular, they strained Iran's relations with the Arab states at a time when the Foreign Ministry was trying to calm down their fears and dissuade them from supporting Saddam.[39] In addition, much to the alarm of Rafsanjani, Ali Meshkini (the president of the Assembly of Experts) and Ahmad Khomeini, Hashemi and his radical friends were attempting to turn Montazeri's office into a power centre from which to seize control of the leadership should Khomeini die, and their attempts to radicalise the theological centres were causing much resentment amongst the powerful conservative clergy of Qom.

On 12 October 1986, Hashemi and a large number of his followers, including Montazeri's son-in-law, were arrested on a variety of charges, including treason, sabotage and involvement in a political murder that took place before the revolution. The real reason for the arrest, however, was that Hashemi and his supporters had come to know about McFarlane's secret visit to Tehran and had attempted to sabotage the negotiations. Too late. The information was already in the hands of Hashemi's friends in Beirut who, hearing of his arrest, promptly leaked information about the secret American–Iranian deals to the Lebanese newspaper *al-Shiraa*. The news was published on 3 November 1986 and on the following day, ironically the anniversary of the hostage-taking at the American Embassy, Rafsanjani was forced to disclose the story of secret arms-for-hostages deals which came to be known as 'Irangate'.

Other Iranian politicians have met their downfall for even suggesting a rapprochement with America. Rafsanjani not only survived but went on the offensive, skilfully exploiting his rivals' weaknesses and, with Khomeini's support, and that of his son Ahmad, putting Hashemi on trial. The Special Court for the Clergy which, by Khomeini's edict, was set up at the time of the Hashemi affair, tried him and sentenced him to death. His execution on 27 September 1987 was seen as a victory for Rafsanjani, killing two birds with one stone by humiliating Montazeri's secretariat and sending a strong signal to the radicals that he would not tolerate their interference.

It was now Rafsanjani's strategy to keep the situation under control which he did by keeping his lines of communication with all factions open and presenting himself as the defender of the radicals, although he was actually a pragmatist by nature. As Khomeini's representative on the Supreme Defence Council, Rafsanjani was effectively in charge of the war, but any military gains by the Revolutionary Guards meant he would become further imprisoned by the very body he had been patronising. While helping them to acquire more weapons and establish their naval and air force units, he moved to curb their political ambitions. In this affair, as in most others, he had the support of Khomeini.

Khomeini would not, however, allow pinpricks like the Irangate scandal to trouble him. He moved instead to intensify his war on another front. By 1986 he was focusing ever more boldly on Islamic internationalism. For him, the export of the revolution was becoming increasingly important. He wanted to turn Iran into a power base for Islam in the world, for without power, he believed, the Islamic movement would get nowhere. The establishment of an Islamic government in Iran was not enough; the 'Islamic homeland' (*vatan-e Islami*) which had been 'divided by the imperialists and ambitious, tyrannical rulers',[40] had also to be liberated. In Bazargan's view, until the revolution, Khomeini's strategy was 'to serve Iran through Islam', but after gaining power in Iran his strategy was 'serving Islam through Iran.'[41]

From the time he returned to his country in triumph, visitors from across the world and messages from one or another branch of the Islamic movement had poured into his office. In his speeches to foreign guests he gradually developed a kind of Islamic internationalism with contemporary relevance. The subjects most dear to him were disunity, colonialism and Palestine and he constantly called for action. Yet he was also careful to separate the issue of Iranian Jews from that of Israel. 'Islam will treat Jews as it treats other groups of the nation. They should not be put under pressure. It is the Zionists who act contrary to Moses' teaching.'[42] He repeatedly told his audience that, 'God willing [other] oppressed nations would learn from Iran and rid themselves of their oppressors.'[43] As time went by he became bolder and began to talk about 'the creation of a worldwide party' which he called the 'Party of the Oppressed' or 'Hezb-e Mostaza'fin'.[44]

For many years Khomeini had been sending messages to participants in the Haj, the annual pilgrimage to Mecca, encouraging them to form a front for the oppressed and to promote unity for Muslims and liberation from satanic powers.[45] His message in 1987 entitled 'The Manifesto of the Islamic Revolution' was seventy pages long. It began with the Qor'anic verse: 'And he who goes forth from his house, a migrant to God and his Apostle, should he die his reward becomes due and sure with God.' This verse, which speaks of death in the path of God, was an unusual choice for the occasion. But Khomeini regarded the Haj as a 'repentance' and a 'disavowal'. The only *sureh* in the Qor'an not beginning with *bismillah* ('in the name of God'), is the last chapter revealed to the Prophet. Known as 'Tawbah' or 'Bara'at' ('Repentance' or 'Disavowal'), it is basically the Prophet's final word on pagans, infidels and hypocrites. It is 'an announcement from God and his Apostle to the people assembled on the day of the great pilgrimage; God and his Apostle dissolve treaty obligations with the pagans.'

Khomeini called on all Muslims to renew this message by joining in a demonstration to disavow 'pagans' such as 'the Soviet Union, the USA and Israel, as well as their servants in the Muslim world, the [Arab] Kings.' To him the idea that Saudi Arabia was a sovereign state with its own laws and regulations which foreign visitors should respect was irrelevant. He saw himself as the righteous interpreter and implementer of the divine law. The belief that the Haj should be respected as a religious ceremony designed to cleanse the pilgrim of selfish and worldly desires was as immaterial to the old patriarch as it had been to the Prophet himself:

Some ignorant people might even say that one should not dishonour the House of God and the Ka'ba with slogans, demonstrations, marches and disavowal. They might even say that the Haj is a time for worship, not a battlefield ... [but Muslims must] echo the crushing slogan of disavowing the pagan apostates of world arrogance ... in the house of monotheism and remember to express their hatred toward the enemies of God and mankind.[46]

The pilgrims' disavowal of the pagans, Khomeini asserted, was to be carried out with as much zeal as possible in the course of the rituals of the Haj, such as throwing stones at the symbol of Satan.

Fired by their leader's rhetoric, the Iranian pilgrims, who included Khomeini's wife Qodsi, rushed into the streets of Mecca and towards the Great Mosque, which they wanted to take over, chanting slogans. The Saudi authorities, determined to contain them, panicked and began to fire on the crowd. A tragedy followed and around 400 people were killed.

The incident caused a crisis in Iranian–Saudi relations which dragged on for several months, culminating a month later in attacks by the crowd on the Saudi embassy in Tehran in which a Saudi diplomat was killed. The ensuing deterioration of relations with the Saudis and the Kuwaitis, and the presence of the United States and Western European navies in the Persian Gulf, changed the political and social climate further.

By the beginning of 1988 long months of stagnation on the battle front, mounting economic problems, and progressive demoralisation among the troops and the civilian population alike, were exacting a heavy political toll. Soldiers were deserting the war front and new volunteers were not coming forward, forcing the government to increase the conscription period from two years to twenty-eight months. Expenditure on the war was beginning to outstrip state revenues, pushing the country into debt. Inflation was eroding personal incomes and the rate of unemployment was climbing to unprecedented heights. Furthermore, diplomatic pressures to end the conflict had by this time tightened the loopholes on the international black market in arms on which Iran was buying weapons and spare parts at back-breaking premiums. Yet Western countries and the Soviet Union continued to supply Iraq with conventional weaponry and the materials it used for chemical warfare while the Arab countries of the Persian Gulf supplied credit.

Iraq began its endgame on 28 February with the first of a series of missile attacks on Tehran for which specially boosted Scuds were deployed posing a threat of a quite different order to the bombing raids that had characterised the 'war of the cities' in 1984 when its distance from the border had protected the capital. The fear produced by the month-long raids lead to the abandonment of the city by an estimated quarter of its inhabitants, including government officials. Among those who remained, each missile triggered a new wave of resentment over the inability of the regime to protect its citizens. Meanwhile, after a lull that had lasted for several months, Iran began a new, limited offensive in the northern sector of the front, occupying the border town of Halabja in Iraqi Kurdestan. Iraq countered with chemical weapons, successfully repulsing the Iranian advance but also killing some 3–5,000 innocent Kurdish civilians. A month later Iraq, helped by American intelligence reports, began new offensives against

Iranian positions inside its own borders and, again using chemical weapons, managed to drive Iranian troops from the dearly won Faw peninsula. At about the same time the American navy, roaming in the Persian Gulf under different pretexts, blew up two Iranian oil rigs, destroyed a frigate, immobilised another and sank a missile boat.

The defeats of the Spring of 1988 emboldened critics of the government and of the war. Montazeri, who openly criticised the security and intelligence forces for mistreating people, also said that the revolution was in danger from misguided counter-revolutionaries, as well as from 'discrimination, official incompetence and self-centredness.' As he was addressing the clerics who had come to see him, he specifically focused the issue of self-centredness among the ruling clergy. Bazargan also wrote an open letter giving voice to the people's resentment:

If you [Khomeini] think that we should sacrifice our lives and our rights to export and impose Islam by war ... you are free to think in this way ... but not at the cost of the lives of those who do not think in this way and who have not said they are ready to sacrifice their lives and homes. Since 1986 you have not stopped proclaiming victory and now you are calling on the people to resist until victory. Isn't that an admission of failure on your part? ... You have spoken of the failure of Iraq and the crumbling of its regime, but thanks to your misguided policies Iraq has fortified itself, its economy has not collapsed and it is we who are on the edge of bankruptcy. You say that you have a responsibility to those whose blood has been spilt. To this, I say, 'When will you stop the commerce with the blood of our martyrs?'[47]

Khomeini's defensive tone was evident in a speech read by his son Ahmad at the inauguration of the third session of the Islamic parliament on 28 May. He referred to the need to remove bottlenecks, limitations and problems, pointing out that there was no greater sin than forsaking the revolution. Khomeini was feeling the heat both at home and abroad. But defying popular pressure to put an end to hostilities, he categorically stated that the 'fate of the war would be decided on the battlefields and not at the negotiating table'. Five days later, in an attempt to limit the damage, he appointed his most trusted lieutenant Hashemi Rafsanjani as acting commander-in-chief of the armed forces. But there was little Rafsanjani could do to rescue the deteriorating situation at the front, where the Iraqis kept up their pressure on the retreating Iranian troops. In desperation, the Revolutionary Guard proposed that Iran should use its own chemical weapons in response to their deployment by the Iraqis. Khomeini had, however, been convinced by Rafsanjani that such a move would provoke more missile attacks, possibly with chemical warheads, against the already demoralised citizens of Tehran.

The last straw for Iran came on 3 July 1988, when an American warship, claiming that it had mistaken the plane for an attacking jet fighter, shot down an Iran Air flight, killing 290 civilians on board. Such an incident would, even in the very recent past, have precipitated a massive popular and official reaction. But for all the anti-American demonstrations and speeches that followed the incident, the reaction was comparatively quiet. Key figures in the government, if not Khomeini himself, had clearly decided that Iran could take no more. The only course was a diplomatic solution.

Ahmad Khomeini, Rafsanjani and Khamene'i played a key role in making such a solution palatable to Khomeini. In the biannual meeting of the Assembly of Experts on 16 July convened at the presidential residence in Tehran, a statement from the Ayatollah indicating his willingness to accept diplomacy was discussed and approved. Rafsanjani and others told the entire leadership that Iran had isolated itself and presented itself as a warmonger, while Iraq, despite the fact that it had started the war, was now regarded as a peace lover. He used the tragic destruction of the Iran Air jet to illustrate America's determination to prevent Iran from winning the war. On 18 July, a year after the United Nations had adopted it, Iran announced that it would unconditionally accept United Nations Security Council resolution 598. Khomeini had finally realised that his revolution was in serious trouble, and faced with the choice between its survival and the continuation of the revolutionary struggle, he chose the former.

The announcement took the world by surprise and was a massive psychological shock to the astonished Iranians. Two days later, Khomeini issued a long statement declaring that:

Had it not been in the interests of Islam and Muslims, I would never have accepted this, and would have preferred death and martyrdom instead. But we have no choice and we should give in to what God wants us to do ... I reiterate that the acceptance of this issue is more bitter than poison for me, but I drink this chalice of poison for the Almighty and for His satisfaction.[48]

14

The Rise of the Phoenix
Khomeini's Last Months

When, on balance, he felt he should accept the ceasefire, when he drank the poisonous chalice, I was with him. The television was showing our soldiers and he kept hitting himself with his fists saying 'ah'. No one dared to see him. After accepting the ceasefire he could no longer walk. He kept saying 'My Lord, I submit to your will.' He never again spoke in public. He never again went to speak at the Jamaran mosque and [eventually] he fell ill and was taken to the hospital.[1]

By the summer of 1988, when the war ended, Khomeini's health had been on the decline for some time. He had cancer as well as the heart problems that had been with him since his exile in Iraq and had intensified in the early 1980s. In the last months of his life his failing eyesight made him more dependent on his children, Ahmad and Zahra, and on Ahmad's wife Fatemeh, to read newspapers, official reports and books for him. Fatemeh and Ahmad lived with Khomeini and he often took their children with him on his daily walks in the high-walled garden of his house in Jamaran. It was his only distraction from a heavy schedule.

Fatemeh was Khomeini's favourite companion. During the early 1980s she had begun to study for a degree in philosophy. She was interested in mysticism and would often ask Khomeini, a former teacher of the subject, to explain difficult points in the texts she was reading.[2] Khomeini would devote regular twenty-minute sessions to her work and on 26 May 1984, in the thick of the war, while Iraq was targeting Iranian cities and tankers in the Persian Gulf, he began to compose a twelve-page letter for her dealing with a number of philosophical, mystical and ethical issues. The letter, published just after Khomeini's death under the title *Rah-e Eshq* (The Path of Love),[3] took him nearly three weeks to complete. Written with love and care, serious yet informal, witty and self effacing it provides a glimpse of a Khomeini rarely seen in public:

Finally you forced me, with your persistence, to parrot something of what my heart is unfamiliar. Old age and daily engagements which are better left unmentioned have made me forget the little I knew. To show you the circumstances in which I started this letter so as not to refuse your request, just look at its date: 26 May 1984.

Where should I begin? *Fitrat* (innate nature).

The person who seeks perfection in what is there loves absolute not defective perfection. Defective perfection is limited by nothingness and innate nature hates nothingness. The seeker of knowledge seeks absolute knowledge and loves absolute knowledge, and the seeker of power seeks absolute power and loves absolute power ...

Alas ... that the life of this broken-pen-man has passed and I have gained nothing from the seminary and its teachings.

My daughter, the subject of philosophy is absolute existence, that is all existence from God to all other forms of existence and the subject of scientific mysticism is the existence of the absolute, that is God ...

With Fatemeh's encouragement Khomeini had also returned after 1984 to his poetry writing. 'One morning when I went for my [philosophy] lesson,' she recalls 'He gave me a *ruba'i* (quatrain) It was a warning of a kind in the form of *tanz* (fun, banter) which goes:

> Hope, with the light of God,
> That she will liberate herself from the veil of philosophy.

Then I began to insist on more poems and few days later he gave me another:

> Fati, we must travel towards the Friend,
> We must pass over the ego of the self,

> Any knowledge that remotely reminds you of your self
> Is a devil you should avoid at any cost.

The kindness he showed towards me enabled me to ask for more and I finally gave him a notebook in which he could write his poems.[4]

Until then Khomeini, who often described himself as a *ma'er* or 'non-poet', had mostly scribbled on whatever scrap of paper was to hand – the corner of a newspaper or the back of an envelope.

Samples of Khomeini's poems from this period, published after his death, show the extent to which he was still, as he had been in his days as a student and junior *mojtahed*, influenced by mystical poets, particularly Hafez of Shiraz. The following sonnet is a good example:

> Oh, I desire a cup of wine from the Beloved's own hands.
> In whom can I confide this secret?
> Where am I to take my grief?
> I have yearned a lifetime to see the Beloved's face;
> I am a frenzied moth circling the flame,
> A wild rue seed pod roasting in the fire.
> See my stained cloak and this prayer-rug of hypocrisy;
> Can I, one day, tear them to shreds at the tavern door?
> If the Beloved allowed me one sip from the Jug of Love, intoxicated,
> I would break loose from the bonds of my existence.
> Old as I am, one signal of hope from those eyes would
>   turn me young again.
> Graciously bestow me this favour, and I will transcend
>   this earthly abode.[5]

Khomeini was not a creative poet but, like many Iranians, he had learned to compose well enough to give voice to his innermost thoughts and feelings in verse. His poetry is significant because it shows how deeply his mysticism is enshrined in his own world of personal experience. As a mystic he is imaginative, tender and gentle, touching upon the ethereal world. He is compassionate and even 'avoids killing flies, instead gently persuading them with the fringe of his cloak to fly away.'[6] His poetic writings are a world apart from his public persona, full of rambling passages, obscurity and allegory, particularly when he expresses his personal impressions of the intangible and abstract domain of perfection and oneness with God. The picture he presents in them of an ascetic who is in love with his creator is overwhelming.

The octogenarian Khomeini, like the young student, once more took up the metaphor of the opposition of the tavern on the one hand – the moment of divine communication – and the mosque and the seminary – the jurist and the preacher – on the other hand. In the poetry of his last months he vehemently rejected the self-righteousness of the mollahs and organised Sufis. Here again he is inspired by Hafez who, in a lament for Mansur Hallaj, a Sufi famously martyred for declaring 'I am the truth', wrote:

> The friend who, being raised sublime upon the gallows,
> Glorified the tree that slew him for his crime,
> This was the sin for which he died,
> That, having secrets in his charge,
> He told them to the world at large.[7]

At a time when he was sending scores of his opponents to the gallows, Khomeini himself felt the rope of the orthodox around his neck when he raved, like Mansur:

> Even while I have shunned love of myself
> Now truth is none but me
> I will see the gallows also
> As did Mansur see.[8]

Khomeini, according to the Iranian scholar Mehdi Ha'eri, 'was a man who saw himself as the truth and believed that, like Hallaj, he had completed the fourth journey which means being with God among the people.' Ha'eri argues that 'had the orthodox clergy been in charge, Khomeini would have been sent to the gallows as Hallaj was.'[9]

Besides his poetry, in the last phase of his life Khomeini also seems to have taken increasing refuge in his mysticism. A few months after the revolution, evidently believing that his new found power meant that he could be less discrete about his mystical views than had been the case during the long years in Qom and Najaf when, for fear of orthodox opinion, he concealed many of his writings on the subject, he had ventured into discoursing openly on the subject. During 1979 Ayatollah Taleqani had delivered a successful series of talks on television and, after his death in September that year, the producers of the programme had approached Khomeini for a similar series. He eventually agreed to provide a commentary on the Qor'an.

Khomeini's sermons dealt with the first few words of the Fatiha, the opening chapter of the Qor'an known as the Sureh-ye Hamd. He discoursed on the significance of each word from all possible textual, theological, philosophical and ethical angles. But he also engaged in lengthy digressions into his mystical world – never before exposed to the public, let alone to millions of television viewers, including many who were almost certainly critical of his beliefs. In orthodox Shi'i eschatology, man's room for manoeuvre is very limited as his affairs are mainly pre-determined. In Khomeini's mystical view, man has more room to develop towards perfection and unity with God. In his sermons on the Sureh-ye Hamd he dealt with a number of unorthodox views such as 'infallibility based in belief' and 'faith is belief'. He also spoke of 'man's path to perfection', of prayer as a way of developing man, and of the development of man involving the institution of justice. He told his audience that an 'uprising for God is a step towards God' and that 'prayer leads man out of darkness and once he emerges he works for God, he wields his sword for God, he fights for God and he rises up for the sake of God.'[10] In his fifth sermon Khomeini became more specific and began to speak about his old instructors in Qom and the difficulties of teaching mysticism without suffering accusations of heresy and blasphemy.

Khomeini must have felt confident that his old enemies could no longer touch him. He was wrong. Although the matter was kept quiet, his sermons caused an uproar among the orthodox clergy who protested that he was restating old views that they had condemned as heretical.[11] At the end of his fifth, broadcast on 11 January 1980, Khomeini promised his audience that he would continue.[12] But a week later he was taken to hospital in Tehran suffering from what appeared to be a serious heart ailment. Whether or not his illness was used as an occasion to allow the television series to come to a quiet end is hard to determine. But in any event Khomeini did not, over the next nine years, return in any systematic way to the topic of mysticism, although he allowed his mystical writings, mostly from the 1930s and 1940s, to be slowly published.

In early January 1989, however, he threw all caution to the winds in a letter to the Soviet leader Mikhael Gorbachev in which he declared that communism belonged to the museum of history and that, before falling into the trap of materialistic capitalism, Gorbachev should study Islam seriously as a way of life. He could do no better, Khomeini continued, than to read the works of Ibn Arabi, Avicenna and Sohravardi, all famous mystical philosophers. Khomeini underlined the personal significance the letter held for him by appointing three emissaries to deliver it, two of them from his inner circle: Tahereh Hadidchi Dabbagh, a family friend who had accompanied the Khomeinis in Paris, then became a Revolutionary Guard commander in Hamadan and was now a woman MP; Ayatollah Javadi Amoli, a student of Khomeini's mysticism, and Javad Larijani, a deputy foreign minister. The delegation was officially received at the Kremlin and Gorbachev is reported to have told them how proud he felt to be the only world leader to whom the Ayatollah had written a personal letter.

Khomeini was, in his own light, following in the footsteps of the Prophet who once wrote to the emperors of Byzantium, Ethiopia and Persia calling on them to submit to Islam. But for the orthodox clergy to invite Gorbachev to study mysticism was an unforgivable crime. From Qom members of a fringe organisation which called itself 'The Protectors of Jerusalem', unable to contain their sense of shock, composed an open letter: 'Your Holiness,' they wrote, 'you have not referred Mr Gorbachev to the truth of the holy Qor'an, but have asked him to read [the works of] the condemned heretic Avicenna, the Sunni pantheist and arch-mystic Ibn al-Arabi, the works of Sohravardi who was executed by the Muslims for his ideological deviations, and the writing of Mollah Sadra, who was exiled to the village of Kahak near Qom because of his intellectual deviations.' They also reminded Khomeini that 'Your Holiness's lectures at the Feiziyeh School of theology were cancelled for exactly the same reason.' It continued:

In view of all this, we fail to understand why you refer the gentleman to deviant philosophers and mystics for the study of Islam. Are there not sufficient reasons in the Qor'an to prove the existence of God and to explain the principles and precepts of religion? Does it mean that the leaders of Islam are unable to explain the truth of the Qor'an without resorting to philosophy and mysticism? You know that both Greek philosophy and Indian mysticism existed long before the advent of either the Prophet Mohammad or Moses and Jesus. If philosophy and mysticism were sufficient to guide mankind, then was there any need for the Almighty to grace us with the mission of the prophets?[13]

A few weeks later, in an audience granted to the Soviet foreign minister and transmitted live on Iranian television, Khomeini, casually dressed without his turban, and visibly frail, explained carefully that he had wanted 'to open a new window for Mr Gorbachev to another world.' He had already vented his wrath on his orthodox critics in one section of a long 'letter to the clergy', completed and signed the previous day:[14]

This old father of yours has suffered more from stupid reactionary mollahs than anyone else. When theology meant no interference in politics, stupidity became a virtue. If a clergyman was able, and aware of what was going on [in the world around him], they searched for a plot behind it. You were considered more pious if you walked in a clumsy way. Learning foreign languages was blasphemy, philosophy and mysticism were considered to be sin and infidelity. In the Feiziyeh my young son Mostafa drank water from a jar. Since I was teaching philosophy, my son was considered to be religiously impure, so they washed the jar to purify it afterwards. Had this trend continued, I have no doubt the clergy and seminaries would have trodden the same path as the Christian Church did in the Middle Ages.[15]

Khomeini's hatred of the orthodox clergy was second only to, and perhaps even surpassed, his hatred of the United States. It made a deep impression on his son Ahmad who believed that his father's greatest achievement was his fight against them:

We have had many *faqihs*, mystics and philosophers. We have had many politicians who fought America. But none were the Imam. Was his greatest art to set up the Islamic Republic? No. What made him the Imam and led to the historic and victorious Islamic movement was the fact that he fought the backward, stupid, pretentious, reactionary clergy … He fought them with theology, mysticism and jurisprudence, philosophy, art and poetry … All this he did to liberate the oppressed from the yoke of the backward clergy. It was [the forces of the oppressed], liberated by the Imam, who brought about the victory of the movement. The feeling was mutual and the orthodox clergy retained their [absolute] opposition to Khomeini's 'mystical ravings' and 'troublesome politics'.[16]

But it was not only the 'reactionaries' who were critical of the 'state of the republic' after the end of the Iran–Iraq War. The absolute power exercised in the name of the *faqih* or his representatives was viewed as unacceptable in many circles and led numerous Khomeini loyalists to withdraw from revolutionary institutions. Some of his very best students and followers, who had been dissatisfied during the war years with the lack of clear strategy in economic, social and political issues, felt that, with the war over, they could express themselves without being accused of helping the enemy. On the street level too there was unrest and dissatisfaction over shortages and over the whole handling of the war. Questions on these issues began to filter down through the society as a whole producing pressures on the government to follow a more relaxed social and political policy.

Montazeri, Khomeini's designated successor, was as critical of the situation as Khomeini's liberal foes. A reluctant politician who stood by his principles, Montazeri was sometimes described by his detractors, including, eventually, Khomeini himself, as a political 'simpleton' and an 'impressionable' person whose judgement could be coloured by his emotions. His position within the labyrinthine power structure of the Islamic constitution was, moreover, ambiguous. He held no office except the title of deputy leader and had, therefore, only moral influence as the most senior revolutionary clergyman after Khomeini. Moreover, the most important responsibility Khomeini had delegated to him – the task of supervising, in the difficult circumstances of post-revolutionary violence and chaos, recommendations for the pardon of prisoners – often brought him into conflict with the intelligence apparatus, the Revolutionary Courts, the judiciary, and a whole web of vested interests. This situation, together with the emotional attachment Montazeri developed to some of his relatives and students, such as Mehdi Hashemi, who came into conflict with other institutions and ultimately with Khomeini's office, created an explosive situation which came to a head in the first three months of 1989.

Montazeri remained a passionate believer in the *velayat-e faqih*. Even so, in a series of lectures to his students in Qom, which during 1988 and early 1989 were serialised in the daily *Kayhan*, he elaborated a view of Islamic government that was far more open, and gave far more scope for popular participation than the polity that had developed over the previous decade under Khomeini. He also made no secret of his belief that the country had become a new kind of dictatorship and in November 1987 he challenged the claim that political parties were irrelevant because there could be no differences of opinion within the Islamic republic by demanding that the 'law on political parties' passed in late 1981 should be implemented.[17]

This was a highly restrictive piece of legislation and Montazeri's advocacy could hardly have been defined as subversive. A year later, however, he began to raise infinitely more sensitive issues, which hit at the heart of the regime and at the policies of his old teacher. The first major question in which he intervened after the end of the war was a new reign of terror unleashed against political prisoners during the late summer and early autumn of 1988. Two days after Iran accepted the ceasefire with Iraq, the People's Mojahedin who, since their leader Mas'ud Rajavi's flight to exile in 1982, had built up a military base in Iraq from which they hoped to overthrow the Islamic Republic, invaded the western border. In a badly conceived offensive, politically as well as militarily, the Mojahedin advanced some 80 miles into Iran, briefly occupied a few border towns and villages, and announced that they were on their way to Tehran. Their action triggered a new surge of zeal. Parliament was closed and Khomeini issued an appeal to all able-bodied Iranians to defend the Islamic homeland. People readied themselves to go to the front and there were widespread denunciations of the Mojahedin. The advance, however, was defeated within two days. Several hundred from both sides were killed and those of the Mojahedin who did not have time to retreat were surrounded and wiped out on the spot either in fighting or in summary executions.

The Mojahedin's invasion gave the hard-liners a chance to clear the prisons of activists. Justifying the plan with a claim that there was a country-wide plot for an uprising, Khomeini appointed a three-man commission consisting of the public prosecutor, the head of the intelligence services and the supervisor of prisons and ordered it to take firm action over political prisoners. His secret brief to them, according to a recent report of the affair written by Hojjat al-Islam Mohammad Reishahri, the Minister of Intelligence of the time, was to decide whether prisoners still adhered to their past beliefs and, if freed, would simply rejoin their organisations, in which case they should be executed immediately, or whether they had genuinely repented and were sorry for their past deeds, in which case they should be freed.[18]

According to international human rights bodies, over little more than two months several thousands were executed as a result of this order.[19] Although the majority were members or supporters of the Mojahedin, a great many prisoners from other, quite separate, political factions were also killed. Many of the victims of this massacre had been in prison for some years, often in parts of the country remote from the National Liberation Army incursion in which they could therefore have played no part. Some were arrested while still at high school for nothing more than distributing leaflets, others were serving prison sentences, while still others had remained in detention for years without ever having been tried. In some cases, former prisoners who had been released after serving their sentences were re-arrested and executed although they had not taken part in banned political activities since their release.

The vengeance that was wreaked in the prisons in the Autumn of 1988 was, in Montazeri's view, against the interests of the Islamic state. It was, he said in three private letters written at the beginning of August, two to Khomeini and a third copied to the various authorities who organised the terror, wrong to execute people who had already been tried and received lesser sentences in the past, and it was against the principles of Islam to execute those who were one's 'captives'.[20] Additionally, the circumstances in which the executions were carried out meant that there was a danger of completely innocent people being murdered. The whole affair, he declared, would turn world opinion against Iran and result in condemnation of the Islamic Republic by future generations, the more so because there was, in the circumstances, a distinct risk of executing entirely innocent people.

In the second of his letters to Khomeini, Montazeri spelt out in some detail just how easily the innocent could fall victim to the arbitrary power to make life and death decisions that had been given to the three-man commission:

Three days ago, a religious judge from one of the provinces, who is a trust-worthy man, visited me in Qom to express concern about the way your recent orders have been carried out. He said that an intelligence officer, or a prosecutor – I don't know which – was interrogating a prisoner to determine whether he still maintained his [old] position. Was he prepared to condemn the hypocrite organisation [the Mojahedin]? The prisoner said 'Yes'. Was he prepared to take part in a [television] interview? 'Yes' said the prisoner. Was he prepared to go to the front to fight the Iraqis? 'Yes,' he said. Was he prepared to walk into a minefield? The inmate replied that not everyone was prepared to walk over mines and, furthermore, the newly converted could not be expected to do so. The inmate was told that it was clear that he still maintained his [old] position, and he was duly dealt with. The religious judge's insistence that a decision should be based on a unanimous, and not a major-ity, vote fell on deaf ears. He said that intelligence officials have the largest say everywhere and in practice influence others. Your Holiness might take note of how your orders, that concern the lives of thousands of people, are carried out.[21]

Montazeri's pleas had fallen on deaf ears. Khomeini believed that anyone who took up arms, directly or indirectly, against the Islamic government should suffer the death penalty. Whereas in defence of his arguments Montazeri cited examples of the clemency the Prophet had shown towards his enemies,[22] to Khomeini it was a religious duty to follow the example of the Prophet's decisive action against the Jews of the Bani Qureizah, 700 of whom were, on a single day, beheaded for constant plotting against Islam.[23] Nor did the condemnation of human rights conditions in Iran by international bodies concern him. He repeatedly denounced their statements, suggesting that they showed double standards. 'We live at a time,' Khomeini said in one such declaration, 'when criminals are supported and praised rather than punished. We live in a time when the so-called human rights organisations support the illegitimate interests of the superpowers, provide legitimacy for their crimes and try to destroy Islam.'[24] Khomeini called Amnesty International 'Travesty International'.

In the early weeks of 1989 Montazeri stepped up his criticism, this time publicly, in an interview published in the daily *Kayhan*:

Unfortunately we produced more slogans instead of getting things moving and instead of keeping our values. Instead of giving more values to the people and keeping them on the scene, we put aside and shunned the bright among them and made them dissatisfied and isolated. Finally, we came to a point at which we were forced to take steps that contradicted our early slogans and to forget all our principles … I agree with the new generation of the revolution that there is a great distance between what we promised and what we have achieved … mismanagement, a failure to give jobs to the right people, exaggeration, self-centredness, monopolisation, factionalism, the denial of people's rights, injustice and disregard for the revolution's true values have delivered the most severe blows against the revolution to date. Before any reconstruction [takes place], there must first be a reconstruction of the country's thinking about administration and its quality, and there must be a political and ideological reconstruction in the management of the country. This is something that the people expect of the leader.'[25]

He continued this attack three days later in a speech to mark the tenth anniversary of the revolution: 'The tenth anniversary of the revolution must remind us of the original aims of revolution,' he told his audience in Qom. He believed, he said, in an open society in which critics would be allowed to express themselves adding, sadly, 'if they censor me what can others expect?' Montazeri continued:

Let us see what slogans we have used over the past ten years that have made us so isolated in the world and made the people pessimistic about us ... Let us see what happened to all the unity, co-ordination, devotion ... that we enjoyed at the beginning of the revolution ... Did we do a good job during the war? Our enemies, who imposed the war on us, emerged victorious. Let us count the forces we lost, the young people we lost, how many towns were destroyed ... and then let us repent recognising that we made these mistakes. On many occasions we showed obstinacy, shouted slogans, and frightened the people of the world who thought our only task here in Iran was to kill. We should not stop at making promises about freedom of speech and freedom for political parties. Our behaviour and actions should be such that all devoted revolutionaries who have ideals can state them in the interests of the revolution and for the development of the country without fear of persecution. Unfortunately, we see good people who are afraid of persecution; they cannot breath in peace. This is wrong.[26]

Towards the end of his speech Montazeri went so far as to say that if the government meant to compromise 'our values and principles', we had better not have government. The statement hit at the heart of Khomeini's world-view. For Khomeini valued ideology only if it could be translated into power and to him the only road to holiness was through action.

Montazeri had delivered by far the most important attack on Khomeini's record ever to have come from within the system.

Pressure had meanwhile been growing on Khomeini from hard-line quarters which saw the relative social relaxation of the post-war period as a road to moral degeneration. The special tenth anniversary issue of the newspaper Pasdar-e Islam, makes a fascinating reading for its harsh criticism of what its authors regarded as deviations from very modest social concessions extracted by moderates from Khomeini such as the permission to play some kinds of music on state radio and television, to play chess, or to use eau de cologne.[27] 'Save Islam and rescue the revolution' was their war cry.

If the war has ended because of the Imam's maslahat [prudence], does it mean that the cruel offensive of world arrogance, from more narrow and undetectable angles has come to an end? Would they leave us alone? The wounded snakes of world arrogance led by America with its external and internal agents are plotting to undermine our revolution in its moral and cultural aspects. These plots are far more dangerous and destructive than their war fleets, missiles, air and land offensives and chemical bombs. If we do not pay attention and remain on our guard, God forbid, they will destroy us by our very own hand.[28]

The journal even accused some politicians of encouraging moral laxity to hide their administrative shortcomings:

... as do the un-Godly regimes which promote corruption and prostitution to keep people busy and stop them complaining. If they have such ideas they are mistaken. Because the supporters of the revolution – the faithful, the Hezbollahis, the families of martyrs and the war veterans – are angry, disappointed and fed-up with this situation; the singers, dancers, musicians and their friends and cronies, on the other hand, will never be happy with this system. The more concessions you make to them, the more their 'elephant feels homesick for India' [the more they want] ... Stop it before it's too late. If you are politicians, you must know that your support is in the Friday prayer congregations which should not be empty, not in music halls; and if you are men of faith, and your trust is in God and the Muslim people, then you must know that this trend will not help the piety of society.[29]

Khomeini was obviously pulled in different directions. Was there to be 'reconstruction' or more revolution? We have seen how American hostages and the war with Iraq were used for domestic purposes. At yet another critical juncture, a frail Khomeini opted for the path of confrontation with the outside world. On the morning of 14 February he issued a *fatwa* (edict) against the British author, Salman Rushdie for his book *The Satanic Verses*. The book took for its theme an obscure episode allegedly from the life of the Prophet, mentioned in several of the traditional Islamic histories. The episode was supposed to concern the Prophet's apparent inability on one occasion to distinguish between revelation and the 'whisperings of Satan', an occasion which, for a very short while, until his error had been made clear to him by the Angel Gabriel, gave his enemies in Mecca hope that he was prepared to compromise with them.

Khomeini's edict, broadcast on Tehran Radio, was short and to the point:

In the name of God the Almighty. We belong to God and to Him we shall return. I would like to inform all intrepid Muslims in the world that the author of the book *Satanic Verses*, which has been compiled, printed, and published in opposition to Islam, the Prophet, and the Qor'an, and those publishers who were aware of its contents, are sentenced to death. I call on all zealous Muslims to execute them quickly, where they find them, so that no one will dare to insult the Islamic sanctities. Whoever is killed on this path will be regarded as a martyr, God willing. In addition, if anyone has access to the author of the book but does not possess the power to execute him, he should point him out to the people so that he may be punished for his actions. May God's blessing be on you all. Ruhollah Musavi al-Khomeini

The format of the letter, and particularly the use of the Qor'anic verse 'We belong to God and to Him we shall return', a verse usually used for mourning and major calamities, was designed to emphasise the gravity of the matter. So too was the declaration that 15 February would be a 'national day of mourning', a signal for thousands of demonstrators chanting 'death to Britain' to pour into the streets and stone the British Embassy.

We will probably never know exactly what considerations were uppermost in Khomeini's mind when he issued the *fatwa*. Khomeini had almost certainly been aware of the content of *The Satanic Verses* for at least several weeks. Salman Rushdie's work was well-known in educated circles in Iran. A translation of his earlier novel *Shame* had won a literary prize from the government for the year's best translation and enjoyed a good sale. The first copies of *The Satanic Verses* seem to have reached Iran in September 1988, soon after it was published. Reviews of the book and extracts from it had been broadcast from Persian language radios abroad – to which Khomeini listened regularly – and reviews had even appeared in the Iranian press. Furthermore, an unnamed scholar is reported to have spent a month – on his own initiative – writing a well-documented refutation nearly 700 pages long which he presented, together with a shorter digest of his findings, to Khomeini's office. Khomeini read the digest, but dismissed the issue with the words: 'The world has always been full of lunatics who have talked nonsense. It is not worth replying to this sort of thing. Do not take it seriously.'[30] He did not even recommend a ban in the import of the book.

In any event, the timing for Khomeini served both domestic and foreign policy ends. Unrest over the book had been building up for some months throughout the Muslim world and among Muslim communities in England. It had crescendoed in Pakistan on 12 February with protesters attempting to storm the American Embassy in Islamabad, and in Kashmir on 13 February when a man was killed and over 100 were injured in riots.

By issuing the *fatwa*, Khomeini had made a serious bid for the leadership of the entire Islamic world, while, at the same time, finding a way to refocus the energies of those his supporters at home who had been demoralised by the long, bloody inconclusive war. From being regarded by most non-Shi'a as merely a renewer of Islam, through the *fatwa* he became a spokesman for the frustrations and ambitions of Muslims in general, and not just those in Islamic countries. Compromise with the society around them was becoming a less and less attractive option among militant Muslims in Europe, and in the art of refusing to compromise there was no mentor more reliable than Khomeini. In the wake of the *fatwa* the Islamic Conference Organisation condemned the book but refused to condone the death sentence, as also did the other main Islamic religious bodies, the Al-Azhar Mosque and university in Cairo and the Saudi Arabian ulema. But no voice had been more effective than Khomeini's in triggering the great wave of indignation that swept round the world.

Soon after Khomeini's *fatwa* was issued, some elements in the political elite wanted to bring the issue under control, but they failed. In his Friday prayer sermon of 16 February, President Khamene'i suggested that 'If he [Rushdie] apologises and disowns the book, people may forgive him.' On 18 February Rushdie issued a carefully-worded statement, regretting 'profoundly the distress the publication has occasioned to the sincere followers of Islam. Living as we do in a world of many faiths, this experience has served to remind us that we must all be conscious of the sensibilities of others.' This short statement, obtained from the author by the Archbishop of Canterbury's aides, was relayed to the Ministry of Foreign Affairs in Tehran via official channels before being released to the press. But it was not accepted. Instead Khomeini's office issued a statement which said that even an apology could not overrule the death sentence:

The imperialist foreign media falsely allege that the officials of the Islamic Republic have said the sentence of death on the author of *The Satanic Verses* will be retracted if he repents. His Excellency, Imam Khomeini, long may he live, has said: 'This is denied 100 per cent. Even if Salman Rushdie repents and becomes the most pious man of all time, it is incumbent on every Muslim to employ everything he has got, his life and wealth, to send him to Hell.' His excellency the Imam added: 'If a non-Muslim becomes aware of Rushdie's whereabouts and has the ability to execute him quicker than Muslims, it is incumbent on Muslims to pay a reward or a fee in return for this action.'

As the controversy that surrounded the *fatwa* in the outside world gained momentum, Khomeini, oblivious to the outcry around the world on fundamental issues of free speech and freedom of expression, turned his attention once more to the domestic situation. He was still fighting to tame the waves of discontent that were sweeping the country. Ten days after Montazeri's anniversary speech, and a week after his *fatwa*, he went on the offensive against his critics in a long 'Letter to the Clergy' dated 22 February.

The letter, which shows Khomeini at his most unyielding, was in effect a response to the 'board of governors' by a chief executive who needed to defend his record and a set of guidelines for the future. First, he answered those of his critics who questioned the achievements of the revolution: 'the revolution has been successful in most aspects and objectives,' he wrote. As for the war:

With God's assistance we have not been defeated and conquered in any way ... of course, had we the means and equipment we would have achieved even higher goals; but this does not mean that we were defeated over our main aim: to repulse aggression and protect Islam ... Each day of the war brought a blessing which we used to the full. Through the war we demonstrated our oppression and the aggressor's tyranny. Through the war we unveiled the deceitful face of the world-devourers. It was during the war that we concluded that we must stand on our own feet. It was through the war that we broke the backs of both Eastern and Western superpowers. It was through the war that we consolidated the roots of our Islamic revolution.

Then, in an obvious reference to Montazeri's criticisms, Khomeini offered an 'official apology' to the relatives of 'the martyrs and self-sacrificing devotees' for the 'erroneous analyses made these days':

I pray to God that he will accept me alongside the martyrs of the imposed war ... we do not repent, nor are we sorry for even a single moment for our performance during the war. Have we forgotten that we fought to fulfil our religious duty and that the result is a marginal issue?

He went on, in yet another veiled reference to Montazeri, to warn the clergy about the dangers of listening to liberals such as Bazargan:

We must not act wrongfully ... in the expression of our views in order to please a handful of sell-out liberals lest our dear Hezbollah feel that the Islamic Republic is deviating from its principled stand. Does it not lead to the loss of people's confidence if we say ... that the Islamic Republic has not achieved anything or that it has not been successful? A delay in the achievement of our goals is not a reason for a retreat from our principles ...

As if what he had already said was not enough Khomeini elaborated at some length on his view of the liberals, cautioning seminarians to be vigilant over the 'pseudo-pious' and the 'pseudo-revolutionaries'. They must, he said,

... learn from the bitter experience of the so-called statesmen who have never reconciled themselves to the principles and objectives of the clergy. Otherwise their past reputation for treason will be forgotten and [through] baseless sympathy and naïveté [they will] make their way back to important positions in the system. We are not sorry at all that they are not alongside us today because they were not with us from the start. The revolution owes no debt to any group. We are still suffering the consequences of the ample confidence which we had in those groups and the liberals.

He turned next to the issue of a general amnesty which, it had been suggested by those who were trying to promote post-war reconstruction, should include the many Iranians with capital and skill who had fled the country after the revolution. They might be allowed home, wrote Khomeini, but only on condition that they say nothing:

The country's embrace is always open to those who seek to return home in order to give their service, but not at the price of their having claims on the revolution, if they question why you have said 'Death to America', why you have had a war, why have you issued the decree of God on the Monafeqin [the Mojahedin-e Khalq] and the counter-revolutionaries, why do you shout the slogan of neither East nor West, why did you occupy the nest of spies, and hundreds of other whys. The important point in that respect is that we should not be influenced by superficial sympathy for the enemies of God, for the opposition and for offenders against the system, and thereby question God's decrees and divine punishments. Not only do I not consider some of these cases to be in the interest of the country, but I believe that enemies benefit from them.

The assault on Montazeri, who was never named in this letter, was a taste of things to come. Khomeini may well at this point have made up his mind to dismiss his successor. But if he was still wavering at the end of

February, the publication abroad in early March of the letters Montazeri had written about the post-war wave of executions was the last straw. The letters, which provided an unprecedented revelation of an affair that had been shrouded in secrecy, had turned up in Abolhassan Bani Sadr's office in Paris and Khomeini was incensed to hear them broadcast back to Iran on the BBC.[31] He immediately ordered the Assembly of Experts to meet and sort out the future of the leadership[32] and on 22 March, in a message to families displaced by the war, he issued a final public warning to Montazeri: 'I have not signed a contract of brotherhood with anyone; the framework of my friendship depends on the correct behaviour of each individual.' Four days later, on 26 March, he summoned the most senior members of his circle, Ali Meshkini, Ebrahim Amini, Akbar Hashemi Rafsanjani and Ali Khamene'i to discuss the matter. They were doubtful, arguing that the public removal of Montazeri would harm the republic since there was no qualified candidate to succeed him. Khomeini reportedly replied '[but] you have Mr Khamene'i who is eligible'.[33] The four men were also very anxious that Khomeini should not go public with a fiery letter he had already prepared for Montazeri and wanted to have read in full on the media. They had the utmost difficulty in dissuading him, but eventually it was agreed that the letter would be taken to Montazeri by Abdollah Nuri who would return with a reply. When Ahmad saw Montazeri's response, it was agreed not to publish Khomeini's letter and it remained in private domain for about 10 years – until 22 November 1997.[34]

The letter read as follows:

I am heartbroken to have to write these few words to you. Perhaps one day the people will realise the facts by reading this letter.

In your recent letter to me, you said that, in accordance with the *sharia*, you give priority to my views over your own. I consider God my witness when I point out the following issues:

Since it has become clear that after me you are going to hand over this country, our dear Islamic revolution, and the Muslim people of Iran to the liberals, and through that channel to the hypocrites [the Mojahedin-e Khalq], you are no longer eligible to succeed me as the legitimate leader of the state. You, in most of your letters, speeches and stances, have shown that you believe the liberals and hypocrites should rule in this country. It is so clear that your remarks have been dictated by the hypocrites that I did not see any point in sending a reply. For instance, thanks to your speeches and written work, the hypocrites took advantage of your stance in defence of their ilk to promote a number of their comrades – who had been condemned to death on charges of waging an armed struggle against Islam and the revolution – to positions of authority. Can you see what valuable services you have offered to arrogance? On the issue of the murderer Mehdi Hashemi, you considered him to be the most religious person on earth. Despite the fact that it was proved to you that he was a murderer, you kept sending messages to me to spare his life. There are so many other examples similar to that of Mehdi Hashemi that I cannot be bothered to mention them all.

You no longer have the power of attorney on my behalf. Tell the people who bring you gold and money to take them to Mr Pasandideh's residence in Qom or to me in Jamaran. Praise be to God, you yourself will not have any financial commitments from this date.

If, in accordance with the *shari'a*, you consider my views to be superior to yours (the hypocrites will certainly advise you that it is against your interests to do so; and no doubt you will become busy writing things which will further deteriorate your future), then you should listen to the following words of advice. It breaks my heart and my breast is full of agonising pain when I see that you, the fruit of my life's labour, are so ungrateful. However, relying on Almighty God, I give you the following words of advice, and it will be up to you whether you make a note of them or not:

One: Try to change the members of your office so as to avoid feeding the hypocrites, Mehdi Hashemi's clique, and the liberals from the sacred charity funds donated to the Imam.

Two: Since you are a gullible person and are provoked easily, do not interfere in political matters, and perhaps then God will forgive you for your sins.

Three: Do not write to me ever again, and do not allow the hypocrites to pass state secrets to foreign radio stations.

Four: Since you became a spokesman of the hypocrites and your speeches have conveyed their wishes and letters to the people via the mass media, you have inflicted heavy blows on Islam and the revolution. This is a great act of treason against the unknown soldiers of the Lord of the Age [intelligence officials], may our souls be sacrificed for him, and against the sacrifices made by the illustrious martyrs of Islam and the revolution. If you wish to save yourself from hell fire, you had better confess to all your sins and mistakes and maybe then God will help you.

I swear to God that from the start I was against choosing you as my successor, but at the time I did not realise you were so gullible. To me you were not a resourceful manager but an educated person who could benefit the religious seminaries. If you continue your deeds I will definitely be obliged to do something about you. And you know me, I never neglect my obligation.

I swear to God that I was against appointing Mehdi Bazargan as the first prime minister, too, but I considered him to be a decent person. I also swear to God that I did not vote for Bani Sadr to become president either. On all these occasions I submitted to the advice of my friends. In the midst of my pain and suffering, I wish to address our dear people from the bottom of my broken heart:

I have made a pledge with my God never to forgive evil individuals if I am not obliged to do so. I have made a pledge with my God that pleasing Him is much greater priority than pleasing my friends and other people. If the entire world were to rise against me, I would never abandon justice and the truth. I do not care about history and current developments. I am only interested in performing my religious duties. In addition to my pledge to God, I have promised the decent, noble, and honest people to inform them of the facts when the time is appropriate. Islamic history is full of examples of treasonable acts by prominent figures of Islam against the religion. Try to make sure that you are not influenced by the lies broadcast by foreign radio stations. These radio stations dictate their lies with so much joy and enthusiasm these days. I beseech Almighty God to grant patience and tolerance to this old father of the dear Iranian people. I beseech God to forgive me and to take me away from this world so that I no longer have to experience the bitter taste of my friends' treachery. We all submit to God's will. We have no power without God's will. Everything comes from Him. Wishing you peace: Ruhollah Musavi Khomeini.[35]

The vehemence of Khomeini's denunciation must have come as a great shock to Montazeri, but his reply on 27 March 1989 was humble, impeccably polite, and above all accommodating. He would, he said, do whatever Khomeini asked, adding that he had not been interested in the job from the start.

Considering the heavy responsibilities, it was not in the interest of the system. And now I announce that I am not ready to take this job. If there have been weakness and mistakes, which are part of human nature, I hope they will be rectified with Your Holiness's leadership. I ask all brothers and sisters not to utter a word in my support.'[36]

Somewhat mollified, on 28 March Khomeini wrote an acceptance of Montazeri's resignation designed for public consumption:

As you have stated, the Leadership of the Islamic Republic is a grave responsibility and a heavy duty which requires an endurance beyond your energy and that is why, from the very beginning, I was against your appointment; and in this regard we were both of the same opinion. You have announced that you do not want the post of deputy leader. I accept this and sincerely thank you for it.'[37]

The publication of this letter was the first that people in Iran heard about the dramatic struggle that had, for a long time, been raging behind the scenes and to which Khomeini referred more explicitly some two weeks later when, on 15 April, he wrote to the Majles:

I have heard that you are not aware of the affair relating to the revered Montazeri and do not know what it is all about. Know then that your old father has been trying, without success, for two years by messages or in statements to prevent the matter from reaching this stage ... My religious duty has obliged me to take a decision in the interests of Islam and the system. Therefore, with deep regret and a heavy heart, I have dismissed the fruit of my heart from his office to safeguard the government and Islam ....[38]

After these exchanges Montazeri's title of grand ayatollah was withdrawn overnight, the publication of his lectures in *Kayhan* and references to him on the state radio were stopped, his portraits were collected from offices and mosques, his security guards were withdrawn and the high security walls of his office in Qom were dismantled. The same preachers who, just a day earlier, had asked their congregations to pray for Montazeri as the 'sublime jurist' (*faqih-e aliqadr*) and the 'hope of the Imam and the People', now had to explain why he had to go. There were divisions within most revolutionary institutions and student bodies over his removal and demonstrations took place in Najafabad, Qom and other places in his support. But they were fruitless.

With Khomeini's health now deteriorating rapidly, Montazeri's departure created a major political crisis. Unlike other leading personalities of the Islamic Republic who had fallen from favour, his revolutionary credentials were impeccable. Ayatollah Shari'atmadari could be challenged as a man who had tolerated the Shah's regime and had allegedly plotted to overthrow Khomeini; Bani Sadr could be labelled a 'Westoxicated nationalist', and Mehdi Bazargan, neither a clergyman nor a hardliner, could be written off as a 'treacherous liberal'. But Montazeri was a pious ayatollah who had been acclaimed since the early 1950s as one of the best teachers of Qom. He had an unblemished record of political activity; he had played a major role in organising support for Khomeini's claim to become a *marja'*, and had often been referred to by the revolutionary mollahs as the best man after the Imam. Even after his removal as deputy leader, he was still a *marja'* in his own right who had firm roots in Qom. To justify his removal, Montazeri's reputation had to be destroyed.

Articles and editorials soon appeared in various newspapers all aimed at dismantling Montazeri's aura. But the principle attack was mounted by Ahmad Khomeini who, on 29 April, produced a hastily drafted 'open letter' entitled *Ranj-nameh*, 'A Book of Suffering' which, together with its appended documents, was some 130 pages long. The letter was distributed first to members of parliament, officials and newspaper editors. It was published in parts in some daily newspapers and eventually as a book with Ahmad's photograph on the cover captioned with a quotation from his father: 'You (Ahmad) are honest and intelligent and I consider you an expert in social and political matters.'[39]

Ahmad's long rambling letter was a revelation, showing the rivalry between Khomeini's office and that of Montazeri. 'For someone who has loved you all his life,' Ahmad said, 'it is hard and incredible to write this letter. But I feel I am indebted to the Imam, who is being wronged, and also bound to serve the people who are in search of truth.' Ahmad admits that he is writing in haste, but because he is aware of all his father did to save Montazeri from the claws of 'plotters' and 'infiltrators', he is obliged to tell the truth rather than betray Islam, the Imam, the people and the revolution. He reminds Montazeri of his final meeting with Khomeini on 19 January at which, Ahmad seems to indicate, most of the time was taken up with Montazeri's criticisms:

Do you remember that in your last meeting with the Imam you talked for half hour and Imam was silent? At the very end of the meeting when you stood up to go, the Imam uttered two sentences. 'Most of what you said was not correct. May God forgive me and bring about my death'.[40]

The decision on the future of the leadership was not, however, taken hastily or overnight even though 'some people might still ask why those who were aware of weaknesses in your character did not act earlier?'

The answer to this question lies in the fact that the Imam was constantly trying to provide you with guidance and prevent you from falling into the hands of the counter-revolutionaries. However, in the light of recent events, the Imam was left with no option but to agree to a change in his choice of successor.'[41]

Using letters and intelligence documents selectively Ahmad went on to speak of matters that had never before been mentioned in public and which revealed rivalries between Khomeini's office in Tehran and Montazeri's office in Qom reminiscent of the rivalry in Qajar Persia between the shah's court in Tehran and the crown prince's in Tabriz with the same sort of family connections and webs of patronage permeating each. One such document shows that on 4 October 1986 Khomeini wrote a letter to Montazeri warning him about Mehdi Hashemi:

Islam and the Islamic Republic is in a dire need of people like you. Therefore your holy personality and dignity should remain intact. I sense danger from your connection with Mr Mehdi Hashemi who is accused of killing people – directly or indirectly. Even if he is innocent it would effect your sanctity. You should ask the Intelligence Ministry to deal with the issue and should not be seen to be defending him even in private.[42]

Montazeri had replied two weeks later, on 17 October 1986, that 'if I did not criticise officials the people would rise up against them ... under the Shah's regime Mehdi Hashemi was condemned to death three times as a result of Savak pressure on the Isfahan court. But the Shah's supreme court had the independence and the gut to overturn that decision. I am not afraid of telling the truth. I know that truth is bitter. I have brought up Mehdi Hashemi. He is articulate, intelligent, and a better manager than your Minister of Intelligence [Reishahri] and your Commander of the Revolutionary Guards [Mohsen Reza'i]. He is no less pious either. His only difference is that he does not want to be a yes man and a pawn.'[43] When Montazeri later read out to Mehdi Hashemi a letter Khomeini had written about him, he remarked: 'the Imam's letter wiped the sleep from my eyes and I have written a reply that will wipe the sleep from his eyes.'[44]

With Khomeini's health failing rapidly, and the propaganda campaign over Montazeri highlighting the splits in the leadership, the question of the succession had to be resolved rapidly. But it posed a seemingly

insurmountable difficulty because those among the clergy who were recognised *marja'* – the principle qualification laid down by the constitution
for the position of leader – did not have the kind of political credentials
that would recommend them to Khomeini. The only recourse was to
change the constitution and so, acting in characteristically decisive fashion, on 24 April 1989, within three weeks of Montazeri's dismissal, Khomeini used his special powers as *vali-ye faqih* to issue a decree convening an
'Assembly for Revising the Constitution' (Showra-ye Baznegari-ye Qanun-
e Asasi).[45] The twenty-five-man Assembly – twenty members were appointed by Khomeini himself and another five by the parliament – began
work immediately. Khomeini had already made it known to his inner circle that Ali Khamene'i was now his favoured candidate for the succession.
In religious terms, however, Khamene'i was too junior and his scholarly
qualifications insufficient for even the ingenious political strategists who
surrounded the Imam to find a way to have him declared a *marja'*. On
Khomeini's own instructions, therefore, Article 109 of the constitution
requiring that the leader should be a *marja'-e taqlid* was removed, as were
the provisions that allowed, in the absence of a single, qualified individual,
for a collegiate leadership.[46] The assembly also took the opportunity to
streamline the relationships between different branches of the executive
that had caused so much trouble over the years. Most importantly, it elimi-
nated the post of prime minister whose responsibilities were attached to
the presidency. Meanwhile, the presidency was weakened by the transfer
of one of its key functions – the co-ordination of the three constitutional
powers – to the leader and abolished the high judicial council which was
elected by members of the judiciary, creating in its stead a single head of
the judiciary appointed by the leader.

The change was immense. Khomeini, in giving his instructions, had
justified himself, firstly, by reference to the concept of *maslehat*, expediency, but, secondly, by claiming that he had always believed that the
marja'iyat was not a requirement of the office of the leader.[47] And yet his
theory of Islamic government was based on the principle that the right to
rule is the exclusive right of the *faqih*, the expert on Islamic law. Accordingly,
the *maraje'-e taqlid*, those who are recognised as the most learned and mor-
ally qualified among the clergy, would be the only valid candidates.[48] Instead of this the Assembly required, in four rambling articles (5, 107 and
109, 111), that the Assembly of Leadership Experts should choose 'a pious
and just *faqih*, aware of the exigencies of the time, courageous, and with

good managerial skills and foresight.' If there are a number of candidates with these qualities, the person with the stronger 'political and jurisprudential' vision should have the priority. Moreover, under the new arrangements, if the leader did not live up to the requirements of his office he could, as before, be dismissed by the Assembly of Experts. But now, under the changes, his function could be temporarily taken over by a council consisting of the president, the head of the judiciary, and a theologian from the Council of Guardians until a new individual could be chosen by the Assembly.

The position of *vali-ye faqih* in the 1979 constitution was tailored, as in the case of Khomeini, to fit primarily a *marja'* and a revolutionary leader who was 'recognised' by the majority of the people (in the sense of *umma*). The *vali-ye faqih* was placed above the state and gave legitimacy to the state. But after ten years of Islamic rule, Khomeini's principle concern was the survival of the Islamic state he had created. If the 1979 constitution was a cloak made for a *marja'*, it had to be re-tailored and made smaller to fit a simple *faqih* to succeed Khomeini who, although still above the constitution, now had to draw his legitimacy from the state. Thus, Khomeini's theory of the rule of the clergy, despite appearances to the contrary, received a blow, as it effectively, in the long run, separated the position of the 'leader' from the institution of *marja'iyat*, subordinating the latter to the state.

Khomeini's historic role was to legitimise the notion of the temporal state for the Shi'i clergy who traditionally rejected it until the reappearance of the Hidden Imam. In so doing he undermined their historical oppositionist role and made it inevitable that any future challenge would be from 'citizens' whose allegiance to the state is expressed through the vote they cast out of political interest, and not from a population which perceives itself as 'imitators' or 'followers' of a sacred clerical establishment to whom they donate alms out of religious duty.

The Shi'i clergy was for some seven centuries in opposition to the Sunni majority rule; for over four centuries it shared power with a traditional Shi'i monarchy; for half a century it opposed the secularised monarchy until it could remove it from power and replace it. A decade of clerical rule under Khomeini may prove to have had more impact on the clergy itself than the five centuries or so that followed the creation of a Shi'i state in Iran by the Safavids in 1500.

Intoxicated by the cosmic vision of a mystic and bound by the firm belief of a jurisprudent who carries out God's command, Khomeini the politician was a powerful fusion. As a mystic, Khomeini was an elitist, but as a theologian he was expedient and as a politician a calculating populist to the point of being opportunistic. He believed in the use of force and, if need be, violence. He felt he was entitled to order the execution of thousands of infidels without shedding a tear. For Khomeini the mystic, when Man reaches a state of unity with God, his anger becomes that of God.

The three facets of Khomeini's personality should not be regarded as three separate personalities in one. For Khomeini there was no distinction between the persona of the jurist, the mystic and the politician. Driven by his personal experience as a mystic and theologian, even in politics he strove to push the community towards a general good, or towards a state of perfection.

As a jurisprudent Khomeini was deeply influenced by the cosmic vision he had acquired through his practise of mysticism. And yet, in this persona he embodied conventional doctrine and faith. To the faithful he preached in the common tongue of the clergy, a precise, legalistic and uninspiring language. Explaining, in minute detail, the procedures to be followed when a man is discovered to have had intercourse with a sheep in his *Towzih al-Masa'el*, Khomeini merely reproduces a topic which has appeared in legal compendia for centuries and which every *faqih* repeats.

Velayat-e Faqih for Khomeini is a suitable peg on which to hang a theory of Islamic government, it clearly names a God-given duty which the *faqih* is obliged to carry out and which everyone else must therefore accept. The problem comes, however, when the concept is examined in detail and one realises that it is a theory put forward by one man and disputed by virtually every one of his peers.

In Shi'i Islam, the Imam is considered to have a wide range of responsibilities, from being the guardian (*vali*) of the orphans and the insane to declaring an offensive war, implementing fixed penalties, i.e. amputation of the hand for theft, stoning for adultery, capital punishment for murder and so on. But whether the *faqih*, as the deputy of the Imam in his absence, should assume responsibility for these legal powers, has been a matter of dispute among Shi'i jurists.

It was Khomeini's impatience and dissatisfaction with the guiding role of the clergy which prompted him to justify the *faqih*'s assumption of political power. Whether he managed to construct an enduring basis for argument and for extending the *faqih's* power remains to be seen, and will, no doubt, eventually become an established topic in the teaching of Islamic law. But the period in which Khomeini ruled as *faqih* produced little public debate on the topic, and practically no response from the teaching clergy.[49]

However, Khomeini's treatment of the issue of the *vilayat* in its political, theological and legal aspects has been further complicated by his mystical commentaries on the subject, and there can be little doubt that he sometimes failed to draw a clear line between the legal meaning of *vilayat* (guardianship over others) and its mystical sense of closeness to God and spiritual participation in the governance of the universe. This mystical strain is in the line of Shi'i gnosis, in which the intellectual development of Sufi thought has been grafted onto the inherent spiritual content of Shi'ism. The hub of this mysticism is the consideration of the Imam as the Perfect Man, that supreme exemplar of the human spirit who acts as a vessel through which the divine outpourings reach Man and Man rises to attain his spiritual perfection. The Imam as the Perfect Man participates in *velayat-e takvini*, creational *velayat*, by virtue of the fact that his perceptions, his will, and his actions have become so permeated with the divine that there is a perfect congruence with their divine counterparts.

Although Khomeini always distinguished between this creational *velayat*, to which he says the *faqih* can lay no claim, and the *velayat-e tashri'i*, or legislative *velayat*, the connection between the two seemed to be so firmly established in his mind that the legislative *velayat* began to take on for him an almost supernatural quality. Perhaps it is in the very nature of the absolute sense which Khomeini gives to the term *velayat-e faqih* that it must transcend the bounds of a legal system, even that of a religion, and assume the spiritual status of divine grace.

Mystical literature in Islam abounds with definitions of *velayat*. Khomeini believed in mystical guardianship, *velayat-e erfani*. This in effect gives the *vali* the power over the precepts of religion, even to the point of suspending them, which is exactly what he did in 1987. This view clearly contradicts the orthodox view of Islam in which the divine rules cannot be tampered with. The question of Khomeini's involvement in the 'fourth journey' in which the *vali's* action is indistinguishable from that of God's, may well have been in Khomeini's mind when he justified his view on the absolute guardianship or *velayat-e motlaqeh*.

But there can be no doubt that here the mystic was taking over from the legist: Khomeini seemed to believe that he was a participator – to what degree only he knew – in that spiritual *velayat* which enabled him to perceive the true causes of events, and therefore to be able to act not only to influence political history, but to bring about the unfolding of the divine scheme. Or, to put it in terms which might be more acceptable, Khomeini seemed to think that the *vali-ye faqih* is, by virtue of being entrusted by God with the responsibility of preserving the Islamic community and the law, empowered with more than what the traditional, rationally-based jurists had supposed; God's will, in the time of the occultation of the Imam, did not manifest itself exclusively through the law, but also in the very will of the *faqih*.

To a certain extent his followers also held this belief about Khomeini's abilities, though not in such a systematic form as he did, and it was, to a certain extent, a belief which was founded on ambiguity. The 'Imam', it was generally believed, had shown by his uncanny sweep to power, that he knew how to act in ways which others could not begin to understand. His timing was extraordinary, and his insight into the motivation of others, those around him as well as his enemies, could not be explained as ordinary knowledge. This emergent belief in Khomeini as a divinely-guided figure was carefully fostered by the clerics who supported him and spoke up for him in front of the people. They were always careful that their words should not exceed proper theological bounds, but they were also careful not to state explicitly the nature of his power and knowledge. In this they followed Khomeini himself.

It is not yet possible to give any precise chronology of the spiritual aspects of Khomeini's life, although the signs are there, and this book has attempted to indicate them. Khomeini held the view, which can be traced back through Mollah Sadra, that the outward observance of the law of Islam was of no value if it was not combined with spiritual development, and he clearly strove for this spiritual ideal throughout his life.

His uniqueness lay, however, not in this, but in his belief that he could change the political fortunes of Islam. There is no way of knowing how much he believed he could do because of certainties he developed in his spiritual life, and to what extent he had developed an astute practical political sense. These are two sides of the same coin. But it is clear that he was in no small sense helped by the perception which his followers had of him, a perception which was every bit as carefully directed as was their perception of the political unfolding of the revolution. The way an Iranian sees the revolution has been inextricably connected with the way he or she sees Khomeini, and the unravelling of these two perceptions will perhaps be the story of Iranian politics for some time to come.

15

Khomeini's End
Death of a Patriarch

The end came just before midnight on Saturday 3 June 1989 and as shock to all, throwing Khomeini's supporters into frenzied commotion and his opponents into hilarious joy. The creator of the Islamic government was gone. Now there was time for change, or for his legacy to be continued. But what was that legacy? While alive, Khomeini the populist 'modified his rhetoric depending on political circumstances'.[1] Now the leaders of the Islamic Republic were faced with the classical problem of how to preserve the system without a successor or successors of the same stature as its architect.

The final crisis on that fateful day began at 8.30 in the morning. At 1 o'clock in the afternoon Khomeini called his wife and children to his deathbed in the north Tehran clinic next to his residence. He had told his family the day before that he was dying. Now he bade them farewell with the words of a man who felt he was soon to meet his creator, a tone not uncharacteristic for a preacher who had given sermons all his life:

This is a very difficult path ... Watch all your words and deeds ... I have nothing more to add. Those who want to stay, may do so; those who don't may go. Put the light out. I want to sleep.

These were the final words of the man who instigated one of the far-reaching revolutions in modern history. Attended only by his son Ahmad and his daughter Zahra, Khomeini fell into a deep slumber. During his sleep, at about 3 o'clock in the afternoon, he lost consciousness, and half an hour later he suffered a second heart attack. Khomeini's office, which had previously announced that the medical team was optimistic, realised that it had to prepare Iran for the inevitable news of the Imam's death.

That evening rumours about his health abounded on the streets of Tehran. In its 8.30 pm bulletin, Tehran television broadcast that there had been some 'complications', and admitted that things were not going as smoothly as they had so far led the people to believe. 'Pray for the Imam,' was the message, 'in the hope that your prayers may be heard to by God Almighty.'

On the same day, by the time that Khomeini was speaking his final words, the leading politicians of the Islamic Republic were still busy re-moulding the constitution in the Shah's old Senate building, now renamed the Islamic Consultative Assembly. Their first move after they were informed that Khomeini was on the verge of death was to call all eighty-three members of the Assembly of Experts to an early meeting on Sunday 4 June to discuss the choice of leader or leaders. Planes were dispatched to bring members from all over the country, and the security forces were put on a state of alert.

Rafsanjani recalled later that:

On the last day the danger was serious for us. The doctors were giving us hope. But his son Ahmad told me that he knew the Imam's condition better since he had been at his bedside, and he was very concerned. Ahmad told me to tell the councillors who were reviewing the constitution to finish the job as soon as possible while the Imam was alive. We then had a session attended by members of the review council in the president's office and decided to leave everything else aside until the work was done. The meeting was temporarily closed at two o'clock in the afternoon, and at 3.30, when we were gathering to continue the revision of the constitution, I received a phone call from the Imam's residence and was told to go there immediately.[2]

Some twenty leading politicians went to the hospital and gathered in a room next to the Imam. That room came to be the first seat of power of post-Khomeini Iran. Rafsanjani was the key player and decision-maker. Besides Rafsanjani, the president, the chief justice, the prime minister and

all the other important government leaders were present. The doctors revived Khomeini, but he was still unable to speak to the relatives and officials at his bedside. 'When I arrived,' said Rafsanjani, 'there was the Imam,
in the last moments of his natural life. We were all by the bedside and His
Holiness opened his eyes for a moment and looked at the sky, after which
there was nothing left that we could count on.'[3]

The doctors continued with their efforts to revive his heart with elec-
tric shock treatment and to resuscitate his lungs; they said the condition
could last for anything from twenty-four to forty-eight hours.[4] But, as the
night closed in, he slid further into oblivion. He had another heart attack
at about 10 pm and at 10.20 a flat line on the monitor pronounced him
dead. Ahmad and Zahra were the first to go to their dead father to kiss
him goodbye.

The commotion of grief had already engulfed the hospital. Everyone
wept. Karrubi, Rafsanjani's deputy, fainted several times. Rafsanjani himself sobbed quietly even as he considered what the next move should be.
Later he recalled:

We were drawing up the agenda for the Assembly of Experts, and while we
were busy talking, all of a sudden we heard the sound of weeping and wailing
from inside the hospital and places nearby. It would have created major problems if the news of the passing away of the Imam had reached people. Those
who were gathered there, the doctors, staff, relatives and the ulema, were sobbing their hearts out. It was not an easy thing to ask people who were crying
in that way to remain silent.[5]

Rafsanjani was uneasy lest the news break throughout the city and the
country before they could gain complete control of the situation. Khomeini's successors, who had not quite concluded the meeting and were
not sure what their next move should be, were under extreme pressure.
Rafsanjani finally pulled himself together and went to Khomeini's family,
some of whom had come from different parts of the country and abroad.
He argued that the Imam would not be pleased if, after his demise, the
society which he had created faced difficulties, and that in the interests of
the system they should remain calm. Khomeini himself had appealed to
his family not to cry after his death. 'I'm going and I'm not coming back,'
Khomeini had told them before he was taken into hospital. 'Don't cry for
me. It is God's will.'[6]

Nevertheless, thousands of distressed supporters had already begun to pour into the village of Jamaran in the north of Tehran towards Khomeini's home and the adjacent clinic. There was a large crowd in the nearby streets. Sobbing officials and security men were mixed with relatives. The situation had already spun beyond Rafsanjani's control. But any evidence of the bad news had to be stopped. The government eventually decided to cordon off the Jamaran area, telling supporters that the family were saying the do'a-ye tawassol, an urgent prayer, for the Imam's recovery.

This ruse gave the politicians time to put the finishing touches to the measures for a state of emergency to be declared, paving the way for the succession and the funeral arrangements. Food, transport and other needs had to be catered for. Airports, borders and key installations as well as international telephone lines were the first public services to be closed down. Rafsanjani later said: 'We had problems on our borders, the war had not yet ended, there were security issues involved when deciding on how to govern on the days when a complete close down came into effect. We had to decide on issues of transport and the general life of the population.'[7]

At this time Rafsanjani had one eye on what was happening in Tehran and another on sorting out the question of the succession without causing undue alarm in the provinces. Undoubtedly, since the gravitas of Khomeini's presence was no longer with them, the new leadership was very nervous indeed. Major decisions, which had often been reached after a long process of consultation with Khomeini, now had to be taken within minutes. The next question which loomed was the exact moment at which the news of Khomeini's death should be made public. Psychological initiative was very important. On previous occasions when they had tried to keep quiet about major developments, the news had been leaked to the people by the foreign media with adverse effects – like the time Khomeini himself heard the news of the Islamic Republican Party headquarters explosion and Beheshti's death from foreign radio stations.

At first the ruling cabal decided not to announce the news until the following day, Sunday 4 June 1989, as they wanted to wait until the Assembly of Experts had convened to choose the new leadership. Eventually the wishes of Khomeini's family and those who had argued that he must be buried as soon as possible, according to Islamic law, prevailed. Some argued that the news could not possibly be kept secret for more than a few hours. Even before telephone lines were cut that night, many Iranians abroad had been told by their friends about the prevailing sombre mood,

and reports of Khomeini's death were proliferating amongst his supporters. Had it not been for previous repeated false alarms in the Western
media about his death, many radio stations would have broadcast these
still unconfirmed reports.

It was a very long night for those who had to remain silent. Even for
hardened politicians such as Rafsanjani, it was not an easy task:

The state I was in that night was the hardest I have ever endured ... During
those few hours I could see that the whole world, all of Iran and all Muslims
were filled with different feelings, but that there were only a few of us who
felt as if we had a hornet's nest inside us which hurt us from within, and yet
we could do nothing about it. Certainly all those who were there felt the
same. In any case, I regard that night as the hardest in my entire life, and it
may have been the same for others who did not allow themselves to cry.[8]

All those who went from north Tehran to the south were observed
carefully by the waiting crowd to see whether they had been crying or not,
or whether they had brought good tidings. Khomeini's most ardent supporters, the war-wounded, were among the first to fill the streets to find
out what had become of their leader. Hundreds of revolutionary committee members were moving towards Khomeini's residence. Revolutionary
Guards and other security services were mobilised. For those who were
waiting in the streets, anything was a sign of hope or despair. By 5.30 in
the morning of 4 June, people in the streets near Jamaran were certain that
the Imam was dead. Radio broadcasts began to change their tune towards
dawn and a more sombre mood prevailed. Normal radio programmes were
suspended and recitations of the Qor'an replaced them.

Meanwhile, the body of the Imam was undergoing the religious rituals.
It was positioned facing Mecca, with the mouth closed and the limbs
straightened, covered with a piece of cloth. Soon came the sound of the
Qor'an recited over the Imam's body to comfort the soul. As morning
approached, the body was prepared for ablution according to religious rites.

Khomeini's body was washed in the manner he himself had prescribed,[9]
while there was a struggle to hide his surgical incisions. Freshly ground
camphor was placed on his forehead, palms, knees, and the tips of his big
toes. No scent was applied, as Khomeini and other clerics had strictly
forbidden the use of musk, ambergris, aloe or any fragrance except camphor.[10] Two pieces of wet, fresh wood were also placed under his arms as
required. Then he was shrouded with three pieces of thick cloth: a waist

cloth which must cover the body from the chest down to knee, a shirt to cover the body from the shoulder to the upper part of the shins, and an all-encompassing large shroud which could be sewn shut at both ends and wide enough to allow one side to overlap the other.

It was some nine hours after Khomeini's death that Iranians and the world at large reliably learned the news. It came in a single historic sentence on Tehran Radio at 7 am. The announcer sobbed openly as he cried: 'The lofty Spirit of Allah has joined the celestial heaven.' Khomeini's opponents were less complimentary. 'The long night of tyranny is over,' said one, adding: 'We are at the threshold of a new dawn.'

Speaker Rafsanjani, President Khamene'i, Chief Justice Ardebili and Prime Minister Musavi issued a joint statement read over the radio after the announcement. The statement was interesting not only because it showed absolute unity at a sensitive hour, but also because it set the tone for what was to come in the eulogies for the dead leader, 'the most divine personality in the history of Islam after the Prophet and the Imams'. The government declared five national days of mourning which were to be followed by forty days of official mourning. Apart from essential services, everything everywhere was closed.

Draped in black, people poured into the streets and the mosques to mourn the death of their Imam. Hundreds of thousands set out for Tehran to attend the funeral clad in black, waving black flags and some carrying a photograph of the old man. Officials, who were anticipating mass hysteria, asked the crowds to keep away from the Ayatollah's residence. Not since his return from exile in February 1979 had such a public outpouring for the person of Khomeini been displayed. Possibly even the most hardened supporters of Khomeini had begun to doubt his popularity, given the extent of public complaints by ordinary men and women about shortages in their daily life. Even among the clergy there were murmurs suggesting that he should be buried at night so that the small number of mourners would not adversely effect his successors. These were real worries. But they were unfounded. The sheer numbers of mourners, not to mention the unfinished task of choosing a successor and the desire to facilitate the attendance of as many foreign guests as possible at the funeral, forced the government to postpone the event for several days, until Sunday 11 June 1989.

On the day after Khomeini's death the focus in government circles was as much on the task of choosing a successor as on the arrangements for the funeral. The first sign of continuity came when the Revolutionary Guards and the army issued a joint statement pledging allegiance to Rafsanjani as acting commander-in-chief of the armed forces. In the morning at nine o'clock sharp, the Assembly of Experts began its session to choose the new leadership, but before that Khomeini's religious and political will had to be read. It was brought to the chairman of the assembly, Ayatollah Ali Meshkini, who publicly broke the seal of the handwritten will, signed and sealed by Khomeini himself. In its introduction it asked that it should be read by Ahmad Khomeini. If he asked to be excused, then the president was to read it. In the event, Ahmad sent his apologies, pleading that he was too upset to honour his father's wish. Rafsanjani telephoned him and begged him to change his mind, but again Ahmad refused.

Perhaps it was fortunate that the second choice to read the 29-page will was Khamene'i, an accomplished literary figure and a very good speaker. Khomeini's handwriting was beautiful, but not the most legible. A sobbing Khamene'i had to endure three hours reading the will in that charged atmosphere while the members of the Assembly wept. For the most part the will was religious. Khomeini began, as would be expected from a believer, with his profession of faith in the Qor'an, the Prophet and the Imams. But he soon departed from this by saying that: 'We are proud to be trying to implement the rules of Holy Qor'an and the *hadith* [traditions] of the Prophet.'

The document was disappointing for those who were expecting a policy statement. It did not contain new or specific issues but was a general reminder and a plea for continuity. The Ayatollah warned his successors not to be mesmerised by their office – their duty was to serve the nation. But the main targets for stinging attack were the usual culprits in Khomeini's long demonology. His strongest assault was on the Saudi king whom he described as a 'traitor to God'. Muslims, he said, 'should curse tyrants, including the Saudi royal family, these traitors to God's great shrine, may God's curse and that of his prophets and angels be upon them ... King Fahd spends a large part of the people's wealth every year on the anti-Qor'anic, totally baseless and superstitious faith of Wahhabism. He abuses Islam and the dear Qor'an.' Khomeini also denounced the leadership of the United States as terrorists who 'terrorise the powerless nations of the world'. The will had been written in 1982 and updated in 1987, when Iran's relations with the Soviets, who were still occupying Afghanistan and arming Iraq against Iran, were at a very low ebb. The Ayatollah asked Muslims all over the world to defend their rights with force and to protect the Islamic Republic, describing it as a 'divine gift'.

Towards the end of the will Khomeini stated:

Therefore, with God's blessing, I bid farewell to the dear sisters and brothers with a calm heart, a happy soul and a mind full of hope in God's blessing. And thus I shall travel to the eternal place. I am in dire need of your good prayers. I beseech the compassionate and merciful God and the nation to accept my apologies for my shortcomings and failures. I hope the nation will march ahead in a determined bid. The nation must know that the departure of a servant will not dent the iron bulwark of the nation. There are greater and more honourable servants at your service. Verily God is the protector of this nation and the oppressed of the world.

As a postscript, he added a few points which were an eye opener to the turmoil of the post-revolutionary years:

Even now, when I am alive, some false claims are being made concerning me. [The sound of loud and mass weeping of the Assembly members prevented Khamene'i from reading] It is possible that they may grow in extent after me. Therefore, I must proclaim that the allegations which have been made or will be made regarding me are not acceptable, unless they are proven with my own voice, or my own writing and my own signature confirmed by experts, or what I have said on the Islamic Republic's television.

Khomeini, as we have already seen, often had his words quoted selectively by his followers to prove their own points. Here he was himself rewriting his own words:

During my lifetime, certain individuals claimed that they used to write my announcements. I strongly deny this allegation. None of my announcements have been prepared by anyone except myself personally.

Khomeini continued:

According to rumours, certain people have claimed that they were responsible for my going to Paris. This is a lie. After I was turned back from Kuwait, I chose Paris after consulting Ahmad because there was the possibility of not being admitted to Islamic countries. They were under the influence of the Shah, but this possibility did not exist in Paris.

Khomeini was excluding his former aides in Paris, people like Bani Sadr, who was now back in his Paris exile, Sadeq Qotbzadeh, who had been executed for plotting against him, and Dr Ebrahim Yazdi, who was now a disgraced liberal. As if this was not enough Khomeini clarified his point:

In the course of the movement and the revolution, some individuals' hypocrisy and their Islamic pretensions, led me to mention them and to praise them. Later, I discovered that I had been the target of their deceit. My praise was given at a time when they pretended to be committed and faithful to the Islamic Republic. The yardstick for everyone is his present condition.

In general, there was very little that was new in the will, but the timing of its public reading was very effective in preparing the ground for Khomeini's circle to reach a consensus very quickly in choosing a successor. Rafsanjani recalls:

The reading of the Imam's will solved many problems. Of course, we had repeatedly heard him speak of the issues mentioned in it. But his words in those circumstances had more effect than in the past. Whenever we had a chance to listen to what was being read, the words shook our brains like a hammer and illuminated our heart. If the reading of the will had no other benefit, it played a great role in solving the problems of the country by creating a climate of beatitude and a psychological condition in everyone so that decisions were taken wisely and were free from personal ambitions and passions. However, it is a great treasure which will remain as the most important historical document of our revolution. Indeed, a second copy of the will had already been put in the museum of the Shrine of the Imam Reza in Mashhad.[11]

In the afternoon, the Assembly of Experts once again gathered in the parliament building to choose Khomeini's successor or successors. It was, reportedly, a difficult meeting. The leader was dead, his designated successor had been sacked just a few weeks earlier and the rules for choosing a new successor, devised under Khomeini's direct instructions by the Assembly for Revising the Constitution, had not yet been announced or ratified. The members of the Assembly did not know whether they should elect a temporary council until the revision of the constitution was completed. Furthermore, it was not clear whether they should, or indeed could, under the new rules, opt for a leadership council of three or five rather than a single leader. These were the themes of the discussion on that unusual afternoon.

The first part of the debate was about the virtues of a single or collective leadership. About a dozen people spoke for and against. Having been through a decade of division within a variety of councils, however, the majority were all too willing to approve the proposal that in future the only option should be for a single leadership. It was also obvious to most members of the Assembly, as it had been for some time to Khomeini's immediate circle, that, in the absence of Ayatollah Montazeri, they would have to elect someone who was not a grand ayatollah.

The argument went back and forth without reaching any conclusion. As the debate was getting nowhere, some members of the Assembly asked for an interval to give people time to think, but this idea was rejected. In the end it was decided that since they could not elect a council, it would be better to have a single leader, and once again the religious seniority issue became the focus of discussion. At this point Ayatollah Amini, the vice-chairman of the Assembly, read, for the first time in public, the letter that Khomeini had written to Meshkini, the president of the Assembly for Revising the Constitution, in which he had set out his instructions for the future of the leadership:

We cannot let our Islamic regime go on without a supervisor. You must elect an individual who can defend our Islamic honour in the world of politics and deceit. Since from the very beginning I was of the opinion and I insisted that the condition of *marja'iyat* [sources of emulation] was not necessary, a righteous or just *mojtahed* who is confirmed by the honourable experts of the whole country will be sufficient. If the people vote for the experts to appoint a just *mojtahed* as the leader of their government and they appoint an individual to take over the leadership, he is of necessity acceptable to the people. In such a case he becomes the elected *vali* of the people and his edict is enforceable.[12]

In fact, Khomeini added in his letter that he had been of this opinion for a long time but did not want to impose his views. 'In the early days of the constitution I used to say so. But friends insisted on laying down the condition of the *marja'iyat*. Then I, too, agreed. But at the time I knew that in the not too distant future, it could not be implemented.'[13]

While the Assembly of Experts was still in session on the Sunday, Tehran television got hold of President Khamene'i, who stated: 'We could perhaps fill the leadership vacuum, although temporarily, because we still have some time before the new articles of the constitution are ratified. We should be able to fill this vacuum. As to whether this will be permanent or temporary, the present session will – God willing – make a decision today, and affairs will progress in their natural course.'[14]

When it came to a vote for the new leader – who had to be a learned theologian (*mojtahed*) with administrative and other abilities – Sheikh Sadeq Khalkhali was the man who publicly mentioned Khamene'i's name for the first time. He gave an account of a conversation with Khamene'i, in which he had made this suggestion and received the reply: 'I won't accept it. This is a grave responsibility.' Khalkhali added: 'I then told him: "Let us discuss the matter, then you can say what you feel." I told him that he had been our president for eight years, that he knew all the problems of the country.' Khalkhali had added: 'We want you to be our leader and we will follow you as we followed Imam Khomeini. The experts will vote for you. And you will have to accept it.' At this point, according to Khalkhali, 'Khamene'i showed humility and began to cry.'[15]

The Assembly now began to discuss the choice of Khamene'i, and one of the members asked the presidium to tell them what was known about Khamene'i and his suitability for leadership, and whether Khomeini had written anything about Khamene'i. It was at this point that Speaker Rafsanjani began to speak about Khamene'i. Rafsanjani later reported that:

We repeatedly debated with the Imam over the issue of the deputy leadership. In one session, the heads of the three branches [of government], Ayatollah Ardebili, myself, the prime minister, Mr Ahmad Khomeini and Khamene'i were present. A discussion ensued and we said to the Imam, if the need arose for a successor to you we would have difficulties, because with the present constitution we could have a leadership vacuum. He said that this would not be the case since we had the right people. When we asked who, he pointed to Mr Khamene'i.[16]

According to Rafsanjani this had happened some months before Khomeini's death, at the time when some of Montazeri's supporters were still on trial. Even then the feeling was that Montazeri would not be the future leader:

It was then that he had decided to solve the issue of the leadership and that is when we were debating the matter. Following that session Mr Khamene'i asked us, in fact insisted, that we did not talk about this issue outside. We did not repeat it anywhere.[17]

In his first Friday prayer sermon after Khomeini's death, Rafsanjani recounted his conversation with Khomeini after Montazeri's dismissal: 'I went to him. He told me clearly that we would not have any problems because we had such an individual amongst us and we should realise it.' Rafsanjani also quoted Ahmad Khomeini as saying: 'While Khamene'i was in North Korea, the Imam, saw him on television – his approach, his speeches and his discussions. It was very interesting for the Imam, who said that he [Khamene'i] was truly worthy of the leadership.' He continued:

The Assembly of Experts, with its deep realisation of its historic responsibility ... in the light of the situation at home and abroad, convened an emergency session on 4 June and with a majority of more than four-fifths of the members present and with sixty votes out of the seventy members present in favour, selected Ayatollah Seyyed Ali Khamene'i as the leader of the Islamic Republic of Iran.[18]

And that is how Ali Khamene'i, at the age of fifty, was chosen to be the leader of Iran. He was thirty-six years younger than Khomeini and a different personality. The Council of Experts elevated him there and then from hojjat al-Islam to ayatollah. A member of the council put it this way: 'Grand ayatollah is for the 'source of emulation', ayatollah is for a very learned jurisprudent and theologian and hojjat al-Islam for the "nearly very learned."'[19]

At dawn on Monday 5 June, Khomeini's body was transferred from his residence in Jamaran to a vast wasteland in the hills of north Tehran, an area known as Mosalla which is designated as a place of prayer. The body lay on top of a temporary podium made out of containers. Khomeini, in an air-conditioned glass case, was covered in a white shroud, his feet facing Mecca. His black turban was on his chest, indicating his religious status and his lineage from the Prophet Mohammad. Within hours there were thousands upon thousands of mourners trying to get a final glimpse of the man they adored. It was a mighty ocean of black-clad mourners, women, men, young and old. The authorities who had planned the occasion must have been as astonished as outsiders at the sheer volume of people. The arrangements made were so inadequate for the size of the crowd that at least eight people lost their lives and several hundred were reported injured in their eagerness to see the Imam's body. Words were inadequate to describe the event. 'Sheer frenzy', 'orgy of emotion', 'emotional orgasm' and a host of other phrases were used, but none could really describe the occasion.

It was a peculiarly Shi'i Iranian state of mind which happens to generate the best kind of Iranian art: *ta'zieh* or mourning. Go to any village or remote tribal area and you will find people replaying the martyrdom of Hossein. In the national psyche of the Shi'a, crying to relieve one's pain and frustration is very common and acceptable. Even the birthday ceremonies of various saints and Imams, which should be joyous occasions, end in tears because the speakers often finish their sermons by mentioning the plain of Karbala where Hossein was martyred. For many of the mourners Khomeini was a living Imam, seen on their television sets every day. He was the embodiment of their religious belief. Without doubt many of them were very critical of the regime and its shortcomings, but once he was dead all could be forgiven.

The heat of the summer in that northern wasteland was so overpowering that the Tehran fire brigade was employed to spray water over the excited crowd to stop them from fainting. Revolutionary Guards stood above the people between them and the coffin. Men pressed together at the front beat their heads and chests and worked themselves into a frenzy of grief. Many collapsed and were passed on stretchers over the heads of the crowd. Behind the men, women's wailing filled the air. Leading politicians came one by one to pay their last respects to the founder of the republic as the mourners continued to chant slogans about him. Rafsanjani, who flew in by helicopter, could not get close to the platform. Khomeini himself had not specified where he should be buried and it had been decided not to take his body to Qom, but to bury it, after a procession through the streets of Tehran, in the graveyard of the martyrs of the revolution and the war known as Behesht-e Zahra.

On Tuesday, early in the morning of 6 June, the leading Shi'i source of emulation in Iran, Grand Ayatollah Golpayegani, led the prayer over Khomeini's body. The organisers expected him to do so while the body lay in glass enclosure high on the platform, but he refused, arguing that it was too high; so the enclosure was brought down. Golpayegani argued that the body must be brought out of it. The officials grudgingly complied. The body, now wrapped in the shroud and inside an open coffin, was set in front of the congregation led by the old Ayatollah. It was the most solemn moment of the whole occasion. Everything in this twenty minutes was at a standstill.

The size of the crowd was even greater than on the previous day. Elderly clerics and foreign guests feared for their lives as the number of mourners increased. The idea was to move in an orderly fashion through Tehran's streets to reach the graveyard. As one official had put it the day before: 'The arrangements have been planned so that, while maintaining the traditional funeral, it will be possible to allow the presence of people, foreign guests and officials.' But the procession could not move more than a few miles and the organising committee had to admit its failure to manage the crowd. No matter how hard the Revolutionary Guards tried, it was impossible to move. Firing into the air and using water-cannons did not help.

Khomeini's hearse was almost lost in the enormous crush which seemed beyond control. Tehran television stopped transmitting live coverage of the events. Swamped by the people, the Revolutionary Guards just managed to rescue the guests. It was then officially announced that the funeral had been postponed. But this move did not help either, and people continued to flood towards Behesht-e Zahra in the hope of seeing the body.

From the north of Tehran to Behesht-e Zahra nothing could be seen but a black sea of mourners dotted only by the white turbans of some mollahs. There were several million in this completely spontaneous and unorchestrated outpouring of grief. The body was taken by helicopter to the graveyard. There the crowd took control of it as soon as the helicopter landed. Its white shroud was torn to pieces and taken by the mourners as holy relics. The Ayatollah's frail white leg was uncovered. Shots were fired into the air to push the crowd back, and the frenzy reached its peak when the Revolutionary Guards were unable to retrieve the body.

Eventually the body was recovered and placed in an ambulance to take it back to the helicopter, but even as the helicopter tried to leave the mourners clung on, preventing it from taking off. Finally the body was taken to north Tehran to go through the shrouding ritual once again. To reduce the numbers of the crowd it was announced that the funeral would not take place that day. To no avail.

When Khomeini's body was brought back from north Tehran, this time inside a sealed metal container, the Revolutionary Guards took more precautions. Increased numbers and fast action helped the situation. Even though the crowd once again broke the security cordons and reached the container, the Guards finally managed to take the body out of the container and put it in the grave, a simple horizontal hole which accommodated the body so that it faced Mecca.

In the cemetery some of the mourners climbed from the top of the walls onto trees and the roofs of double decker buses. The roof of one bus collapsed, injuring those inside. Khomeini had recommended that mourners be patient in face of death: 'Scratching one's face and body on the death of anyone and causing harm to oneself are not acceptable ... Baring the chest is not acceptable except on the death of one's father or brother. It is an obligatory caution not to raise the voice too loudly while crying for the dead.'[20] It is ironic to compare this with what happened in Tehran during his own funeral and the first seven days of mourning. The Iranian media reported over 10,000 people suffering from self-inflicted injuries, exhaustion, heat, loss of consciousness and the crush. Dozens of people lost their lives. It was an extraordinary event. But, after all, Khomeini, viewed from whatever perspective, was not an ordinary man.

Notes

Chapter One

1. Morteza Pasandideh, 'Khaterat-e Ayatollah Pasandideh'. *Pasdar-e Islam*, no. 84, p. 27, 1988, Qom.
2. Ahmad Khomeini in an interview with Hamed Algar, 12 September 1982. In this interview Ahmed Khomeini speaks about his father and family based on his recollection of family stories. Professor Algar has kindly provided me with a copy of the tape. Ahmad has also spoken about his father in a number of speeches and interviews see *Majmu'eh-ye Asar-e Yadegar-e Imam*, 2 vols, Tehran, 1996.
3. Chief among them is Fereidun Adamiyyat.
4. Pasandideh in *Pasdar-e Islam*, no. 84, p. 28.
5. Ibid.
6. Ibid. no. 85, p. 26.
7. Ahmad Khomeini, interview with Hamed Algar.
8. Pasandideh, *Khaterat* pp. 18–21. The style of Pasandideh's memoir is somewhat telegraphic and a direct translation would not mean much to the non-Iranian reader. My paraphrase leaves out some detail but adds brief explanations of a few personalities and customs. It is occasionally supplemented by in-

formation from a report of the episode that appeared in the newspaper *Adab* on 15 May 1905, the only contemporary account of the episode.

9. *Adab*, 15 May 1905.

10. Ibid.

11. Ahmad Khomeini, interview with Hamed Algar.

12. Hassan Roshdiyeh, *Sawaneh-e Omr*, p. 17.

13. Nader Naderpur, a contemporary Iranian poet who met Khomeini in Qom in the early 1960s has said: 'For four hours we recited poetry. Every single line I recited from any poet, he recited the next.' Personal communication.

14. Pasandideh in *Pasdar-e Islam*, no. 86, p. 27.

15. Ibid.

16. Vanessa Martin, *Islam and Modernism, The Iranian Revolution of* 1906, London, 1989, p. 97.

17. The account of Sheikh Fazlollah in this and the following paragraphs is taken from, Ibid., pp. 165–200.

18. Ibid., p. 187.

Chapter Two

1. For an account of Ha'eri's life see Abdolhadi Ha'eri, *Tashayyu' va Mashrutiyat dar Iran*, Tehran, 1364/1985 pp. 188–9.

2. Haj Mohammad Taqi Bushehri, *Cheshmandaz*, vol. 4, p. 26.

3. Aqa Najafi Quchani, *Siyahat-e Sharq*, Tehran, 1362/1984, pp. 366–7.

4. Biography of Ha'eri in *Nur-e Elm*, no. 11, August 1985.

5. Ibid.

6. H. Soltanzadeh, *Tarikh-e Madares-e Iran*, Tehran, 1985. This is a comprehensive survey of schools of Islamic learning.

7. Algar, 'Imam Khomeini: the Pre-Revolutionary Years', in Edmund Burke, III, and Ira M. Lapidus, *Islam, Politics and Social Movements*, p. 285.

8. Morteza chose the surname Pasandideh for himself.

9. See Abdolhadi Ha'eri, *Tashayyu' va Mashrutiyat dar Iran*, for an account of Najaf clergy's role in this period and Ha'eri's life.

10. Sadeqi Tehrani in an interview, *Yad*, vol. 1, no. 4, (August 1356/1977), p. 47.

11. Amin Banani, *The Modernization of Iran: 1921–1941*, Stanford 1961, pp. 28–43. This book provides a lucid account of Reza Shah's rise to power.

12. Ruhollah Khomeini, *Sahifeh-ye Nur*, Tehran 1361/1982, vol. 15, p. 143. (Hereafter *Sahifeh-ye Nur*).

13. Ha'eri, *Tashayyu' va Mashrutiyat*, p. 198.

14. Shahrough Akhavi, *Religion and Politics in Contemporary Iran*, New York,

1980, p. 29.

15.   Ha'eri, *Tashayyu' va Mashrutiyat*, p 189. See also Muhammad Hassan Faghfoory, 'The Role of the Ulama in Twentieth Century Iran with Particular Reference to Ayatollah Haj Sayyid Abul-Qasim Kashani', Ph.D. dissertation, University of Wisconsin, 1978, p. 67.

16.   Ibid., p. 68.

17.   Hassan Morsalvand, *Zendeginameh-ye Rejal va Mashahir-e Iran*, Tehran, 1990, vol. 2, pp.17–18.

18.   Najafi Quchani, *Siyahat-e Sharq*, pp. 399–401.

19.   According to his wife Khomeini was a virgin when he married. *Resalat*, 1 February 1994.

20.   Hamid Ruhani Ziyarati, *Barresi va Tahlil az Nehzat-e Emam Khomeini*, Tehran 1360/1981, vol. 6, p. 30.

21.   Ruhollah Khomeini, *Sabu-ye Eshq*, Tehran, 1368/1989. p. 15.

22.   Qor'an: 9:122.

23.   In 1972 a critical book published by a cleric reported that there were 8,000 students receiving money in theological centres of whom only 2,000 were genuine students. Mir-Mohammad Sadeqi *Hayahu*, Isfahan 1351, p. 206.

24.   Haj Mohammad Taqi Bushehri, *Cheshmandaz*, vol. 4. Khomeini obtained permission to relate *hadith* from four leading teachers: 1. Mohsen Amin 'Ameli (1952), a leading clergy from Lebanon. Imam Musa Sadr succeeded Amin in becoming the leader of Lebanese Shi'i. 2. Sheikh Abbas Qomi (1959), a leading narrator of *hadith* and Shi'i historian. Qomi is a best-selling author in modern Iran, especially his book of common prayer known as *Mafatih al-Jenan* (Keys to Paradise). A copy of this book was given to each volunteer during the Iran–Iraq war, a practice misinterpreted by the opponents of Khomeini and fed to the gullible Western press as a gift of the 'plastic key to heaven'. 3. Abolqassem Dehkordi Isfahani (1934), a leading mollah in Isfahan. 4. Mohammad Reza Najafi Masjed Shahi (1943) who settled in Qom in 1925 in protest against Reza Shah.

25.   Ruhani Ziyarati, *Barresi va Tahlil az Nehzat-e Emam Khomeini*, p. 31 as quoted by Ja'far Sobhani, *Kayhan-e Farhangi*, June, 1989, p. 2. See also Sobhani in *Howzeh*, no. 32, Qom, July 1989.

26.   Interview with Qods-e Iran Saqafi, Khomeini's wife, by her daughter Dr Zahra Mostafavi, published in *Resalat*, 1 February 1994, on the 15th anniversary of Khomeini's return to Iran.

27.   *Resalat*, 11 July 1989.

28.   *Resalat*, 1 February 1994.

Chapter Three

1. In the last months of his life Khomeini openly criticised the traditional clergy for regarding the learning of philosophy and mysticism as a heresy. See chapter 14 and *Sahifeh-ye Nur*, vol. 18, pp. 79–80. A decade or so earlier Aqa Najafi wrote a vivid account of how studying *erfan* or Rumi's *Mathnavi* was seen as a sin by many mollahs. His account of the opposition to studying philosophy and mysticism late last century is an accurate reflection of the situation in most theological circles. See Najafi Quchani, *Siyahat-e Sharq*, p. 72.

2. Ahmad Khomeini in Reza Sha'rbaf (ed.), *Sargozashtha-ye Vizheh az Zendegi Hazrat-e Emam Khomeini beh Ravayat-e Jam'i az Fozala*, (Tehran, 1364/1985) vol. 1, p. 127. This is a five volume collection of interviews, quotations and writings by Khomeini's students, family members and friends. The first four volumes are edited by Mostafa Vejdani and volume five by Reza Sha'rbaf. Ahmad Khomeini quotes a verbatim interview with his father on Khomeini's first books and his interest in mysticism.

3. *Nur-e Elm*, no. 9, April 1985, p. 125.

4. Ibid.

6. Mirza Mohammad Tonekabani, *Qesas al-'Olama*, Tehran nd, pp. 334–5.

7. Ibid.

8. Ibid., p. 82; Shafi'i Kadkani, in the notes to his Persian translation of *The Idea of Personality in Sufism* by R. A. Nicholson, has a summary of views on the logos and perfect man. *Tasavvof-e Eslami va Rabeteh-ye Ensan va Khoda*. pp. 223–37, Tehran, 1979.

9. Ruhollah Khomeini, *Sharh-e Do'a al-Sahar*, ed. Ahmad Fehri, Beirut, 1982, p. 68.

10. Morteza Motahhari, *Ashna'i ba 'Olum*, Qom, 1358/1979.

11. Ruhollah Khomeini, *Mesbah al-Hedaya*, pp. 205–7.

12. Khomeini in *Yadnameh-ye Ostad-e Shahid Morteza Motahhari*, vol. 1, Tehran, pp. 30–100.

13. Ruhollah Khomeini, *Me'raj al-Salekin*, pp. 98–9.

14. Ruhollah Khomeini, *Tafsir-e Sureh-ye Hamd*, Tehran, nd, p. 89.

15. Ahmad Khomeini in *Sargozashtha-ye Vizheh*, vol. 1, pp. 1–4.

16. A. Fehri in his introduction to Khomeini, *Do'a al-Sahar*, p. 7.

Chapter Four

1. Ja'far Sobhani, *Kayhan-e Farhangi*, June 1989.

2. Khomeini, *Kashf al-Asrar*, n.d., p. 9.

3. Ruhani, *Nehzat*, vol. 1, p. 39.

4. Jalal al-Din Madani, *Tarikh-e Siyasi-ye Mo'aser-e Iran*, Qom 1361/1982, vol.1, p. 120; Banani, *The Modernization of Iran*, p. 46.

5. Azari Qomi in an interview published in *Yad* Quarterly, vol. 1, no. 4, 1356/1977, p. 30.

6. Khomeini, *Sahifeh-ye Nur*, vol. 8, p. 31.

7. Ayatollah Mohammad Saduqi in *Sargozashtha-ye Vizheh*, vol. 3, p. 134.

8. *Yad* Quarterly, vol. 4, 1986, interview with Mohammad Sadeqi Tehrani.

9. Mohammad Taqi Haj Bushehri, 'Az Kashf al-Asrar ta Asrar-e Hezar-saleh', in *Cheshmandaz*, Summer 1368/1989, no. 6, p. 9.

10. E. Abrahamian, 'Kasravi, the Integrative Nationalist of Iran', in Eli Kedourie and S. Haim (eds), *Towards a Modern Iran*, London, 1980, pp. 96–131.

11. Faghfoory, 'The Role of the Ulama', pp. 171–8.

12. Algar, 'Imam Khomeini', p. 129. Algar quotes from a newspaper interview with the widow of Navvab Safavi published in *Sorush*, 26 Dey 1360/16 January 1982. Algar goes on to point out that there is a similarity between Khomeini's remarks on monarchy in *Kashf al-Asrar* and the section on monarchy in the programme of the Fada'iyan, *Rahnama-ye Haqa'eq*. See note 97, p. 288.

13. *Sahifeh-ye Nur*, vol. 1, p. 3.

14. The first edition of *Kashf al-Asrar* had no date, no publisher and no reference to the author. In the post revolutionary reprint the name of the author i.e Ayatollah Khomeini has been added with no date or publisher.

15. *Kashf al-Asrar*, p. 9.

16. Ibid., p. 9.

17. Ibid., p. 10.

18. Ibid.

19. Ibid., p. 6.

20. Ibid., p. 100.

21. Ibid., p. 17.

22. Ibid.

23. Ibid.

24. Ibid., pp. 94–5.

25. Ibid., p. 105.

26. Ibid., p. 291.

27. Ibid., pp. 185 and 233.

28. Ibid., p. 105.

29. Ibid., p. 105.

30. Faghfoory, 'The Role of the Ulama', p. 97.

31. Ruhani, *Nehzat*, vol. 1, p. 96.

32. *Sahifeh-ye Nur*, vol. 3, p. 36.

33. Mohmammad Sharif Razi, *Athar al-Hojjat*, Qom 1332/1953, vol. 2, pp. 11–13.

34. Michael Cook, *Mohammad*, Oxford, 1986, p. 51.

35. A. K. S. Lambton, *The Persian Land Reform*, Oxford, 1969.

Chapter Five

1. Ruhani, *Nehzat*, vol. 1, pp. 98–109.

2. Ibid., pp. 142–50.

3. Ibid., p. 195.

4. Hassan Shari'atmadari, in an interview from Germany, November 1989. Story of the Iranian Revolution, Programme 12. BBC Persian Service, 1992.

5. Ruhani, *Nehzat*, vol. 1, p. 151.

6. *Maktab-e Islam*, Qom, 1962.

7. Ruhani, *Nehzat*, vol. 1, pp. 165–6.

8. Ibid., p. 183.

9. Ibid.

10. Ibid.

11. Asgar Owladi, *Resalat*, 'Heyatha-ye Mo'talefeh'.

12. Asadollah Badamchian, *Negahi Gozara beh Jami'at-e Mo'talefeh-ye Islami*, Tehran 1375/1996.

13. The first group included: 1. Sadeq Amani who was implicated in the assassination of Mansur and executed. 2. Mohammad Sadeq Eslami who played a major role in supporting Khomeini throughout his years of exile. He was killed in 1981 in the Islamic Republican Party headquarters explosion in Tehran. 3. Asadollah Lajevardi who was imprisoned by the Shah and played a major role in the revolution. He became Tehran's Revolutionary Prosecutor and later Evin prisons notorious supervisor. He sent hundreds of Khomeini's opponents to the firing squads. Others included Ahmad Ghadirian, Abbas Modarresifar, Hossein Rahmani, Abdollah Mahdian. The second group included Asgar Owladi, Habibollah (Mehdi) Shafiq, Abolfazl Tavakkoli, Mehdi Eraqi, Mostafa Ha'eri, Mehdi Ahmad, Mahmud Mohtashami and Hashem Amani; and the third, Mahmud Mir Fendereski, Alaeddin Mir Mohammad Sadeqi, Mehdi Bahadoran, Ezzatollah Khalili, Mohammad Matin and Asadollah Badamchian.

14. Khomeini to Asgar Owladi quoted in 'Heyatha-ye Mo'talefeh'.

15. Ibid.

16. Ibid.

17. Ibid.

18. Khomeini, *Sahifeh-ye Nur*, vol. 1, p. 16.

19. Ibid., p. 17.
20. F. Mahallati in *Sargozashtha-ye Vizheh*, vol. 4, p. 87.
21. Ruhani, *Nehzat*, vol. 1, p. 224.
22. Ibid., p. 225.
23. Ali Davani, *Nehzat-e Ruhaniyat-e Iran*, Tehran, 1358/1979, vol. 3, p. 220.
24. Ruhani, *Nehzat*, vol. 1, p. 265.
25. I personally witnessed this in the village of Darrud, north east of Neishabur, where primary pupils were taken to vote.
26. Ruhani, *Nehzat*, vol. 1, p. 262.
27. Ibid.
28. Ibid.
29. Ibid., p. 309.

Chapter Six

1. Author's interview with Golpayegani's aides. Also see Ruhani, *Nehzat*, vol. 1, p. 364; Davani, *Nehzat*, vol. 3, p. 263–5.
2. *Sargozashtha-ye Vizheh*, vol. 2, p. 34.
3. Ruhani, *Nehzat*, vol. 1, p. 377.
4. Ibid.
5. Ibid., p. 393.
6. Ibid., p. 399.
7. Ibid., p. 403.
8. Rafsanjani in *Yadnameh-ye Shahid Motahhari*, vol. 2, p. 10.
9. Ibid., p. 12.
10. Ibid.
11. Khomeini, *Sahifeh-ye Nur*, vol. 1, pp. 46–8.
12. Ruhani, *Nehzat*, vol. 1, p. 425.
13. A. Dehnovi, *Qiyam-e Khunin-e Panzdah-e Khordad-e 42 beh Ravayat-e Asnad*, Tehran, 1360/1981.
14. Ruhani, *Nehzat*, vol. 1, p. 451.
15. Author's interview with General Mobasser (19 May 1988).
16. Dehnovi, *Qiyam-e Khunin*, p. 186.
17. Dehnovi has reprinted in his book police and military governors' reports concerning these events. The figures given here are the most reliable available.

Chapter Seven

1. Ruhani, *Nehzat*, vol. 1, p. 470.
2. Ibid.
3. Ibid., vol. 1, p. 472.
4. Author's interview with General Mobasser, London 19 May 1988.
5. Ibid.
6. Dehnovi, *Qiyam-e Khunin*, p. 79. This is the most detailed account from the police archives on the events of 15 Khordad. There is also a new account by Gh. Nejati, *Tarikh-e Siasi*, which, based on reports by Western journalists, gives much higher figures for the dead and the injured. The police reports reproduced by Dehnovi give lower figures than all sources. Popular stories believed by the religious sources have even put the figure up to 15, 000.
7. Ibid., p. 97.
8. Ibid., p. 112. Dehnovi reproduces a copy of the order signed by Nassiri as Military Governor of Greater Tehran on 15 Khordad 1342 at 8.00 pm.
9. Ibid., pp. 77–8.
10. Ibid., p. 138.
11. Ibid., p. 24. Also Iraj Pezeshkzad, *Moruri Bar Vaqe'h-ye Panzdah-e Khordad-e Chehel-o-Dow*, p. 63, Paris 1986.
12. Ruhani, *Nehzat*, vol. 1, pp. 562–77.
13. *Sahifeh-ye Nur*, vol. 1, pp. 109–11.
14. Ruhani, *Nehzat*, vol. 1, p. 662.
15. *Sahifeh-ye Nur*, vol. 1, pp. 109–11. This is an abridged version reprinted from Hamed Algar's translation. See Algar, *Islam and Revolution*, pp. 181–8.

Chapter Eight

1. Dr Mahmud Borujerdi in *Sargozashtha–ye Vizheh*, vol. 3, p. 30.
2. Ruhani, *Nehzat*, vol. 2, p. 3.
3. Ibid., vol.1, p. 742.
4. Ibid., vol. 2, pp. 722–3.
5. Ibid., p. 723.
6. Ibid., p. 5.
7. Ruhani, *Nehzat*, vol. 2, p. 728.
8. The Cetiner family's recollections of Khomeini's stay with them are taken from a memoir by Ali Bey Cetiner published in *Melliyat*, 16–22 August 1987.
9. Ruhani, *Nehzat*, vol. 2, p. 57.
10. Ibid., Introduction, photos.

11. Cetiner, Ali Bey, *Melliyat*, 16–22 August 1987.

12. Ruhollah Khomeini, *Tahrir al–Wasilah*, Beirut, 1987, vols 1&2.

13. Savak report reproduced in Ruhani, *Nehzat*, vol. 2, p. 750.

14. Ibid., p. 751.

15. Ibid., p. 117.

16. Do'a'i in *Sargozashtha–ye Vizheh*, vol. 1, p. 75. Seyyed Mahmud Do'a'i was one of Khomeini's students who was active in the sixties against the Shah. In 1967 he fled to Iraq to join Khomeini and was in charge of anti-Shah broadcasts from Baghdad. Do'a'i became Iran's first envoy to Iraq after the revolution and later a member of parliament. He remained close to Khomeini and is now editor in chief of Ettela'at publications.

17. Ibid., p. 118.

18. Ruhani, quoting Savak files: *Nehzat*, vol. 2, pp. 120–1.

19. Ibid.

20. Ibid., p. 122.

21. Ibid., p. 151.

22. Ibid., pp. 151–2.

23. Marion Farouk Sluglett and Peter Sluglett, *Iraq Since 1958: From Revolution to Dictatorship*, London, 1987, p. 192.

24. Ofra Bengio, 'Shiite Politics in Ba'thi Iraq', *Middle Eastern Studies*, January, 1985.

25. Ruhani, *Nehzat*, vol. 2, p. 406.

26. Khomeini, *Sahifeh-ye Nur*, vol. 1, p. 160.

27. Ruhani, *Nehzat*, vol. 2, pp. 428–9.

28. Ibid., p. 442.

29. Ibid., p. 120.

30. Ibid., p. 492.

31. Ibid., p. 125.

32. Ibid., p.156.

33. Khomeini, *Sahifeh-ye Nur*, vol. 1, p. 99.

34. Ibid., p. 129.

35. Ibid.

36. Ibid., pp. 126–7.

37. Ruhani, *Nehzat*, vol. 2, pp. 143–4.

38. Ibid., p. 553.

39. Ibid.

40. Hamid Enayat in *Islam in the Political Process*, pp.160–80, edited by J. Piscatori, Cambridge, 1983.

41. Ruhollah Khomeini, *Islam and Revolution: Writings and Declarations*, tr. by Hamid Algar, London, 1981, p. 25.

42. Ibid., p. 41.

43. Ibid., p. 55.
44. Ibid., pp. 55–6.
45. Ibid., p. 143.
46. Ibid., p. 145.
47. Ibid., p. 146.
48. Khomeini, *Islam and Revolution*, p. 420.
49. Khomeini, *Jehad-e Akbar*, p. 46.
50. Hamid Dabbashi, *The Theology of Discontent*, New York, 1993, p. 438.
51. A. Baqi, *Dar Shenakht-e Hezb-e Qa'edin-e Zaman*, Qom, 1363/1984, pp. 297–8.

Chapter Nine

1. Abrahamian, *Iran Between Two Revolutions*, Princeton, NJ, 1982, p. 325. Abrahamian notes that over 3,000 party members were arrested in this period, forty were executed and another fourteen tortured to death.
2. Houchang Chehabi, *Iranian Politics and Religious Modernism: The Liberation Movement of Iran under the Shah and Khomeini*, London, 1990. pp. 175–6 and p. 186.
3. See Chapter 5.
4. Madani, *Tarikh-e Siasi-ye Mo'aser-e Iran*, vol. 2. p. 106; Ruhani, *Nehzat*, vol. 1, p. 810.
5. Asadollah Badamchian, *Shohada-ye 26 Khordad: Jami'at-e Mo'talefeh-ye Islam*, Tehran 1375/1996, p. 17.
6. *Yadnameh Shahid Motahhari*, vol. 2, pp. 8–14.
7. Bahram Afrasiyabi and Sa'id Dehqan, *Taleqani va Tarikh*, Tehran, 1359/1981. p. 481.
8. Ervand Abrahamian, *Radical Islam, The Iranian Mojahedin*, London, 1989, p. 128.
9. Chehabi, *Iranian Politics and Religious Modernism*, p. 123.
10. For a detailed account of the Freedom Movement's ideology in this period see ibid. pp. 64–6 and 156–60.
11. Quoted from ibid. p. 158.
12. Allameh Seyyed Mohammad Hossein Tabataba'i, *Osul-e Falsafeh va Ravesh-e Realism*, with an introduction and annotations by Morteza Motahhari, 5 vols, Qom 1332–64/1953–85.
13. This account of the Monthly Talks Society is based on Chehabi, *Iranian Politics and Religious Modernism*, pp. 170–2.
14. Ali Rahnema, 'Ali Shari'ati' in A. Rahnema (ed.) *Pioneers of Islamic Revival*, London, 1994, pp. 208–10.

15. Ibid., pp. 214–15.

16. See Chehabi, *Iranian Politics and Religious Modernism*, p. 205 and Ali Rahnema, *An Islamic Utopian: A Political Biography of Ali Shari'ati*, London, 1998, pp. 254–9 for an account of the conflict between Motahhari and Shari'ati.

17. See Rahnema, 'Ali Shari'ati', pp. 227–38 for a concise account of Shari'ati's thought.

18. Ibid.

19. Shari'ati translated two works by Louis Massignon on al-Hallaj, the mystic, and Salman Farsi, the Persian companion of the Prophet whom Shi'is revere for his devotion to the family of the Prophet.

20. Rahnema, 'Ali Shari'ati', p. 237.

21. Rahnema, *An Islamic Utopian*, p. 265.

22. Ibid.

23. Mohammad Reza Pahlavi, *Pasokh beh Tarikh*, Paris, 1366/1987, p 229.

24. *Sahifeh-ye Nur*, vol. 1, p. 211.

25. Ibid.

26. Ibid., p. 215.

27. Ibid., p. 223.

28. Ibid., p. 143.

29. Mojahedin-e Khalq-e Iran, 15 *Khordad, Noqteh-ye Atf-e Mobarezat*, n.p., n.d., p. 17.

30. Abrahamian, *Radical Islam*, pp. 149–51 provides a detailed account of this interview based on 'Interviews with Comrades Hossein Ruhani and Torab Haqshenas' *Paykar* 70–84, 1 September–23 November 1980 and on an interview Abrahamian conducted in Paris with Mas'ud Rajavi.

31. *Sahifeh-ye Nur*, vol. 6, p. 179; Madani, *Tarikh-e Siasi-ye Mo'aser-e Iran*, vol. 2, p. 221.

32. Abrahamian, *Radical Islam*, p. 150.

33. *Sahifeh-ye Nur*, vol. 6, p. 179; Madani, *Tarikh-e Siasi-ye Mo'aser-e Iran*, vol. 2, p. 221.

34. Chehabi, *Iranian Politics and Religious Modernism*, p. 171

35. Rahnema, *An Islamic Utopian*, p. 275. Rahnema quotes an article by Do'a'i published in *Howzeh*, no. 45, Mordad &Shahrivar 1370 and Jalaleddin Farsi's *Zavaya-ye Tarikh*, Tehran, 1373.

36. Hossein Akhavan-e Towhidi, *Dar Pas-e Pardeh-ye Tazvir*, Paris, 1364/1986, p. 158.

37. *Sahifeh-ye Nur*, vol. 1, p. 227.

38. Akhavan-e Towhidi, *Dar Pas-e Pardeh-ye Tazvir*, pp. 158–9.

39. Ruhani, *Nehzat*, vol. 3, pp. 267–70.

40. *Sahifeh-ye Nur*, vol. 1, p. 229.

41. Akhavan-e Towhidi, *Dar Pas-e Pardeh-ye Tazvir*. See also Badamchian, *Negahi*

Gozara beh Jami'at-e Mo'talefeh.

42. *Ta'limat-e Dini, Sal-e Sevvom-e Dabirestan*, Ministry of Education, Tehran 1977.

43. M. Razavi, *Hashemi va Enqelab*, Tehran 1998, p. 192.

44. *Sahifeh-ye Nur*, vol. 1, p. 142.

45. Razavi, *Hashemi va Enqelab*, p. 192.

46. *Sahifeh-ye Nur*, vol. 1, p. 216.

47. Badamchian, *Negahi Gozara beh Jami'at-e Mo'talefeh*, pp. 4–6.

48. Razavi, *Hashemi va Enqlelab*, p. 135.

49. Ibid., p 192.

50. *Sahifeh-ye Nur*, vol. 1, p. 221.

51. Ali Khamene'i, *Khaterat va Hekayatha*, Tehran, 1995, p. 67.

Chapter Ten

1. Author's interview with Cyrus Vance.

2. Author's interviews with Bakhtiar, Foruhar, Sanjabi and Bazargan.

3. *Sahifeh-ye Nur*, vol. 1, p. 243.

4. Akhavan-e Towhidi, *Dar Pas-e Pardeh-ye Tazvir*, p. 52.

5. *Sahifeh-ye Nur*, vol. 1, p. 249.

6. John D. Stempel, *Inside the Iranian Revolution*, Bloomington, 1981. pp. 89–90.

7. Madani, *Tarikh-e Siasi-ye Mo'aser-e Iran*, vol. 2, p. 246.

8. *Sahifeh-ye Nur*, vol. 2, p. 46.

9. Ibid., p. 98.

10. Ibid., p. 114.

11. Ibid., vol. 4, p. 216.

12. Akhavan-e Towhidi, *Dar Pas-e Pardeh-ye Tazvir*, p. 200.

13. Madani, *Tarikh-e Siasi-ye Mo'aser-e Iran*, vol. 2, p. 281.

14. Stephen Jessell.

15. Related by Ziba Hindi who personally witnessed the event.

16. Dabbagh in *Sargozashtha-ye Vizheh*, vol. 4, p. 34.

17. *Sahifeh-ye Nur*, vol. 5, p. 168.

18. Akhavan-e Towhidi, *Dar Pas-e Pardeh-ye Tazvir*, p. 212.

19. *Sahifeh-ye Nur*, vol. 2, p. 259.

20. Ebrahim Yazdi, *Akharin Talash-ha dar Akharin Ruzha*, Tehran 1363/1984, p. 119.

21. *Sahifeh-ye Nur*, vol. 4, p. 60.

22. *Sahifeh-ye Nur*, vol. 4, p. 207.

23. Yazdi, *Akharin Talash-ha*, p. 117.

Chapter Eleven

1. 'The Story of the Revolution: Iran 1906–1979', a 36-part radio documentary produced by B. Moin and B. Afagh, BBC Persian Section; Bani Sadr in an interview with the author.

2. *Sahifeh-ye Nur*, vol. 4, p. 280.

3. Ibid., p. 284.

4. *Sargozashtha-ye Vizheh*, vol. 3, p. 100.

5. Bazargan, *Dow Sal-e Akhar*, pp. 293–4

6. *Sahifeh-ye Nur*, vol. 5, p. 31. For the full text of Khomeini's letter to Bazargan on the formation of the Provisional Government see Ibid, vol. 5, p. 27.

7. BBC Persian Section, 'The Story of the Revolution', programme 36.

8. *Sahifeh-ye Nur*, vol. 5, p. 71.

9. Khalkhali, BBC Interview, Qom, May 1997.

10. *Sahifeh-ye Nur*, vol. 5, p. 236.

11. *Negahi Gozara beh Jami'at-e Mo'talefeh*. The Coalition claims that it was able to mobilise 60,000 people for this purpose.

12. Razavi, *Hashemi va Enqelab*, pp. 190–3.

13. Bani Sadr, *Khianat be Omid*, p. 402, cites evidence that they operated with Khomeini's approval.

14. *The Guardian*, quoted in Homa Omid, *Islam and the Post-Revolutionary State in Iran*, New York, 1994, p. 72.

15. This account mostly comes from *Hashemi va Enqelab*, p. 174.

16. Figures from Kenneth Katzman, *The Warriors of Islam: Iran's Revolutionary Guards*, Oxford, 1993, p. 81.

17. *Sahifeh-ye Nur*, vol. 5, p.119.

18. Ibid, vol. 7, p. 104.

19. Ibid., vol. 5, p. 125.

20. Abdol Ali Bazargan (ed.), *Masa'el va Moshkelat-e Nakhostin Sal-e Enqelab*, Tehran, 1983, p. 227.

21. Bazargan's statement issued on 7 May 1979 in Abdol Ali Bazargan (ed.), *Masa'el va Moshkelat-e Nakhostin Sal-e Enqelab*, Tehran 1983, p. 36.

22. Schirazi, *The Constitution of Iran*, pp. 22–3. Schirazi quotes Nehzat-e Azadi, *Barkhord ba Nehzat va Pasokh-ha-ye Ma*, Tehran, 1983.

23. Schirazi, *The Constitution of Iran*, p. 23. Schirazi quotes Khomeini's speech to the Jame'eh-ye Rowhaniyat-e Tehran delivered on 17/6/79.

24. For a carefully documented account of the manouevres, public and private

over the constitution and the constituent assembly see Schirazi, *The Constitution of Iran*, pp. 27–33. Schirazi pinpoints the origin of the proposal for an 'Assembly of Experts' to a meeting of the Revolutionary Council, held in Khomeini's house in Qom on 22 May which excluded non-clerical members.

25. Ibid. pp. 29–30.
26. Quoted in ibid. p. 30.
27. Ibid.
28. Ibid., p. 32.
29. *Sahifeh-ye Nur*, vol. 8, p. 245.
30. Quoted in Ali Rahnema and Farhad Nomani, *The Secular Miracle: Religion, Politics and Economic Policy in Iran*, London, 1990, p. 5.
31. *Sahifeh-ye Nur*, vol. 8, p. 256.
32. *Sargozashtha-ye Vizheh*, vol. 4, pp. 105–6.
33. *Sahifeh-ye Nur*, vol. 10, p. 147.
34. Bazargan, *Enqelab-e Iran dar Dow Harekat*.
35. *Sahifeh-ye Nur*, vol. 12, p. 253.
36. Ibid., vol. 10, p. 150.

Chapter Twelve

1.   Davani, *Sargozashtha-ye Vizheh*, vol. 6, p. 54.
2.   See Chapter 1.
3.   *Sahifeh-ye Nur*, vol. 6, p. 258.
4.   Yusef Sane'i, *Velayat-e Faqih*, Tehran, 1364/1986, p. 247.
5.   Ibid., pp. 72–3.
6.   M. E. Asgharzadeh, *Kayhan-e Sal*, Tehran, 1364/1986.
7.   *Sahifeh-ye Nur*, vol. 10, p. 149.
8.   Ibid., pp. 148–57
9.   Bani Sadr, *Khiyanat beh Omid*, p, 169.
10. Ibid., pp. 170–1.
11. Ibid., p. 168.
12. Bazargan, *Enqelab dar Dow Harekat*, p. 84.
13. Schirazi, *The Constitution of Iran*, p. 48.
14. Ibid.
15. Ibid., p. 49
16. Ibid. and Ali Rahnema and Farhad Nomani, *The Secular Miracle*, p. 197.
17. See ibid., pp. 197–9 for a detailed account of the campaign against Shari'atmadari.
18. *Sahifeh-ye Nur*, vol. 10, p. 260.

19. Razavi, *Hashemi va Enqelab*, pp. 306–7.

20. Ibid.

21. Ibid.

22. Rahnema and Nomani, *The Secular Miracle*, p. 198.

23. *Sahifeh-ye Nur*, vol. 11, p. 257.

24. Ibid., p. 260.

25. Abrahamian, *Radical Islam*, p. 204.

26. See, for instance, *Sahifeh-ye Nur*, vol. 14, pp. 124, 182–3, 239–41.

27. Ibid., p. 243.

28. Ibid. vol. 12, pp. 280–2; Khomeini, Tehran Radio, 22 September 1980.

29. Shaul Bakhash, *The Reign of the Ayatollahs: Iran and the Islamic Revolution*, London 1985, pp.127–8.

30. Ali Amir Hoseini, Bani Sadr's advisor, in an interview with the author, London, 1986.

31. Ibid.

32. Abrahamian, *Radical Islam*, p. 216.

33. Bakhash, *Reign of the Ayatollahs*, pp. 153–4.

34. Abrahamian, *Radical Islam*, p. 199.

35. Ibid., p. 202.

36. Ibid., p. 217.

37. *Sahifeh-ye Nur*, vol. 14, pp. 267–71.

38. Bani Sadr, *Khiyanat beh Omid*, p. 19.

39. According to some reports, over eighty people were killed. But to ensure the eternal grace of martyrdom for Beheshti and those who died with him, the number was officially scaled down to seventy-two – the number of Imam Hossein's companions who were martyred in 680 AD in Karbala.

40. *Sahifeh-ye Nur*, vol. 15, p. 44.

41. *Sargozashtha*, vol. 2.

42. *Sahifeh-ye Nur*, vol. 15, pp. 116–22.

43. Ibid., p. 140.

44. Schirazi, *The Constitution of Iran*, p. 127 quoting Amnesty International says that there were 2,444 executions in the first half of 1981 alone but may have meant the second half. Abrahamian, *Radical Islam* (p. 220) gives the figures as 600 by September, 1,700 by October and 2,500 by December.

45. Ahmad Khomeini, *Majmu'eh-ye Yadegar-e Imam*, vol. 6, p. 318.

46. *Sahifeh-ye Nur*, vol. 15, pp. 139–40.

Chapter Thirteen

1. *Sahifeh-ye Nur*, vol. 15, p. 139.

2. Ibid., vol. 10, p. 103.

3. Ibid., vol. 11, p. 245.

4. Ibid., vol. 15, p. 41.

5. Ibid., p. 284.

6. Bazargan, *Enqelab-e Iran dar Dow Harekat*, p. 13.

7. Ibid., p. 202. Bazargan uses the untranslated French term 'regence clericale' in his text.

8. *Sahifeh-ye Nur*, vol. 21, p. 98.

9. A frequent theme in Khomeini's speeches. See, for example, his 'Letter to the Clergy' which is quoted at length in chapter 14.

10. *Sahifeh-ye Nur*, vol. 18, p. 178.

11. Ibid., vol. 14, p. 291.

12. Ahmad Khomeini, *Yadegar-e Imam*, vol. 6, p. 716.

13. *Sahifeh-ye Nur*, vol. 16, p. 154.

14. Ahmad Khomeini, *Yadegar-e Imam*, vol. 1, p. 717.

15. Ian Brown, *Khomeini's Forgotten Sons: The Story of Iran's Boy Soldiers*, London 1990, p. 84.

16. Ibid., p. 89.

17. Ibid., pp. 31–2.

18. *Sahifeh-ye Nur*, vol. 16, p. 212.

19. Ahmad Khomeini, *Yadegar-e Imam*, vol. 1, p. 718.

20. A frequently repeated phrase, almost Khomeini's motto.

21. *Sahifeh-ye Nur*, vol. 18, pp. 194–5.

22. Helen Chapin Metz (ed.): *Iran–A Country Study*, Washington, 1989, pp. 283–4.

23. Ibid.

24. Ibid.

25. Author's interview with scholars from Qom.

26. *Sahifeh-ye Nur*, vol. 14, p. 63.

27. Ibid., vol. 10, p. 103.

28. Ibid., vol. 10, p. 98.

29. Ibid., vol. 15, p. 107.

30. See Chapter 4.

31. Rahnema and Nomani, *The Secular Miracle*, p. 212.

32. *Sahifeh-ye Nur*, vol. 18, pp. 18–38.

33. Schirazi, *The Constitution of Iran*, pp. 86–7.

34. Ahmad Khomeini, *Yadegar-e Imam*, vol. 1, p. 586.

35. Schirazi, *The Constitution of Iran*, p. 65.

36. Tehran Radio, Friday Prayer Sermon, January 1988.

37. *Sahifeh-ye Nur*, vol. 18, p. 42.

38. *Echo of Iran*, March 1999, p. 27, Tehran. The house belonged to a colonel of the imperial army. It was purchased by one of the foundations and let to Rafsanjani. He still lives there.

39. Katzman, *The Warriors of Islam*, p. 82.

40. Ruhollah Khomeini, *Kalam-e Imam, Melligara'i*, Tehran, 1983, p. 30.

41. Bazargan, *Enqelab-e Iran dar Dow Harekat*, p. 111.

42. *Sahifeh-ye Nur*, vol. 6, p 164.

43. Ibid., p. 52.

44. Ibid., vol. 8, p. 278.

45. See, for example, Ibid., vol. 9, p. 225.

46. Quoted in Robin Wright, *In the Name of God*, London, 1990, p. 165.

47. Rahnema and Nomani, *The Secular Miracle*, p. 341. See also Wright, *In the Name of God*, p. 176.

48. Tehran Radio, 20 July 1988.

Chapter Fourteen

1. Ahmad Khomeini, *Yadegar-e Imam*, vol. 6, p. 468.

2. *Divan-e Imam*, 4th edition, pp. 34–5, Tehran, 1995.

3. *Rah-e Eshq*, Tehran, 1989.

4. Fatemeh Tabataba'i in her Introduction to *Divan-e Imam*, 4th edition, pp. 34–5, Tehran 1995.

5. *Divan-e Imam*, p. 151.

6. Akhavan-e Towhidi, *Dar Pas-e Pardeh-ye Tazvir*, p. 226.

7. Translation by Mehrdad Nabili.

8. *Divan-e Imam*, p. 42. Translation by Roger Cooper.

9. Author's interview with Mehdi Ha'eri, London, 1986.

10. Khomeini, *Tafsir-e Sureh-ye Hamd*, Qom 1984, p. 54.

11. Interview with Ahmad Salamatian, Paris, 9 January 1999. Salamatian says that he was told about the uproar by Ahmad Khomeini.

12. *Tafsir-e Sureh-ye Hamd*, p. 84.

13. A copy of this letter is in the author's possession.

14. The letter, written on 22 February, was published in *Resalat*, 25 February 1989.

15. *Resalat*, 25 February 1989.

16. Ahmad Khomeini, *Yadegar-e Imam*, vol. 1, pp. 497–8.

17.   Schirazi, *The Constitution of Iran*, p. 131. Montazeri reiterated this demand at the end of January 1989. See *Kayhan* 25 January 1989. Schirazi provides a detailed and interesting account of the debate that followed this demand in the ruling circles and press of the Islamic Republic.

18.   *Payam-e Emruz*, no. 18, p. 22.

19.   Amnesty International has documented 3,000 names but has said that the real number of prisoners executed was probably much higher. Other estimates range from a minimum of 6,000 (*Cheshmandaz*, vol. 6, Summer 1368/1989) to as many as 10,000.

20.   *Payam-e Emruz*, no. 22, March 1377/1998, p. 22. For the text of three of Montazeri's letters, see *Cheshmandaz*, vol. 6, Summer 1368/1989, pp. 35-7.

21.   Quoted in Ahmad Khomeini, *Ranjnameh*, Tehran, 1368/1989. See also *Cheshmandaz*, vol. 6, p. 36.

22.   *Cheshmandaz*, vol. 6, p. 37.

23.   *Payam-e Emruz*, p. 22.

24.   *Sahifeh-ye Nur*, vol. 18, p. 23.

25.   *Kayhan Hava'i*, 8 February 1989.

26.   *Kayhan*, 12 February 1989.

27.   *Pasdar-e Islam* monthly, no. 86, January/February 1989.

28.   Ibid. p. 41.

29.   Ibid. p. 17.

30.   From a private source.

31.   *Payam-e Emruz*, no. 25, 1998, p. 20.

32.   Ibid.

33.   *Payam-e Emruz*, no. 21, 1997, p. 15.

34.   Ibid., p. 8, 1997. The letter, dated 6 Farvardin 1368/26 March 1989, was published by *Abrar*, 22 November 1997.

35.   Edited version of translation taken from www.eurasiannews.com/iran/montazeri

36.   *Pasdar-e Islam*, no. 89, p. 8, 1989.

37.   Ibid. p. 9.

38.   Quoted in Schirazi, *The Constitution of Iran*, p. 72.

39.   Ahmad Khomeini, *Ranj-nameh*.

40.   Ahmad Khomeini, *Yadegar-e Imam*, vol. 1, p 202.

41.   Ahmad Khomeini, *Ranj-nameh*, pp. 14-15.

42.   Ibid.

43.   Ibid.

44.   Ahmad Khomeini, *Yadegar-e Imam*, vol. 1, p. 178.

45.   Schirazi, *The Constitution of Iran*, pp. 110-11.

46.   Ibid., p. 107.

47.   Ibid., p. 240.

48. Ibid., p. 108.
49. Some who fell from political favour, such as Bazargan and Bani Sadr, tried to question the validity of Khomeini's rule by attacking the concept of *velayat-e faqih*. Such criticism carries little weight because it comes from a political rather than a juridical point of view. Both men pointed out the debt which the theory of *velayat-i faqih* owes to the Platonic ideal of the philosopher-king.

Chapter Fifteen

1. Ervand Abrahamian, *Khomeinism*, London 1993, p. 132.
2. Tehran Radio, Friday 10 June 1989; *Summary of World Broadcasts*, 12 June 1989.
3. Ibid.
4. Khomeini suffered a total of five heart attacks in one day. In addition, his cancer had advanced in his last weeks and a number of tumours had been removed two weeks before his death. In an interview televised a few days, his personal physicians Hasan Arefi and Iraj Fazel, revealed that on 26 March 1986 he had almost died of a heart attack.
5. Tehran Radio, Friday 10 June 1989; SWB, 12 June 1989.
6. Ibid.
7. Ibid.
8. Ibid.
9 'It is obligatory to bathe the dead three times; first with water mixed with the dried leaves of the lotus tree,' Khomeini had written. 'Second with water mixed with camphor and third with pure water.'
10. The only substance that can, under religious rulings, be mixed with the camphor is a little earth from the grave of Imam Hussein.
11. Tehran Radio, Friday 10 June, 1989; SWB, 12 June, 1989.
12. Tehran Radio, 4 June 1989, SWB, 6 June 1989.
13. Ibid.
14. Ibid.
15. Khalkhali, BBC interview, Qom, May 1997 and numerous interviews in the Tehran press during 1989.
16. Tehran Radio, Friday 10 June, 1989; SWB 12 June, 1989.
17. Ibid.
18. Ibid.
19. *Kayhan*, 20 June 1989.
20. Khomeini, *Resaleh-ye Towzih al-Masa'el*, Baghdad 1398/1978, problems 633-7.

Select Bibliography

Abrahamian, Ervand, 'Kasravi, the Integrative Nationalist of Iran', in Eli Kedourie
   and S. Haim (eds), *Towards a Modern Iran*, London, 1980.
—*Iran Between Two Revolutions*, Princeton, N.J., 1982.
—*Radical Islam, The Iranian Mojahedin*, London, 1989.
—*Khomeinism*, London, 1993
Afrasiyabi, Bahram & Dehqan, Sa'id, *Taleqani va Tarikh*, Tehran, 1359/1981.
Akhavan-e Towhidi, Hossein, *Dar Pas-e Pardeh-ye Tazvir*, Paris, 1364/1986.
Akhavi, Shahrough, *Religion and Politics in Contemporary Iran*, New York, 1980.
Algar, Hamed, *Religion and State in Iran 1785-1906: The Role of the Ulama in the
   Qajar Period*, Berkeley, 1969.
—*Enqelab-e Eslami dar Iran*, tr. into Persian by Morteza As'adi and Hassan
   Chidari, Tehran, 1360 /1981.
—*The Roots of the Islamic Revolution*, London, 1983.
—'Imam Khomeini, 1902–1962: The Pre-Revolutionary Years' in Edmund Burke
   and Ira Lapidus (eds), *Islam, Politics and Social Movements*, London, 1988.
Aqiqi Bakhshayeshi, *Ten Decades of the Ulama's Struggle*, tr. into English by Alaedin
   Pazargadi, Tehran, 1405/1985.
Ashtiani, Mirza Mehdi, *Asas al-Towhid*, Tehran, 1330/1951.
Azari Qomi, Ahmad, *Rahbari va Jang va Solh*, Tehran, 1366/1987.
Badamchian, Asadollah, *Negahi Gozara beh Jami'at-e Mo'talefeh-ye Islami*, Tehran
   1375/1996.

—*Shohada-ye 26 Khordad: Jami'at-e Mo'talefeh-ye Islam*, Tehran 1375/1996.

Bakhash, Shaul, *The Reign of the Ayatollahs: Iran and the Islamic Revolution*, London, 1985.

Banani, Amin, *The Modernization of Iran: 1921–1941*, Stanford 1961.

Bani Sadr, Abolhassan, *Khianat beh Omid*, Paris, 1361/1982.

Baqi, A., *Dar Shenakht-e Hezb-e Qa'edin-e Zaman*, Qom, 1363/1984.

Bazargan, Mehdi, *Enqelab-e Iran dar Dow Harekat*, Tehran, 1363/1984.

—*Showra-ye Enqelab va Dowlat-e Movaqqat*, Tehran, 1361/1982.

—*Gomrahan*, Tehran, 1362/1983.

Bonyad-e Farhangi-ye Ayatollah Taleqani, *Yadnameh-ye Abuzar-e Zaman*, Tehran, 2nd ed. 1360/1981.

Borujerdi, Hossein Tabataba'i et al., *Resaleh-ye Towzih al-Masa'el*, Qom, n.d.

Brown, Ian, *Khomeini's Forgotten Sons: The Story of Iran's Boy Soldiers*, London 1990.

Cook, Michael, *Muhammad*, Oxford, 1986.

Chehabi, Houchang, *Iranian Politics and Religious Modernism: The Liberation Movement of Iran under the Shah and Khomeini*, London, 1990.

Dahbashi, Hamid, *The Theology of Discontent*, New York, 1993.

Davani, Ali, *Nehzat-e Ruhaniyat-e Iran*, 10 vols, Tehran, 1360/1981.

Davari, Reza, *Vaz'-e Konuni-ye Tafakkor dar Iran*, Tehran, 1357/1978.

Dehnovi, A, *Qiyam-e Khunin-e Panzdah-e Khordad-e 42 beh Ravayat-e Asnad*, Tehran, 1360/1981.

Enayat, Hamid, *Andisheh-ye Siyasi dar Eslam-e Mo'aser*, tr. by Baha' al-Din Khorramshahi, Tehran, 1362/1983.

Faghfoory, M. H.,'The Role of the Ulama in Twentieth Century Iran with Particular Reference to Ayatollah Haj Sayyid Abul-Qasim Khahsani', Ph.D. dissertation, University of Wisconsin, 1978.

al-Fakhuri, Hana and al-Jarr, Khalil, *Tarikh-e Falsafeh dar Jahan-e Eslami*, tr. from Arabic by Abdol Mohammad Ayati, Tehran, 2535 Shahanshahi/1976.

Farouk Sluglett, Marion and Sluglett, Peter, *Iraq Since 1958: From Revolution to Dictatorship*, London, 1987.

Fazeltuni, Mohammad Hossein, *Ta'liqeh bar Fosus*, Tehran, 1360/1981.

Fehri, Ahmad, *Ta'lim va Ta'allom az Didgah-e Shahid-e Sani va Emam Khomeini*, Tehran, 1362/1983.

Fischer, Michael M. J., *Iran From Religious Dispute to Revolution*, Cambridge, Mass., 1980.

Ha'eri, Abdolhadi, *Tashayyu' va Mashrutiyat dar Iran*, Tehran, 1364/1985.

—*Hoviyat-e Senfi-ye Ruhani*, Qom, 1361/1982.

Hiro, Dillip, *Iran Under the Ayatollahs*, London, 1987.

Huyser, Robert E., *Mission to Tehran*, London, 1986.

Jombesh-e Azadi Bakhsh-e Mardom-e Iran, *Gozashteh Cheragh-e Rah-e Ayandeh*

Ast, Tehran, n.d.

Jorfadeqani, M., *'Olama-ye Bozorg-e Shi'a az Koleini ta Khomeini*, Qom,1364/1985.

Kasravi, Ahmad, *Tarikh-e Mashruteh-ye Iran*, Tehran, 1363/1984.

Katzman, Kenneth, *The Warriors of Islam: Iran's Revolutionary Guards*, Oxford, 1993.

Keddie, Nikki R., *Roots of Revolution*, New Haven, 1981.

Khamene'i, Ali, *Didgah-ha*, Qom, 1362/1983.

—*Khaterat va Hekayatha*, Tehran, 1374/1995.

Khomeini, Ahmad, *Majmu'eh-ye Asar-e Yadegar-e Imam*, Tehran, 1375/1996.

Khomeini, Ruhollah, *Kashf al-Asrar*, n.p., n.d.

—*Tafsir-e Sureh-ye Hamd*, Tehran, n.d.

—*Hokumat-e Eslami*, Najaf, 1391/1971.

—*Me'raj al-Salekin*.

—*Mesbah al-Hedaya*.

—*Resaleh-ye Towzih al-Masa'el*, Baghdad, 1398/1978.

—*Resaleh-ye Novin*, 4 vols, Tehran, 1359/1981.

—*Sahifeh-ye Nur*, 16 vols, Tehran 1361/1982.

—*Tafsir-e Sureh-ye Hamd*,

—*Islam and Revolution: Writings and Declarations*, tr. by Hamid Algar, London: Mizan Press, 1981.

—*Sabu-ye Eshq*, Tehran 1368/1989.

—*Sharh-e Do'a al-Sahar*, ed. Ahmad Fehri, Beirut, 1363/1984.

—*Manasek-e Haj*, Tehran, 1361/1982.

—*Ruhaniyat, Talayeh-dar-e Eslam-e Faqahati az Didgah-e Emam Khomeini*, Tehran, 1361/1982.

—*Jehad-e Akbar*, Tehran, 1361/1982.

—*A Clarification of Questions* (An unabridged English translation of *Resaleh-ye Towzih al-Masa'el* by J. Borujerdi) Boulder Co., 1984.

—*Tahrir al-Wasileh*, Beirut, 2 vols. 1407/1987.

Lambton A. K. S., *The Persian Land Reform 1962–1966*, Oxford, 1969.

Madani, Jalal al-Din, *Tarikh-e Siasi-ye Mo'aser-e Iran*, Qom, 1361/1982.

Martin, Vanessa, *Islam and Modernism, The Iranian Revolution of 1906*, London, 1989.

Masjed Jame'i, Mohammad, *Ideolozhi va Enqelab*, Tehran, 1361/1983.

Metz, Helen Chapin (ed.): *Iran- A Country Study*, Washington, 1989.

Meshkat al-Dini, Abdolmohsen, *Falsafeh-ye Sadr al-Din Shirazi*, Tehran, 1361/1983.

Moghniyeh, Mohammad Javad, *Falsafat al-Velayat*, Beirut, 1984.

Momen, Moojan, *An Introduction to Shi'i Islam*, London, 1985.

Montazeri, Ayatollah Hossein Ali, *Resaleh-ye Towzih al-Masa'el*, Tehran, 1363/1985.

Moqimi, Mohammad, *Velayat az Didgah-e Marja'iyat-e Shi'a*, Tehran, 2535 Shahanshahi/1976.

Morad, A. et al., *Nehzat-e Bidadgari dar Jahan-e Eslam*, tr. by Seyyed Mohammad Mehdi Ja'fari, Tehran, 1362/1983.

Morsalvand, Hassan, *Zendeginameh-ye Rejal va Mashahir-e Iran*, Tehran 1369/1990.

Mortimer, Edward, *Faith and Power: The Politics of Islam*, London, 1982.

Motahhari, Morteza, *Moqaddameh bar Jahanbini-ye Eslami*, Qom, n.d.

—*Nehzatha-ye Eslami dar Sad Sal-e Akhir*, Qom, 1363/1984.

—*Ashna'i ba 'Olum-e Eslami*, Qom, 1358/1979.

Mottahedeh, Roy, *The Mantle of the Prophet*, London, 1985.

Najafi Quchani, *Siyahat-e Sharq*, Tehran, 1362/1984.

Na'ini, Mohammad Hossein, *Tanbih al-Ummah va Tanzih al-Milla: Hokumat az Nazar-e Eslam*, Tehran, 1358/1980.

Nasr, Seyyed Hossein, *Shi'ite Islam*, London, 1975.

Nehzat-e Azadi-ye Iran, *Tafsil va Tahlil-e Velayat-e Motlaqeh-ye Faqih*, Tehran, 1367/1988.

—*Barrasi-ye Safar-e Hoveizer beh Iran*, Tehran, 1362/1983.

Nicholson, R. A., *The Idea of Personality in Sufism*, Cambridge, 1970.

Nurbakhsh, Seyyed Hassan, *Yadvareh-ye Nehzat-e Eslami*, Tehran, 1360/1982.

Omid, Homa, *Islam and the Post-Revolutionary State in Iran*, New York, 1994.

Pahlavi, Mohammad Reza, *Ma'muriyat Bara-ye Vatanam*, Paris, 1366/1987.

—*Pasokh beh Tarikh*, Paris, 1366/1987.

Pezeshkzad, Iraj, *Moruri bar Vaqe'eh-ye 15 Khordad 42*, Paris, 1365/1986.

Piscatori, James P. (ed.) *Islam in the Political Process*, Cambridge, 1983.

Qarebaghi, Abbas, *E'terafat-e Zheneral, Khaterat-e Arteshbod Abbas Qarebaghi (Mordad-Bahman 57)*, Tehran, 1365/1986.

al-Rahman, Afzal, *Mohammad as a Military Leader*, London, 1980.

Rahimi, Mostafa, *Dar Bareh-ye Jomhuri-ye Eslami*, Tehran, 1355/1979.

Rajaee, Farhang, *Islamic Values and World View*, London, 1983.

Rahnema, A., *An Islamic Utopian: A Political Biography of Ali Shari'ati*, London, 1998.

—'Ali Shari'ati' in A. Rahnema (ed.) *Pioneers of Islamic Revival*, London, 1994.

—and Nomani, F., *The Secular Miracle: Religion, Politics and Economic Policy in Iran*, London, 1990.

Rasa'i, Davud, *Hokumat-e Eslami az Nazar-e Ibn-e Khaldun*, Tehran, n.p., n.d.

Razavi, M., *Hashemi va Enqelab*, Tehran 1998.

Rodinson, Maxime, *Mohammad*, London, 1971.

Ruhani Ziyarati, Hamid, *Shari'atmadari dar Dadgah-e Tarikh*, Qom, 1361/1982.

—*Barrasi va Tahlil az Nehzat-e Emam Khomeini*, Tehran, 1360/1981.

—*Nehzat-e Emam Khomeini*, Tehran, 3 vols, 1360/1981, 1364/1986, 1374/1995.

Sadr, Mohsen, *Khaterat-e Sadr al-Ashraf*, Tehran, 1364/1986.

Sadr al-Din Shirazi (Mullah Sadra) *Masha'er*, Tr. from Arabic by Gholam Hossein Ahani, Tehran, 1340/1961.

—'Arshiyeh, tr. from Arabic by Gholam Hossein Ahani, Tehran, 1361/1983.

Sadeqi, Mir-Muhhamad, Hayahu, Isfahan, 1351/1972.

Safi Golpayegani, Lotfallah, Velayat-e Takvini va Velayat-e Tashri'i, Tehran, 1360/1981.

Salehi Najaf-Abadi, Shahid-e Javid, Tehran, 1349/1971.

Sha'rbaf, Reza (ed.), Sargozashtha-ye Vizheh az Zendegi Hazrat-e Emam Khomeini beh Ravayat-e Jam'i az Fozala, Tehran, 1364/1985.

Sharif Razi, Muhammad, Athar al-Hojjat, Qom 1332/1953.

Sane'i, Yusef, Velayat-e Faqih, Tehran, 1364/1986.

Sangalaji, Shari'at, Kelid-e Fahm-e Qor'an, Tehran, 1345/1966.

Shirazi, R. M., Nosus al-Khosus fi Tarjomat al-Fosus, Tehran, 1359/1980.

Soltanzadeh, Hossein, Tarikh-e Madares-e Iran, Tehran, 1364/1985.

Sorush, Abdolkarim (ed.) Yadnameh-ye Ostad-e Shahid Morteza Motahhari, Tehran, 1363/1985).

Stempel, John D., Inside the Iranian Revolution, Bloomington, 1981.

Tabari, Ehsan, Jahanbiniha va Jonbeshha-ye Ejtema'i dar Iran, East Berlin, 1348/1970.

Tabataba'i, Allameh Mohammad Hossein, Osul-e Falsafeh va Ravesh-e Realism, Qom 1332–64/1953–85.

—et. al., Marja'iyat va Ruhaniyat, Qom, 1341/1962.

Taheri Khorramabadi, Hassan, Velayat-e Faqih va Hakemiyat-e Mellat, Qom, 1362/1983.

Taleqani, Mahmud, Eslam va Malekiyat, Houston, 1355/1977.

Tonekaboni, Mirza Mohammad, Qesas al-'Olama', n.p., n.d.

Wright, Robin, In the Name of God, London, 1990.

Yazdi, Ebrahim, Akharin Talash-ha dar Akharin Ruzha, Tehran, 1363/1984.

Zavabeti, Mehdi, Pazhuheshi dar Nezam-e Talabegi, Tehran, 1359/1980.

Index

Abadan 187, 248
Abaqat al-Anwar (Neishaburi) 3
Abarqu'i, Abbasqoli 10
Abolqassem, Akhund Mollah 14
Abu Bakr, (1st Rashidun caliph) 15
Abu Zarr 172
Achaeminids 163
Acre (Palestine) 66
Adab 9
Adib Tehrani, Mirza Mohammad 29
Afghani, Seyyed Jamaleddin 140, 148
Afghanistan 41, 215, 306
Afzali, Colonel 129, 132
Ahmad, Seyyed (Khomeini's
    grandfather) 2, 3
Ahmad Shah 25, 26, 27, 64
Ahmadabad 120, 218
Ahmadzadeh, Mas'ud 164
A'in al-Qozat 45
Air France 200
al-Azhar mosque, Cairo 284
Al-e Ahmad, Jalal 166, 189
al-Futuhat al-Makkiyya (Ibn Arabi) 40

Ala, Hossein 113
Alam, Asadollah 72, 76, 77, 78, 79,
    86, 96, 104, 111, 113, 114
Alavi, Hojjat al-Islam 94
Alfiyya 24
Algeria 220, Algerian Revolution 173
Ali ibn Abi Talib (1st Shi'i Imam) 15,
    16, 30, 72, 74, 82, 157, 158, 165, 179,
    191, 192
Ali Asghar (son of Imam Hossein)
    16
Aligudarz 8
Amal (Lebanon) 180, 212
Amin al-Soltan 8
Amini, Ali 71, 72, 73, 75, 83, 182
Amini, Ayatollah Ebrahim 287, 308
Amir Bahador-e Jang 9
Amnesty International 242, 280
Amol 252
Amoli, Seyyed Heidar 41
Amuzegar, Jamshid 183, 187
Andalucia (Spain) 40
Andarzgu 180

Anglo-Iranian Oil Comapny 65
Ankara 130, 135, 138
Ansari, Haj Morteza 91
Ansari of Herat 43
Ansari Qomi, Sheikh Morteza 92
Anvari, Mohyeddin 81, 161
Arab–Israeli war (1973) 163
Arak (Sultanabad) 1, 6, 7, 8, 9, 22, 25
Araqi, Mehdi 105, 106, 180, 194
Araqi, Haj Aqa Mohsen 22
Archbishop of Canterbury 284
Aref, Abdol Rahman 144
Arsanjani, Hassan 71, 72
Arya Mehr Industrial University 184
al-Asfar al-Arba'a (Mollah Sadra) 41
Asgar Owladi, Habibollah 180
Asghar (Tayyeb Haj Reza'i) 110
Asrar-e Hezar Saleh (Hakamizadeh)
   61
Assembly for Revising the Constitu-
   tion (Showra-ye Baznegari-ye
   Qanun-e Asasi) 293, 307, 308
Assembly of Experts (Majles-e
   Khobregan) 217, 218, 219, 224,
   225, 226, 230, 261, 262, 263, 264,
   269, 287, 293, 300, 301, 302, 305,
   307, 308, 310
Atatürk, Kemal 130, 134, 142
Avicenna (Ibn Sina) 40, 48, 275
Ayadi, General 161
Ayandegan 218, 219
Ayat, Dr Hassan 180, 242
Ayesha (wife of the Prophet) 16
Ayn al-Dowleh 8, 9, 10, 12
Azarbaijan 134, 229, 231, 232
Azari Qomi, Ayatollah Ahmad 219
Azhari, General Gholamreza 195
Azod al-Soltan, Prince Abolfazl 7

Bab, Mirza Ali Mohammad 66
Badi', Colonel 96
Bafqi, Ayatollah 28, 56, 88

Baghdad 139, 144, 145, 146, 152, 189
Baha'is, Baha'ism 66, 95, 255
Baha'ollah (Mirza Hossein Ali Nuri)
   66
Bahonar, Mohammad Javad 81, 111,
   178, 179, 180, 181, 210, 221, 235, 242,
   245
Bahram Khan 7
Bakhtiar, General Teimur 109, 183,
   197, 198, 202, 203, 204, 205, 221
Bakhtiyari tribe 19
al-Bakr, General Ahmad Hassan 144
Balkh 41
Bani Qureizah 280
Bani Sadr, President Abolhassan
   149, 200, 241, 242, 246, 248, 289,
   290, 307; alliance with Mojahedin
   243; election and confirmation as
   president 233–5; conflict with IRP
   and Khomeini 238–40; and
   hostage crisis 227–8; impeached
   240; with Khomeini in Paris 189–
   93 passim, delegate to Assembly of
   Experts 219; and war with Iraq
   236–7
Baqerabad 112
Basij 249, 250, 257
Basra 16, 250
Ba'th Party 144, 145, 146, 147, 148,
   152, 153, 322, 334, 339
Bazargan, Mehdi 59, 68, 77, 150, 165,
   166, 172, 173, 178, 183, 197, 218, 219,
   224, 237, 238, 246, 262; appointed
   prime minister 203–4, 206; and
   Bakhtiar 204–5; biography 167–
   8; criticism of Khomeini 247, 265,
   268; and executions 206–8; and
   Freedom Movement of Iran 167–
   8, 255; imprisonment 160; and
   Islamic constitution 216–17;
   Khomeini's rejection of 289, 291;
   resigns from government 220–2;

sidelined 215, 216; as vehicle of
Khomeini's plans 209–10
Behbehani, Ayatollah Seyyed
Mohammad 67, 70, 85
Behesht-e Zahra cemetery 201, 210,
311, 312
Beheshti, Ayatollah Mohammad
Hossein 166, 235, 243, 245, 246,
262, 263, 302; and assassination of
Mansur 161; and Coalition of
Islamic Societies 81, 187, 210;
employee of Ministry of Educa-
tion 179; formation of Society of
Militant Clergy 180–1; member
of Revolutionary Council 221; as
head of IRP 234; appointed chief
justice 234; assassinated 241
Beirut 177
Bibi Khanum 3
Bojnurdi, Mohammad Kazem 161,
162, 212
Bokhara'i, Mohammad 161
Borqa'i, Seyyed Ali Akbar 57
Borujerdi, Grand Ayatollah Moham-
mad Hossein 59, 60, 64, 65, 66,
67, 68, 69, 70, 73, 74, 75, 81, 83, 141,
151, 152
Britain, British 3, 12, 22, 60, 104, 121,
123, 149, 155, 174, 188; and 1921
coup 26; oil interests in Iran 64–
5; and Salman Rushdie affair
282–3
British Broadcasting Corporation
(BBC) 192, 287, 319, 326, 340
Brzezinski, Zbigniew 196, 220
Byzantium 275
Bulvar Palace Hotel (Ankara) 130
Bursa (Turkey) 131, 132, 134, 135, 136,
137, 138

caliphate 26
Carlyle, Thomas 166

Canada 149
Carter, President Jimmy 182, 183, 185,
186, 188, 196
Caspian Sea 252
Central Treaty Organisation
(CENTO) 138
Cetiner, Colonel Ali Bey 131–9 passim
Cetiner, Mellahat 131–8 passim
Cetiner, Payan 133
Cetiner, Tanju 133, 135, 136
Cetiner, Tulga 133
Chamran, Mustafa 212
China 263
Christians, Christianity 33, 148, 154,
276
CIA coup against Mosaddeq 66, 219
Coalition of Islamic Societies 80, 81,
82, 110, 161, 178, 180, 181, 187, 188,
210, 211, 233, 235, 258
Communist Party (Iraq) 144
Confederation of Iranian Students
185
Constituent Assembly; of 1926 27,
64; promise of after 1979 revolu-
tion 203; conflict over after 1979
revolution 216–18
Constitution of 1906 12, 77, 119, 168,
175, 183, 187, 196, 217,
Constitution of Islamic Republic
179, 194, 216–34 passim, 254, 260,
261, 262, 277, 293–4, 300, 307–8,
309
Constitutional Revolution of 1905-6
11, 12, 18, 22, 26, 36, 58, 77, 223
Corbin, Henry 173
Cossack Brigade 12, 25
Council of Guardians 225, 247, 257,
258, 259, 260, 261, 294, 340
A Critique of Darwin's Philosophy
(Masjed Shahi) 28

Damascus 16, 40, 194

Danesh Amuz 167
Dar al-Shafa, Qom 28
Da'wa Party 144, 152
Derakhshesh, Mohammad 72
*A Discussion on the Marja'iyat and
    Clergy* 171
Divan of Shams-e Tabrizi (Rumi) 42
Divine Justice (Motahhari) 170
Do'a al-Sahar (Khomeini) 44
Do'a'i, Mahmud 176
Doshan Tappeh air base 205
Duzduzani, Abbas 212

Eftekhar al-Ulama, Mirza Mahmud
    18
Egypt 148, 246
ejtehad 4, 36, 167, 247, 350
Emami Kashani, Ayatollah Moham-
    mad 180
Enlightenment 20, 168
Enqelab-e Islami 237, 238
Eqbal, Manuchehr 69, 71, 161
erfan (gnosis) 39, 40, 41, 42, 44, 48
Eshraqi, Ayatollah Mohammad Taqi
    (Khomeini's son-in-law) 57, 190,
    192
Eslami, Sadeq 80, 180
Eslamshenasi (Shari'ati) 173
Ethiopia 275
Ettela'at 115, 120, 121, 186
Evin prison 194, 206
executions 204, 328; after revolu-
    tion 207–8; after June 1981
    demonstrations 240–1; Kho-
    meini's response to International
    Human Rights bodies 208, 242;
    mass executions of 1988 278–9

Fahd, King of Saudi Arabia 305
'faith' v. 'expertise', debate on 235–6
Fakhr al-Dowleh 71
Falsafi, Hojjat al-Islam Mohammad

Taqi 66, 78, 85, 86
Fanon, Franz 173
Farahabad 205
Farahan 3
Farrokhi Yazdi, Mohammad 91
Farsi, Jalaleddin 178, 233, 235
Fatemeh Ma'sumeh, shrine of (Qom)
    25
Fatemeh al-Zahra 15, 157, 179
Fath Ali Shah 28
Faw peninsula 251
Feda'iyan-e Islam 59, 60, 63, 65, 69,
    79, 120, 161, 224, 233
Feda'iyan-e Khalq 164, 165, 209, 220,
    226, 239, 255
Fehri, Seyyed Ahmad 44
Feiz Qomi, Ayatollah 25
Feiziyeh Seminary (*madraseh*) 43, 54,
    95, 96, 98, 99, 102, 103, 106, 107, 118,
    119, 120, 167, 201, 216, 275, 276;
    ransacked 92–4
feqh 29, 35, 36, 138; *feqh-e puya* 259;
    feqh-e sonnati 258
Ferdowsi 17, 106, 240
First World War 18, 21, 26, 64
Florya (Turkey) 136
Forqan 216
Foruhar, Dariush 183
Foundation for the Oppressed
    (Bonyad-e Mostaz'afin) 201
*Foundations of Metaphysics and the
    Method of Realism* (Allameh
    Tabataba'i) 170
France 149, 164, 167, 189, 191, 251
Freedom Movement of Iran
    (Nehzat-e Azadi-ye Iran) 77, 150,
    160, 165, 168, 171, 183, 203, 216, 217,
    219, 254
French Revolution 168
Fusus al-Hikam (Ibn Arabi) 43

Gabriel 157

Germany 149
Ghaffari, Hojjat al-Islam Hadi 211
Ghaffari, Hossein 179
Gharani, General 216
Gharbzadegi (Al-e Ahmad) 166, 189
Gharebaghi, General 205
al-Ghazali, Imam Mohammad 40
Goethe Institute 183
Golpayegan (province) 1, 8
Golpayegani, Grand Ayatollah
    Mohammad Reza 70, 72, 75, 76,
    78, 79, 83, 92, 93, 94, 97, 121, 152,
    186, 230, 253, 257, 260, 311
Goltappeh, Major 105
Golzadeh Ghafuri, Ali 166, 179
Gorbachev, Mikhael 274, 275, 276
Gowharshad mosque (Mashhad) 55
The Guardian 211
Guevara, Che 173
Gurvitch, George 173

Habibi, Hassan 190, 194, 216, 233
Hadidchi Dabbagh, Tahereh 191, 198,
    275
hadith 56, 305
Ha'eri Yazdi, Mehdi 51, 273
Ha'eri, Sheikh Abdolkarim 22, 24,
    25, 27, 28, 32, 35, 36, 55, 57, 68, 75
Hafez 17, 32, 42, 48, 272, 273
Haifa (Israel) 66
Hajieh Agha Khanum 2, 3, 10
Haj Mollah Sadeq School of Theol-
    ogy 54
Haj Reza'i, Tayyeb 105, 110, 115, 118
Hakamizadeh, Ali Akbar 57, 61, 62
Hakim, Mirza Ali Akbar 51
al-Hakim, Grand Ayatollah Mohsen
    70, 76, 96, 97, 141, 142, 143, 144,
    145, 147, 151, 152, 153
Hakimi, Mohammad Reza 166
Halabi, Sheikh Mahmud 66, 67, 256
Hallaj, Mansur 45, 51, 273

Hamadan 149, 275
Harun al-Rashid, (Abbasid caliph)
    90, 92
Hashemi, Hadi 264
Hashemi, Mehdi 263, 277, 292
Hashemi Rafsanjani, Akbar 97–8,
    179, 180, 203, 212, 241, 245, 249,
    262, 300–11 *passim*; and Coalition
    of Islamic Societies 161, 210, 235;
    and assassination of Mansur 161;
    Mojahedin-e Khalq sympathiser
    176; speaker of Majles 260, 261;
    relations with Khomeini 263, 287;
    Irangate affair 263–5; and Iran-
    Iraq war 265, 268–9
Hashemi-Nejad, Hojjat al-Islam A.
    K. 180, 242
Hassan (Second Shi'i Imam) 16, 142,
    143
Hejazi, Fakhreddin 172
hekmat 39, 40, 41, 42
Heshmat al-Dowleh 7, 9
Heshmatieh 9
Hezbollah 211, 218, 219, 220, 226, 234,
    238, 239, 240, 254
Hezbollah (Lebanon) 263, 264
Hidden Imam 140, 153, 154, 158, 199,
    200, 201, 256, 294
Hindi, Nureddin (Khomeini's
    brother) 4
Hindi Neishaburi, Mir Hamed
    Hossein 3
Hojjati Kermani, Mohammad Javad
    180
Hojjatieh Mahdavieh Society 66,
    254, 255, 256
Hojjatieh seminary 91
Homayun 57, 61
Horr 118
Hossein, (3rd Shi'i Imam) 9, 15, 16,
    17, 35, 68, 85, 98, 101, 103, 104, 106,
    112, 118, 140, 142, 143, 157, 165, 241,

311

Hossein, King of Jordan 249
Hosseiniyeh Ershad 171, 173
Hoveida, Amir Abbas 183, 207;
  execution of 208–9

Ibn Arabi 40, 41, 43, 45, 47, 48, 50,
  275
Ibn Malik 24
Ibn Sina see Avicenna
Imam Reza, shrine of (Mashhad) 52
Imperial Guard 92, 93, 101, 105, 205,
  206
Imperial Tobacco Company 3
International Monetary Fund 70, 75
Iran Novin Party 118, 119
Iran–Iraq War 44, 235, 236, 276, 306
Irangate affair 265
Iranian Committee for the Defence
  of Freedom and Human Rights
  186
Iraq 3, 4, 16, 22, 27, 55, 58, 64, 70, 76,
  129, 161, 185, 191, 207, 255, Khomei-
  ni's exile in 138–59, 188; expulsion
  of residents of Iranian origin 146;
  expulsion of Shi'i leadership from
  25, 27 see also Iran–Iraq war
Isfahan 1, 3, 8, 18, 22, 27, 36, 45, 58, 81,
  111, 153, 162, 222, 262, 292
Isfahani, Grand Ayatollah Seyyed
  Abolhassan 27
Islam and Ownership (Taleqani) 171
Islamabad (Pakistan) 283
Islamic Nations Party (Hezb-e
  Mellal-e Islami) 161, 212
Islamic Republican Party (Hezb-e
  Jomhuri-ye Islami) 80, 162, 210,
  211, 212, 215, 216, 218, 221, 233, 234,
  237, 238, 239, 240, 241, 246, 255,
  302; bombing of headquarters
  241
Islamic Society (The) 167

The Islamic State (Khomeini) 156–8
Israel 66, 95, 99, 100, 101, 104, 115, 120,
  123, 126, 163, 208, 249, 263, 265, 266

Ja'afar Qoli Sultan 7–9, 11
Ja'far al-Sadeq (6th Shi'i Imam) 90,
  92
Ja'far, Sheikh (Khomeini's tutor) 18
Ja'fari school of jurisprudence 92
Ja'fari, Sha'ban (Bimokh) 104, 106, 111
Jaleh Square massacre 188
Jamaran (Tehran) 249, 253, 263, 270,
  302, 303, 310; Khomeini takes
  residence at 237
Jannati, Ayatollah Ahmad 180
Japan 263
Javadi Amoli, Ayatollah 275
Jazani, Bijan 164
Jehad-e Akbar (Khomeini) 156, 157
Jesus 184, 275
Jews, Judaism 99, 154, 265, 280
Jigaraki, Nasser 104, 106
Johnson, President Lyndon 182
Jojo, Abdolqeis 115
Jomhuri-ye Islami 237
jurisprudence (osul-e feqh) 23, 29

Kahak 275
Kamalvand, Ayatollah Ruhollah 83,
  84, 114
Kamareh 1, 2
Kamareh'i, Seyyed Mohammad 8
Kamareh'i, Yusef Khan 3
Karbala 3, 16, 17, 22, 85, 97, 103, 106,
  112, 118, 140, 141; plain of 311;
  battle of 15, 17, 95
Karrubi, Ayatollah Mehdi 301
Kashani, Ayatollah Seyyed
  Abolqasem 63–4, 65, 69, 79
Kashf al-Asrar (Khomeini) 60–3, 137,
  189
Kashmir 149, 283

Kashmiri, Mas'ud 242
Kasravi, Ahmad 57, 62
Kayhan 277, 280, 290
Kennedy, President John F. 69, 71, 72, 75, 89, 182, 183
Ketab al-Bai' (Khomeini) 153
Khalkhali, Sheikh Sadeq 91, 111, 194, 207, 208, 309
Khalq-e Mosalman 230
Khamene'i, Ayatollah Ali 111, 179, 181, 210, 310; biography 245–6; and formation of Society of Militant Clergy 180; as president 245, 249, 263, 269, 284, 304, 305; designated as leader 287, 309, 310; and *velayat-e motlaqeh-ye faqih* 260
Kharijites 16
Kharrazi, Ja'far 171
Khatami, Ayatollah Mohammad 194
Kho'i, Grand Ayatollah Abolqassem 76, 84, 141, 151, 152, 158, 159, 180, 227, 257
Khomein 1, 3, 4, 6, 7, 8, 9, 12, 13, 14, 18, 22, 31, 32, 34, 37, 45
Khomeini 72, 263, 290
Khomeini, Ahmad (Khomeini's son) 130, 152, 182, 201, 208, 227, 241, 242, 249, 251, 260, 264, 268, 269, 276; on family background 2, 6, 13, 24, 52; in Khomeini's last days 270, 300, 301, 305, 306, 309, 310; in Paris 189–94 *passim*; and Montazeri 287, 291–2; *Ranjnameh*, 291–2
Khomeini, Mostafa (Khomeini's son) 94, 100, 130–1, 134, 276; and father's arrest 107–8; and father's exile 136–58 *passim*; death of 184–5
Khomeini, Ruhollah anti-American-ism 122–7, 188, 220, 221; arrest and imprisonment 107–28;

attitude to Reza Shah 60–1; and Bani Sadr 190, 233–4, 238, 239–40; and Bazargan 204, 209, 205, 221–2; and Borujerdi 60, 68, 73, 74; and Coalition of Islamic Societies 80–1, 110, 161, 178, 180, 210; childhood 2, 12–20 ; consti-tution of Islamic state 216–18, 224, 225–6, 293–5; December 1981 decree 254; death and funeral 299–313; death of Mostafa 184–5; education 21–38; exile in Iraq 139–59; exile in Turkey 130–9; export of revolution 236, 265 265–6; family background 2–11; and Feda'iyan-e Islam 59–60, 65, 67, 79–80, 161, 223–4; in France 189–98; and al-Hakim 142–3, 151–2; and Iranian students abroad 149–50; and Iran–Iraq war 236–7, 249, 251, 269; *and* IRP *explosion* 241–2; *The Islamic State* (*Velayat-e Faqih*) 153–56, 158; and Kashani 63–4, 66, 68–9; *Kashf al-Asrar* 60–3; and Khamene'i 246; and Kho'i 158–9; 'letter to the clergy' 285–7; and local councils bill (1962) 75–80; marriage 37–8; and 1988 mass executions 279–80; and Mojahe-din-e Khalq 176, 238–43 *passim*; and Montazeri 262, 263, 277–82, 285–9; and Motahhari 179–80, 180–1, 206; moves to Jamaran (Tehran) 237; mysticism 39–51, 271–6, 295–8; and occupation of American Embassy 226–9; poetry 32, 272–3; and Rastakhiz Party 175; religious network 85, 111, 150–51, 177–81, 187–8; returns to Iran 199–203; returns to Qom 203–5; Salman Rushdie 282–4; and Shari'ati 177; and

Shari'atmadari 82–3, 97, 116, 121
186, 229–32, 252; and structure of
Islamic Republic 247–8, 253, 257,
258, 259, 260–1; as teacher of
theology
Khonsar 8
Khonsari, Grand Ayatollah Ahmad
65, 85, 86, 114, 152
Khonsari, Haj Mirza Mohammad
Mehdi 8
Khonsari, Mohammad Taqi 29
Khorasan province 172
Khorasani, Akhund Mohammad
Kazem 22
Khorramabad 83
Khorramshahr 248, 249, 250
Kianuri, Nureddin 255
Kintur (India) 2
Konya (Turkey) 42
Kufa (Iraq) 16, 247
Kumla (Turkey) 137
Kurdish Democratic Party of Iran
(KDPI) 219
Kuwait 150, 185, 189, 306

Lahuti, Ayatollah Hassan 212
Lajevardi, Asadollah 194
land refom 69–70
Larijani, Javad 275
Lavasan 31
Lavasani, Mohammad Sadeq 31, 37,
38
Le Bon, Gustave 166
Le Monde 187
League for the Freedom of the
Iranian People 172
Lebanon 65, 70, 100, 115, 150, 180, 184,
185, 201, 212, 249, 263
Lilian 2
Lions Club 100
Local Council Election Bill 75, 77,
79, 81

logos (the Perfect Man) 47
Lucknow 2
Luristan 6, 83
Lurs 1, 13

Madani, Vice-Admiral Ahmad 233
Madani, Ayatollah Baha al-Din 242
madraseh architecture 22; curriculum 24, 29, 34–5, 36, 39, 42;
finances 32; history 23–4
Maeterlinck, Maurice 166
Mafatih al-Gheib 43
Mahallati, Ayatollah Baha al-Din
101, 114, 117
Mahallati, Sheikh Hamza 18
Mahdavi Kani, Mohammad Reza
179, 185
Majles (National Consultative
Assembly) 12, 19, 20, 26, 27, 58,
64, 65, 69, 71, 72, 78, 79, 83, 95, 119,
160, 121, 122 123, 124, 125, 126, 127,
162; (Islamic Consultative Assem-
bly) 234, 239, 241, 257, 258, 259,
260, 261, 268, 290, 291, 293, 307,
300, 322
Majma'-e Tashkhis-e Maslahat-e
Nezam (Assembly for Assessing
the Interests of the System) 261
Makarem Shirazi, Nasser 166
Maktab-e Islam 76
Maku 55
Maleki Tabrizi, Mirza Javad Aqa 42
Manazel al-Sa'erin (Ansari) 43
Manichaeism 46
Mansur, Hassan Ali 119, 161, 162, 194
Mansuri, Javad 212
Manzarieh barracks 87
Mara'shi Najafi, Grand Ayatollah
Shahab al-Din 70, 72, 83, 98, 150,
186, 230, 257
Mardom Party 118, 237
marja', marja'iyat 33, 34, 35, 36, 58, 59,

60, 68, 70, 75, 122, 127, 151, 152, 229, 230, 231, 247, 261, 291, 293, 294, 308, 310, 311

Mashhad 2, 36, 51, 55, 66, 81, 101, 111, 114, 124, 147, 153, 161, 172, 180, 195, 216, 242, 246, 307; University of 173

Masjed-e Ark (Tehran) 185

Masjed Shahi, Mohammad Reza Najafi 28

Mathnavi (Rumi) 46

Massignon, Louis 173

Matin Daftari, Hedayat 220

Mazandarani, Sheikh Abdollah 22

McFarlane, Robert 263

Mecca 15, 16, 68, 175, 199, 202, 303, 310

Medina 15, 16, 68, 175, 202, 203

Mevleviyya (Whirling Dervishes) 42

Me'raj al-Salekin wa Salat al-'Arefin (Khomeini) 49

Meshkini, Ayatollah Ali Akbar 180, 264, 287, 305, 308

Milani, Grand Ayatollah Hadi 113, 116, 161

Mir-Damad 45, 46

Mirza Qoli Soltan 7-9

Mizan 237

Mo'awiya (Umayyad caliph) 16, 82, 142

Mobarak, President Hosni 249

Mobasser, General Mohsen 102, 103, 104, 109, 110

Modarres, Seyyed Hassan 27, 60, 126, 214

Mofattah, Ayatollah Mohammad 181, 210

Moghaddam, Colonel Nasser 102, 151

Mohammad, the Prophet 2, 14, 15, 16, 17, 23, 35, 38, 39, 44, 45, 46, 47, 48, 51, 68, 77, 78, 81, 90, 103, 122, 153, 154, 155, 157, 175, 184, 192, 200, 202, 204, 236, 245, 246, 247, 259, 260,

262, 266, 275, 280, 282, 304, 305, 310

Mohammad Ali Shah 11, 19

Mohtashami, Ali Akbar 194

Mojahed 237

Mojahedin-e Khalq-e Iran 79, 164, 165, 174, 175, 176, 177, 205, 210, 212, 220, 226, 234, 237, 238, 239, 241, 242, 243, 252, 264, 278, 279, 286, 287; 30 Khordad (20 June 1980) demonstration 240

Mojahedin of Islam 79

Mojahedin of the Islamic Revolution (Omir) 180, 210

Mojtahed-e Khonsari, Mirza Ahmad 3

Mollah Sadra (Sadr al-Din Shirazi) 41, 45, 46, 48, 50, 275, 297

Mongols 41

Montazeri, Ayatollah Hossein Ali 150, 179, 180, 194, 308, 309, 310; appointed deputy leader 262-3; biography 262; dispute with Khomeini 264, 268, 277-81, 285-6; dismissed 287-93 *passim*; and first Assembly of Experts 218; on 1988 mass executions 279-80

Montazeri, Mohammad 194

Monthly Talks Society 171

Morvarid, Sheikh Ali Asghar 194

Mosaddeq, Mohammad 69, 71, 77, 84, 105, 106, 109, 120, 172, 209; and commemorations of death 218, 238; National Front 64; and nationalisation of oil industry 65; relations with clergy 65, 66; CIA *coup* against 66, 67, 182

Mosalla (Tehran) 310

Moses 184, 275

Moshir al-Saltaneh 10

Mossayyeb (Iraq) 140

Mostafa, Seyyed (Khomeini's father)

3, 4, 5, 6, 7, 8, 9, 10
Mostafavi, Dr Zahra (Khomeini's
    daughter) 270, 300, 301
Mostanbet, Ayatollah 141
Motahhari, Ayatollah Morteza 111,
    166, 173, 177, 246, 262; assassinated
    216, 223; biography 168–9; thought
    169–72; and Coalition of Islamic
    Societies 81, 161, 185, 187; as
    Khomeini's closest ally 178–81
    passim, 194; Chairman of Revolu-
    tionary Council 200
Movahhedi Kermani, Mohammad
    Ali 180
Movement of God-Worshipping
    Socialists 172
Mowla'i, Abdollah 81, 161
Mowlavi, Colonel 107, 109, 120
Mozaffar al-Din Shah 9, 10, 12, 19, 71
Musa al-Kazem, (7th Shi'i Imam) 2
Musa Sadr, Imam 201
Musavi Ardebili, Ayatollah Abdol
    Karim 179, 210, 221, 260, 304, 309
Musavi Hindi, Seyyed Ahmad
    (Khomeini's great grandfather) 2
Musavi Kho'iniha, Hojjat al-Islam
    Mohammad 180, 194, 227
Musavi, Mir Hossein 249, 257, 258,
    260, 263, 304
Muslim Brotherhood 246
Muslim People's Republican Party
    (Hezb-e Jomhuri-ye Khalq-e
    Mosalman, MPRP) 218, 226, 229,
    230, 231, 232
Muslim Students Association 167
mut'a marriage 29
mysticism 29, 39, 40, 42, 43, 44, 45,
    46, 47, 51, 52, 53, 168, 169, 271, 272,
    273, 274, 275, 276, 295, 296

Nabavi, Behzad 212
Nahj al-Balaghah 257

Na'ini, Mirza Mohammad Hossein
    27, 68
Najaf 3, 4, 21, 22, 25, 27, 30, 36, 64, 70,
    72, 76, 83, 96, 97, 98, 99, 114, 124,
    125, 139, 140, 141–58 passim, 167,
    175, 176, 177, 180, 184, 186, 187, 188,
    192, 194, 203, 204, 210, 230, 262,
    273, 290
Najd (Saudi Arabia) 62
Naneh Khavar (Khomeini's nurse)
    13
Nasser al-Din Shah 3, 9
Nasser, Gamal Abdul 100
Nassiri, General Ne'matollah 104,
    105, 109, 110, 111, 114, 115, 147, 161,
    162, 207
National Democratic Front 218, 239
National Front 64, 65, 71, 72, 86, 95,
    149, 160, 164, 165, 168, 172, 183, 185,
    193, 210, 212, 218, 233, 241
National Iranian Oil Company 168
National Liberation Army 278
National Security Council 242
Naus, Monsieur 11
Navvab Safavi, Mohammad 59, 60,
    67, 79, 223, 224
Neauphle-le-Château (France) 189,
    192, 200
Neishabur 2, 195
New York 227
North American Islamic Students
    Associations 177
North Korea 310
Nuri, Ayatollah Abdollah 287
Nuri, Sheikh Fazlollah 19, 223

Office for World Islamic Liberation
    Movements 264
oil industry 70, 138, 163, 168, 172, 195,
    208, 236, 248, 252, 268, 340, 346,
    347, British ownership of 64;
    nationalisation of 65

Omar Khayyam 32, 42
Omar (2nd Rashidun caliph) 15
Ommat 237
Osman ibn Affan (3rd Rashidun
  caliph) 15
Ottoman Empire 21
Oudh (India) 2

Pahlavi 202, 258
Pahlavi, Crown Prince Reza 105
Pahlavi, Shahbanu Farah 3, 105, 179;
  visit to Ayatollah Kho'i in Najaf
  158
Pahlavi, Mohammad Reza, Shah of
  Iran 57–8, 65, 67, 136, 138, 139, 141,
  143, 145, 146, 148, 150, 152, 161, 165,
  201, 207, 227, 229; succeeds to
  throne 57; and Americans 71, 163,
  185–6, 188, 197; and Borujerdi 70,
  74; fall of 195–8; and conflict with
  religious leaders over reform 75–
  128 *passim*; Khomeini on 75, 122,
  184, 201; and religious opposition
  158, 178, 187, 188; and secular
  opposition 72, 149, 160, 162, 183,
  185, 188; twenty-fifth anniversary
  celebrations 164; and Rastakhiz
  Party 174–5; and 1953 coup d'etat,
  66, 69; and 15th Khordad uprising
  106, 109, 114–15, 116, 119, 121
Pahlavi, Reza Shah 1, 43, 57, 58, 64,
  71, 75, 93, 174; abdication 57–8;
  Khomeini on 54, 60, 61, 104;
  modernising policies 55–6, 59;
  relations with religious establishment 27–8, 56, 84; 1921 coup 25–
  6
Pahlavi, Queen Taj al-Moluk 28
Pahlavi dynasty 187
Pahlavi Foundation 187
Pa'inshahri, Sheikh Mehdi 57
Pakravan, General Hassan 113, 114,

115, 116, 117, 162
Palestine 66, 149
Paris 138, 172, 182, 189, 190, 191, 192,
  193, 200, 202, 203, 210, 212, 216, 219,
  233, 243, 252, 306, 307
parliament *see* Majles
Partow, Colonel 96
Pasandideh, Ayatollah Morteza
  (Khomeini's brother) 4, 184, 200,
  214, 234
Pasdar-e Islam 281
The Prayer of the Mystics (Khomeini)
  50
Peikar Organisation 237
Peiman, Dr Habibollah 172, 237
Persian Gulf 1, 57, 163
Persian language 138
Pishva 112

Qajar dynasty 3, 7, 8, 26, 27, 28, 64, 71
Qasemlu, Abdolrahman 219
Qazvini, Sheikh Mujtaba 51, 52
Qeisari, Sharaf al-Din Davud 43
Qom 21–38 *passim*; 42, 48–59 *passim*,
  64–72 *passim*, 76, 80, 83, 84, 101,
  107, 109, 124, 125, 130, 140, 141,
  147–53 *passim*, 168, 169, 173, 180,
  194, 213, 214, 215, 216, 219, 221, 223,
  229, 230, 231, 248, 260, 264, 273,
  274, 275, 277, 279, 280, 288, 290,
  291, 292, 311; revival of seminary
  25; Khomeini's school in 28;
  political tension in 87–91; 92–9,
  102–6, 110–22 *passim*, 184–5, 186,
  187, 232
Qomi, Ayatollah Hossein 55, 58, 59,
  101
Qomi, Mirza-ye 25, 28
Qor'an 8, 14, 16, 19, 23, 25, 29, 33, 35,
  46, 50, 51, 60, 61, 75, 78, 85, 87, 90,
  93, 122, 125, 126, 127, 130, 132, 143,
  153, 155, 167, 170, 184, 202, 225, 229,

257, 274, 275, 282, 303, 305
Qotb, Seyyed 246
Qotbzadeh, Sadeq 200, 252, 307;
    arrest and execution 252; in
    Iranian student movement in
    exile 150; in Paris 190–4 passim;
    plot to overthrow Khomeini 252
Qurna (Iraq) 250

Rabbani Amlashi, Mohammad
    Mehdi 180
Rafi'i Qazvini, Seyyed Abolhassan
    42
Rafiqdust, Mohsen 180, 201, 210
Rafsanjani see Hashemi Rafsanjani
Rah-e Eshq (Khomeini) 271
Rahimi, Dr Mostafa 196
Raja'i, Sheikh Fazlollah 10
Raja'i, Mohammad Ali 10, 178, 180,
    235, 242, 243, 245
Rajavi, Mas'ud 243, 278
Ranj-nameh (Ahmad Khomeini) 291
Rasht 19
Rastakhiz Party 174, 175, 183
The Rational Order of the Rights of
    Women in Islam (Motahhari) 170
Reagan, President Ronald 263
Refah School 202, 205, 207
Regional Co-operation and Develop-
    ment 138
referendum (White Revolution, 1963)
    83, 84, 85, 86, 87, 88, 89, 95, 99, 114,
    160
referendum (3 March 1979) 203, 212,
    213, 215, 217
referendum (10 December 1979) 221,
    226, 231, 232, 256
Reishahri, Hojjat al-Islam Moham-
    mad 278, 292
Revolutionary Council 111, 197, 198,
    200, 202, 203, 211, 212, 215, 216, 217,
    221

Revolutionary Courts 277
Revolutionary Guards 201, 211, 235,
    240, 257, 264, 303, 305, 312
Rex cinema (Abadan) 187;
Rey 43
Reza (8th Shi'i Imam) 25
Reza Khan 143
Reza'i, Haj Esma'il 115, 118
Reza'i, Mohsen 212, 292
Riyadh (Saudi Arabia) 62
Rowghani, Haj 117
Rumi, Jalal al-Din 41, 48, 50
Rushdie, Salman 282, 283, 284
Russia intervention in Iran 12, 19, 126

Sabet, Habib 67
Sabzevari, Haj Mollah Hadi 42
Saddam Hossein 236, 249
Sa'di 17
Sadr al-Ulema 7
Sadr, Javad 119
Sadr, Ayatollah Mohammad Baqer
    152
Saduqi, Ayatollah Ali Mohammad.
    55, 194
Sa'idi, Gholam Reza 179
Safavid dynasty 1, 2, 9, 41, 45, 294
Safi Golpayegani, Ayatollah Lotfollah
    260
Sahabi, Ezatollah 219
Sahabi, Dr Yadollah 77, 168, 216
Sahebeh (Khomeini's paternal aunt)
    6, 7, 10, 13
Sakineh (Khomeini's grandmother)
    3
Salam, Abdol 144
Samarra (Iraq) 3, 140
Sami, Kazem 171
Sangelaj (Tehran) 19
Sanjabi, Dr Karim 183, 212, 216
Saqafi, Ayatollah Mirza Mohammad
    37

Saqafi, Qods-e Iran (Khomeini's
   wife) 37, 38, 266
Sarbedaran 252
Sardar Heshmat, Nasrollah Khan 9
Sartre, Jean Paul 173
Sassanid dynasty 163
Satanic Verses (Rushdie) 282–3
Saudi Arabia 62, 305
Savak (State Intelligence and
   Security Organisation) 101, 102,
   107, 108, 109, 111, 113, 115, 117, 118,
   128, 129, 130, 131, 138, 139, 146, 150,
   151, 152, 161, 162, 163, 164, 172, 174,
   184, 185, 187, 199, 207, 208, 241, 292
schools, Islamic 178–9
Second World War 57, 104, 165
Seyyed Abolqassem (Imam Jom'eh of
   Tehran) 9
Seyyed Azizollah mosque 79, 85, 86
Seyyed Mohammad (Imam Jome'eh
   of Tehran) 9
Shah Abdolazim, Shrine of 11, 43, 55,
   113
Shah mosque, Tehran 12, 106, 111
Shahabadi, Mirza Mohammad Ali
   42, 43, 44
Shahnameh (Ferdowsi) 17
Shahrudi, Grand Ayatollah Mahmud
   141
Shahzdeh Agha 10
Shame (Rushdie) 283
Shamkhani, Ali 212
Sharh Do'a al-Sahar (Khomeini) 44
Sharh-e Fusus (Gheisari) 43
Sharh-e Manzumeh (Mollah Hadi
   Sabzevari) 42
shari'a 5, 13, 19, 23, 35, 44, 54, 56, 59,
   60, 63, 65, 69, 70, 72, 75, 76, 78, 79,
   82, 83, 91, 92, 96, 97, 98, 113, 116, 121,
   152, 153, 166, 171, 172, 173, 174, 175,
   177, 186, 204, 213, 216, 217, 218, 219,
   223, 226, 229, 230, 231, 232, 238,

   239, 241, 242, 252, 253, 258, 259,
   287, 288, 290
Shari'at-Sangelaji 56
Shari'ati, Ali 166, 172, 177
Shari'ati, Mohammad Taqi 59, 166,
   171, 172
Shari'ati-Fard, Hojjat al-Islam 242
Shari'atmadari, Grand Ayatollah
   Kazem 70, 72, 75, 76, 78, 79, 82,
   83, 91, 92, 96, 97, 98, 113, 116, 121, 151,
   152, 186, 216, 218, 226, 229, 230, 231,
   232, 238, 239, 252, 290
Sharif Emami, Ja'far 187, 195
Shatt al-Arab 145, 249
Shemr 157
Shi'is, Shi'ism principles of reli-
   gion 14; early history 15–18;
   structure of clerical institution
   33–5, 36; *world-view* 95; *see also*
   ejtehad, feqh, madraseh, marja'iyat,
   mysticism, velayat-e faqih
Shiraz 42, 45, 101, 111, 123, 124, 239,
   272
Shirazi, Mirza Hassan 3, 140
Shirazi, Qotb al-Din 41
Shirin Khanum 3
Shokrollah Khan 13
Shrine of the Imam Reza (Mashhad)
   307
Siahkal (Gilan) 164
Siffin (Iraq) 16
Sobhani, Ayatollah Ja'far 37
Society of Militant Clergy (Jame'eh-
   ye Rowhaniyat-e Mobarez) 180,
   211
Sohravardi 41, 45, 48, 275
Soltanpur, Sa'id 242
Soviet Union 57, 174, 266, 267, 306;
   ambassador's audience with
   Khomeini 215; influence in Iran
   58, 104, 188; Khomeini on 125;
   Khomeini's mission to Gorbachev

274-6; Tudeh party links with 255 *see also* Russia

Special Court for the Clergy 264

Students Following the Imam's Line 227

Sufism, Sufis 10, 39, 40, 41, 42, 43, 44, 45, 47, 50, 62, 273, 296

Sultanabad *see* Arak

sunna 23, 46, 153, 155

Sunni Islam 15, 41, 59, 84

Supreme Court 254

Supreme Defence Council 237, 246, 265

Sureh-ye Hamd 274

Suyuti, Jalaleddin 24

Switzerland 57

Syria 16, 150, 184, 185, 189

Tabari, Ehsan 255

Tabataba'i, Allameh Mohammad Hossein 166

Tabataba'i, Fatemeh (Khomeini's daughter-in-law) 270-2

Tabataba'i, Sadeq 150, 194

Tabataba'i, Seyyed Ziaeddin 26

Tabriz 19, 81, 187, 231, 232, 242, 292

Taheri Khorramabadi, Hassan 180

Tahrir al-Wasilah (Khomeini) 137

Taleqani, Ayatollah Seyyed Mahmud 59, 69, 77, 160, 165, 166, 167, 168, 171, 172, 175, 183, 196, 207, 216, 219, 273

Taraki, President Nur Mohammad 215

Tayyeb *see* Haj Reza'i

ta'zieh 17, 311

Tehran 201, 215 110-14; demonstrations in 85, 101, 104-6, 121, 184-5 (pro-Bakhtiar 205; Jaleh Square 188; 15 Khordad 110-14; Tasu'a and Ashura 1978 196; opposition to Khomeini 218, 220, 238, 240);

Khomeini's funeral in 310-13; street fighting in 205; American embassy in 221

Tehran Radio 66, 110, 111, 128, 198, 206, 237, 248, 282, 304

Tehran University 106, 111, 214; National Front and demonstrations at 71-2; Bani Sadr's rally at 238

Tehrani, Haj Mirza Hossein Khalil 22

theocracy 224

theosophy 45, 48, 52, 67

A Thousand and One Nights 17

Towzih al-Masa'el (Khomeini) 119

Tudeh Party 58, 88, 102, 109, 114, 160, 165, 167, 172, 209, 218, 237, 255

Turkey 26, 41, 128, 129, 130, 132, 136, 137, 138, 139, 142, 148, 149, 160, 161, 252

Tusi, Nassir al-Din 40

Twelfth Imam *see* Hidden Imam

Ulucami mosque (Turkey) 135

Umayyad dynasty 16, 101

United Nations 139, 186, 269; Security Council Resolution 598 269

United States 104, 149, 202; Carter administration 182, 227; hostage crisis 221, 226-7, 229; Irangate affair 263-4; and Iranian revolution 188, 196-7, 198, 202, 205, 206, 220-1, 236, 269; Kennedy administration 71; Khomeini on 122-7 *passim*, 129, 155, 156, 184, 220, 241, 249, 276, 282, 286, 305; relationships with Iran in Pahlavi era 70, 121-2, 163, 182, 183, 184

Universal Declaration of Human Rights 183

Universal House of Justice 66

Va'ez-e Tabasi 180
vali-ye faqih 225, 261, 293, 294, 297, 350
Vance, Cyrus 182, 197
Varamin 112
Vasiq, Colonel Abdollah 101
velayat-e faqih 153, 156, 158, 195, 204, 217, 218, 222, 225, 227, 230, 231, 256, 261, 277
Velayat-e Faqih (Khomeini) 157 *see also* (*The*) *Islamic State*
Vinogradov, Vladimir 214

Wahhabis, Wahhabism 62, 305
White House 185
White Revolution 83, 88, 100, 106, 113, 114, 125, 160, 162, 165, 175
The White Revolution (Mohammad Reza Shah Pahlavi) 114
Writers' Association 183

Yasrebi-Kashani, Ayatollah Ali 35
Yazd 187
Yazdi, Dr Ebrahim 49, 177, 189, 190,
193, 200, 307
Yazdi, Mirza Ali Akbar 42
Yazid (Umayyad caliph) 16, 17, 98, 102, 104, 118, 142, 187
Yujan 8, 9

Zagros mountains 2
Zahedi, Ardeshir 196
Zahedi, General Fazlollah 66
Zahir al-Islam (Javad Emami) 9, 10
Zamani, Abbas 212
Zanjani, Abu Abdollah 141
Zanjani, Ayatollah Seyyed Abolfazl 69
Zanjani, Ayatollah Seyyed Reza 68, 229
Zanjani, Sheikh Ebrahim 20
Zein al-Abedin (4th Shi'i Imam) 16
Zeinab (daughter of 1st Shi'i Imam) 17
Zionism, Zionists 119, 213, 232, 251, 265, 351

28 ~~14~~ DAYS